THE WAR AND COLONEL WARDEN

Please return to.

A.J. Roberts.

By the same author:
THE SECRET WAR, 1939–45

GERALD PAWLE

The War and Colonel Warden

Based on the recollections of
Commander C. R. Thompson
C.M.G., O.B.E., R.N. (ret.)
Personal Assistant to the Prime Minister 1940–45

WHITE LION PUBLISHERS
London, New York, Sydney and Toronto

First published in the United Kingdom by
George G. Harrap and Co. Ltd., 1963

White Lion edition, 1974

ISBN 0 85617 637 0

Printed in Great Britain by
Biddles Ltd., Guildford, Surrey,
for White Lion Publishers Ltd.,
138 Park Lane, London W1Y 3DD

TO
TWO ARCHITECTS OF THE SEA VICTORY

Admiral of the Fleet
VISCOUNT CUNNINGHAM OF HYNDHOPE
K.T., G.C.B., O.M., D.S.O.
Commander-in-Chief Mediterranean 1939–42 and 1943
First Sea Lord 1943–46

AND

Admiral of the Fleet
SIR JOHN H. D. CUNNINGHAM G.C.B.
Commander-in-Chief Mediterranean 1943–46
First Sea Lord 1946–48

NULLA FLUIT CUJUS MEMINISSE NON JUVET

Foreword

COMMANDER C. R. Thompson was one of the most intimate and essential members of Winston Churchill's personal entourage during the war. I am grateful to Tommy for having undertaken to assist Gerald Pawle in writing this book. It brings back many cherished moments that I shared. While I cannot agree with some of the political conclusions which the author expresses, I find the book a valuable contribution to an understanding of the personal side of Churchill's life during the war years.

Tommy was responsible for the arrangements for the Prime Minister's many travels to four continents, often proposed on short notice, as well as for day-to-day arrangements. This was not an easy task, as Sir Winston was not always predictable in his movements. He must have been an endless source of concern to his devoted security staff. Churchill had no personal fear and believed that his best security was unannounced appearances. Assassination plots, the Prime Minister once explained to me, took a great deal of planning to have a chance of success. I was with him on a number of these unannounced appearances.

During the winter of 1941 when the British cities were subjected to heavy bombing raids, Churchill considered, and quite rightly, that his visiting these cities would contribute to the morale of the people. I remember once he showed up at the port of Swansea, which had been hit a few days before. He went directly into the port area and was immediately surrounded by several hundred dockers. In the excitement of wanting to see the Prime Minister, they closed in on him. His security guards were, of course, gravely concerned that he would be injured in the jam. But it didn't worry Churchill. He simply called out: "Stand back, my men—let the others have a chance to see too." They pulled back and gave him room. Churchill had an intuitive understanding of how people would react. He put his unique square-shaped bowler on his cane and held it up for all to see. This led to laughter and cheers and he was able to move quietly out of the crowd.

Another difficulty of Tommy's was to get the different organizations dealing with Churchill's travel plans to work in concert. I remember once I was the "cover" in the plan for the Prime Minister's trip to meet President Roosevelt at Casablanca. I went with some of the members of my staff to the airfield near Oxford and had dinner in the R.A.F. Officers' Mess. We sat about, talked freely with the officers about our alleged plans to go to Algiers to look into certain supply questions. At the proper moment, we drove out to the plane. The automobile parked in the dark under the shadow of the wings and we waited in silence for the Prime Minister. When he arrived my associates were to leave in the automobile and I would board the plane with the Prime Minister. Some time later there was a tremendous noise of sounding sirens and the lights of an approaching convoy some miles away. The Air Force security officer, who had carefully worked out these plans, was utterly disgusted by the lack of care of the police and exclaimed, "There goes all of our cover plan! No one but the Prime Minister could make so much noise!"

In any event, we took off and arrived safely at Casablanca. The Prime Minister was supposed to step directly from the plane into a closed armoured car. There were many Arabs working in the field with no way to screen them. However, he heard another plane in the sky and was told that it was bringing General Ismay and some of his party. So he insisted on remaining to welcome them. He maintained there was no danger as he was disguised in the uniform of an Air Force commodore. He calmly walked over to Ismay's plane and greeted the passengers as they disembarked. In spite of Churchill's "uniform" there could be no mistaking his contour. Pug Ismay was dismayed and commented that he "looked like an Air Force commodore disguised as the Prime Minister."

I knew Tommy from the moment I arrived in England in early March 1941. He met me at the airfield and took me directly to Chequers. At this time, when Britain was standing alone, President Roosevelt had sent me to England to consult the Prime Minister and other members of his government and to report to the President on everything we could do to assist Britain, short of war.

Churchill considered that the best way that I could carry out my mission was for me to be given the most intimate information on the British military situation and supply problems. The battle of the Atlantic was raging. Sinkings were averaging about 10 per cent. per convoy. Since

Britain depended upon imports for half her food and most of her raw materials, it didn't take much calculation to figure out how soon her situation would become extremely grave. President Roosevelt took a series of actions in quick succession: one clearly unneutral act was the repairing of British naval vessels in American shipyards. Also, our naval ships extended their patrol in the Atlantic. We transferred two million tons of surplus shipping, and through Lend-Lease and otherwise stepped up our shipments of the most critically needed items of raw materials and food, bearing in mind conservation of shipping. We rapidly increased arms shipments.

I had not been in England long before the Prime Minister told me that his determined aim was to hold out in Britain and in the Middle East until we came into the war. He did not conceal from me the fact that there was a limit to the length of time Britain could hold out alone. Yet he showed complete confidence to the British people in all of his speeches and public statements. The British people never wavered in that year they stood alone. Every man, woman and child had but one thought: to do their part. It was inspiring to be in Britain at that time.

As I had been widely publicized as the President's personal representative, Churchill thought that my going with him on his trips to severely bombed communities would add confidence.

I recall one day he visited Bristol, which had been badly "beaten up" by bombings just before he arrived. As he walked through the streets, it naturally created tremendous excitement. Women rushed to the doors of their homes shouting, "There he is—dear old Winnie!" He waved to everyone and he told me that he tried to catch a person's eye as this gave a direct communication with the individual.

At the end of this day, I happened to be alone with him in his railway car as we pulled out of the station to return to London. By that time everyone knew he was in town and people were leaning out of their windows in the hope of seeing him. Again he waved and tried to catch their eyes. As we left the city behind us, he picked up a newspaper to conceal his emotion. He had been deeply touched by the reception he had received all day from the people of Bristol. Tears came to his eyes and he said quite simply, "They have such faith—it is a grave responsibility." He then buried himself in his newspaper. It was his custom to read the newspapers carefully, in spite of the constant flow of government dispatches.

The Prime Minister's mind was always on the war, but on occasion, particularly while travelling, he liked to play bezique, as something of a relief from the constant pressures. He told me that while it might not be altogether appropriate for the Prime Minister to play cards with his British colleagues, he thought it was quite proper to do so with the "President's personal envoy." It was invariably fascinating to play with him. While we shuffled the six packs of cards between hands, he would talk of things which were particularly on his mind.

The Prime Minister was deeply attached to Tommy and grateful for his devotion. But sometimes he became upset when things didn't go exactly as he wished. Somewhat in jest, but I think also to let off steam without being unduly unkind, he would announce that he had given Tommy a certain number of demerits, as a teacher might to a school boy. These would accumulate until something went unexpectedly well which pleased the Prime Minister. Then the demerits would be cleared off the books. Unhappily, Tommy was never able to get ahead of the game.

An amusing incident occurred on our trip from Tehran to Moscow in August of 1942. This was Churchill's first meeting with Stalin and the first face-to-face military discussion. The plane we travelled in was a converted B 24 bomber with no insulation and the noise was so loud that it was impossible to talk. The Prime Minister wrote notes to each of us when he had something he wanted to say. When it came to opening the lunch basket, prepared by the British Embassy in Tehran, the first item was ham sandwiches. Churchill demanded mustard, and Tommy rummaged in the basket but couldn't produce any mustard. Churchill wrote "Ten demerits! You should know no gentleman eats ham sandwiches without mustard." However, on the return trip the Kremlin service had supplied the lunch, and it included caviar and champagne. The Prime Minister was pleased and all Tommy's past demerits were erased.

On the way to Moscow, these frivolous messages were interspersed with serious comments on the approaching encounter with Stalin. Knowing that I had negotiated with Stalin in Moscow the year before, he asked my comment on how best to break the news to Stalin that there could be no Second Front in Europe and to explain the plans for the invasion of North Africa. Although Churchill was, of course, extremely quick and alert in debate, he planned his strategy carefully in advance. The Stalin talks turned out to have moments of agreement and moments of violent argument.

At one point, Churchill explained why the North Russian convoys had to be discontinued on account of devastative German air and submarine attack. In the July convoy 25 per cent. of the ships had been lost. The Admiralty had considered there was a better chance for the ships to get through if the convoy dispersed and the naval vessels returned to Britain. Stalin said gruffly, "This is the first time in history that the British Navy turned back from a battle." As for the Second Front, he commented that the Germans were not invincible, and if the British would only fight they would find the Germans were not supermen.

Churchill was highly incensed. Nevertheless he kept his temper, and never mentioned what must have been uppermost in his mind—the perfidy of Stalin in the Ribbentrop treaty for the division of Poland, which gave Hitler a free hand to attack the West. In a sober but dramatic way Churchill described what Britain had done during the year she had stood alone, the manner in which the British forces and people had heroically dealt with every crisis, and the total effort which was now being put forth. Churchill never recognized the difficulties of interpretation of his vivid English into Russian, and he proceeded without pause. The interpreter, an elderly member of the British Embassy staff, tried to take notes but became so enthralled by the Prime Minister's eloquent speech, that he finally put down his pencil. Churchill suddenly noticed this and told him to proceed with the interpretation. This he attempted to do from his notes in a somewhat halting manner. Churchill would interrupt and say—"Did you tell him this?" or "Did you remember that?" All this utterly flustered the poor fellow. Stalin listened for a time and then started to laugh, saying, "Your words are of no importance—what I like is your spirit."

I believe that incident formed the basis of the wartime relationship between the two men. Each knew the other disagreed utterly in ideology, but Stalin would frequently refer to Churchill in toasts as "My staunch comrade-in-arms during this war." I have always regretted that there was not a verbatim transcript of Churchill's reply to Stalin. It was perhaps one of the most vigorous and moving of his many historic statements.

During the course of the war, I was present at all but one of the meetings between Churchill and Roosevelt, and all of the tripartite talks with Stalin. As I travelled with Churchill on many of his trips by sea and air, including those to the United States, and saw the Prime Minister frequently while I was in London, I recall many of the incidents described in this book, but with some differences in detail.

For example, a dramatic moment was the dinner at Chequers on Sunday, December 7, 1941. Mrs Churchill was not feeling well and was having dinner upstairs. My daughter Kathleen was the only woman present. She had been asked because it was her birthday. Only Tommy, Pug Ismay, John Martin (the Prime Minister's private secretary), Gil Winant, and myself were there. During dinner, at nine o'clock, Sawyers, the butler, would always bring in a small radio, a present from Harry Hopkins. It turned on by lifting up the lid. Churchill was a bit despondent that evening and was immersed in his thoughts. The news started with unimportant events. Suddenly there was a pause and the announcer said he had a special dispatch: "The Japanese have bombed Pearl Harbour." He then calmly continued with another item. I was startled and said, "What's that about bombing Pearl Harbour?" Tommy said, no, it was Pearl River. This I disputed. At that moment, John Martin returned from a telephone call and said that the Admiralty wanted to speak to the Prime Minister. For some reason, the Prime Minister slammed down the top of the radio and went rapidly out of the room. Winant and I followed. The reports of the attack on Pearl Harbour were confirmed by the Admiralty. He then immediately telephoned President Roosevelt in Washington. In that conversation he told the President without hesitation that the next day he would announce that Britain was in a state of war with Japan.

This was the first exchange between the two heads of Government, now allied in war. The intimate personal relationship between Roosevelt and Churchill led to the integration, unparalleled in history, of our mutual military and civilian war effort. I wish to add at this point that I disagree with some of the personal judgments which the author expresses on certain decisions made by the President and the Prime Minister, and on the way these decisions were reached.

My final wartime talk with Sir Winston was in London in July 1945, just after the Potsdam meeting. The election had gone against the Conservative Party and Attlee and Bevin had taken Churchill and Eden's place in the middle of the Conference. Before going back to my post in Moscow, I wanted to see Churchill and pay him my respects. So I went to London and he asked me to lunch. He was living temporarily in a penthouse apartment on the top floor of Claridges. Mrs Churchill, Brendan Bracken and I were the only ones present. Churchill talked about the election. The repudiation by the British people had been a very deep shock to him. He told me that the week since I had seen him in Potsdam had been the longest in his life but that he was now adjusted to these events. In order to make some consoling comment, I pointed to the fact that the Labour Party had not gained a majority of the popular vote, that if there had been proportional representation in Britain as in France, the Conservative and Liberal Parties would have the majority of seats in the Commons and then he would no doubt still be Prime Minister. Churchill indignantly rejected this idea saying: "I will fight against the evils of proportional representation with all my strength." He explained that one could not have responsible government with proportional representation. He said it was essential that one Party have responsibility for government so that the people would know whom to hold accountable. Otherwise democracy cannot succeed.

To me, it was completely in character that at this time of great personal disappointment he was as vigorous as ever in upholding his basic concept of the great traditions of the British democratic system of government, which he understood so well.

I also suggested that his retirement would give him an opportunity to write the history of the war as no one else could. "Yes," Churchill replied, "but there is other work to be done." I knew then that this turn in events had cast only a passing shadow on his indomitable spirit.

W. AVERELL HARRIMAN

Preface

MANY books have already been written about the Second World War and the part played in it by Sir Winston Churchill as First Lord of the Admiralty, Prime Minister, and Minister of Defence. Most of them have, however, dealt mainly with the political or military aspects of the war. Here I have attempted to fill in some of the gaps, concentrating in particular on the Prime Minister's life, day by day, as he directed the war effort, and his journeys throughout the world.

My principal source has been Commander C. R. Thompson, who spent the whole war at the Prime Minister's side. Living with him in Downing Street and at Chequers, organizing all his journeys by land, sea, and air, and accompanying him everywhere he went, Tommy had, perhaps, a closer view of decisive events and the men who played a leading part in them than any other observer. Unlike some others, however, he did not keep a diary, and when Sir Winston Churchill encouraged him to tell his story we set to work, converting my Cornish study into a small-scale reproduction of the Downing Street Map Room and prompting and checking his recollections with the aid of a wall chart covering every day from September 1939 to August 1945.

To supplement Tommy's own notes, compiled during several hundred hours of discussions, I have talked, both in this country and abroad, to many others whose war-time service brought them into close contact with the Prime Minister. In setting down this account, which touches the last war at so many points, I gratefully acknowledge the assistance I have received from them, and, in particular, from members of the Churchill family.

My special thanks are due to Lord Willoughby de Broke, A.F.C., D.L., J.P.; Miss Irene Boyle, formerly personal secretary to H.M. Ambassador to the United States; Commander F. Barley, R.N.R., of the Admiralty's Historical Section; Mr E. A. Bell; Major N. W. Chavasse, M.C.; Mr J. R. Colville, C.B., C.V.O.; Sir Edward Cottrell, C.B.E., J.P.; Admiral of the Fleet Viscount Cunningham of Hyndhope, K.T., G.C.B., O.M., D.S.O.; Group Captain John Cunningham, D.S.O., O.B.E., D.F.C., who commanded 604 and 85 Night Fighter Squadrons; the Right Hon. Anthony Eden (now Earl of Avon, K.G., P.C., M.C.); Air Chief Marshal Sir William Elliot, G.C.V.O., K.C.B., K.B.E., D.F.C.; Detective-Inspector Cyril Davies; Rear-Admiral R. S. Foster-Brown, C.B.; Wing Commander E. G. Fraser, M.V.O., A.F.C.; the Hon. T. G. D. Galbraith, M.A., M.P.; Brigadier Sir James Gault, K.C.M.G., O.B.E., M.V.O., formerly Military Assistant to General Eisenhower; Admiral Sir Guy Grantham, G.C.B., C.B.E., D.S.O.; the Right Hon. Sir James Grigg, P.C., K.C.B., K.C.S.I., Secretary of State for War 1942–45; the late Admiral Sir Cecil Harcourt, G.B.E., K.C.B.; Sir Alan Herbert; Mrs Kathleen Hill; Brigadier Godfrey Hobbs, C.B.E.; Mr H. S. Hobday, D.F.C.; the Hon. Mrs Alexander Hood; General Sir Leslie Hollis, K.C.B., K.B.E., R.M.; Sir Adrian Holman, K.B.E., C.M.G., M.C.; Detective-Superintendent W. L. Hughes; the Right Hon. Viscount Ingleby, P.C., Parliamentary Under-Secretary of State, Home Office, 1939–44; Major-General Sir Millis Jefferis, K.B.E., M.C.; Group Captain G. J. H. Jeffs, O.B.E., M.V.O.; the Right Hon. Lord Killearn, P.C., G.C.M.G., C.B., M.V.O., H.M. Ambassador to Egypt and High Commissioner for the Sudan 1936–46; Mr Patrick Kinna, M.B.E.; Major-General J. M. Kirkman, C.B., C.B.E.; Sir Reginald Leeper, G.B.E., K.C.M.G., H.M. Ambassador to Greece 1943–46; Captain R. C. Lewis, D.S.O., O.B.E., R.N.; Mr C. H. Lowery and Mr L. Marshall, of Ruston Bucyrus Ltd, Lincoln; Lord Mancroft, K.B.E., T.D., M.A.; Major-General Sir Stewart Menzies, K.C.B., K.C.M.G., D.S.O., M.C.; Major Sir Desmond Morton, K.C.B., C.M.G., M.C.; Mr B. J. M. Nairn, O.B.E., H.M. Consul-General at Tangier, and Mrs Nairn, who has kindly allowed me to reproduce her drawing of Sir Winston Churchill as an illustration for this book; Mrs Elizabeth Nel, who as Miss Layton was a member of the Prime Minister's war-time Secretariat; Miss D. Palmer, secretary to the Director of Naval Construction, Admiralty; Captain Sir Richard Pim, K.B.E., V.R.D., R.N.R.; Mr M. W. Perrin, C.B.E., chairman of the Wellcome Foundation; Lieutenant-General Sir Harold Redman, K.C.B., C.B.E.; the Duke of Richmond and Gordon; Sir Leslie Rowan, K.C.B., C.V.O.; Wing Commander J. S. Schreiber, H.M. Air Attaché at Lisbon 1941–44; Marshal of the R.A.F. Sir John Slessor, G.C.B., D.S.O., M.C.; Mr W. F. Spanner, M.I.N.A.; Mr Howard

Spring; the Right Hon. Viscount Stuart of Findhorn, P.C., C.H., M.V.O., M.C.; Admiral Sir William Tennant, K.C.B., C.B.E., M.V.O.; Lieutenant-General Sir Francis Tuker, K.C.I.E., C.B., D.S.O., O.B.E., F.R.G.S.; Admiral of the Fleet Sir Philip Vian, G.C.B., D.S.O.; Brigadier Lionel Bootle-Wilbraham, D.S.O., M.C.; the Right Hon. Richard Wood, P.C., M.P.; and Mr Philip de Zulueta.

My thanks are also due to Mrs Hilary St George Saunders, of Writers and Speakers Research, for her invaluable assistance in connexion with various important Parliamentary debates between 1942 and 1945, and the General Election of 1945; to the proprietors of Thomson Newspapers and the *Yorkshire Post* for permission to use their libraries; and, finally, to Miss Frances Webb for her untiring and conscientious help with the checking and typing of my manuscript.

GERALD PAWLE

TREWORGAN,
MAWNAN
December 1962

Introductory Note

I HAVE long thought that some comprehensive account of Sir Winston's war-time life and, in particular, his journeys to many parts of the world during that period, should be recorded. Since I always accompanied him I felt that I could make a contribution to such a book, and Sir Winston very kindly gave me his permission to do so. I therefore welcomed Gerald Pawle's suggestion that he should undertake the writing of it.

I did not keep a private diary, for this would have inevitably contained much Top Secret information and, indeed, I doubt whether as a serving officer it would have been permissible for me to maintain a record of this kind. As a result, however, Pawle was faced with the need for a vast amount of research, not only to check my recollections but in order to provide continuity of narrative and an adequate background to events which happened so many years ago.

This book is not an essay in collaboration. Pawle alone is the author. Beyond providing a basis on which he could build, my only contributions have been suggestions and general concurrence.

C. R. THOMPSON

Contents

Illustrations

between pages 204 and 205

PLATES

IN THE TEXT

[*A number of photographs reproduced as illustrations in this volume have come from Sir Winston Churchill's private collection and in certain cases their source is not known.*]

I

"This is Tommy!"

ON THE afternoon of September 3, 1939, a report reached the Admiralty that German warships had been sighted by reconnaissance aircraft of the Royal Navy in the Schillig Roads, off Wilhelmshaven. The First Sea Lord, Admiral of the Fleet Sir Dudley Pound, had already left the War Room to attend a Cabinet meeting, and, taking the signal with him, Captain Guy Grantham, his Naval Assistant, went to Downing Street in search of him.[1]

All that day there had been much conjecture throughout Whitehall about imminent changes in the Government, and when Grantham entered the Cabinet Room he noticed with more than usual interest that in front of each person seated round the long table was a printed card proclaiming the office he held. Next to Admiral Pound was Winston Churchill, bending his own card to and fro, but he replaced it on the table as he took the signal from Pound. And in large block letters Grantham saw:

FIRST LORD OF THE ADMIRALTY

Armed with approval for an attack on the German ships, Grantham dashed back to tell the Admiralty that the operation was on, and that the new First Lord would be arriving as soon as the meeting was over. An hour later he accompanied him to the room which Churchill had left "in pain and sorrow almost exactly a quarter of a century before," following Lord Fisher's resignation. Walking over to the sofa, the First Lord dragged out a long box, and from it he produced some old charts of the North Sea. "I used these last time," he said. He then asked for a certain octagonal

[1] Now Admiral Sir Guy Grantham, G.C.B., C.B.E., D.S.O., Governor and Commander-in-chief, Malta, 1959–62.

table which he remembered, and when, to Grantham's surprise, this was immediately produced by the office-keeper from some secret store near by, they set to work, Admiral Pound explaining the disposition of the Fleet.

Early next morning Lieutenant-Commander C. R. Thompson, Flag Lieutenant to the Board of Admiralty, was working in his office when the door opened and he saw Brendan Bracken. He knew Bracken well, for they had visited the Mediterranean and the Baltic together in the Admiralty yacht *Enchantress* during Duff Cooper's term as First Lord.

"This is Tommy," said Bracken. A nod, a quick glance round the room, and Mr Churchill continued his tour of inspection. With that briefest of introductions began an association which was to continue unbroken through all the years of war which lay ahead.

Once, from a landing-stage in Bermuda in 1942, a disconsolate naval officer had to watch a flying-boat take off for Britain without him. It was a long and potentially hazardous flight, and to make way for extra fuel the passenger list had to be drastically reduced.

The naval officer was "Tommy" Thompson, left "lamenting as bitterly as Lord Ullin in the poem," wrote Churchill later. "Never before and never afterwards were we separated."[2]

* * * * *

At the time when Mr Churchill arrived at the Admiralty Lieutenant-Commander Charles Ralfe Thompson had no reason to expect any dramatic change in his career. Aged forty-five, he was, in fact, due to retire from the Active List in a few weeks, for although at one stage he had commanded submarines for thirteen years almost without a break, he had not been promoted.

In the early thirties, when he had been in the zone for promotion, competition was particularly keen, and any adverse entry on a Service record was bound to attract close attention. At this critical juncture Lieutenant-Commander Thompson incurred Their Lordships' displeasure by running the submarine *Oberon* on to a sandbank.

On passage to Chatham he had anchored in dense fog close to the first Lightship in the main Thames Channel. Up to this point he had not sighted the Lightship, and, as it transpired, he had anchored on the wrong side of it. When the fog lifted six hours later his bows were resting firmly on the sandbank in full view of a row of interested spectators, and although *Oberon* floated off easily enough with the tide, Tommy arrived in Chatham to find that the Lightship had already reported the incident.

"Quite rightly," he remarked afterwards, "I didn't get away with it, but in retrospect it seems the luckiest thing that ever happened to me;

[2] Churchill, *The Second World War*, Vol. III, p. 628.

otherwise, the most interesting period of my life would never have come my way."

While this is true, Tommy Thompson's early days in the Royal Navy had been far from uneventful. Born in the little Durham village of Shiney Row, he came of a shipbuilding family. Although this influenced his choice of career, the first thing which really captured his imagination, and became an absorbing passion in his life, was flying. Passing through Osborne and Dartmouth, he went to sea as a midshipman in the battleship *Monarch* in 1911. Soon afterwards he was spending most of his leaves at a private flying school at Shoreham. In those days the pupil often had to make his first apprehensive circuits of the field alone, and after a few ground hops Tommy took to the air in an old single-seater Avro. Later he graduated to a Henry Farman Box Kite—the only really dependable aircraft which the school owned. Unfortunately, this was smashed up by another pupil before Tommy could qualify for his pilot's certificate.

There was a delightful air of informality about flying at Shoreham. Two brothers, Cecil and Eric Pashley, supplemented their finances by giving joy-rides in the Box Kite at a sovereign a time. Normally they alternated between flying the plane and taking the money, but Cecil Pashley broke his leg while trying to win a bet which involved driving a motorcycle and sidecar through a maze of petrol-cans. After this he had to remain in the plane and do all the flying himself, as he was unable to walk and it was felt that the sight of a partially disabled pilot might discourage the public who queued up to fly with him.

Two other notable characters there were Cedric Lee, managing director of a firm which rented a hangar on the field, and Gordon Bell, a large, cheerful man with a pronounced stutter, who was making a name as a test pilot. Lee designed and built one aircraft which greatly intrigued Tommy; it had semicircular wings which left a void on either side of the fuselage. When Bell took off in the plane on its maiden flight he found to his dismay that it was almost impossible to fly in any direction but a straight line. After fighting with the controls for several miles he managed to make a wide turn and, arriving in sight of Shoreham again, he side-slipped the aircraft through the telegraph wires bordering the field and dived straight into the nearest ditch. His only comment as he emerged wrathfully from the wreckage was—"Burn it!" This advice was ignored, and when the plane was rebuilt it was flown successfully by Gordon England, later well known as a racing motorist, but the war put an end to further development of an interesting design.

The war put an end, too, to Tommy's hopes of specializing in flying. He had not yet done the necessary amount of sea-time to qualify for a watch-keeping certificate, and, faced by an Admiralty ruling that all volunteer pilots must first possess one, he persuaded an influential relation to intercede with the First Lord of the Admiralty.

His hopes of joining the Royal Naval Air Service were shortlived. Back came—in Mr Winston Churchill's own handwriting—the discouraging reply that it was most undesirable for any young officer to try to short-circuit established procedure. Reflecting wryly that this seemed strange advice to come from Mr Churchill, whose own exploits in India, the Sudan, and South Africa had been largely made possible by consistent rejection of "established procedure," Tommy abandoned his first choice and joined the Submarine service. Twenty years were to pass before he had the chance to take up flying again and get his pilot's certificate. From 1918 he was in command of submarines almost continuously until 1931. It was an era of retrenchment in the Royal Navy; following the Washington Naval Agreement of 1921 the British and American Governments vied with each other in scrapping major warships, but Britain still possessed the greatest fleet in the world. And for the young officer on the Mediterranean or China Stations, where Tommy spent most of his service, life had much to offer. A keen and accomplished horseman, he played polo for the Navy and won many flat races; riding and shooting filled many happy hours of shore leave.

At sea, with his own command, a submarine officer had every opportunity for developing self-reliance and initiative, and developing too the faculty for getting on with his fellow-men. The cramped living conditions in the early submarines imposed their own test of leadership and self-control. Even with the world at peace seagoing officers in small craft could rarely complain of any lack of adventure. Leaving Hong Kong in the submarine L 19 to rejoin his flotilla one day in the early twenties, Tommy had entered the channel between Formosa and the Chinese mainland when the barometer began to fall with astonishing speed. A yellow sky and an ominous swell indicated an approaching typhoon, but avoiding action was out of the question; the water was too shallow to allow him to dive, and he continued on the surface right through the centre of the typhoon. Mountainous seas smashed L 19's casing, and when he reached port he found that even the hydroplane shafts, eight inches thick, had been bent as much as 35 degrees.

Back in England again, in 1931 Tommy was posted to Fort Blockhouse, headquarters of the Submarine service. His unfortunate encounter with the sandbank made it seem all too likely that he would now serve out his time in a series of routine shore appointments, but after a short spell at Blockhouse he was asked by Admiral Sir Arthur Waistell, Commander-in-Chief, Portsmouth, and himself an ex-submariner, to come as his Flag Lieutenant.

In peace-time a Commander-in-Chief ashore has a heavy programme of official engagements. There are inspections to carry out ashore and afloat; staff meetings to preside over, at which all manner of operational and administrative matters are decided; courtesy calls to pay on visiting ships of foreign navies; and countless distinguished visitors to entertain. Apart from engagements involving the three Services there are a host of civilian functions which he is expected to support in his official capacity.

For the smooth running of this daily programme the Flag Lieutenant is largely responsible. And to succeed in this exacting rôle calls for much more than the social poise and charm needed to attract or repel the advances of the Admiral's daughter. The efficient Flag Lieutenant needs to possess organizing ability, a high degree of tact, and initiative; he must mix easily, and yet be discriminating and unobtrusive; he must also be punctual and patient, conscientious and imperturbable. Since Tommy possessed all these qualities to a marked degree, he was asked to stay on when Admiral Sir John D. Kelly went to Portsmouth in 1934, and in all he served five years there.

To stay the course with "Joe" Kelly called for considerable resilience. The Flag Lieutenant now had to cope with the eccentricities of one of the great characters of the Navy. The new Commander-in-Chief was a huge man with a hooked nose, a jutting chin, and the physique of a heavy-weight boxer. A bluff, irascible seaman who affected to despise the technical advances of the modern Navy—because, in truth, he could not really understand them—he was a stern disciplinarian who insisted on smart boats, clean ships, and well-dressed sailors. He had quelled the Invergordon Mutiny by sheer force of personality; his rough, unsubtle wit became a legend in the Fleet, and the sailors loved him.[3]

When he came to Portsmouth he was a tired, rather lonely old man of unpredictable moods, and to keep the machinery of Admiralty House running smoothly required all the Flag Lieutenant's diplomacy. But they got on well together. Joe Kelly liked originality, and was intrigued that Tommy, who had just bought a second-hand Gipsy Moth, could fly his own aircraft to Worthy Down, clad in frockcoat and sword, to return the Group Captain's call on the Commander-in-Chief.

In August 1936 Kelly hauled down his flag. The first Lord, Sir Samuel Hoare, was then about to pay an official visit to the Mediterranean in the Admiralty yacht *Enchantress*, and Tommy was appointed Flag Lieutenant for the cruise. They visited Gibraltar and Malta, passing en route another Yacht, *Nahlin*, with the King and Mrs Simpson on board. At Malta there were lengthy discussions about the lack of anti-aircraft defences, and the

[3]A revealing portrait of Admiral Kelly is given by Commander Geoffrey Lowis, A.F.C., R.N.(ret.), in his book *Fabulous Admirals*.

Admiral Superintendent of the Dockyard[4] urged that caves should be hewn at Marsa Scirocco to provide aircraft workshops and hangars for fighters. In the end nothing whatever was done to improve any aspect of Malta's defences, for at this time, with war already raging in Spain and the shadow of a far greater conflict looming ever larger over Central Europe, the British Government were still—in the words of Mr Churchill, their unrelenting critic—"resolved to be irresolute, adamant for drift."[5] And if they were not prepared to spend money at home on expanding a pitifully inadequate Air Force and Navy, Hoare, who confessed that he himself only learnt the lesson of Malta's "extreme importance as a strategic centre" for the first time on this tour, must have realized even as he listened to the arguments of his naval advisers on the spot that there was little chance of implementing any recommendations on behalf of a remote Mediterranean island.[6]

To the officers of the yacht the First Lord was pleasant and considerate. Rather precise in manner and speech, he was inclined too to be pernickety over dress. One day at Malta he had changed for an official lunch, and Bill Astor, his Parliamentary Private Secretary, offered to mix a special cocktail called a "French 75." This consisted largely of champagne, and while Astor was shaking it it exploded, covering the First Lord, immaculate in his white tropical suit, from top to toe in a sticky foam at the very moment he was due to go ashore. The only person who appeared completely unmoved by this embarrassing mishap was Hoare himself.

By the time *Enchantress* returned to England the value of having a permanent Flag Lieutenant to the Board of Admiralty had been realized. This new post was offered to Tommy in the winter of 1936, and he moved to London. Thenceforward much of his time was occupied in liaison with the various home ports, and making the arrangements for all official visits which came under the ægis of the Admiralty.

At the Coronation Naval Review in 1937 all living past First Lords of the Admiralty were invited to go afloat in *Enchantress*, and for the first time Tommy met Winston Churchill. What impact, if any, his future Personal Assistant made on Mr Churchill is not known, but Churchill made a distinct impression on Tommy because of an incident which took place just before the start of the traditional fireworks display and illumination of the Fleet.

Restless and obviously bored by this time, Churchill announced that he wished to return to London. Aware of an order from the Commander-in-Chief, Tommy asked if he would mind waiting for a short while. "No

[4] Admiral Sir Wilbraham Ford, K.C.B., K.B.E.
[5] In a speech in the House of Commons (November 12, 1936).
[6] Viscount Templewood, *Nine Troubled Years*, p. 214.

boats are supposed to move until the fireworks finish," he explained. "Rubbish!" said Churchill gruffly, and, calling for the Admiralty barge, he went ashore.

Duff Cooper had replaced Hoare at the Admiralty, and with him Tommy again visited the Mediterranean in *Enchantress*. Much of Duff Cooper's time was spent fighting the Navy's battles in a Cabinet which obstinately refused to sanction the most modest estimates for new warship construction, and trying to iron out problems arising from the transfer of the Fleet Air Arm from Air Ministry control.[7] But there were compensations for the long days in Whitehall. "To visit ships was a great pleasure. . . . I had not been long at the Admiralty before I knew the age and tonnage of every capital ship in the Fleet and could have repeated from memory the various classes of cruisers and destroyers."[8]

Tommy accompanied Duff Cooper on many visits to the Fleet in home waters, but their last voyage together in *Enchantress*—in August 1938—was to the Baltic. When they set out the Munich Crisis and the First Lord's dramatic resignation were only a few weeks distant, but it was a happy cruise. Tommy enjoyed serving with Duff Cooper, who was quick-tempered but a man of great charm—a lover of good books, good wine, and good conversation. One day they were walking down a street in Copenhagen to the hotel where they were lunching when the First Lord drew his Flag Lieutenant's attention to a shop front shared by two different firms—a bookseller and a wine merchant. "Look at that," he said; "two of the finest things of life in one window!"

At Danzig a ceremonial duck-shoot was arranged in the First Lord's honour. This proved something of an anticlimax as the only birds to appear were a few enormously fat tame ducks which seemed to find some difficulty in flying at all. They also visited Gdynia, where they paid an official call on Poland's Foreign Minister, Colonel Beck, "an intense and concentrated bore," who became very drunk while entertaining them to dinner and remained in an advanced state of intoxication throughout their stay in the port.[9]

They called at Helsingfors and Stockholm, but the programme was never completed. While they lay off the coast of Denmark on August 28 a signal was received summoning the First Lord back to England. After a dash through the Kiel Canal the yacht entered the Thames early on the morning of August 30, and Duff Cooper went straight ashore.

[7] Expert advisers to the First Lord considered the £70,000,000 put forward by the Admiralty in 1938 as the bare minimum needed for new construction. However, Sir Thomas Inskip, then Minister for Co-ordination of Defence, recommended to the Cabinet that this should be reduced by no less than £58,000,000. (Duff Cooper, *Old Men Forget*, p. 216.)

[8] *Ibid.*, p. 217.

[9] Lady Diana Cooper, *The Light of Common Day*.

The purpose of the Cabinet meeting which he attended that morning was to consider Germany's attitude towards Czecho-Slovakia. Duff Cooper wrote later:

> If Hitler was at that time still in some uncertainty as to what action Great Britain would take . . . I thought that we should do everything in our power to indicate by action the line we meant to adopt. A suitable warning would be to bring the crews of our ships up to full complement, which would amount to semi-mobilization. No such decisions were, however, taken at that time, and after this first Cabinet meeting I began to feel that my views were not in agreement with those of the majority and the most important of my colleagues.[10]

One month later Duff Cooper left the Government, and Lord Stanhope took his place at the Admiralty. When war broke out Neville Chamberlain, who had accepted with such relief the resignation of his chief critic in the Cabinet, was obliged to send for an even more persistent and outspoken opponent of his policies—the man who had said in the debate on Munich: "We have sustained a total and unmitigated defeat." On the morning of September 3, 1939, Winston Churchill became First Lord of the Admiralty once again.

* * * * *

Throughout the Admiralty and, indeed, every ship and shore station, to which the news had been immediately signalled, Churchill's return brought a new and heartening sense of purpose. While his grasp of defence matters entitled him to be regarded at this time as the complete 'triphibian,' he had in his previous spell at the Admiralty identified himself so wholeheartedly with the problems of the Navy that Lloyd George had said to him reproachfully: "You have become a water creature. You think we all live in the sea, and all your thoughts are devoted to sea life, fishes, and other aquatic creatures. You forget that most of us live on land."[11]

In the struggle now joined Churchill's attitude to the naval task could be summed up in a characteristic phrase of his own. "If you should be thrown into a quarrel you should bear yourself so that an opponent may be aware of it . . . pugnacity and will-power cannot be dispensed with."[12] From the outset he was determined to make the Germans aware that he was at the head of the Navy.

To the Admiralty planning staff he put forward a succession of imaginative ideas of his own—the provision of a special squadron to force an entry into the Baltic (Operation *Catherine*); the construction of dummy battleships for use in the Firth of Forth; attacks on the enemy's inland

[10] Duff Cooper, *op cit.*, p. 225.
[11] Riddell, *More Pages from my Diary.*
[12] In a speech in the House of Commons (January 31, 1947).

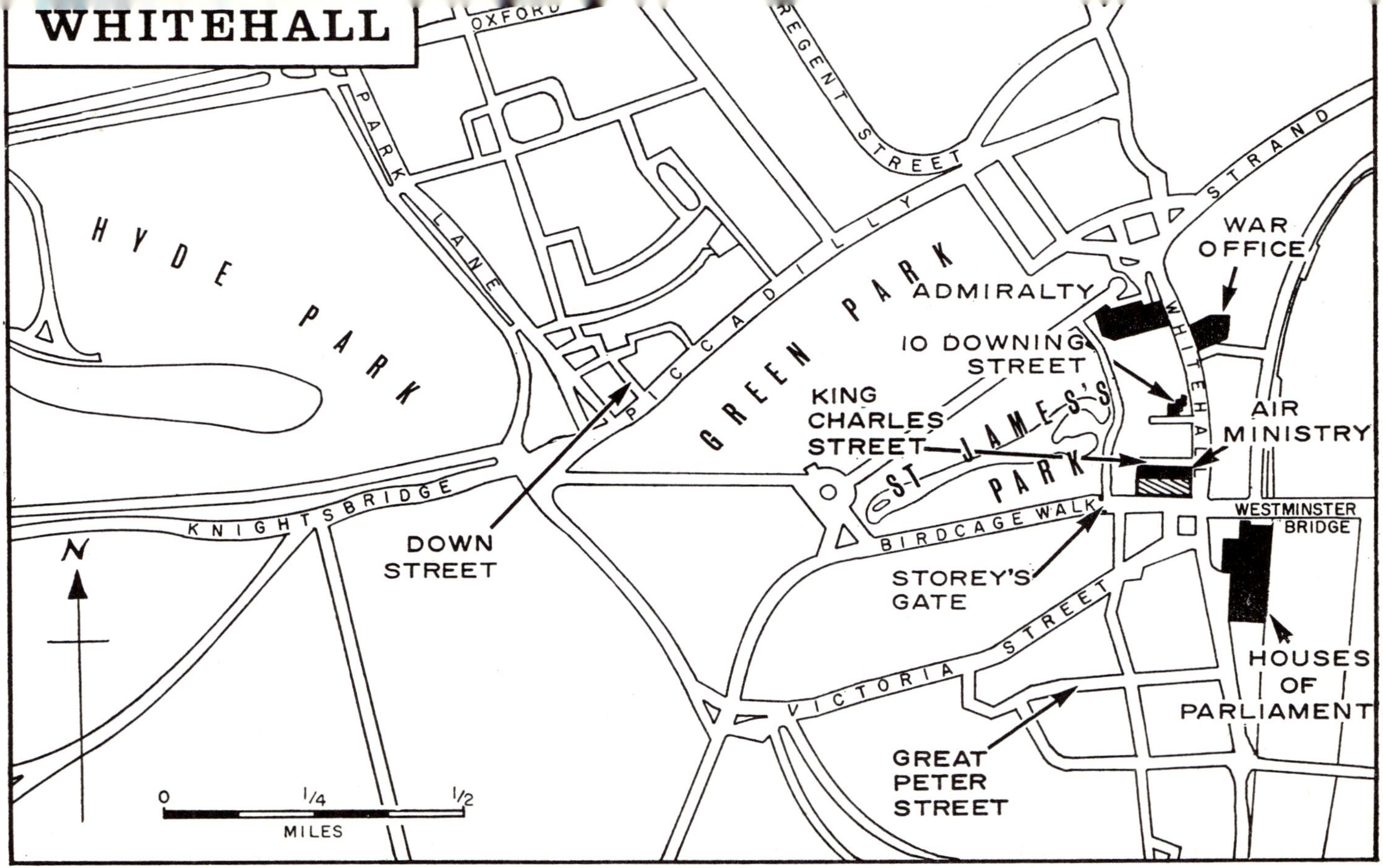
WHITEHALL
OXFORD
REGENT STREET
STRAND
PARK LANE
HYDE PARK
PICCADILLY
GREEN PARK
WAR OFFICE
ADMIRALTY
WHITEHALL
10 DOWNING STREET
KING CHARLES STREET
ST JAMES'S PARK
AIR MINISTRY
WESTMINSTER BRIDGE
KNIGHTSBRIDGE
DOWN STREET
BIRDCAGE WALK
STOREY'S GATE
VICTORIA STREET
HOUSES OF PARLIAMENT
GREAT PETER STREET
N
0
1/4
1/2
MILES

waterways with fluvial mines; and a plan for occupying Lulea to deny Germany the use of the ore from Gallivare, to mention only a few of them. In the early months, however, the Royal Navy were desperately hard-pressed to carry out even their essential commitments.

A convoy system had to be set in motion, but there was a desperate shortage of escort vessels and virtually no air support; enemy minelaying and air attacks took a heavy toll of coastal shipping, but a saving mercy was the strange fact that the enemy began the war without a single torpedo bomber. Even so, our survival at sea depended largely on "bows, arrows, and guts," as one harassed naval captain remarked after a meeting at which Admiral Pound had once again underlined the danger of earmarking twenty-five valuable ships for Operation Catherine.

This particular plan was, indeed, impractical at such a juncture, for it called for a reduction in the draught of the *Revenge* Class battleships to enable them to pass through the Great Belt—this necessitated the building of special 'blisters' or caissons on to the ships' sides—and the conversion of four Clan Line vessels to carry fuel and ammunition. The bows of the destroyers and other ships of the squadron had to be strengthened against the Baltic ice, and, in all, the modifications involved would have taken a year to carry out.

Churchill's insistence on a detailed examination of projects like this, at a time when the Admiralty's resources were stretched to breaking-point, provoked criticism. To the ultra-conservative the new First Lord, with his "wild ideas," was a force to be resisted, but he jolted many stereotyped Service minds into thinking on new and original lines. Where his own thinking was concerned he respected opposition and would invariably accept it if it was shown to be well-founded, but those who opposed him had to contend with two factors—the First Lord's persuasive powers when a plan of his own was involved, and his tendency to suspect obstruction for obstruction's sake. On the first score even the redoubtable Admiral Fisher had been moved to complain: "I am sure I am right . . . I am sure I am right, but he is always convincing me against my will. I hear him talk and he seems to make difficulties vanish."[13] Dudley Pound, who was destined to be Churchill's chief naval adviser throughout the first four years of the war, was a far less forceful character than Fisher; but he was tough and imperturbable in the face of disaster, and he fought his battles at the conference table with great tactical skill.

Completely devoted to the naval service, Pound was something of an enigma to subordinates, who found him cold, remote, and impersonal. He disliked delegating responsibility—as an instance of this, he invariably wrote out his signals himself—and Admirals junior to him were often

[13] Admiral of the Fleet Lord Fisher of Kilverstone, *Memories*.

disconcerted to be treated as if they were still Midshipmen. But they respected his great professional knowledge and his honesty.

All through his career Pound had over-worked. By the time war came he never allowed himself more than four hours' sleep at night. Even if he retired early the Royal Marine sentries used to see his light burning hour after hour, and Churchill, on his own way to bed, would often throw in the early editions of the morning papers as he passed Pound's room. On one occasion, when the First Sea Lord had been particularly advised to rest, it was discovered that he had gone to bed just as late as usual, leaving instructions for his car to be ready at 4.0 A.M., as he had decided to go duck-shooting.

In the circumstances it was not surprising that he fell asleep from time to time when evening meetings dragged on, but those who knew him well noticed that his spells of somnolence coincided suspiciously often with arguments which were not going his way! Churchill, who became very fond of him, once remarked: "Dudley Pound's a funny old boy. People think he's *always* asleep, but you've only got to suggest reducing the naval estimates by a million and he's awake in a flash."

In addition to Pound much responsibility at this period fell upon Rear-Admiral Tom Phillips, Deputy Chief of the Naval Staff; Rear-Admiral B. A. Fraser, the Third Sea Lord, who was responsible for the building and refitting of ships and the efficiency of the naval dockyards; Captain C. S. Daniel and Captain C. H. J. Harcourt, Directors respectively of Plans and Operations; and Captain W. G. Tennant, who held a somewhat anomalous and ill-defined post as Chief Staff Officer to Admiral Pound.[14]

All were subjected to what became known as "The First Lord's Morning Prayer"—the memoranda which invariably began "Pray inform me . . ." Papers on which Churchill required action or comment were circulated in dockets bearing a red label. There were, Tommy recalls, three gradings officially in existence for Churchill's papers—"Action This Day," "Report within Three Days," and "Report as soon as Possible." The second and third were, however, rarely used. When his minutes were typed he used to stick the red labels on himself, and from that moment things moved with quite remarkable speed. One day Sir James Lithgow, the Glasgow shipbuilder who was Controller of Merchant Shipbuilding and Repairs, seized the chance to smuggle a few of the magic labels out of the First Lord's room, and was highly elated with the results they produced. He was soon found out, however, and was made to disgorge the remainder.

For a while the First Lord's personal staff saw little of him. The War

[14] Phillips was later promoted to Admiral and appointed C.-in-C., Eastern Fleet, losing his life when his flagship, *Prince of Wales*, was sunk off the Malayan coast on December 10, 1941; Fraser became an Admiral of the Fleet and First Sea Lord; and Daniel, Harcourt, and Tennant all became Admirals.

Cabinet was meeting sometimes twice a day, and when he was not at Downing Street Churchill spent much of his time in the Admiralty War Room. When he moved from his flat in Morpeth Mansions into Admiralty House the library, close to his bedroom, was transformed into an Upper War Room, and Commander Richard Pim, a tall, shrewd Ulsterman who had served in the R.N.V.R. since the First World War, was placed in charge of this.

The Admiralty War Room staff plotted the position of every British and Allied warship throughout the world. The whereabouts of each convoy, together with its escort, speed, and number of ships, was shown, as was the position of every British, Allied, and neutral merchant ship at sea or in port. Churchill asked that ships equipped with Asdic gear should be specially marked on the map, which was revised twice daily; he liked to know the names of all escort group commanders; and he wanted the latest information about the weather prevailing in the North Atlantic. When a gale warning was received a cardboard dolphin would go up on the board.

If a raider or U-boat was reported the War Room plot enabled him to see what British ships were near by and what was their speed. He could also find out at a glance if ships were being delayed in any part of the world. In the middle of one night Sir John Gilmour, then Minister of Shipping, was woken by a telephone call. "It seems to me," said Mr Churchill, "that those ships loading in the River Plate should have sailed by now. Please let me have a report."

The First Lord used maps for many purposes. One day he noticed that a certain ship was crossing the Atlantic with 7000 tons of eggs. "How many eggs go to the ton?" he demanded. Pim, who had no idea, hurriedly rang up the Ministry of Agriculture. When he returned with the answer Churchill looked thoughtful. "Do you realize that cargo represents one egg for every second person in the British Isles," he remarked.

As his demands for information increased Pim had to rope in a special staff of R.N.V.R. officers to man the room in watches. Among them were a former journalist who had survived the sinking of *Courageous*, a barrister, a Bond Street jeweller, and a member of the B.B.C. Clad in his dressing-gown, Churchill would often pay his first visit to the War Room soon after seven in the morning. The information it provided became indispensable to him, as did the analyses, tables, and diagrams which flowed from the statistical department now at work in the Admiralty under the direction of Professor Lindemann, who for many years had been his chief adviser on all scientific matters.

A close friend of the Churchill family from the days when he had been Professor of Experimental Philosophy at Oxford in the early thirties,

Lindemann, a brilliant mathematician and physicist, had the gift of explaining the most complicated scientific phenomena in words of one syllable. The briefings prepared by his small band of statisticians and economists were particularly helpful to Churchill during his inspection tours, when he might be confronted by some alleged difficulty over shortage of manpower, a bottleneck in armament supply, or delay in the turn-round of a convoy.

For some time after he arrived at the Admiralty Lindemann was regarded with suspicion—even hostility—by heads of departments subjected to his close and critical scrutiny. And when it was rumoured, quite correctly, that he was a vegetarian who, if he drank at all, asked for his brandy to be measured out by the cubic centimetre, they thought his favoured position with Mr Churchill was even more surprising. Few realized that this association had already stood the test of years. In the campaign for rearmament which Churchill had fought over the past decade Lindemann's wisdom and prescience, and his courageous independence of mind, had made a vital contribution.

* * * * *

A weekly event at Admiralty House was initiated even before Churchill moved into the flat on the top floor. Sending for the Flag Lieutenant, he asked him to arrange a special dinner-party every Tuesday. Each of these gatherings had a definite object. Either the First Lord wanted to become better acquainted with certain naval officers or politicians, or he wished to bring together men of influence in different spheres—quite often people who were reputed to be at loggerheads. He began by inviting members of the Board of Admiralty and the Army Council, whose relationship was amicable enough; later he was host to the Board of Admiralty and members of the Air Council, who at that time were somewhat antagonistic.

Before these dinners—usually limited to fourteen—a Swedish milk punch was provided. This concoction proved a great success as a 'party-starter,' and as Cabinet Ministers, senior civil servants, and the heads of the fighting Services got to know each other in an atmosphere of easy informality a more co-operative attitude was manifest in many quarters of Whitehall.

On Churchill's arrival at the Admiralty he knew precisely what was required, but he lacked knowledge of the personal characteristics and capabilities of the various naval commanders, their needs and difficulties. He preferred to see them against their own background and among their own staff. Accordingly Tommy was told to arrange for a series of visits—to Chatham, Scapa and Loch Ewe, Portsmouth, Plymouth, and Greenock. On September 14, taking with him Sir Archibald Sinclair and Brendan Bracken, Churchill set out for Wick.

"On this first journey north he was preoccupied with precisely the same problem that had faced him twenty-five years earlier. Was the fleet secure at Scapa? We were given an immediate answer on our arrival," Tommy recalls, "for although Admiral Sir Charles Forbes, the Commander-in-Chief, was there in his flagship, H.M.S. *Nelson*, the rest of the fleet were hiding in Loch Ewe, which we visited two days later. They were there for the same reason which had driven them from Scapa at the time Mr Churchill visited Admiral Jellicoe in 1914—lack of preparedness against an enemy attack on the main fleet anchorage. None of the entrance channels had been properly netted. A naval fighter station was being built at Wick, but although the runways were almost ready there were no buildings; at a near-by R.A.F. station the buildings were complete, but there were no runways!

"On the 18th, a beautiful, sunny September day, we left Loch Ewe by road to join the train at Inverness, and during a picnic lunch Mr Churchill pointed out a hill in the distance. He then recalled a strange incident in the First World War.

"A powerful light had been seen flashing intermittently from this hillside at night, and it was believed that a German spy was signalling information about Fleet movements. When the area was searched the suspected spy turned out to be a London businessman who had installed a portable searchlight on the roof of his shooting lodge. This enabled him to shoot stags in comfort from his bedroom window—a form of sport which he had hitherto managed to conceal from his remote neighbours."

Churchill's uneasiness over the Scapa defences was justified. Within a month Lieutenant Prien, in U 47, entered the Flow on the surface through Kirk Sound and sank the battleship *Royal Oak*.[15]

This led to a further visit to Admiral Forbes at Scapa, when priority was given for extensive reinforcement of the sea and anti-aircraft defences. On this occasion Churchill was accompanied by Admiral Pound and the Deputy Chief of the Air Staff, Air Marshal Sir Richard Peirse. During the train journey to Scotland Churchill was extolling the merits of a new kind of pill which his doctor had recommended—it was a mild form of sleeping

[15]According to Schellenberg, who succeeded Canaris as head of the German Secret Service, this feat was greatly helped by long-range planning, spread over fifteen years. A former German naval captain named Alfred Wehring, who transferred to the military section of the Secret Service, learnt the trade of watchmaker. After changing his name to Oertel and gaining a Swiss passport he became a naturalized Briton and settled in Kirkwall, where he opened a small jeweller's shop. Early in October 1939 he sent information that the eastern approach to Scapa through Kirk Sound was not fully sealed off, and Prien was therefore ordered to proceed straight to Scapa and attack any shipping he could reach in the Flow. (*The Schellenberg Memoirs.*) In point of fact, research by the Foreign Documents Section of the Admiralty has failed to establish the existence of any German naval captain named Alfred Wehring. In the Admiralty view Schellenberg has created a fictitious naval officer and made him the original of an equally imaginary Swiss watchmaker.

tablet, to be used on train or air journeys—and, sending his detective for the box, he handed one pill to each of his companions. Hardly had they swallowed these when to their dismay the detective announced that he had handed them the wrong box. To the Admiral and the Air Marshal Churchill had dealt out a homely cure for constipation!

* * * * *

At the beginning of November Churchill visited France for the first time since taking office. Despite free and friendly discussions between staff officers of the Admiralty and the French Ministry of Marine, the French Navy had so far made little contribution to the war effort. The First Lord therefore felt that the time had come for a frank review of the whole naval situation with his opposite number, M. Campinchi. If some sense of urgency could be infused into the French programme for building and refitting anti-submarine craft they would be able to play a much more active part in the protection of the Allied convoys. To help them the Admiralty were prepared to equip with Asdic gear any French warships which could be sent to British ports.

Churchill took an immediate liking to Campinchi, a courageous Corsican, but when he drove out of Paris to Darlan's headquarters in the grounds of a château near Rambouillet he soon found there was little accord between the Admiral and his Minister. The French Naval Staff seemed largely divorced from the civil and political side of the Ministry of Marine, and Darlan went to tedious lengths to emphasize his own independence. He seemed, indeed, more interested in establishing his superiority to politicians in general than in discussing the problems of the naval war. Undeterred, Churchill invited both the Admiral and the Minister of Marine to a dinner-party he gave that evening at the Ritz.

To this he also asked several prominent French political leaders, irrespective of party; they included Daladier (the French Premier); Reynaud, Blum, Mandel, and Léger. When Tommy visited the British Embassy to enlist their aid in making the invitations Sir Ronald Campbell's private secretary showed some alarm at the prospect of the Ambassador being involved in any way with such an explosive gathering, but only one man refused. When the invitation reached Daladier he rang up and asked for the guest list to be read out to him. He then expressed his regret that a previous engagement would prevent him from attending. Nevertheless the dinner was a great success. Sir Edward Spears, who was present, noted that, although Churchill had by this time received disturbing reports about the state of French morale, he was not in the least depressed. "We are quite capable of beating the Germans singlehanded," he was heard to remark.[16]

Before returning to England he spent a final night with Gort at Arras.

[16] Major-General Sir Edward Spears, *Prelude to Dunkirk*, p. 62.

Unlike some military commanders, Lord Gort held somewhat austere views about the feeding and accommodation of himself and his staff. He lived very simply and had no use for frills of any kind. From his Military Assistant Tommy heard of a recent incident which had caused much amusement at the British G.H.Q.

In the sparsely furnished room which Gort's staff used as an office his Military Assistant would march to and fro as he dictated orders and reports, and his hobnailed boots made such a thunderous noise on the bare boards that the A.D.C.'s working near by found it difficult to concentrate on their own tasks. At length they had a bright idea. After searching the building they discovered a tattered strip of carpet, and this was nailed down in the M.A.'s path. When Gort entered the room next day he glared at the offending object as though he could hardly believe his eyes. "Carpets?" he barked. His Military Assistant began to explain, but he cut him short with one withering word. "Pansy!" he said. And with a snort of contempt he left the room.

* * * * *

Although the first German bombs fell on Britain a few days after Churchill's return, the Shetlands were too remote a target to attract more than passing interest. The reporting of naval operations was often necessarily delayed for security reasons, and, with the stalemate on land, news of offensive action was confined to the bombardment of Germany with propaganda leaflets. In many minds grew a conviction that the war was not going to prove such an ordeal after all, and this mood of unreasoning optimism was encouraged by the predictions of 'military experts,' who proved almost daily in print that the Maginot Line was impregnable and that Hitler had overreached himself.

In this state of affairs there was no parallel to the apathy already manifest in certain circles in France, but the situation cried out for leadership. And since no clarion call came from Neville Chamberlain—once acidly described by Lloyd George as "a good Lord Mayor of Birmingham in a lean year"—Winston Churchill's first major broadcast, with its shrewd appraisal of Russian motives, commanded wide attention.

He spoke of successes against the U-boats. "The Royal Navy is hunting them night and day—I will not say without mercy, because God forbid we should ever part company with that, but at any rate with zeal and not altogether without relish." In his next broadcast came characteristic references to Hitler ("that evil man") and the "prodigious contortionist," Ribbentrop. It was plain to his listeners that the affairs of the Admiralty at least were in resolute hands.

Soon he was to announce the first notable victory in battle, but before then the Royal Navy faced a crisis which might well have decided the war at sea.

2

A Night on the Mud Flats

ONE evening just after his return from France Churchill was at his home at Chartwell when Admiral Pound arrived. He reported that the mysterious sinking of ships in waters already searched by our minesweepers had now assumed serious proportions. Six more vessels had just gone down in the mouth of the Thames, and it might be necessary to close the Port of London.

The news came as no surprise to the First Lord. These unexplained casualties had been occurring off various South Coast ports for the past two months, and although some form of magnetic mine was suspected, counter-measures could not be devised until the precise nature of the mechanism was known.

As the sinkings increased in early November Pound called a late-night meeting to consider what further steps, if any, could be taken to meet this threat. "It had been a pretty grim day in the Admiralty," recalls one officer who was present, "and the First Sea Lord must have noticed that we didn't look very cheerful. He lit his pipe rather more deliberately than usual and then remarked, with one of his rare smiles, 'Well, gentlemen, the war's beginning to get interesting at last.' But I don't think he felt any better about it than we did, for there seemed to be absolutely nothing we could do to stop the sinkings."

Rear-Admiral A. L. St G. Lyster had already been working for some weeks, sifting every scrap of evidence which might yield a clue to pass on to H.M.S. *Vernon*, the Torpedo and Mining establishment at Portsmouth, but the search brought little reward until the evening of Monday, November 20, when a ship which had been mined managed to struggle into the

Humber. At the same time reports reached the Admiralty that low-flying aircraft had just dropped large objects into the sea off Hull and Southend.

Lieutenant-Commander R. C. Lewis, a torpedo specialist, was immediately dispatched to Southend, where he spent all the following day questioning masters of ships at anchor in the roads. Several told him they had seen strange things, "looking like seamen's kitbags," falling from enemy aircraft, and this was confirmed by the Naval Officer-in-Charge there. An ex-gunnery officer, he explained in some exasperation that he had been unable to open fire on the German planes: all anti-aircraft fire was co-ordinated with radar plots and controlled from Uxbridge. Deciding at length to act on his own initiative, he had asked for a number of Bisley marksmen to be posted to Southend from Whale Island, the Navy's gunnery school. The men had just arrived, and that night he planned to station them at intervals along the pier.

Lewis returned to London to write his report, and he was still working in the Admiralty late that evening when word came from Southend that the Bisley marksmen had just 'winged' an aircraft. It had promptly dropped something on the mud flats off Shoeburyness, and this would be visible at low tide.

Asking the N.O.I.C. to arrange for a photographer, Lewis set out again. He took with him Lieutenant-Commander J. G. D. Ouvry, who had just arrived in the Admiralty after four days' exhausting work in rendering safe mines which had broken adrift from our own East Coast barrage. The journey seemed endless, for dense fog blanketed the forty-mile route to the sea. While Ouvry snatched some sleep on the back seat Lewis guided the Admiralty driver. At the large hotel which served as the naval headquarters at Southend they picked up the photographer and set off across the beach.

They soon found the mine, which was lying on the Shoeburyness Artillery Range, but the tide was flowing in fast and they had only thirty minutes before the sea would cover it. They photographed it from various angles, measured it, and then, with a signal pad and pencil, took an impression of a small silvery-coloured object which protruded from the casing of the mine. On their way back they found a parachute which had parted company from the mine when it struck the water.

After sitting up for the rest of the night in the hotel, writing an interim report, they went back to the mud flats. What followed can now be described in Roger Lewis's own words.

"We had about four hours to play with. First we took a jolly good look at the mine. Then we decided to take out the little object we had examined earlier. We didn't like the look of it, and thought it probably housed the detonator.

"Ouvry said to me, 'I'm senior to you, and it's my job to do this. You'd better go back three hundred yards and stand by.'

"I did this, and he and a Petty Officer named Baldwin, using a spanner which the Army had made for us overnight after they had looked at the rubbings we had taken on the signal pad, began unscrewing the small cap. Ouvry spoke to me every now and then over a telephone we had rigged up, and I made notes.

"When he got the object out we assumed the detonator was now in our hands and the mine was therefore safe. One thing puzzled us, however—the object we had extracted seemed to have no visible connexion with the rest of the mine . . . there were no wires or anything leading from it. It was, admittedly, in *contact* with the mine, but not with any mechanism immediately inside it. It did, however, have a little thing underneath it which we recognized as a gaine, so we concluded we must be right."[1]

They carried the small object to the beach and laid it down. Then Ouvry and Lewis, accompanied by Baldwin and Leading Seaman Vearncombe, went back to the mine to take out any other movable parts they could reach.

"The tide was now coming in again. First we got out some of the spring mechanism for releasing the parachute. Then we rolled the mine over. Immediately we found another piece which could obviously be unscrewed, for it had two indents in the head. Gradually we turned this, driving it round and round with blows from a hammer and screwdriver. We were bashing it about with no misgivings, for we were certain the mine was safe, but when it came free at last we saw to our horror that it was a perfectly normal mine detonator-carrier, with two detonators protruding from its base. We were absolutely shattered!

"We cut the leads with a penknife, extracted two primer systems and two detonator systems, and carried them all back to the shore. On the dome in front of the mine we had noticed four mysterious metal discs, about six inches in diameter, but we didn't take these off because our main consideration at this stage was to make the mine safe for the journey to H.M.S. *Vernon*, where it could be examined more thoroughly."

They had just got back to the hotel when the discovery of a second mine was reported, but the sea covered this before Ouvry and Lewis could reach it. "It was then two o'clock. As we had had no sleep and little to eat we were glad of a glass of champagne which the N.O.I.C. produced for us."

The mine was loaded on to a lorry. Ouvry, taking with him the mysterious small object he had first removed from the mine-casing, went to Woolwich Arsenal to get it X-rayed; Lewis headed for London to report to Admiral Lyster.

*   *   *   *   *

[1] A gaine is a small primer which builds up the explosive power of a detonator.

In the Admiralty there was intense excitement. Every one realized that the bravery of the four men concerned had almost certainly brought deliverance from disaster. It was a historic moment, and Churchill, greatly moved, marked it in a fitting way. At 11.30 that night he called a meeting, over which he himself presided, in the Admiralty's largest room, and to a gathering which included almost every flag officer serving in the Admiralty and the Directors of every division and department, Lewis told his story. Since he had had no sleep for forty-eight hours he found it "a bit of an ordeal." At the end Churchill turned to him and asked, "Were you frightened?" Before he could reply, however, Admiral Pound, who evidently considered the question an affront to any naval officer, said indignantly, "Frightened? Of course he wasn't frightened!"

Churchill then asked Lewis what kind of a mine he thought it was. Knowing that the Royal Navy had laid magnetic mines of their own off the Dutch coast in 1918, Lewis had come to the conclusion that the Germans were unlikely to have copied something we had developed ourselves. At this stage, therefore, he suspected it was not a magnetic mine which they had found, but an acoustic mine, actuated by mechanism hidden behind the four metal discs they had noticed in the nose.

He explained his reasons, and then Churchill pushed back his chair. To the gathering at large he said, "You have heard a very exciting and brave story. We can trust the technical staff and the scientists at H.M.S. *Vernon* to give us the answer in a short time." And he sent Lewis off to bed.

As it turned out, Roger Lewis was wrong, but his mistake had an interesting sequel. Germany's secret weapon was found to be an improved version of Britain's magnetic mine of twenty years earlier, and its designers had incorporated one special refinement. In case the mine dropped in very shallow water, where it might be seen by the human eye, they had installed a gadget which would destroy it automatically. This consisted of an ordinary Luftwaffe bomb fuse, which could be set to detonate at a depth of seven feet or less—and it was this object which had so puzzled Ouvry and Lewis from the start. It had not functioned on this occasion because when the machine-gunners strung out along the pier opened fire on the German plane the captain ordered the mines to be jettisoned. In their anxiety to get rid of them the crew forgot to set the special mechanism to the firing position.

Lewis's mistaken belief that the mine was acoustic prompted Churchill to issue an order which had far-reaching consequences. Soon afterwards he decreed, "The right department to deal with noises under water must develop an acoustic minesweeping gear." H.M.S. *Osprey* were told to tackle this problem without delay, and by the time the first Allied ship was sunk by an acoustic mine some four months later the scientists in *Osprey* and *Vernon*, working in collaboration, had their answer ready.

The final postcript to the conquest of the magnetic mine was written on the parade ground of H.M.S. *Vernon* on the morning of December 21, when His Majesty the King invested Ouvry and Lewis with the D.S.O., and also decorated Baldwin and Vearncombe for their courage and devotion to duty.

* * * * *

By this time Mr Churchill's working routine had fallen into the pattern which was to become familiar in the days ahead. Naval officers bringing the latest signals to him in the morning would find him sitting up in a bed strewn with papers, dictating to two secretaries after an early breakfast. His energy and the range of his interests were remarkable, for in addition to keeping closely in touch with day-to-day operations, developments in the Fleet Air Arm (on which he had written a very far-sighted memorandum for Inskip three years earlier), the progress of naval construction and repairs, and the organization of supplies, he found time to dictate memoranda to the Prime Minister about the 'black-out,' to the First Sea Lord about court-martial procedure, and to the Secretary of the Admiralty about the destruction of confidential books, the removal of rubbish which might block the ventilators of the Citadel—the hideous new bomb-proof annexe which housed the operational and Intelligence staffs—and the provision of emergency stocks of candles in case of air-raid damage.

He kept a vigilant eye on personnel problems. Why should it be difficult for men in certain branches of the Navy to rise to commissioned rank? ("If a telegraphist may rise, why not a painter? Apparently there is no difficulty about painters rising in Germany.") Surely Admirals of the Fleet should not be penalized for gaining early promotion ("What is the value of being made an Admiral of the Fleet if it is only to hoist the Union Flag for one day and retire to Cheltenham, writing occasional letters to *The Times*?").

We also find him badgering the Fourth Sea Lord about decorations for minesweeping personnel, telling the Second Sea Lord to provide more backgammon sets for the sailors, and busily trying to discover what has happened to "the £1000 which Lord Rothermere gave me for various kinds of amusements."[2]

Although he continued working through the day and a large part of the night, he seemed to thrive on toil; responsibility, which others found a burden, was a stimulus to him. Geoffrey Dawson, the editor of *The Times*, who lunched with the First Lord in the flat at Admiralty House during the most anxious period of the magnetic mine casualties, found him

[2] Churchill, Vol. I, pp. 656–692.

at the top of his form. "I left him about to take his regular hour's sleep," he recorded in his diary.[3]

This brief rest in the afternoon, when he undressed and went to bed, was all he needed to recharge his physical vitality. Mentally he drew fresh inspiration from the gravity of his task and his close contact with men of action. He liked to hear about naval operations at first hand, and one young officer for whom he formed a particular regard was Commander E. O. Bickford, captain of the submarine *Salmon*.

Bickford, a gay, talented, and attractive personality, who gained immediate promotion and the D.S.O. for torpedoing the cruisers *Nurnberg* and *Leipzig*, was often invited to the flat for meals. After a while the Churchill family noticed that he was looking drawn and tired; the strain of the long winter patrols was beginning to tell on him. Mr Churchill, greatly distressed, tried to get him rested from operations, but Bickford firmly refused to leave his ship. Not long afterwards he was reported missing.

Early in December came the Battle of the River Plate. Throughout the 13th, as Commodore Harwood's three battered but defiant cruisers continued to engage the *Graf Spee*, the First Lord hardly left the War Room. Four days later he sat hunched up in his dressing-gown in front of a huge chart of South America, enthralled by an eyewitness account, broadcast by an American radio commentator, of the scene on the waterfront at Montevideo as Captain Langsdorf prepared to put to sea in the pocket battleship.

Harwood's own reports to the Admiralty were considerably delayed. They had to be sent in cipher via a network of relay stations, and the time-lag between them and the colourful commentary to which he was listening exasperated the First Lord, who kept urging Admiral Pound to revise his orders to the Commodore. Pound was horrified at the very idea. At length he said sternly, "You simply can't rely on information in an American broadcast to order the disposition of our ships. You must leave it to the man on the spot." Reluctantly Churchill had to admit that he was right.

The news of the *Graf Spee*'s end was received in the War Room with considerable emotion. The significance of this first victory at sea was not lost on anyone present, particularly the First Lord of the Admiralty, who immediately dictated a sheaf of personal messages to the ships which had taken part in the battle.

[3] Sir Evelyn Wrench, *Geoffrey Dawson and our Times*, p. 404.

3

Operation Royal Marine—and the White Rabbit

THE first week of January 1940 found Churchill again in France. In addition to Professor Lindemann and Tommy, he took with him two men who had recently been engaged in some very interesting secret experiments. One was Mr C. J. W. Hopkins, an Assistant Director of Naval Construction at the Admiralty; the other was a Sapper major named Millis Jefferis, a short, dynamic man with sandy hair who after serving for many years in India had been brought back shortly before the war to command the First Field Squadron of the Royal Engineers at Aldershot. Their baggage, which was closely guarded, contained several boxes of working mechanical models which they were to demonstrate to the French High Command.

Although he had had no formal training in science or engineering, Churchill's imagination, his inquiring mind, and his passionate interest in all new things had long endowed him with unusual insight into what the scientist and the machine could achieve. In the First World War critics who lacked imagination themselves accused him of wasting time and public money on such fanciful ideas as a caterpillar tractor which carried its own bridge for negotiating special obstacles, and a monster steam-roller designed to crush in the sides of trenches and bury their occupants. But this latter idea had led to the 'land battleship,' which in its turn became the prototype of the tank introduced with such spectacular success in the Battle of the Somme.

Since those early days his association with Lindemann had made him even more aware of the part which science could play in military operations, and when at General Gamelin's invitation he visited units of the

French Army in the Rhine sector just before the outbreak of the war he had talked till far into the night about such problems as the use of artificial fog and the possibilities of disrupting barge traffic on the Rhine with fluvial mines.[1] Now he was returning to France to enlist support for two unusual projects.

One, known by the code name of *Royal Marine*, was the selfsame plan to bring Rhine traffic to a standstill by feeding into the river from French territory thousands of mines of a special type. The launching of these mines would be carried out by the Navy, while other mines with a similar function would be dropped from the air into the Ruhr section of the river. The latter plan had not been received with much enthusiasm by the Air Ministry, who considered the airborne mine too small to be really effective, but Jefferis had designed a most ingenious naval version. Shaped like a pineapple, it bobbed along just under the surface, making it difficult to detect, and after it had been in the water a short time it emitted a cluster of hooks which would claw on to any passing object. For demonstration purposes Jefferis had produced a miniature specimen which greatly intrigued Churchill. Placed in a bucket of water, it would lie there inert until a soluble plug had absorbed sufficient moisture; then out sprang the hooks, and the winking of a small electric bulb showed the moment of explosion.

Charles Hopkins had an even more ingenious object to demonstrate. Although he was an Assistant Director of Naval Construction at the Admiralty, the machine for which he was responsible had no naval rôle. It was a tracked vehicle of strange appearance. On the list of Top Secret projects it was known as "White Rabbit No. 6." Of it Churchill has written:

> I believed that a machine could be made which could cut a groove in the earth sufficiently deep and broad through which assaulting infantry and presently assaulting tanks could advance in comparative safety across No-man's-land and wire entanglements and come to grips with the enemy in his defences on equal terms and in superior strength. . . . If this method could be applied on a front of perhaps 20 or 25 miles, for which two or three hundred trench cutters might suffice, dawn would find an overwhelming force of determined infantry established on or in the German defences, with hundreds of lines-of-communication trenches stretching back behind them, along which reinforcements could flow. Thus we should establish ourselves in the enemy's front line by surprise and with little loss.[2]

The creation of this mechanical monster had begun only a few weeks earlier, when Churchill had outlined his idea to Sir Stanley Goodall,

[1] Spears, *op. cit.*, p. 9.
[2] Churchill, Vol. I, p. 644.

Director of Naval Construction at the Admiralty.[3] Goodall picked on Hopkins, a man of great energy and organizing ability, to direct operations, and Hopkins then sent for a young naval architect named Spanner who had just joined his staff. Having stressed the need for secrecy, he explained that he wanted, as soon as possible, several alternative designs for a "trench-cutting tank" which would first burrow its way below ground level and then proceed steadily forward, cleaving a channel over six feet wide and six feet deep.

The young naval architect and three draughtsmen were shut in an empty bedroom in the Grand Pump Room Hotel at Bath and left severely alone to study this complicated problem. After a month of solitary seclusion the two junior draughtsmen ventured the opinion that the whole scheme was "crack-brained" and that Spanner must have been entrusted with it because he was the youngest and most inexperienced member of D.N.C.'s staff. But he was making progress. He found some drawings made by Sir William Tritton when designing Churchill's original tank, and these proved of great value in deciding on the method of drive and the kind of caterpillar track to be used for propelling the monster. Eventually he was able to show Goodall and Hopkins six designs in sketch form, and the most promising one was passed to Basset-Lowke's, who made toy trains in peace-time. In six weeks they built a working model. While this was happening other callers descended on the hotel room at Bath, including Mr William Savage, chief engineer of Ruston Bucyrus, the Lincolnshire firm selected to build the full-sized 'White Rabbit,' and a team of his own draughtsmen.

When the working model was ready Spanner put it through its paces in a room in the basement of the Admiralty. A pile of sawdust had been dumped on the floor and watched by a fascinated group, which included Mr Chamberlain, General Ironside (the C.I.G.S.), and the Chancellor of the Exchequer, the long, squat machine churned its way through this with effortless precision. Hopkins outlined his plans, and Cabinet approval was soon given for the construction of 240 of these trench-cutters.

It was a vast undertaking, for each full-sized machine would weigh 130 tons; it would be nearly 80 feet long and 10 feet high. The power to be generated was colossal; 'White Rabbit' had to be capable of excavating earth and stones at the rate of about 100 tons a minute, and forcing a way through all manner of obstacles which the enemy might place in its path.

[3] When Churchill had first begun thinking about the construction of a 'landship' a quarter of a century earlier he had turned for advice to Sir Eustace Tennyson d'Eyncourt, the Chief Constructor of the Navy. The Landships Committee of the Admiralty was formed under the latter's chairmanship, and in 1915 H.M. Landship *Centipede* was built under Admiralty supervision. As already mentioned, this proved the prototype of the first tank.

Since a department of the Admiralty, already fully occupied with warship construction, could not possibly take on as a sideline a venture which was soon to occupy a large staff of its own and 350 civilian firms making various components, a special organization was set up in the Ministry of Supply. Hopkins and Savage became the chief executives of the Department of Naval Land Equipment, and since 'White Rabbit'—originally chosen to salute Churchill's reputation for pulling things 'out of the hat'—was already attracting too much attention as a code name this was abandoned. The monster about to be born at Lincoln was allotted the more prosaic title of 'Cultivator.'

Coming events were soon to deprive this remarkable project of the significance rightly attached to it at this stage, but since there were many who proclaimed that 'Cultivator' would never achieve what Churchill predicted the story of what was eventually accomplished at Lincoln deserves to be told.

Soon after work began there a major crisis arose, because the Rolls Royce Merlin engines proposed for it could not be spared. They were desperately needed for the R.A.F., so the design was recast, and two 600-h.p. Paxman Diesels—one to drive the trench-cutter along and the other to provide power for the excavators—were introduced. The cutting apparatus, which consisted of eight specially treated steel blades mounted on a revolving cylinder, was successfully demonstrated to Mr Churchill on a deserted airfield near the Ruston works only a few weeks after his visit to France. But this was only one facet which occupied Leonard Marshall, Ruston's chief draughtsman, Savage, Spanner, and a growing army of technicians working night and day, through week-ends and holidays, for many months to come.

The fantastic stresses involved in hewing a way through miles and miles of solid ground raised formidable cooling problems; the design of an adequate gearbox, and any form of accurate directional control of the monster once it had buried itself below ground level, proved extraordinarily difficult; and for a time the earth displaced by the huge rotary churn in front of the machine threatened to bring 'Cultivator' to a standstill. While most of the spoil was hurled sideways to form a protective parapet along the top of the trench some of it obstinately remained to clog up the conveyor system.

Elaborate security arrangements were in force in the factory area where Marshall had his drawing-office and some of the major construction was taking place. This inevitably slowed up progress, for every time there was an air-raid warning all drawings had to be removed from the boards and taken to a place of safety. In a room in the upper gallery of Ruston's Anchor Street works, which overlooked the River Witham, a full-scale wooden mock-up of 'Cultivator' was built. Several large axes were kept there. If an airborne attack was made on the factory a team was ready to destroy the mock-up and hurl the debris into the river flowing below. Fortunately the axes were never needed.

Although the plan which called for 'Cultivator' to cut a *curving* trench, which would give additional cover to infantry advancing behind it, had to be modified, every other major problem was overcome.

Churchill went to Clumber Park, in the Dukeries, to watch its trials. When the engines were started 'Cultivator' did not make an excessive noise, much of the sound coming from two high-speed fans mounted for cooling purposes between the tracks at the rear of the machine. It moved slowly forward, and then plunged down into the ground. In a minute or so all that was visible to the fascinated observers was the small, squat structure, like the conning-tower of a submarine, housing the driver. Upward, and to either side of this, poured streams of earth which formed an ever-lengthening bank three feet high. Barbed wire entanglements and land-mines sown in the path of the monster were hurled aside and buried in the cascade of soil spewed out by the steel conveyors.

At the end of its trial run the great machine emerged with perfect precision on to the surface of the Park, leaving behind it a clean, well-formed trench along which Mr Churchill slowly walked. Although he knew by then that 'Cultivator' no longer had an immediate rôle in the Allied war plan, the ingenuity and speed of its creation was a heartening symbol of British technical skill.

* * * * *

When Churchill showed the models of 'Cultivator' and the fluvial mines to General Gamelin at Vincennes, the French supreme military commander was politely non-committal. Like Daladier, he seemed reluctant to support any project which might invite enemy reprisals, but the reaction of General Georges, who commanded the northern group of French armies, was characteristically different. He was much intrigued by the trench-cutter, and when the mining operation was explained to him he said instantly, "We *must* try it."

Churchill spent a night with Georges at La Ferté-sous-Jouarre, examined a sector of the Maginot Line near Metz with considerable interest, and then went on to Gort's headquarters at Arras. There he attended a ceremony which to British eyes had a somewhat incongruous finale. General Gamelin had come to invest both Gort and Ironside with the Grand Cross of the Legion of Honour, and after the ribbon had been placed round his neck Ironside, who towered above the tiny Frenchman, had to bend almost double before Gamelin could kiss him on both cheeks!

Apart from the staunch attitude of General Georges, whom he greatly admired, Churchill's five days in France increased his uneasiness over

French morale. At home there were other disquieting factors to consider. War production was lagging, and he was distressed by resistance to his plans for aiding Finland—now fighting for her life against Russia—and securing at the same time control of the Gallivare ore. Undeniably the objections raised by the Joint Planning Committee to the series of ventures which Mr Churchill urged in Scandinavia was based on the solid fact that our forces were totally inadequate, and the material aid which we could offer to the Finns, or to Sweden—if she could be persuaded to come in on the Allied side—was insignificant. But in his anxiety for positive action the First Lord was apt to consider the end rather than the means. Travelling back in the Royal train from Clydeside after the launching of H.M.S. *Duke of York*, he observed to the King that his fellow Ministers spent all their time telling him he was wrong and that such a project could not be carried out.

"Perhaps they're sometimes right," said the King, with a smile.

"Nine times out of ten," replied Mr Churchill, unabashed.

If some of his strategic conceptions were not sufficiently related to the resources available the First Lord of the Admiralty could, nevertheless, rightly claim that a policy of complete inaction would merely play into the enemy's hands. His views received little practical encouragement in the Cabinet, however, and the reluctance of industrial firms to switch over to war work seemed yet another pointer to the growing apathy in the country. He was greatly cheered by the unexpectedly warm reception given to a speech which he made at Manchester. Addressing a mass meeting in the Free Trade Hall, he called for greater efforts from war workers and the recruitment of a million women into industry. It was an outspoken speech, but when he finished there was a tremendous ovation. Randolph and Mary had accompanied their father, and at a family dinner-party on the train returning to London he was happier and more at ease than they had seen him for some time.

Mary was now seventeen and a half—an attractive and intelligent girl already developing her parents' strength of character. Since the Churchills were a particularly united family, her father, for all his pre-occupations, took a proud interest in his youngest daughter, and her companionship meant much to him. When she left the Admiralty flat one evening to go to Queen Charlotte's Ball—almost the only survival of pre-war gaiety in the blacked-out London of early 1940—Mr Churchill was still hard at work. Just before midnight, however, he arrived unexpectedly at Grosvenor House, bringing with him Brendan Bracken, Richard Pim, and Tommy, and they all joined her table. Not thinking that he was even aware of the ball taking place that night it was a surprise which greatly touched her.

A few days later she watched a moving ceremony outside the Admiralty, when her father inspected contingents of the ships' companies which had taken part in the River Plate battle. As the men fell in on the parade ground Mrs Churchill noticed a small group of people being shepherded to a special enclosure. They were the widows and orphans of the men who had lost their lives in the battle. Instantly Mary was sent racing to the nearest Lyons Corner House to organize refreshments for them. The King and Queen inspected the sailors, and then as the Royal Marine Band played the King decorated many of the officers and men before they marched through wildly cheering crowds to Guildhall for a civic luncheon.

By then the Royal Navy had again distinguished itself. The boarding of the *Graf Spee*'s supply ship, the *Altmark*, in Josing Fjord and the release of three hundred British merchant seamen imprisoned in her holds has often been described, but Churchill's part in this stirring incident is not so widely known.

Captain Philip Vian's destroyer flotilla had withdrawn to the mouth of the fjord after a Norwegian gun-boat had assured them that the *Altmark* had already been searched and no prisoners were on board. In view of this, and the possible repercussions from launching an attack in Norwegian territorial waters, Vian signalled to the Admiralty requesting further instructions, and Admiral Pound was himself struggling to frame some clear orders for him when the First Lord came into the War Room. He had in his hand a brilliantly concise signal which he had already written on his own. It covered every contingency which Vian might face if the Norwegians intervened again.

"I have already shown this to Lord Halifax. He has agreed to it, but I have to speak to him again in five minutes," Churchill added. When he did so the Foreign Secretary confirmed his approval, but asked for one sentence to be added—"Honour will be satisfied if they bow to superior force."

For most of that night the First Lord and Pound remained in the Upper War Room waiting for a signal from H.M.S. *Cossack*. There was much jubilation when it came, reporting the rescue of the prisoners after hand-to-hand fighting. In Vian's own view the success of this action was largely due to the "crystal clear" directive which he received so promptly from the Admiralty.

4

The Storm Breaks

IN BRITAIN early spring brought no outward sign of coming catastrophe, but the enemy plans were moving inexorably forward. On the first day of March Hitler made his decision to invade Norway before launching Case Yellow—the attack in the West—and when he met Mussolini on the Brenner Pass on March 18 he had already decided on the date for an advance into Norway and Denmark. To Mussolini, whose misgivings about the ill-starred alliance he had formed had already prompted him to lecture the German leader on his lack of principles, Hitler characteristically did not disclose his intention to attack France.[1]

The continued lull on the home front enabled Mr Churchill to revisit the Home Fleet at Scapa Flow. Since the torpedoing of *Royal Oak* the defences of the base had been completely overhauled, but much still remained to be done, including the provision of more blockships and the reinforcement of the anti-aircraft screen. The First Lord also wanted to see for himself what facilities were being provided for the welfare and recreation of the sailors in this bleak outpost.

When he arrived off Scapa from the Clyde in H.M.S. *Rodney* an air-raid warning was in force, and the battleship could not enter the Flow. The First Lord was therefore transferred in a cutter to H.M.S. *Lion*, flagship of Vice-Admiral W. J. Whitworth, who was commanding the Battle Cruiser Squadron. For two days he made a typically thorough inspection

[1] On January 3 Mussolini had written to Hitler criticizing the pact with Russia. "I, who was born a revolutionary and have not modified my revolutionary mentality, tell you that you cannot permanently sacrifice the principles of your revolution to the tactical requirements of a given moment." (Churchill, Vol. I, p. 496.)

of the base with the Civil Engineer-in-Chief, and it was while he was looking into welfare problems that he first heard of the extraordinary generosity of an American citizen towards the Sixth Destroyer Flotilla.

Mrs Mary Hanrahan, widow of a Captain in the United States Navy, had decided on the outbreak of war that she, for one, was not going to remain neutral and she adopted the ship's company of H.M.S. *Somali.* Soon sixteen Tribal Class destroyers were all receiving comforts from Mrs Hanrahan by the crate—clothing, chocolates, and personal gifts of all kinds, and even pocket money. "Auntie May," as she became affectionately known to thousands of British sailors, continued to act as a fairy godmother to British destroyer crews throughout the war—a gesture which cost her over £50,000.[2]

Apart from a lightning visit to Barrow at the end of March to attend the launching of H.M.S. *Illustrious* by Mrs Churchill, this was to prove the First Lord's last naval tour. Increasingly Churchill's time became concentrated upon problems arising from the general direction of the war, and his efforts to win over the French Government to approval of Operation Royal Marine. Some progress in this direction was made at a meeting of the Supreme War Council in London on March 28, attended by the new French Premier, M. Reynaud, but only qualified agreement was reached, and even this was rapidly withdrawn. The French were still fearful of reprisals on their country, still apparently convinced that if they themselves took no aggressive action the enemy would stay his hand. Churchill had no illusions on this score. In a broadcast directed at the neutral countries of Europe on March 30 he gave a grim warning: "More than a million German soldiers, including all their active divisions and armoured divisions, are drawn up ready to attack, at a few hours' notice, all along the frontiers of Luxembourg, of Belgium, and of Holland. At any moment these neutral countries may be subjected to an avalanche of steel and fire; and the decision rests in the hands of a haunted, morbid being who to their eternal shame the German peoples in their bewilderment have worshipped as a god."

When the French withdrew their assent to the mining of the Rhine Churchill hastened to Paris. On his previous visit to France early in February Tommy had been saddled with all the arrangements for the travel and accommodation of an entire War Cabinet delegation headed by the Prime Minister and Foreign Secretary, and owing to a lightning strike of French railway bed-makers the retreat from Paris had been somewhat disorganized. This time they went by air, only Tommy and General Spears

[2] Mrs Hanrahan came to England in 1946 and was received by the Queen. At a naval ceremony at Devonport she was presented with a scale model in silver of a Tribal destroyer. She died at her home in New York in August 1953.

accompanying the First Lord, and in stormy weather the little Flamingo in which they flew took a severe buffeting as they crossed the Channel.

To Churchill's chagrin the journey brought little reward, for Daladier, who seemed as uncompromisingly hostile as ever towards Reynaud, refused to dine at the British Embassy, and when the First Lord had a long talk with him next day his protestations of future loyalty to Reynaud had an unconvincing ring. Churchill's spirits were raised by a luncheon—privately arranged for him by Spears at a restaurant on the Left Bank, where they could talk undisturbed—with his old friend General Georges. This informal meeting yielded, to Tommy's delight, a memorable phrase of Churchillian French. Complaining to his guest of the lack of unity in the French Government, the First Lord remarked severely, "Nous allons perdre l'omnibus!"

By an odd coincidence the British Prime Minister, addressing a Conservative meeting in London on the very same day, also spoke of "missing the bus," but Mr Chamberlain used the phrase in a singularly unfortunate context. Hitler, he said, had dissipated his strength, and Germany was now no longer in a position to launch a major offensive. Within a week German forces had overrun Norway and Denmark.

* * * * *

The abject failure of the British attempt to gain a firm foothold in Norway was primarily due to lack of proper planning and co-ordination. Various aims were defined without considering whether the resources were available to achieve them, and throughout the eight desperate weeks which the campaign lasted the lack of vigorous and clear-sighted central control left the commanders at sea and ashore in a state of constant confusion.

The initial aim was clear enough. Southern Norway was already held by the enemy, but an Allied landing at Narvik, far to the north, was plainly feasible and would provide a rallying-point for loyal Norwegian forces. Narvik, however, offered very limited resources as a main base, whereas Trondheim, four hundred miles to the south, could provide good port facilities and an airfield. From there the Allies might be able to delay the German advance.

Initially, therefore, it was decided to seize Narvik and prepare a more ambitious assault on Trondheim to follow, but since the War Office orders to Major-General Mackesy conflicted in some respects with the directive which the Admiralty gave to the naval commander, Admiral of the Fleet the Earl of Cork and Orrery, and Mackesy argued that he had no authority to attempt an opposed landing, no progress was made at Narvik, which at that time was only lightly held by German machine-gunners.

A firm decision was then made to press on with attacks on both Narvik and Trondheim, but now the Chiefs of Staff began to have misgivings

NORWAY AND HER NEIGHBOURS
ALTEN FJORD
VESTFJORD
NARVIK
VAAGSÖ
NAMSOS
TRONDHEIM
ANDALSNES
BERGEN
STOCKHOLM
JOSING FJORD
COPENHAGEN
NORWAY
SWEDEN
FINLAND
DENMARK
DENMARK
N
MILES
0 100 200 300 400
DENMARK STRAIT
0 400
N
ICELAND
NORWAY
GREAT BRITAIN

about the feasibility of landing at Trondheim in the face of growing German air superiority. The situation was further confused by the intervention of Sir Roger Keyes, who stoutly maintained that Trondheim could easily be captured by a special naval force which he was anxious to lead. Like Lord Cork, Keyes was an Admiral of the Fleet and senior to both the First Sea Lord and Forbes, the Commander-in-Chief, Home Fleet. Churchill may not have been aware of the fact at this stage, but he had unwittingly caused some tension by making signals to Lord Cork without informing Admiral Forbes, under whom Cork was serving. He *was*, however, fully aware that if he supported Lord Keyes against Pound, who had already declared himself against the Trondheim attack, both Pound and Forbes might well resign. So the direct attack on Trondheim was abandoned in favour of an alternative plan now advanced by the Chiefs of Staff for landing forces at Namsos and Andalsnes, points north and south of Trondheim, and carrying out a pincer movement to envelop the main port.

Both attacks went in, and both failed, for the German Air Force, now present in massive strength, was able to range at will over the British positions. The Andalsnes force, under General Paget, did manage to inflict considerable casualties before they withdrew. Narvik was eventually captured on May 28, but was only held long enough to demolish the port installations and complete the embarkation of the remaining British troops. In the final withdrawal *Illustrious* and her escorting destroyers were sunk by the *Scharnhorst*, but the greater casualties suffered by the German Navy during the Norwegian operations were to have an important bearing on the war at sea.

Throughout "this ramshackle campaign," as he later termed it, Mr Churchill was at the centre of events, and by the force of his personality he undoubtedly exercised some influence on their course. Equally he bore a share of the responsibility for what went wrong, and this he never shirked for a moment. But although for a short time after Lord Chatfield resigned as Minister for Co-ordination of Defence he had taken the chair at the meetings of the Military Co-ordination Committee he had not been in any sense the director of their deliberations. The Chiefs of Staff and their deputies, the three Service Ministers, and Major-General H. L. Ismay, who was to work closely with Churchill for the remainder of the war, all had a voice in the conduct of military operations. It was not until the campaign was virtually at an end that the direction of the war was placed on a surer footing, and a central war staff, owing allegiance to no one particular Service, was formed, with Ismay at its head.

Churchill himself felt that there had been a woeful lack of resolution in the conduct of the Norwegian campaign. Certainly there had been incompetence as well; supply ships, for example, were loaded in such a way that, although guns could be promptly disembarked, it was impossible to reach any ammunition for them.

Major Jefferis, whom the First Lord summoned to the Admiralty just before the final evacuation, had not seen him for some weeks, for he had been ordered to drop work on Royal Marine and go to Norway to carry out sabotage, including the demolition of key railway bridges. Making contact with various Norwegian resistance groups, he distributed supplies of explosive devices, but by the time this was done he found he was cut off by the enemy. Undeterred, he struggled through the deep snow, and, penetrating the German lines at night, he eventually reached Andalsnes, fifty miles away. On landing in England he heard that both Chamberlain and Churchill wanted a personal report.

When Jefferis had finished his story at Downing Street the Prime Minister asked, "Do you think the landing should ever have been attempted?"

"Well," said Jefferis, "something had to be done, and it was better than nothing."

He had still not had breakfast when he was shown into Mr Churchill's room at the Admiralty. The First Lord greeted him warmly, pressed a whisky-and-soda into his hand, and then cross-examined him closely. Churchill was in a belligerent mood, and was all for leaping to the attack again. Within a week, however, greater events had supervened.

The storm of criticism which burst when the campaign was debated in the House of Commons on May 7–8 was not to be allayed by Churchill's courageous defence of the Prime Minister, and a change of Government was already inevitable when on the morning of May 10 the German armies began their invasion in the West.

That morning Churchill and Lord Halifax were summoned to No. 10 Downing Street. The Prime Minister explained that he felt it was no longer possible for him to form a National Government owing to Labour opposition. It was therefore his duty to recommend the name of his successor to the King.

Mr Churchill's own account of this momentous interview suggests that, although Mr Chamberlain continued to review the situation and possible alternatives which seemed open to him, he appeared to invite interjection. Churchill remained silent. To Tommy, whom he saw immediately afterwards, he said, "It was the only time in my life when I have kept my mouth shut."

Lord Halifax made it clear that his position in the House of Lords made it impossible for him to accept office, and at six o'clock that night Mr Churchill was called to the Palace. Of his feelings that night he has written:

I was conscious of a profound sense of relief. At last I had the authority to give directions over the whole scene. I felt as if I were walking with destiny, and that all my past life had been but a preparation for this hour and for this trial. . . . Although impatient for the morning, I slept soundly and had no need for cheering dreams. Facts are better than dreams.[3]

[3] Churchill, Vol. I, p. 601.

5

"Get my Heavy Pistol"

ALTHOUGH the strong sense of destiny which had so often fortified him in the past led Mr Churchill to welcome his new task without any fear of failure, he knew that a substantial body of opinion in the Commons was still critical of him. He had never been popular in the accepted sense of the term, for he was too much of an individualist, and the fact that he had rarely concealed a strong conviction of his own ability had laid him open to charges of vanity and lack of good manners. Many leaders in public life mistrusted him, but at this critical moment none could deny the consistency and wisdom of his long and lonely campaign to warn the nation of its military weakness.

Taking as he did the view that Versailles had heralded not peace for generations to come but a twenty-year Armistice, he, almost alone, had recognized the significance of Hitler's rise to power. Few had been prepared to listen to him with any patience in those early days of the thirties. Indeed, when the Government made belated proposals for strengthening the Royal Air Force in 1934 the Labour Party had put forward a motion deploring this attempt to "jeopardize the prospects of international disarmament and encourage a revival of dangerous and wasteful competition in preparation for war." Supporting these sentiments, Mr Attlee, for one, had said, "We deny the need for increased air armament." And in all seriousness Attlee's colleague, Mr George Lansbury, proclaimed that their party would never *consent* to the rearming of Germany—a statement which drew from Churchill the scathing inquiry, "Is he quite sure that the Germans will come and ask him for his consent before they rearm? Does he not think that they might omit that formality and go ahead without even taking a card vote of the T.U.C.?"

By 1935 Mr Churchill was at least making some headway, for Baldwin invited both him and Lindemann to serve on the newly formed Committee of Imperial Defence dealing with air defence research. The future of air warfare had long exercised his mind; as far back as 1914 his vivid grasp of its possibilities had so impressed Kitchener that he asked Churchill, as First Lord of the Admiralty, to take over the organization of aerial home defence. This strain of prophecy, fortified by his own tireless researches into scientific development, was later to illumine many of his warning speeches, and in November 1934 he spoke of the serious threat offered by an intensive bombing assault on London. "The most dangerous form of air attack," he warned the House, "is the attack by incendiary bombs."

The value of his realistic appraisals of German intentions was enhanced by the practical proposals which he constantly put forward. More than three years before war broke out he was calling for the planning of factories, "not only on paper, but with the necessary jigs, gauges, and appliances handy, hung up on the spot, so that they could turn over at once to some form of war production."

Unhappily the very frequency of his warnings blunted their effect. "Mr Churchill's recurring intimations of the wrath to come were as familiar as the voice of a muezzin announcing the hour of prayer."[1] And until Munich shook the nation out of its lethargy this constant harping on such an uncongenial theme was considered by many to be ill-judged and needlessly provocative towards a foreign Power whom it would be much safer to placate. Only now, when the German armies were rolling forward into Belgium and Holland, and the remnants of a defeated Allied force were fighting their way out of Norway, came the full realization of Churchill's wisdom and foresight.

On the day he became Prime Minister men were seen hurriedly erecting barbed wire round the Admiralty and a posse of Royal Marine sentries took up their posts. Wags in the building said that these precautions had been ordered "to prevent Winston coming back"—a harmless enough jest, but one which nevertheless reflected the relief felt in some quarters at his departure from a post where his unorthodox methods had not been universally appreciated.

To the man in the street, who knew nothing of such matters, Winston Churchill, the embodiment of resolution and confidence, offered a welcome contrast to the tremulous Chamberlain. They looked to him anxiously for some sign of new and vital leadership, and they had not long to wait. On May 13 he made his first, memorable speech as Prime Minister. And it electrified the House.

Paraphrasing at the start words of Garibaldi, he said with grim

[1] Philip Guedalla, *Mr Churchill*, p. 266.

emphasis, "I have nothing to offer but blood, toil, tears, and sweat," and then, with the House hanging on every succeeding sentence, he made his historic declaration of policy—"to wage war by sea, land, and air with all our might and with all the strength that God can give us, . . . to wage war against a monstrous tyranny never surpassed in the dark, lamentable catalogue of human crime." Continuing with great deliberation, he said, "You ask what is our aim? I can answer in one word—Victory! Victory at all costs, victory in spite of all terror, victory however long and hard the road may be. For without victory there is no survival."

With this one speech the new Prime Minister had the Commons at his feet. Of Chatham it was said that "no one ever left his Cabinet without feeling a braver man." Now, two centuries later, a Parliament confused and uncertain in the face of sudden disaster was once again uplifted and given fresh courage by one man's proud defiance.

* * * * *

While he was busy forming his Coalition Government Mr Churchill continued to live at Admiralty House. Then, as No. 10 Downing Street was not yet ready for him, he moved for the time being into a suite in the Carlton Hotel, near by in the Haymarket.

It was soon apparent that the situation in France was much graver than early reports had suggested, for although there was no great disparity on paper between the opposing German and Allied formations many French units bore no relation to their reported strength. When Tommy, who accompanied the Prime Minister to Paris for discussions with Gamelin on May 16, expressed surprise at the rapid rout of the French Ninth Army one of Gamelin's staff officers explained that the figures of those officially 'mobilized' for military service included large numbers of men—postmen, railway workers, municipal employees—who were in fact still at home, carrying on with their normal civilian duties.

In the air the French contribution was negligible, and the R.A.F., who bore the brunt of the fighting, lost 260 of an operational force of 474 aircraft in the first four days, but Gamelin's hopes of checking the German Panzer thrusts seemed to centre solely on reinforcements from the slender fighter reserve still held in England. The strategic reserve of the French Army did not, he revealed, exist except on paper.

The small British party who flew to Paris in a Flamingo were staggered by the atmosphere of complete resignation prevailing at the Quai d'Orsay. Huge fires were burning in the gardens, and to and fro scurried civil servants bearing piles of State documents which they cast into the flames.

Strange stories were circulating. Although Gamelin was supposed to be grappling night and day with a military situation as alarming as any commander in history had faced, friends of Mme Gamelin who had invited her to dinner were surprised to receive a reply in the General's own hand explaining that his wife would not be able to accept as she was 'tellement occupé.' And the French Premier himself was setting a strange example at a time of national crisis, for his intimate friend, the Comtesse de Portes, a violent Anglophobe, was apparently privy to most of the highly confidential negotiations between the British and French Governments. One vital signal from London, for which a frantic search was made, was eventually discovered in her bed, and when on the night of May 16 Colonel Redman, head of the small British liaison unit which Ismay had set up in Paris, went round to Reynaud's flat, where he understood that anxious discussions were taking place on the French plea for more fighter support, he found her with Reynaud. In the days to come she was to prove an implacable enemy of any proposal for continuing the struggle.

Air Chief Marshal Dowding had already warned the War Cabinet that if the wastage of Hurricanes continued at the current rate of thirty a day Fighter Command would have none left in six weeks, but the need to buttress French morale was so desperate that it was decided, after much telephoning between Paris and London, to send a further four squadrons from Britain. Next morning Churchill flew home.[2]

Once back in England it was difficult to discover precisely what was happening on the disorganized French front, but by the following weekend it was plain that the British divisions were in grave danger of being completely cut off. Ironside, who had been sent to confer with Gort, corroborated this, adding that the Belgians were preparing to capitulate.

When the C.I.G.S. had delivered his report on his visit to France the Prime Minister rose from his seat in the War Room and paced to and fro. He recalled the tactics which would have been employed in other wars if the German break-through had been made with cavalry—sealing off the gap so that our own cavalry could deal with the trapped enemy—and then remarked sadly, "To-day there is a difference. This new type of cavalry is heavily armoured and you say we have nothing to counter it. We cannot leave our armies to be slaughtered or surrender. We must get them out and give them the new weapons they need to deal with the enemy."

Warning the Admiralty to prepare for a large-scale evacuation, Churchill returned once more to France. By this time Weygand, hurriedly summoned from Syria, had replaced the indecisive Gamelin as Allied Commander-in-Chief, and Reynaud himself had taken over the War Ministry from Daladier, with whom he had long been at loggerheads.

Initially Weygand made a good impression. He seemed resolute, and determined to launch an attack southward with the French First Army

[2] In point of fact, the situation deteriorated so rapidly that these additional squadrons did not go into action. See Wilmot, *The Struggle for Europe*.

and the British which would destroy the German armour around Arras. So Gort was informed of this, and for the time being the evacuation project was left in abeyance. It was soon to be resurrected, for Weygand rapidly found that the plan he had put forward with such a show of confidence had no chance of success. A few weak Allied counter-attacks were strangled at birth, a promised French thrust from the Somme never materialized at all, and the collapse of the Belgians at Courtrai left Gort with no alternative but a fighting retreat to the coast.

Writing of the climactic week of Dunkirk, an American historian has remarked that Churchill showed how to live with adversity.[3] Certainly none of those in daily contact with the Prime Minister could detect from his bearing and conversation that he held any serious misgivings.

> The courage of the man was, in fact, breath-taking. What enhanced the impression was that he was so completely unconscious of it himself. He was so sure, so certain, so single-minded in his decisions, so unconcerned with anything but the effect any given measure would have on the result of the war that the weight of his staggering responsibilities sat lightly on his shoulders.[4]

He was the very embodiment of confidence and pugnacity, and the War Room staff were much intrigued to hear him say to Detective-Inspector Thompson one morning, as he prepared for one of his flying visits to France, "Get my heavy pistol for me. If we are attacked on the way I may be able to kill at least one German."

Enemy fighters were indeed already patrolling the skies north of Paris when he went to France for a meeting of the Supreme War Council on May 31, and a wide detour was necessary. With the Prime Minister were Mr Attlee, now the Deputy Prime Minister, and General Dill, who had just succeeded Ironside as C.I.G.S. For the first time Marshal Pétain took part in the discussions, which reviewed not only the evacuations now proceeding in Norway and at Dunkirk but future policy towards Italy and Spain, and the prospect of aid from America. Reynaud's cordiality and Darlan's apparent readiness to provide full French naval co-operation at Dunkirk did not dispel an uneasiness in the British party at the attitude of Pétain, who remained an impassive, remote spectator, showing not a flicker of interest or enthusiasm as Churchill outlined British plans. By this time it was all too evident to British observers on the spot that apart from a few honourable exceptions like Mandel, Campinchi, and Colonel de Gaulle, the Under-Secretary for War, few members of the French Government had any heart left for the struggle. Regarding further opposition as

[3] Professor Trumbull Higgins, *Winston Churchill and the Second Front.* The example which the Prime Minister set was reinforced, in the author's opinion, by the national forte of the British for taking up "a morally exalted defensive."

[4] General Sir Edward Spears, *The Fall of France,* p. 117.

futile, and yet at the same time feeling a sense of guilt at their own defeatism, they resented Churchill's obstinate refusal to accept their point of view. It made them feel uncomfortable. Churchill, for his part, recognized that, unless he continued to keep a close personal grasp of the situation, stiffening the waverers and dinning into the defeatists that Britain had no intention of abandoning the fight, the French Government might capitulate before anything could be done to organize resistance from new bases in the French Empire overseas.[5] The French fleet would also be jeopardized. From London he continued, therefore, to keep closely in touch with General Spears, the Paris Embassy, and Ismay's liaison officers.

Churchill's searching questions and his formidable powers of persuasion were feared by men already contemplating a policy of inaction, and the liaison officers in Paris had a difficult task. One day Colonel Redman was rung up by Ismay, who said that the Prime Minister wished to speak to General Weygand. Redman hastened to Vincennes, and, finding Weygand in the middle of lunch, he sent in word that Mr Churchill would like to talk to him on the phone. Back came a curt message that General Weygand refused to take the call.

Redman was in a dilemma. Reluctant to report complete failure, he wrote another note stressing the importance of his mission, and a few minutes later Weygand himself entered the room, napkin in hand. Taking the British officer by the arm, he walked him along a passage and into a bedroom. He shut the door and then said with great emphasis, "Tell Mr Churchill that I will not speak to him. I go each day to the meeting [an inner Cabinet meeting over which Reynaud presided].... Anything which Mr Churchill wants of a political nature he can get from political sources. I am *not* a politician."

The evacuation of the British Army provided more fuel for the French faction who had been hinting that Churchill had no scruples over sacrificing immediate French interests in order to further nebulous British plans for the future. There were, however, still some Frenchmen who were able to take a realistic view of events. De Gaulle, who flew to London on June 9 with yet another urgent plea for fighter reinforcements, accepted Mr Churchill's explanation that, while he was prepared to help France with fighter squadrons based on England, none could leave the country. "As a politician I am disappointed," said de Gaulle; "as a soldier I don't see how you could have come to any other decision."

* * * * *

[5] Mr Churchill had long held a realistic view of the influence likely to be exerted by the "defeatist" element in French Government circles. As far back as 1932 he had said in the Commons (November 23), "France, though armed to the teeth, is pacifist to the core."

If the swift march of events in May had brought a rude awakening from dreams of a victory gained by sitting tight and waiting for the enemy to exhaust his resources the month which followed heralded far greater trials. Operation Dynamo brought 360,000 soldiers out of France, but their arms and equipment were lost; the fighting ended in Norway; Italy entered the war; the fall of Paris was a prelude to the capitulation of France, and by the end of the month the German Army had occupied British territory in the Channel Islands.

As the small craft gathered for Dunkirk even the Prime Minister's War Room supplied its quota of eager volunteers to man them. Captain Pim took command of three Dutch schoots and as many motor-boats as he could round up at Dover and Deal. Working from La Panne, in Belgium, and Bray Dunes, east of Dunkirk, he brought off 3500 men of the B.E.F. Among those he picked up after a heavy spell of dive-bombing which sank the destroyer H.M.S. *Keith*, was Gort's Military Secretary, Brigadier Sir Colin Jardine.

Churchill's indomitable spirit was reflected in the speech which he made in the House of Commons after the evacuation was completed. It has often been quoted before, and one memorable passage, which inspired a demonstration unsurpassed in the long history of the Commons, vividly conveyed his unshaken determination and courage in the face of disaster. After taunting Hitler with the memory of Napoleon waiting vainly at Boulogne for the invasion of England, which he was never able to carry out, he reiterated the British resolve. "We shall not flag or fail. We shall go on to the end. We shall fight in France, we shall fight on the seas and oceans, we shall fight with growing confidence and growing strength in the air. We shall defend our island, whatever the cost may be. We shall fight on the beaches, we shall fight on the landing grounds, we shall fight in the fields and in the streets, we shall fight in the hills. We shall never surrender. And even if, which I do not for a moment believe, this island or a large part of it, were subjugated and starving, then our Empire beyond the seas, armed and guarded by the British Fleet, would carry on the struggle until in God's good time the New World, with all its power and might, steps forth to the rescue of the Old."[6]

While the situation continued to deteriorate in France the Prime Minister urged the Joint Chiefs of Staff to suggest measures for "a vigorous, enterprising and ceaseless offensive against the whole German-occupied coastline. Tanks and armoured fighting vehicles must be made in flat-bottomed boats, out of which they can crawl ashore, do a deep raid inland, cutting at vital communications, and then back, leaving a trail of German

[6] This speech was made in the House of Commons on June 4, the day following the completion of the Dunkirk evacuation.

corpses behind them. It is probable that when the best troops go on to the attack of Paris only the ordinary German troops of the line will be left. The lives of these must be made an intense torment," he wrote in a memorandum to Ismay.[7]

Churchill tried hard to infuse the French leaders with this aggressive spirit when he returned to France on June 11 for a meeting of the Supreme War Council, but by this time Pétain was already talking openly of an armistice. The Government had left Paris and were moving to Tours. Weygand had installed himself in a château at Briare, south-east of Orleans, and it was to Briare that the Prime Minister flew in the Flamingo. The ugly and depressing house which Weygand had taken over as his headquarters could hardly have been less suitable as the scene of a vital Allied conference. Communication with the outside world depended, as Tommy soon discovered, on one ancient telephone fixed to the wall of the butler's pantry. This was connected, not to a military exchange but to the village post office, where the switchboard was only manned for certain hours in the day. There was no accommodation in the house for the British party, which included Eden, Dill, Ismay, and Spears, and they spent the night in a train in a near-by siding, only the Prime Minister staying in the château.

The talks opened in an atmosphere of intense gloom deepened by Weygand, who reported that the last French reserves had been thrown into the battle and that continued resistance was out of the question. Urging the importance of defending Paris, Mr Churchill said he would like to hear the views of General Georges, but when the latter arrived he too gave the impression that the French Army could not hold out much longer. To Churchill's concern Georges appeared to think that there was little possibility either of forming a redoubt in the north-west corner of France or even of carrying on the war in French North Africa.

The discussion which lasted all afternoon and evening was depressing enough, but an incident during dinner showed more plainly than anything how far French morale had deteriorated. Air Chief Marshal Sir Arthur Barratt, commanding the R.A.F. units still operating in France, rang up to say that a move was on foot to stop British bombers carrying out a raid that night on Turin and Milan, on the grounds that this might produce reprisal attacks on Southern France. Since the French Government had been kept fully informed about this raid on Italy, and had agreed to it, Churchill complained vehemently to Reynaud, who issued orders that it should be allowed to take place. Later that night Barratt reported that farm carts and other obstructions had been dragged on to the airfields near Marseilles from which the British bombers were operating and they

[7] Churchill, Vol. II, p. 217.

had been unable to take off. General Vuillemin, Chief of the French Air Staff, denied that any of his subordinates had played a part in this move, but to the British it seemed highly improbable that French peasants, who were said to be responsible, could have known anything about the projected raid unless there had been a calculated leakage of information from the French Air Force.

Next morning there was a further short discussion, at which Churchill stressed the vital need for fighting on until aid was forthcoming from the United States, and then came a hazardous flight home. Cloud over France prevented the Hurricane escort from guarding the Flamingo, but this cleared as the small aircraft reached the coast, and the rest of the journey was made at wave-top height to elude the enemy air patrols.

The Prime Minister's last words to General Doumenc, who saw him to his car at Briare, were, "You may be sure that, whatever happens, England will not abandon France." By this time, however, both Weygand and Pétain were not only determined to conclude an immediate armistice: they regarded all Mr Churchill's suggestions for fighting on, in either France or her Empire overseas, as completely unrealistic. And so it was that on that very evening, while the British Prime Minister was reporting to the War Cabinet in London that there was still hope of preventing an immediate French collapse, General Weygand called upon the French Premier at Tours to surrender to Germany. When Reynaud and others said they must keep their word to Britain Weygand remarked sarcastically that none of the opponents of an armistice were paying any attention to the military situation. "I spoke also of the impossibility of holding our own in the Breton redoubt, which existed only in the imagination of the Prime Minister," wrote Weygand later.[8]

Mr Churchill's guarded optimism had been based on the attitude of Reynaud and de Gaulle at the meetings he had just attended; at the Cabinet meeting at Tours a majority supported Reynaud's call to continue the war from North Africa. But at this critical point, when a further personal appeal by Churchill to the French Cabinet might well have won over the waverers, Reynaud did a surprising thing. He sent a message urging Churchill to return to France next day for a further conference at Tours, but he kept the news to himself. Not even the British Ambassador was aware of any meeting until Tommy rang up Henry Mack, his First Secretary, from the Prefecture at Tours at lunch-time on Thursday, June 13.

On this last momentous journey to France the Flamingo carrying the Prime Minister, Lord Halifax, and Lord Beaverbrook, as well as General Ismay and Tommy, headed far to the west before crossing the Channel. "When we arrived over Tours," Tommy recalls, "we saw that the airfield

[8] General Maxime Weygand, *Rappelé au Service*.

was pock-marked with craters. Most of them appeared to be marked with red flags, but although the bombs had fallen ten days before, no attempt had been made to repair the damage. When we landed we taxied to the control tower, which turned out to be part of the Air France building. There I was told that Air France had closed down and we were directed to some hangars on the far side of the field. We saw no sign of life, but after searching round I discovered two French officers munching sandwiches. They seemed surprised to see us. No arrivals were expected, they said, and every one had gone to lunch. They offered to drive us to Tours in two very small cars of their own. We squeezed in with some difficulty and I had to sit on Lord Beaverbrook's knee.

"For want of a better idea I asked my driver to take us to the Prefecture. This turned out to be a lucky shot, for although, here again, all the officials were at lunch, I caught sight of Revoil, one of Mandel's staff, fighting his way through the crowd which was besieging the Prefecture. He told us that Mandel was expected at any moment. Reynaud, he thought, was still at Orleans, but he had an idea that the British Embassy had taken temporary quarters near by and said I might be able to ring them up from Mandel's office. To my surprise I was put straight through to Henry Mack, who said that the Ambassador was at that moment with Reynaud. I explained that Mr Churchill wanted to hold a meeting as soon as possible after two o'clock and then Revoil took us off to the Hôtel Grande Bretagne, where we lunched in a private room. Just as we were finishing we were joined by Baudouin, who a few days later was to become Foreign Minister in the Pétain Government. Uninvited, he sat down between me and Mr Churchill and straight away began sounding the P.M. as to whether Britain would be prepared to release the French Government from its undertaking not to negotiate a separate peace. Mr Churchill gave him no encouragement whatever. Later that afternoon we heard that Baudouin was already spreading the rumour that the P.M. had agreed to a French surrender if the United States did not come into the war immediately.

"We had entered the hotel by a back entrance, but Mr Churchill insisted on leaving by the main doorway so that the crowds in the streets could see that their Allies had not deserted them. Tours was an amazing sight. The streets were jammed with people who didn't seem to know what to do or where to go. Many were lying exhausted on the pavement. Past the hotel crawled an unending stream of cars festooned with personal belongings. I noticed that a lot of them had smashed windscreens and bodywork riddled with machine-gun fire."

Reynaud was at the Prefecture when they got back. Neither Pétain nor Weygand was present, and de Gaulle, who only heard of the meeting by chance, did not arrive until later in the afternoon. Reynaud, who evidently thought it would be easier for him to put France's case to the Prime Minister on his own, reported that in Weygand's view further organized resistance was impossible. He himself was sending a last appeal to President Roosevelt for American intervention, but if this failed he wanted to know what Britain's attitude would be towards a move by the French Government to come to terms with the enemy. Once again Mr Churchill stressed the British determination to fight on. And once again he pointed out that it was vital to gain time. Surrender now might well persuade America that the Allied cause in Europe was already lost. Surely they could continue to fight southward from Paris to the sea, thereby gaining a breathing-space for establishing a reorganized opposition on the far shore of the Mediterranean. Reynaud, however, returned to the theme that even if he himself voted against capitulation a Government under other leadership would probably abandon the struggle if there seemed to be no reasonable hope of survival. The British party therefore withdrew to discuss the matter among themselves. When Churchill told Reynaud that they could not take the responsibility of releasing France from her pact he asked the French Premier to make no decisive move, at any rate until a reply had been received to the appeal to Roosevelt. To this Reynaud agreed.[9]

In the throng outside the Prefecture while this final meeting of the Supreme War Council was taking place a prominent figure was the Comtesse de Portes, who made repeated attempts to force her way to the conference room. Evidently she was apprehensive as ever of Churchill's powers of persuasion, and her strident cries that Reynaud must be told to surrender were only silenced when a French officer went up to Baudouin and shouted, "Get that woman out of here, for the dignity of France!"[10]

When the Prime Minister's party left the Prefecture and drove back to the airfield there was an unexpected hitch. The pilots of the Hurricanes could not start their cold engines unaided, and all that the French could provide in the way of starter equipment was an odd assortment of car batteries of various sizes hurriedly assembled on a handcart. In the end the Flamingo had to make the return flight to England alone.

* * * * *

[9] Churchill, Vol. II, p. 160. The President's reply stressed that the United States were redoubling their efforts to give all material aid to the Allies. He was not at that time in a position to demand from Congress an immediate declaration of war. Robert Sherwood, an active supporter of William Allen White's "Committee to defend America by Aiding the Allies," which began its campaign against isolationism in May 1940, considers that if Roosevelt *had* taken such a step during that summer he would undoubtedly have been repudiated. It must also be remembered that Roosevelt was in the last year of his second term as President, and "it is one of the classical weaknesses of our American constitutional system that a President who is approaching the end of his tenure of office can exercise little authority in the conduct of foreign affairs." (Robert E. Sherwood, *The White House Papers of Harry L. Hopkins*, Vol. I, p. 138.)

[10] Bois, *Truth on the Tragedy of France*.

From this point the French tragedy moved swiftly to its close. For a brief moment the proposal for a Declaration of Union, whereby Britain offered to France joint citizenship and the sharing of future responsibilities and benefits in every sphere of national life, seemed likely to strengthen Reynaud's hand, and when Mr Churchill spoke to the French Premier on the phone on June 16 he told him he was willing to return to France next day to discuss this. The War Cabinet agreed to this plan, and orders were given for a British destroyer to proceed to Bordeaux to pick up Reynaud and his staff. They would be taken to a rendezvous—in the Baie de la Forest, south of the Brittany peninsula—with the cruiser which would carry the Prime Minister from Portsmouth. The conference would take place at sea.

That evening, having seen the baggage loaded on to the special train waiting at Waterloo, Tommy returned to Downing Street. Several times the departure from Number 10 was delayed by urgent messages from the Foreign Office. "Eventually the P.M. decided that he could not risk waiting longer and we drove to the station. We were sitting in the train, which was about to move off, when one of the Private Secretaries dashed on to the platform with a signal from Sir Ronald Campbell, our Ambassador to France. The French Government was already tottering; a meeting with Reynaud was no longer possible. On the following morning, when we heard that Reynaud had resigned and Marshal Pétain had taken over the Government, it was difficult to see any ray of light. All Mr Churchill's efforts seemed to have been wasted. There would be no question now of fighting on from French bases overseas. In the days to come, however, the P.M. was to remark more than once that perhaps, after all, it was providential that the French Government did not move immediately to North Africa. 'The Germans might well have pursued them through Spain, taken Gibraltar, and crossed the Straits,' he said—'and then the Mediterranean would have been closed to us.' "

6

Invasion Summer

WHEN Mr Churchill first moved to Downing Street Tommy remained at the Admiralty. By now he was regarded as a full-time—if unofficial—member of the Prime Minister's staff, and was, in fact, in charge of the conversion of a building on the outskirts of London as an emergency headquarters for the Cabinet if air attacks compelled a withdrawal from Whitehall. He was not, however, in daily touch with Churchill, and the new arrangement soon proved unsatisfactory. One of the Prime Minister's strongest traits was a marked dislike of new faces. In his own immediate circle he was ill at ease with newcomers who were unused to his working routine and personal foibles, and the sight of a stranger in his secretariat sitting opposite his desk, pencil nervously poised over her notebook as she waited to take dictation, was enough to jolt him sharply from his concentration. Glaring at the unfortunate girl with quite unintentional ferocity, he would growl, "Where's Mrs Hill? Or Miss Shearburn?" By now he had become accustomed to the unobtrusive naval officer who seemed to know without any prompting just how he liked things to be done. He had become almost part of the family. So whenever the Prime Minister decided to go anywhere Commander Thompson would be summoned to accompany him. In July a request came from Downing Street for his permanent attachment to Churchill's staff, and he moved to new quarters in a large building at Storey's Gate, overlooking St James's Park. From now on he was rarely away from the Prime Minister's side.

Mr Churchill also borrowed Captain Pim to set up a new Map Room for him. Later on Pim's organization was extended to provide a travelling map room which could be set up at short notice in any ship or building, at

Chequers, or on long train journeys; up-to-date maps of the fronts likely to be active at the time were always available.

Since no day went by without a visit from the Prime Minister to study enemy dispositions or the movements of Allied ships the Map Room staff, like the secretariat, had their own lessons to learn. Mr Churchill's pronunciation of foreign place-names was robustly British, and when one morning Richard Pim was rash enough to render Walshavn as VALS-HARVERN the Prime Minister looked at him resentfully.

"Don't be so B.B.C.," he said . . . "the place is WALLS-HAVEN."

In secret session Churchill had already warned the Commons that an attempted invasion must be faced. Soon he gave wider warning of ordeals to come. "Here in this strong city of refuge which enshrines the title-deeds of human progress and is of deep consequence to Christian civilization . . . we wait undismayed the impending assault. Perhaps it will come to-night. Perhaps it will come next week. Perhaps it will never come. We must show ourselves equally capable of meeting a sudden violent shock or, what is perhaps a harder test, a prolonged vigil. But, be the ordeal sharp or long, or both, we shall seek no terms . . . we shall tolerate no parley; we may show mercy . . . we shall ask for none."[1]

Leadership of the nation at such a time was a fearful burden to bear, for Churchill more than anyone realized the full extent of Britain's weakness. When he complained of the failure—due to lack of suitable craft and equipment—of Commando raids on Boulogne and Guernsey carried out at the time of the French capitulation, Admiral Pound showed him the Top Secret Admiralty list of H.M. ships damaged and temporarily out of action. "As far as I can see," remarked the Prime Minister, "we have only the *Victoria and Albert* left."

From the moment France fell there were undoubtedly many who felt, with a sudden chill certainty, the fear that we were going to be beaten. By his speeches and actions Churchill had to restore the nation's confidence—in its Government and in itself. With no prospect of imminent successes to announce in any field of operations, and the grim example of Germany's murderous assault on France and the Low Countries still fresh in every one's mind, this was a daunting task, but the Prime Minister's keynote of aggressive defiance brought an instant response.

A firm believer in studying problems at first hand, he was continually on the move throughout July and August. As well as inspecting the Army units re-forming after Dunkirk he visited almost every stretch of the coast where an enemy landing was feasible from St Andrews to Lyme Regis. In no sense were these inspection tours by the Prime Minister aimed merely at showing himself to the troops. Before he descended on each place he had

[1] House of Commons, July 14, 1940.

already studied an elaborate brief prepared for him by Lindemann's staff, or by Admiral Sir Frederic Dreyer, whom—much to the annoyance of some of the generals—he had appointed to survey the coastline and report on defensive weaknesses. He knew precisely what troops, guns, and equipment should be available in each area, and made searching inquiries to find out how they were being deployed. Lindemann's statisticians furnished him with tables showing the number of Bren-gun carriers, light machine-guns, and other weapons earmarked for each battalion, and with these figures in mind generals and subalterns alike were subjected to rigorous cross-examination.

Although he remarked to General Sir Alan Brooke, the newly appointed Commander-in-Chief, Southern Command, that he wondered if England had ever been in such straits since the Armada, the Prime Minister betrayed no outward sign of anxiety.[2] The strain of constant journeys by road, rail, or air, and the need to grapple with fresh problems and fresh personalities in the field, as well as conducting the day-to-day business of Government, seemed to affect him not at all. He was refreshed by his personal contact with the troops preparing feverishly for the coming attack, and no day seemed too long for him.

On a visit to Sussex he was much impressed by Major-General B. L. Montgomery, whom he first met at the latter's Divisional H.Q. near Steyning. Montgomery complained that, although he was in command of "the only fully equipped Division in England, the only Division fit to fight any enemy anywhere," he had nevertheless been allotted a static rôle. It was not right. His Division should be equipped with buses and held in mobile reserve to launch a counter-attack on any invading force. Churchill noted the point, and the buses were soon forthcoming.[3] He was attracted by Montgomery's aggressive self-confidence and his obvious mastery of his job; Montgomery himself was in no way overawed by the Prime Minister and continued to speak his mind freely at subsequent meetings. Churchill once asked Tommy to tell the General that he was expecting him and his A.D.C. to lunch with him in his special train. Montgomery said he would come—by himself. "The right place for an A.D.C. to lunch," he observed, "is in a ditch, off sandwiches." On this occasion the General met with defeat, and the A.D.C. got his lunch after all!

Another area Churchill visited, just before the Battle of Britain, was Lincolnshire, where the 1st Guards Brigade had been sent after Dunkirk. The 2nd Battalions of the Coldstream Guards and Hampshire Regiment were holding an attenuated line along the coast; the 3rd Battalion Grenadier Guards were in reserve at Louth, and after inspecting them on parade there the Prime Minister lunched at Brigade H.Q.

[2] Arthur Bryant, *The Turn of the Tide*, p. 199.
[3] Viscount Montgomery, *Memoirs*, p. 69.

Apologizing for arriving a few minutes late, the Brigade Major added that he had just received the parade state. One man, he mentioned, had been placed under arrest.

"What for?" inquired Mr Churchill.

"Talking on parade, sir."

"What did he say?"

The Brigade Major hesitated, and Mr Churchill leant forward attentively.

"Well, as a matter of fact, sir, just after you passed down the line this man was clearly heard to remark, 'Pugnacious old bugger, ain't he?'"

This unconventional tribute from the ranks delighted the Prime Minister.

* * * * *

On several occasions before the war Tommy had accompanied Darlan on official visits which the French naval Commander-in-Chief had paid to England. He had come to know him well, and after one visit to Portsmouth, when Darlan had commented with some amusement at the sight of British naval officers carrying walking-sticks when they went ashore, a parcel arrived at the Admiralty for the Flag Lieutenant to the Board. It contained a beautifully made malacca stick which Darlan had bought for him at Hermes, the Paris gift shop. Having composed what he thought was an eloquent letter of thanks in French, Tommy kept a copy to show to one of the French liaison officers in the Admiralty. To his chagrin the letter reduced the Liaison Section to helpless merriment, and it was pointed out to him that he had, in fact, thanked Admiral Darlan for the very acceptable present of a female wild duck!

The rôle of Darlan following the French surrender was the subject of much speculation. After the Admiral's repeated assurances to Churchill that he would guarantee the safety of the French fleet it seemed inconceivable that he would himself go over to Vichy, leaving a powerful navy at the mercy of Germany. But by the end of June, with Italy already in the war, the whole balance of naval power was affected by the presence in the Mediterranean of large naval forces acting directly under the orders of the Pétain Government.

Since, as a result of this, Churchill was called upon to make a decision which he considered "the most unnatural and painful with which I have ever been concerned," the action at Oran on July 3 calls for some examination at this point, particularly as it raises certain matters which have never been satisfactorily explained.[4]

[4] Churchill, Vol. II, p. 206. For a detailed account of the sequence of events preceding Force H's bombardment of the French ships see *The Mediterranean and Middle East* (Major-General I.S.O. Playfair), Vol. I, pp. 130–138.

At Mers-el-Kebir, the large anchorage off Oran, lay two of the world's most powerful warships, the battle cruisers *Dunkerque* and *Strasbourg*, two battleships, and several light cruisers, destroyers, and submarines. Vice-Admiral Sir James Somerville was ordered to proceed there with Force H, which included *Hood*, *Valiant*, *Resolution*, and *Ark Royal*, and present a firm demand from the British Government that Admiral Gensoul, the French commander, who was flying his flag in the *Dunkerque*, should comply with one of four courses. He could sail his ships to a British port and fight on the Allied side; proceed to a British port, after which the crews would be repatriated; sail to a French port in the West Indies, where the ships could be demilitarized and the crews could return to France; or sink his ships where they lay, at Mers-el-Kebir. The third course was subsequently amended, allowing Admiral Gensoul to demilitarize his ships there and then if he preferred this to sailing to some port like Martinique. This concession was, however, made meaningless by an additional proviso that the effective disablement of the French squadron had to be completed in six hours—a sheer impossibility. If Admiral Gensoul rejected the alternatives placed before him Somerville, whose actions were controlled by the War Cabinet, was ordered to sink the ships in the roadstead.

For Somerville and Admiral Sir Andrew Cunningham, whose anxious negotiations with a similar French squadron at Alexandria were prejudiced by a series of astonishingly intemperate and illogical directives from the Admiralty, it was an agonizing situation. The British Government could, however, only be guided by known facts. Having measured the threat of a formidable fleet under imminent German domination, they took the only action to counter it which appeared open to them.

When Admiral Somerville was ordered to open fire on the French ships at Mers-el-Kebir the War Cabinet understood that Gensoul had rejected the British ultimatum. By then the Admiralty had intercepted an order by the French naval Chief of Staff, Admiral le Luc, for all French warships in the Western Mediterranean to rally to Gensoul's aid, and there was obviously no time to be lost. Unhappily, neither Somerville nor the War Cabinet knew of the existence of two signals made by the French Admiralty within the previous ten days.

Both were signed "François," indicating that they came from Darlan in person. The first, which Gensoul received on June 23, directed that on no account were French ships to fall into other hands; the moment there was any danger of this they were, without further orders, to proceed to the United States or sink themselves. The second, which reached him three days before the action, stated that enemy agreement had now been received for the demilitarization and internment of the French ships in North African ports.

Subsequent research into these tragic events suggests that, while Admiral Gensoul was admittedly—and inexplicably—at fault in not communicating to the French Admiralty any of the alternative courses offered to him on the morning of July 3, he *did* mention both the "François" signals during his parleys with Somerville's emissary on board the *Dunkerque*. In the stress of the moment their significance does not seem to have been appreciated. It is also averred in some responsible British naval circles that copies of both signals did in fact reach the Admiralty from a Free French source in London. The only official admission since made which has any bearing on this point concedes the receipt of the second message, but the signal is said to have been in a corrupt state, and since it was unintelligible it provided no basis for a reappraisal of policy.

The mystery surrounding the two signals made by Darlan therefore remains unsolved. Lacking any knowledge of them, the War Cabinet had no grounds for temporizing in a desperately critical situation, and although he was faced with a decision as distressing as any in the war, Churchill's firmness in this crisis gave unmistakeable proof of the Allied resolve.

Not surprisingly the British action roused much bitterness, but the understanding felt by many Frenchmen in the Vichy camp was shown by Sir Andrew Cunningham's subsequent relations with Admiral Godfroy, whose squadron lay for the next three years immobilized under the guns of the Mediterranean Fleet at Alexandria. Every British reverse in the war brought a message of eloquent sympathy from the French flag officer; every success of Allied arms brought a note of delighted congratulation. A strange confusion of loyalties kept Godfroy and his men passive observers of the conflict, but they understood and sympathized with Churchill in the dilemma which confronted him at Mers-el-Kebir.

7

The First Victory

ALTHOUGH recurrent German peace feelers suggested a certain hesitancy in the enemy mind, the heavy air attacks which began on July 10 followed a set pattern, and from this it was possible to discern what he hoped to achieve. By harrying the coastal convoys and bombing the Channel ports he imposed a constant strain on Fighter Command which became even more intense when he switched to a concerted series of attacks on the R.A.F. sector stations in the middle of August. If he could wear down the Royal Air Force in combat and disrupt its communications one of the greatest obstacles to a major landing operation would be removed, and in the opening stages of the Battle of Britain there was a disposition on the German side to wait and see how the air fighting went. Little serious planning for the invasion operation itself—Operation Sealion—was carried out, and Hitler did not convene the first staff meeting to discuss it until July 26.

In England, however, nothing was known of this reluctance to prepare for the move which Hitler and the German radio promised so freely. Enemy propaganda grew more and more strident in its attempts to spread dissension, and Goebbels' New British Broadcasting Station concentrated relentlessly on Churchill, proclaiming that the Prime Minister was being handsomely bribed by the Jews to continue the war. It hinted, however, that a highly organized Fifth Column would soon remove him and his friends from power. When this failed to make any impression they urged their listeners to demonstrate for peace by writing chain letters, hissing Churchill on the news reels, and horsewhipping him when he appeared in public.[1] If anything, this childish abuse increased Mr Churchill's popu-

[1] Peter Fleming, *Invasion 1940*, p. 98.

larity, but the constant harping on forthcoming German moves made it evident that the enemy were committing themselves to a major assault. The problem which faced the War Cabinet was to decide where the blow would fall.

With a coastline of 2000 miles, and inadequate forces to defend more than a small part of it at any one time, it was vital to determine where military strength should be concentrated. The Admiralty, too, had to decide how to deploy their forces to the best advantage. Admiral Forbes was understandably reluctant to bring his heavy ships south of the Wash, where they would be subject to air attack and possibly put out of action before the main invasion was launched, and his insistence on this point at one of the daily conferences brought a typically Churchillian reproof. Observing that no undue attention should be paid to what the Royal Navy might say they would do in certain circumstances, the Prime Minister added drily, "It is surely well known that if one hospital nurse was in distress on a rock or island in heavily guarded enemy waters the Admiralty would instantly agree to any number of major war vessels proceeding to the rescue, quite regardless of any possible dangers to them which might arise."

Independently the Prime Minister and the Chiefs of Staff came to the conclusion that the area most liable to invasion lay between the Wash and Dover. Soon evidence of the enemy's intention to launch his attack on the South Coast was provided by aerial photographs of self-propelled barges and other craft making their way to assembly points in Northern France. None could doubt now that the crisis was approaching.

The air attacks grew heavier, and between August 24 and September 6 an average of more than a thousand sorties were made over Britain every twenty-four hours. During one ten-day spell the R.A.F. lost 154 pilots and 213 aircraft; less than 150 new fighters reached the squadrons, and only 63 men who had just completed their training were available to fly them.[2] In the skies over Southern England it was a war of attrition which we seemed to be slowly losing.

As the Battle of Britain increased in ferocity Mr Churchill made many trips into the invasion area, visiting the fighter stations, inspecting the coastal belt around Dover, where 14-inch guns had been mounted to command the sea approaches, and watching the army in training. On these expeditions he generally used the special train which had recently been made available for him.

Soon after becoming Prime Minister he had found that war-time travel created awkward problems. Often he had to be away from London overnight—at times for several days on end—and to stay in hotels involved

[2] Fleming, *op. cit.*, p. 234.

complex security arrangements, embracing not only his own personal protection but the safeguarding of secret documents and telephone communications. Tommy was therefore sent to discuss the difficulty with Sir Harold Hartley, and after he had outlined what was needed a special composite train was built up from rolling-stock not required for normal passenger services.[3]

The key coaches were two 'semi-Royal' saloons, which had a small compartment at each end and a large open lounge in the centre. In the Prime Minister's personal coach a bedroom and bathroom occupied one end; at the other was an office for his Private Secretary and a typist, with a scrambler telephone connected to Mr Churchill's bedroom. The other large coach was unaltered, the lounge being used by the staff and official visitors, while the small compartments were available for V.I.P.'s who wanted to work undisturbed.

In the rear of Mr Churchill's coach was a sleeper coach, fitted with a shower, and following this came a passenger coach and a van carrying a diesel generator. In front of the second 'Royal' coach was a dining-car. Its rear compartment had a long table with seats for a dozen people; the front half of the coach was used by the detectives, photographers, telephone engineers, and others who usually accompanied the Prime Minister on his journeys. The rolling-stock was completed by a kitchen car, a sleeper coach for the retinue and the crew of the train, and another corridor coach and luggage van.

This immediately solved the communication problem, for whenever the train stopped the engineers merely had to plug in one end of a length of wire to a socket on the side of the Prime Minister's coach and unreel the rest of the wire until they reached the nearest telephone line. Number 10, Downing Street, had a special Top Priority number, known to every exchange throughout the country. Once contact had been made with the nearest trunks supervisor it was only necessary to ask for "Rapid Falls 8833," and within a few moments of the train coming to a halt the staff would be speaking to Whitehall. Even on arrival at some remote Scottish moorland siding the system worked with astonishing efficiency; there would sometimes be a brief pause before the operator at the rural exchange recalled the instructions he had received, perhaps many months before, about "Rapid Falls," and then the call went through in a matter of seconds.

On overnight stops the train would generally be shunted into some quiet siding in the depth of the country where the Prime Minister could sleep undisturbed. When close to big cities it was usually placed near some tunnel which could provide refuge in the event of an air raid.

[3] Brigadier-General Sir Harold Hartley was Vice-President and Director of Research, London, Midland, and Scottish Railway, from 1930 to 1945.

Using the train allowed Mr Churchill to carry out a morning inspection and then travel on to his next rendezvous, lunching on the journey and continuing discussions with his advisers. In this way much time was saved, and he could snatch an occasional rest. Both considerations were vital, for the Prime Minister's working day, which began at 8.0 A.M., with the study of the overnight telegrams and the dictation of a stream of minutes and directives from his bedside, proceeded at a tempo which would have exhausted many men half his age. Amid the anxious preparations for meeting a German invasion he was confronted with grave responsibilities in other theatres of war. There was a strong possibility of a German move through Spain to attack Gibraltar; Wavell was calling urgently for reinforcement of the Middle East, where the Italians, who had driven a small British force from Somaliland, were now poised for a major assault on Egypt; and at the same time an expedition was being mounted to land a force of Free French troops, under General de Gaulle's leadership, at Dakar in a bid to check the spread of Vichy influence in West Africa.

In spite of all these preoccupations, Mr Churchill gave no outward sign of anxiety. Geoffrey Dawson, who lunched with him at No. 10, found him "in excellent form, fit and confident and full of Beaverbrook's achievements in production."[4]

* * * * *

Study of the tides and moon made it almost certain that the invasion, if it came at all, must be attempted in the last fortnight of September. General Halder's plan called for an attack by one army between Hythe and Eastbourne and by another in the Worthing area, but although 4000 craft had been collected by the start of the month the naval preparations made little further headway. Every night Bomber Command pounded the assembly areas, and soon Admiral Raeder had to report to Hitler that the earliest date for the attempt would be September 21. Lacking any knowledge of this development, and seeing only the unremitting efforts of the enemy to continue their build-up of ships and barges, the War Cabinet in Britain could only assume that the die was cast. The Royal Air Force were still being pressed to the limit of their endurance, and although Goering's decision to switch the main weight of his air offensive to London itself gave them an unexpected respite, the Prime Minister felt it necessary to warn the nation of the impending assault. "We must regard the next week or so as a very important period in our history," he said in his broadcast; "it ranks with the days when the Spanish Armada was approaching the Channel."

To a tense House of Commons, which went into secret session, he gave

[4] Wrench, *Geoffrey Dawson and Our Times*, p. 425.

further details of the German preparations. Pointing out that the coastline to be defended was almost as long as the whole front in France from the Alps to the sea, he said, "One must expect many lodgments or attempted lodgments to be made on our island simultaneously." Characteristically he added, "I am confident that we shall succeed in defeating and largely destroying this most tremendous onslaught by which we are now threatened."[5]

As it turned out, however, the decisive moment had come two days earlier. On the afternoon of Sunday, September 15, Mr Churchill, who was on his way by road from Downing Street to Chequers, broke his journey at Uxbridge, where No. 11 Group, Fighter Command, had its headquarters. From a balcony in the underground Operations Room which controlled the squadrons covering south-eastern England it was possible to follow every move in the air fighting on a huge plotting-table. On the opposite side of the room was a blackboard in which were set dozens of electric bulbs. The glowing of these lights signalled the state of readiness of the squadrons held in reserve, the aircraft already in contact with the enemy, and those which had just disengaged from the battle to refuel or rearm.

The ceaseless orderly activity of this nerve centre, with the plotters moving their discs to and fro on the table, the Army liaison officers passing information about the anti-aircraft units in action, and the winking of the red and white lights on the far wall, created an instant sense of drama. Mr Churchill had paid one previous visit there. On that occasion he had been accompanied by a member of his secretariat, who had remarked in an awed voice to the officer sitting next to her:

"The old man *will* be fascinated by this. It's the Battle of Blenheim all over again."

"Whatever do you mean?" he asked.

"I was on duty with the P.M. when he stayed at Blenheim Palace last week-end," she explained. "It was terribly interesting. We spent quite a long time on our hands and knees on the library floor while he reconstructed the battle of Blenheim for us with tin soldiers."

She was quite right. The Prime Minister *was* fascinated by the whole intricate control system, and that day he had plied Wing Commander Thomas Lang, the Controller on duty at the time, with questions about the procedure for detecting the enemy aircraft forming up and the method by which the waiting squadrons were alerted and directed to the attack. Eventually the A.O.C., Air Vice-Marshal K. R. Park, felt it was time he

[5] The Prime Minister broadcast his invasion warning on September 11; in his secret session speech on September 17 he declared, "Whatever happens we will all go down fighting to the end."

intervened. He had noticed signs of activity on the plot and did not want his Controller to be distracted. As the Prime Minister was plainly unaware of the situation he could hardly reprove his distinguished visitor, so he said pointedly—"Lang! Lang! If you go on chattering like this I shall have to replace you by a less talkative Controller."

On the afternoon of September 15, however, all was quiet when the Prime Minister entered the Operations Room, and while the Air Vice-Marshal walked about talking to his staff the Duty Controller—this time Group Captain Lord Willoughby de Broke—outlined the procedure he normally followed.

Park believed in giving his Controllers a fairly free hand. He would lecture them on the broad tactics he wanted to adopt, tell them where he wanted the fighters to be up, the way he wanted them grouped, and the heights at which they were to operate. Since the A.O.C. himself might not be within immediate reach when an attack showed signs of developing, it was therefore left to the Controller to set the stage himself, ordering the fighters up to their battle positions, and then report what had been done. Often when the plots began to form on an otherwise blank map table it was a matter for split-second decision whether they indicated the start of a real raid or some decoy move. If the Controller hesitated, and delayed his decision to order up the fighters for two or three minutes, it could make just the difference between the R.A.F. pilots having 2000 feet of extra height over the German raiders or finding themselves at a complete disadvantage far below. Having taken the plunge and made his initial dispositions, he would ring up the A.O.C. "There is a hundred plus assembling over Gris Nez, and a nasty-looking fifty plus over the mouth of the Somme. It rather looks as if they are going to have a go at Plymouth or Bristol . . . one of the West Country entertainments." Park would then come down, and, sitting next to the Controller, he would study the board, which by then would be showing a definite pattern. The radar would be assessing the German aircraft with increasing accuracy, and he could see from the symbols before him the heights to which our own fighters had been ordered, and their relative positions. If he was satisfied with the orders already given he would often leave his Controller to carry on.

Mr Churchill listened intently while this was explained to him. Then, as the attacks began that afternoon, he sat hunched in his chair, silent and absorbed, as Lord Willoughby de Broke spoke to the Fighter Stations. The German Air Force came over in wave after wave, and No. 11 Group fought to a standstill. Not a single squadron was left in reserve when the last German aircraft turned for home. When Park told him this the Prime Minister was deeply affected. As he drove back to Chequers with Ismay he made the remark which has since become part of history—

"Never in the field of human conflict was so much owed by so many to so few."

The heavy losses sustained by the Luftwaffe that afternoon and a shattering attack on the invasion fleet at Antwerp by Bomber Command a few hours later led Hitler to postpone the invasion indefinitely. It was to remain among the German war plans, debated half-heartedly from time to time, for almost two and a half years. But without air superiority and suitable landing-craft there was never any serious likelihood of such a venture succeeding after the day and night of September 15, 1940.

8

Ordeal by Night

WHEN the full fury of the Blitz fell upon London the Churchills were living in Downing Street. Number 10 presented a more substantial target than might be imagined from its deceptively modest frontage, for a passage from the entrance hall leads to a much larger house, formerly owned by King Charles II, which looks out over a walled garden to the Horse Guards Parade. This had been rebuilt in Walpole's time, two centuries earlier. Since then no major structural alterations had been made, and the rambling old building offered scant protection against high-explosive bombs. This fact was brought home to the Prime Minister when, wishing to reassure some members of the Cabinet, he prodded one of the low ceilings with his stick. To every one's amazement it went straight through into the Treasury passage above. Only three inches of crumbling lath and plaster covered the room they were in.

Mr Churchill's own philosophy on the subject of air raids was summed up in the words of advice he had already given to the House of Commons. "Learn to get used to it," he said; "eels get used to skinning." He strongly disliked the idea of being dislodged from his new home by enemy action, for apart from Lord Salisbury every Prime Minister since the days of Disraeli had used No. 10 as his London residence. And so, for the time being, he remained defiantly in occupation. A small dining-room and sitting-room were furnished in the sub-basement, the ceilings of these were shored up, and a new air-raid shelter capable of holding every one who might be caught in No. 10 was built in a corner of the garden next to the Treasury wall.

Soon, however, it became obvious from the weight and duration of the attacks that bombs were bound to fall on Downing Street before long. For fifty-seven nights on end an average of two hundred enemy aircraft arrived over the capital; day and night the sirens—"those banshee howlings," Churchill called them—wailed so often that it was difficult to distinguish between one raid and another. It was therefore decided to transfer the Prime Minister's office and staff to a much stronger Government block near by at Storey's Gate. There during the heaviest raids he could work and sleep, for thirty-five feet below ground was a small bedroom, furnished with monastic austerity.

Facing the bed was a map bearing the legend, "London to Suez." From the rough walls hung other maps, curtained by strips of dingy linen. At the far end was a plain desk with a note pad and, inevitably, a pile of his red labels with the black lettering—ACTION THIS DAY.

His secretaries lived in the same corridor, and another Spartanly furnished room was provided for Mrs Churchill, who insisted on taking her turn with fire-watching duties on the roof far above. Close at hand was the Cabinet Room, a grim, yellow-walled cavern, its ceiling supported by huge steel girders. Covering this whole area was a carapace of reinforced concrete, several feet thick. Even the outside walls of this citadel were fortified so successfully that when one night a bomb fell a few feet away, at the end of King Charles Street, the Annexe, as the new headquarters was now known, sustained no damage at all.

A vulnerable point, however, was the central well of the block. To shield this some one designed an enormous net of steel wire, suspended on pulleys and counter-weighted to take the shock of a descending bomb. The occupants of the Annexe waited with morbid interest for the baptism of this remarkable contraption, but fortunately nothing ever landed in the net. Another possible hazard was the flooding of the basement, for it was below the level of the Thames, and an elaborate pumping system was installed. This could be operated by auxiliary machinery if the main power failed.

During the daytime Churchill much preferred to work at No. 10, but he had an office on the ground floor of the Annexe. To protect this from blast naval paunch mats—normally used during gunnery exercises—were hung over the windows, but the Prime Minister took a strong dislike to these primitive trappings, and they were soon replaced by sliding steel shutters.

When it was safe to go to Downing Street he would work there through the morning and remain for lunch and his afternoon's rest, but an incident on the evening of October 14 persuaded him that it was no longer safe to dine there while the heavy night raids continued. On that particular night he and his guests—Sir Archibald Sinclair, Moore-Brabazon (the Minister of Transport), Oliver Lyttelton, and Colonel Stewart Menzies—were half-way through dinner when a bomb fell on the Treasury.

A few minutes before a strong presentiment of danger had prompted Churchill to send Mrs Landemare, his cook, and the rest of the kitchen staff to the shelter. They had a miraculous escape, for the kitchen at No. 10 is a huge, high-ceilinged room with a glass window covering almost the whole of one end. It was completely wrecked, but the Prime Minister, who immediately hurried in search of his staff, found them unharmed. When he had made sure they were safe he summoned his guests, led them through the India Office quadrangle to Storey's Gate, and up to the sandbagged emplacement which had been built for him as an observation post on the roof of the Air Ministry.

This was his favourite coign of vantage in air raids. On one particularly cold night he was sitting outside this shelter, hunched in his thick coat and staring at the flashes of distant gunfire as a German raid developed, when a Fire Guard emerged choking on to the roof to report that the room below was filling with smoke. This was not surprising, for Mr Churchill was seated firmly on top of its chimney.

To those who accompanied him on his frequent visits to the roof at night the Prime Minister seemed completely unmoved by danger. During one heavy raid shell-fragments were raining down, and an apprehensive member of his staff kept saying, as loudly as he dared, that it was tempting Providence to remain there. When Churchill eventually overheard this he said phlegmatically, "My time will come when it comes."

"You're probably right, sir," came a dejected voice from the darkness, "but there's no need to take half a dozen of us with you."

The Prime Minister's personal disregard of hazards had in it no element of callousness or lack of sensitivity. A vivid imagination reinforced his humanity, and he was readily and intensely moved by misfortune and suffering. His own actions, however, were dictated by a strong sense of fatalism; this, coupled with the invigoration he felt in the presence of danger, often made him oblivious to the risks to which he was exposing himself and those with him.

On the night after Downing Street was hit came the heaviest attack of the month on London, the Luftwaffe dropping nearly four hundred tons of high-explosive and seventy thousand incendiary bombs. The builders were still busy in the Annexe, and Mr Churchill was persuaded for the time being to take shelter at night in the disused Down Street tube station in Piccadilly, where the Railway Executive had a suite of offices. As often as not he would return to Whitehall before daylight, disregarding the bombers still circling overhead, for in this temporary refuge he felt restless and out of touch with events. He steadfastly refused to contemplate a retreat from the capital, but the raids were already imposing a new and threatening pattern on the life of London. The constant 'alerts' were disrupting work; the 'black-out' and the nightly damage to the congested suburban railway system disorganized transport and communications. If the business of government was to be carried on from London most of the major departments of State might have to be housed underground.

With characteristic energy Lord Beaverbrook undertook the task of preparing a number of bomb-proof refuges. One large underground building already equipped with its own extensive communication system was available at Dollis Hill, where the G.P.O. had been constructing a new Continental Telephone Exchange. It was the conversion of this building which had taken up much of Tommy's time before he went to Downing Street. He also laid in stores of tinned food and bedding for the Prime Minister and his staff in the Rotunda, a gloomy dungeon in Great Peter Street, a hundred yards from the Embankment, which had been used as a Government store. This could be reached underground from Whitehall by taking a lift from the basement of the Air Ministry and walking along the tunnel through which ran the Post Office mail trains.

Provisional accommodation for members of the Government was also earmarked at various places in the Midlands, but apart from Chequers the only house where Churchill stayed for any length of time was Ditchley, the home of Ronald Tree, the Member of Parliament for Market Harborough. While invasion seemed imminent the Prime Minister had been strongly advised not to go to his own home at Chartwell, in Kent, owing to its prominent position on a hill and the fact that it could be easily identified from the air by a chain of lakes near by. Then, when the night raids grew heavier, Chequers, too, was found to have serious drawbacks. This Elizabethan mansion, given to the nation twenty years earlier by Lord Lee of Fareham, is set in a large wooded park two miles south-east of Wendover, in Buckinghamshire. The long, straight drive to the house runs up the centre of a small valley, and it was seen that by taking their bearings from certain reservoirs on the London side bomber crews might be able to pin-point the target without much difficulty. There were other aids to navigation, for behind Chequers lay Beacon Hill, 756 feet above sea-level, and Coombe Hill, an even more prominent landmark to the north-east. While the Blitz raged Churchill therefore spent the week-ends of full moon at Ditchley, not far from Blenheim. Scrambler telephone equipment was installed there, and the War Office supplied a special guard, who camped in the old coach house and stables. In some ways it was a most unusual arrangement. On these week-ends Ditchley was occupied partly by the Prime Minister and his official entourage and partly by the Tree family and their friends, but everything ran smoothly, and security was so effective that when Tommy rang up the War Office on one occasion to find out why no guard had arrived he was told it had been dispatched many hours before—to Ditchling, in Sussex!

It was at Ditchley at the end of November that Churchill spent his sixty-sixth birthday—perhaps his most anxious war-time birthday of all, for although the threat of invasion had receded Britain was still naked and alone, under constant assault from the air. By now the raids had widened. The first mass attack on a provincial city—Coventry—was immediately followed by a tremendous moonlight onslaught on London, and then came a series of heavy raids on the Birmingham area. By crippling the Italian Battle Fleet at Taranto the Fleet Air Arm had struck a notable blow, but the situation at sea was very grave, and the danger of a U-boat stranglehold on Allied supplies—"the only thing that ever really frightened me during the war," Churchill wrote afterwards[1]—was constantly in the Prime Minister's mind. The Italian invasion of Greece dangerously extended Allied commitments in the Middle East, and public confidence in the central direction of the war effort, largely restored since the Norwegian debacle, had been undermined once again by the events at Dakar.

* * * * *

In many respects the Dakar operation had been a misconceived and muddled affair, launched with insufficient planning and complicated by a series of unfortunate incidents which were later to yield valuable lessons.

The basic idea was sound enough. To forestall any move by Hitler or Pétain in West Africa it was intended to land a Free French force under the leadership of General de Gaulle at Dakar, in Senegal, thus securing an important naval and air base and a great stretch of Atlantic coast for the Allies, and rallying French resistance over a vast area. No serious opposition was expected, for although Pierre Boisson, the Governor-General of French Equatorial Africa, gave his allegiance to Vichy, it was not thought that he would offer more than token resistance when confronted by a powerful Allied Fleet and a military force composed of his own countrymen.

De Gaulle himself would have preferred to land his troops at Konakry, several hundred miles to the south, and raise French support to his flag as he marched on Dakar with a British naval force covering his seaward flank. It was pointed out to him, however, that a large squadron of warships could not be spared for a campaign of such length. The landing must be attempted at Dakar or not at all.

Unhappily, nothing went right. The original plan recognized that the transporting and covering of the force would be largely a British commitment. Once in the landing zone it was to become a Free French operation

[1] Churchill, Vol. II, p. 529.

involving no extensive Allied contribution in men or equipment. Only when the planners got down to a more detailed examination with de Gaulle and his staff was it realized that British troops would, in fact, outnumber the French.

The force commanders, Vice-Admiral John Cunningham and Major-General N. M. S. Irwin, did not receive their orders until August 12, but they were directed to mount the expedition, sail to West Africa, and be ready to act on September 8. Any untoward delay would, it was emphasized, imperil the success of the whole undertaking. Almost immediately, however, the programme had to be put back by ten days; the ships carrying the transport were half loaded before it was realized that their speed and range were insufficient to take them to Dakar on schedule. They would have to refuel at Freetown.

This was followed by a more serious development. It was reported that the safety of the whole expedition had been compromised by breaches of security. At this time methods of deception were in their infancy as far as the staging of amphibious operations was concerned, and if the Free French troops were briefed at all about "Careless Talk"—the subject of so many effective British posters later on—the warnings could not have made much impression. At the Coq d'Or restaurant, in the heart of the West End of London, French officers sitting round the table at the far end of the dining-room were overheard loudly toasting the success of the landing in Senegal; when de Gaulle's train left Euston it was surrounded by well-wishers shouting, "A Dakar!" If this was not bad enough the train had travelled only a short distance when it was discovered that a huge chest of gold louis had been left on the platform. So it put back to retrieve this, and there was further delay while a dining-car was fetched and hitched on to the train for the General's use.

Perhaps the most surprising breach was unintentionally committed by de Gaulle himself, for he went openly to Simpson's, in Piccadilly, and asked if they could equip him with tropical uniform. At that time Simpson's were besieged by officers wanting uniforms. Many had just escaped from enemy territory with no wearable uniform of any kind, and the firm could not supply de Gaulle, whose height made him a difficult man to fit from stock. In the end he contented himself with the purchase of a light trench coat. The reaction of the assistants in the shop to the arrival of the General, whom they instantly recognized, was one of immediate curiosity. His appearance there led to general discussion of the enterprises upon which the Free French might be likely to embark. The assistant who served de Gaulle said they conjectured that his destination would be "Africa."

All this was bad enough, but worse was to follow. The British intelligence briefing was deplorable. Admiral Cunningham was given no information about the Dakar area and its defences until he was about to sail. When he ploughed through the mass of papers handed to him he found that much of it dated from before the First World War. By contrast, when Schellenberg—later destined to become head of the German Secret Service—joined the German Foreign Office Intelligence Department the first assignment he was given by Heydrich, in the autumn of 1938, was to survey the West African coastal region and compile a full report on Dakar. He photographed the harbour installations and secured up-to-date charts and maps of the whole area.[2]

The expedition sailed on August 31. On September 11, when Admiral Cunningham's force was off the Cape Verde Islands and steaming slowly towards Freetown, three French cruisers crammed with Vichy reinforcements were allowed to pass unhindered through the Straits of Gibraltar, and they headed south. They reached Dakar on September 14—five days before the Allied expedition showed itself off the port—and disembarked their troops. Boisson could now face any Allied move with equanimity.

In England it was instantly realized that this development altered the whole situation, and a signal was sent calling for the expedition to be abandoned. The force commanders took a different view. To them it seemed by no means certain that the arrival of the cruisers had materially changed the situation, and de Gaulle himself was determined to go ahead with the attempt at an unopposed landing in the harbour. If this failed he would put his troops ashore farther up the coast and enter Dakar from the landward side. Impressed by the zeal of his commanders on the spot, the Prime Minister decided to give them a free hand, but they had not reckoned on the implacable hostility of Boisson towards the liberating force. The Governor-General showed no disposition to welcome de Gaulle's various envoys, who were fired upon when they approached by sea and arrested when they landed on the airport. After due warning bombardment of the heavily fortified port began, but dense fog prevented the spotting planes from aiding the ships' gunners, and after three abortive days, during which *Resolution*, Admiral Cunningham's flagship, was torpedoed, and *Barham* and several other ships were damaged, this ill-starred action had to be broken off. The only solid gain was the disablement of the French battleship *Richelieu.*

"To the world at large," wrote Churchill later, "it seemed a glaring example of miscalculation, confusion, timidity and muddle; . . . there was a storm of criticism. . . . I decided, however, that no explanation should be offered and Parliament respected my wish."[3]

[2] Schellenberg, *Memoirs,* pp. 59–60.

[3] Churchill, Vol. II, pp. 436–437. Reviewing the failure of the operation, Churchill points out that "no blame attached to the British naval and military commanders, and both were constantly employed until the end of the war, the Admiral attaining the

The case of Dakar has been examined in some detail because it was the first operation of its kind attempted by the Allies, and Churchill, who drafted the original directive himself and was closely concerned with subsequent decisions, accepted the main responsibility for its failure. In retrospect the prize seems still to justify the risk so boldly accepted, first by the Prime Minister and later by de Gaulle and the British force commanders. And the harsh experience of unco-ordinated planning, unreliable intelligence work, and inattention to security was turned to lasting account. Dakar taught its lessons in the political as well as the military sphere, for it showed how wide was the chasm now dividing the French nation. On the night of October 21 Churchill broadcast a moving appeal to the French people to reject propaganda which sought to widen this breach. Three days later he sent a personal message to Weygand, now Vichy Commander-in-Chief in North Africa, by the hand of Professor Louis Rougier, who was returning to France via Lisbon and Algiers. In this he again stressed the solid advantages to France of setting up an independent Government on the far shore of the Mediterranean; "the Prime Minister is convinced that the opportunity that presents itself is the most brilliant ever offered to men of courage."

Weygand's reaction to this was typical of the illogicality which ruled so many French minds at this time. He was "unfavourably impressed by the call to political adventure," as he termed it, and, taking the attitude that he was "not entitled to communicate with a Foreign Government," he sent copies of the messages he had received from the Prime Minister and Foreign Secretary straight to Pétain.

The Marshal wrote back, "You have done very well in not replying to the letters from W. Churchill and Lord Halifax. . . . I too have received many questions from W. Churchill and Lord Halifax, who are curious to know what was the subject of my conversations with Hitler."[4]

Oran and Dakar gave welcome ammunition to the Vichy leaders. More unfortunately, these two clashes with the French provoked adverse criticism in the United States. Not even the threat of a German invasion of Britain and the bombing of her cities had affected the hard core of American isolationism, and the British cause had no advocate in the United States Ambassador to the Court of St James.

Although he appeared co-operative and helpful in the first few months of the war, Joseph Kennedy's Irish-American background made it difficult

highest distinction. . . . It was one of my rules that errors *towards* the enemy must be lightly judged." Admiral of the Fleet Sir John Cunningham became in turn Fourth Sea Lord in 1941, Commander-in-Chief Mediterranean in 1943, and succeeded his namesake, Admiral of the Fleet Sir Andrew Cunningham, as First Sea Lord in 1946.

[4] Weygand, *op. cit.*, pp. 357–360. Pétain met Hitler at Montoire on October 24, the day after Hitler and Franco had conferred at Hendaye.

for him to take an entirely objective view of events. Lacking any instinctive understanding of the British people, he became readily convinced that their defeat was inevitable, and this conviction was shared by senior Army and Naval officers on his staff.

Colonel Carl Spaatz, of the United States Army Air Corps, who came to England in June to make his own assessment of the situation, formed quite the opposite conclusion. And so did Colonel "Wild Bill" Donovan, who arrived soon afterwards as the personal representative of President Roosevelt.[5] He toured Bomber Command stations and talked to the crews returning from raids on Germany; he met the Prime Minister and leading politicians, and held exhaustive discussions with the heads of all the fighting Services. Reaching the firm conclusion that the Ambassador's advice was unrealistic, he told the President that there was no likelihood of an imminent British collapse. It was largely due to the report he made to Roosevelt on his return that fifty U.S. destroyers were transferred to reinforce the convoy escort groups.

Kennedy continued to spread the doctrine that active support for Britain would be a mistaken policy, but in October he went home. Gilbert Winant, who replaced him, was to prove a man of altogether different temper and calibre.

Before Winant arrived, however, Roosevelt was re-elected President. The election campaign over, he set out on a brief holiday. He was cruising in the Caribbean early in December when he received from Churchill a long and reasoned survey of the war situation. It made a profound impression on him. In it the Prime Minister, having first emphasized the identity of interests between their two countries, referred to the grave and increasing shipping losses which threatened Britain's survival. He pointed out ways in which America might help—by protecting British convoys with U.S. escorts, extending the American naval patrol area, and interceding with Eire for the use of Southern Irish bases. He explained the desperate need of any surplus merchant shipping which the United States might have available, and stressed the critical shortage of combat aircraft and munitions. Immediate payment for all the supplies which the Allies needed to continue the fight was clearly beyond their resources, but since the fate of Western civilization was at stake some equitable means could surely be devised for solving this problem.

Re-election for a third term by a majority of over five million votes had greatly strengthened the President's hand, and at a Press conference held immediately on his return he laid the foundation for public acceptance of

[5] Donovan, a former United States Assistant Attorney-General, became Director of the Office of Strategic Services when America entered the war. In the first war he had won the Congressional Medal of Honour.

the Lease-Lend agreement, which was finally ratified in the following March. From that moment onward Allied war needs were secure—and there was no provision for repayment. In Parliament Churchill was to refer to this as "the most unsordid act in the history of any nation."

Roosevelt followed up his Press conference with a "fireside chat," broadcast to the nation a few days later. "Never," he told them, "has American civilization been in greater danger." There was a new feeling of purpose in the direction of American affairs, and although Churchill spoke gravely of the bombing and the losses at sea when he gave one of his own periodical reviews of the war situation to Parliament, he was able to announce a notable feat of British arms in the Western Desert, where Wavell had driven a large Italian army headlong from Egypt, taking 38,000 prisoners. Broadcasting to Italy two days before Christmas, the Prime Minister promised that this was only a beginning. "Our armies will tear your African empire to shreds and tatters," he said. And to a people already dazed and dismayed by the rout of Graziani's forces the fierce emphasis he put into this particular phrase must have sounded a note of doom.

On Christmas Day 1940 the Churchill family gathered at Chequers. Randolph and his wife were there, and Sarah and her husband and Mary. There was a strange lull on land and sea, and even in the air, and for once the duty secretary, John Martin, had little to do. Hardly a call came through from Whitehall. It seemed unnatural—almost ominous—and into the diary of one of the house party went a pensive entry—"I wonder whether we shall all be together this time next year." It was, in fact, the last Christmas they were destined to spend together for four long years.

9

"Whither Thou Goest I will Go, Even to the End"

ONE grey winter morning a fortnight after Christmas Tommy and Brendan Bracken caught a train to Bournemouth. A B.O.A.C. flying-boat was coming in from Lisbon with an important passenger.

They were on the jetty at Poole when the aircraft appeared, flying low over the harbour. It taxied to the buoy, and then there was a long wait before the tender came in to the shore. From the boat they helped a frail and exhausted man who sank back in the waiting car with obvious relief. During the journey to the station he seemed too tired to talk, and Tommy, who had never met him before, thought how very ill he looked. His name was Harry Lloyd Hopkins. He had come to Britain at President Roosevelt's request to make contact with the Prime Minister.

Hopkins, then in his fiftieth year, was Roosevelt's closest confidant. During the thirties he had administered many New Deal relief agencies on the President's behalf, and from 1938 to 1940 he had been United States Secretary of Commerce. Since resigning from this post he had moved into the White House to become, in effect, a Minister without Portfolio and Roosevelt's most trusted adviser. He *was* a very sick man, and it was a miracle he was still alive, for an attack of typhoid in childhood had weakened his constitution, and later a series of severe internal operations had left him suffering from a wasting malnutrition. Shortly before the war Roosevelt was told that Hopkins could not survive more than a few weeks, and now life hung by a thread. Often it seemed that only will-power sustained him, but even at times of extreme exhaustion his mind remained vividly alert.

On Churchill's instructions a special Pullman coach had been attached to the train. They gave him a light lunch and a large Scotch, and to their relief their guest began to look much better. Soon he was firing questions, and swapping stories with Bracken—no mean story-teller himself—about their previous meetings.

As they neared London in the gathering dusk the sirens sounded. The train kept on, reaching Waterloo dead on schedule, but they were only just in time. Within a minute of their arrival hundreds of incendiaries showered down on the line between Clapham Junction and the terminal, and all tracks were blocked for several hours afterwards.

Hopkins went straight to Claridge's. Next day he lunched at Downing Street, and on the following afternoon Tommy took him to Ditchley. They had an eventful journey, for signposts had been removed at the first threat of invasion, and the chauffeur, trying to take a short cut near Beaconsfield, became hopelessly lost. As they groped uncertainly through the byways of the Chilterns Tommy cursed himself for not bringing a map. To lose the Prime Minister's most important guest in the short distance between London and Ditchley was an unfortunate start to the week-end, but Hopkins, who had no idea of the right direction anyway, said he was thoroughly enjoying himself. He seemed quite disappointed when they regained the main road near Oxford.

During that first week-end in the country the Prime Minister and his guest formed a friendship which endured through all the misunderstandings which were to cloud Harry Hopkins' relationship with Roosevelt in the years ahead. Before his arrival Churchill knew nothing about him; when he first learnt that Hopkins was coming to England Bracken had to explain who he was. The Prime Minister took to him immediately. He found him frank and outspoken, but Hopkins' occasional caustic criticisms were always based on a penetrating study of the problem in hand. From the start of his visit he made it plain that he was there to learn; he would sit quietly weighing up the facts, and then give his views with complete impartiality. One could take them or leave them; he made no attempt to 'sell' a proposition against its merits.

For his part Harry Hopkins was fascinated by Churchill. Before he left Washington he had been advised by Jean Monnet, the Frenchman who was working for the British Purchasing Commission there, to waste no time with the different Ministers in the British Cabinet but to concentrate on Churchill—"for Churchill *is* the British War Cabinet and no one else matters."[1] He soon found this was no exaggeration, and, watching Churchill at work during that first week-end at Ditchley, he was astonished by the Prime Minister's close contact with every facet of the war effort. He was impressed by his buoyancy—even the disturbing news that German

[1] Sherwood, *op. cit.*, p. 233.

dive-bombers had made their first appearance in the Mediterranean was received with apparent unconcern—and he was stimulated by the Prime Minister's methods and the sense of drama which seemed to invest every incident in his working day. To him Churchill "always seemed to be at his command post on the precarious beach-head and the guns were continually blazing in his conversation; wherever he was, there was the battlefront—and he was involved not only in the battles of the current war but of the whole past from Cannae to Gallipoli."[2]

Hopkins had been charged with a remarkable message from Roosevelt to the Prime Minister—"The President is determined that we shall win the war together. . . . He has sent me here to tell you that at all costs and by all means he will carry you through, no matter what happens to him—there is nothing that he will not do so far as he has human power."[3] Deeply moved by this, Churchill was determined that his visitor should carry back with him a complete picture of the British war effort, and he took him on several tours of inspection. The most important of these began at Scapa Flow, where the Prime Minister travelled to bid farewell to Lord Halifax, who was setting out across the Atlantic in H.M.S. *King George V* to take up his new post as British Ambassador to the United States. Lord Lothian had died suddenly in December, and the appointment of the Foreign Secretary to succeed him emphasized the importance which the Government attached to relations with America.

At Scapa, where they visited ships of the Home Fleet, Hopkins had a memorable day. First he lost his foothold when trying to board a destroyer and all but fell into the sea. Then he was standing on the bridge of H.M.S. *Nelson* when the Prime Minister noticed a new rocket device mounted on the top of *Nelson*'s 'B' turret and called for this to be demonstrated.

The device in question was a multiple projector which hurled bombs and masses of wire into the sky to discourage dive-bombers. Unfortunately, not enough allowance was made for the wind on this occasion, and one of the wires drifted back on to the ship, where it became entangled with the wireless spur on the mainmast and exploded violently. Churchill seemed quite unmoved. His cigar remained tightly clenched between his teeth, and, staring up at the mast, he observed drily, "I think there is something not quite right about the way you are using this new weapon."

From Scapa they went to Clydeside and the Newcastle area to visit war factories and inspect the Civil Defence organization. At Glasgow they dined with the Lord Provost, and Hopkins was called upon to say a few words. As the representative of a nation still neutral he was careful to avoid making public speeches in the ordinary way, but this time he rose to his feet and repeated a prophetic passage from the Book of Ruth—"Whither

[2] *Ibid.*, p. 242.

[3] Churchill, Vol. III, p. 21.

thou goest, I will go"—adding, with great feeling, the words "even to the end." For every one present it was an emotional moment.

After their return to London Hopkins spent two week-ends at Chequers. He found this something of an ordeal, for he felt the cold acutely—and Chequers was a quite remarkably cold house. The great hall where the house party spent much of the time stood on the site of an old courtyard which had been roofed in. Even a blazing log-fire scarcely took the chill off this vast, lofty room, and perhaps because of the architect's warning that central heating might warp the oak panelling the few radiators seemed designed to give out a minimum of warmth. Whenever he could find an excuse Hopkins retreated to the only warm place he had discovered in the house—the downstairs bathroom. There, huddled in his overcoat, he would sit for hours working on his papers. He sent back voluminous reports on all he had seen. In one of these he told Roosevelt:

> Your former Navy person is not only the Prime Minister. He is the directing force behind the strategy and conduct of the war in all its essentials. He has an amazing hold on the British people of all classes.

After referring to the conviction that Germany would make another attempt to invade Britain in the spring he continued:

> The spirit of this people and their determination to resist invasion is beyond praise. No matter how fierce the attack may be you can be sure that they will resist it, and effectively. . . . I therefore cannot urge too strongly that any action you may take to meet the immediate needs here must be based on the assumption that invasion will come before May 1. If Germany fails to win this invasion then I believe her sun is set. I am convinced that if we act boldly and promptly on a few major fronts we can get enough material to Britain within the next few weeks to give her the additional strength she needs to turn back Hitler.

He then went on to outline an astonishingly comprehensive list of requirements for the supply of ships, aircraft, and munitions, which he had drafted after lengthy discussions with Lindemann and his statisticians.[4]

At his own request his stay in England was extended to a month. On February 8, the day he went to Chequers to say good-bye, word came through that the House of Representatives had approved the Lease-Lend Bill. He left Churchill hard at work on a speech he was to broadcast to the world on the following evening and set off for Bournemouth. Tommy and Brendan Bracken again went with him; also in the party was a young Guards officer, Lieutenant Anthony McComas, for Hopkins was taking back to America a large number of Top Secret papers, and since he did

[4] Sherwood, *op. cit.*, p. 257.

not want to be solely responsible for their safety the War Office chose McComas to accompany him across the Atlantic.

On their way to the coast the weather closed in. By the following morning flying was out of the question, so they spent that night at Branksome Towers Hotel. After dinner they went into the public lounge to hear Churchill's broadcast. As the crowded room listened to his memorable appeal—"Give us the tools and we'll finish the job"—none of Hopkins' fellow-guests realized that the President's special envoy was sitting there with them.

When Hopkins boarded the Clipper next day for the long flight back to Washington via Lisbon and Brazil he carried an unusual souvenir. Before he left Chequers the Prime Minister had handed him a box of pink pills which, he said, should be taken at intervals throughout the journey. Hopkins gathered that they had remarkable recuperative properties. On his return to the White House he showed them to the President, who was much intrigued and, handing one to his medical adviser, Rear-Admiral Ross McIntire, he asked him to have it analysed. The report was singularly unflattering. As far as they could determine the pill could do no conceivable good, said the analysts. On the other hand, they added encouragingly, it was not likely to inflict actual harm!

* * * * *

Before Hopkins left England another important visitor arrived from America—Wendell Willkie, the defeated candidate in the recent Presidential election. Willkie came with the President's blessing, and Tommy flew to Filton, the airfield near Bristol, to meet him and bring him back to London in the Flamingo aircraft which Churchill often used. At first Willkie seemed tired and hesitant, and Tommy had some difficulty in discovering what he wanted to do. He was accompanied by two of his campaign helpers, John Cowles and Landon K. Thorn, and as they chatted on the airfield Cowles, glancing at Willkie, said apologetically, "He's not all that alert now . . . he's still punch-drunk after the campaign."

It was arranged that Willkie should visit Chequers, but as a private observer he could not be briefed on many of the matters which had been fully discussed with Harry Hopkins, and the Prime Minister could not spare as much time to entertain him as he would have liked. His anxiety to make amends for this was to lead to a somewhat embarrassing incident when Churchill found himself in America a year later.

For a time the weather over England allowed only spasmodic enemy bombing raids. The rout of the Italians continued in the Western Desert, Bardia, Tobruk, and Benghazi being occupied in rapid succession, and Italy's empire on the shore of the Indian Ocean crumpled under the assault of forces brilliantly led by General Sir Alan Cunningham, the younger brother of the naval Commander-in-Chief in the Mediterranean. In the opening weeks of 1941 the prospect seemed fairer than at any time in the past year, but clouds were gathering. German troop movements through the Balkans pointed to an invasion of Greece; their dive-bombers began pounding Malta; and there was evidence of renewed pressure by Hitler to persuade Spain to enter the war. Another piece of intelligence was puzzling and disturbing because it could not be fitted satisfactorily into the existing pattern of possible developments. There was a sudden stir of excitement in Britain's Japanese colony, but this quickly subsided, defying interpretation.

The danger of a German move through Spain prompted the Prime Minister to address further messages to Weygand and Pétain offering an expeditionary force of up to six divisions to help in the defence of French North Africa if the Vichy Government would move there. His letter to Weygand, sent by the hand of a Suez Canal pilot who was passing through Algiers on his way back to Egypt, spoke of the hope that there would soon be active collaboration once more between French and British arms. Weygand again made no reply. His slavish adherence to Pétain apparently precluded even the sending of a sympathetic acknowledgment.

The arrival of German dive-bombers in Sicily led to the cancellation of a project which the Joint Planners had long opposed. First mooted in the autumn, Operation Workshop, as it was called, involved the capture of the small island of Pantelleria, in the Sicilian Channel, by a Commando force under the personal leadership of Admiral of the Fleet Sir Roger Keyes.

Keyes had been appointed Director of Combined Operations in the previous summer, but up to the time when the capture of Pantelleria was raised his specially trained Commandos had found no employment. To Keyes, chafing at inaction, this Mediterranean E-boat lair seemed an ideal target for his picked troops, and no doubt his ardour had some bearing on Churchill's favourable attitude at first towards an operation which in reality offered very few advantages. Dominated by enemy air bases, Pantelleria had a poor harbour and an inadequate airfield of its own. Once seized, the island could easily become a liability.

Admiral Cunningham disliked Keyes' plan from the start and said so in vehement terms—so vehement, in fact, that the Prime Minister was moved to reply, "Surely no such feelings should exist between old comrades." But Cunningham was not alone in condemning the operation, and as the drawbacks became more apparent the Prime Minister realized their force. His admiration and regard for Keyes made him reluctant to abandon the idea, but he was more flexible than many of his advisers believed him to be. He would often urge examination of projects which they considered impracticable, but he never disregarded professional opinion when it was firmly based on valid reasoning. Unlike Keyes, he was, too, in a position to see all sides of a problem, and relate them to strategic needs in other theatres.

By the New Year, when Operation Workshop had already been postponed more than once, he was beginning to find Keyes' insistent appeals something of a trial. The Admiral would employ endless ruses to obtain interviews, often arriving in the Prime Minister's office after he had been told on the phone that Churchill could not see him, and eventually, when the operation was finally cancelled, General Ismay had to inform him that Churchill could not discuss the matter further. Keyes then wrote six pages of typescript denouncing the Naval Staff and imploring that Workshop should be restored to the priority list. "I cannot bear to see you and the country being let down by craven-hearted advisers. . . . Please give me an interview today or tomorrow," he ended. In a firm reply Churchill explained that it was not possible to argue out with him "every decision of the Defence Committee which affects your command. My burden would become intolerable if I were to attempt such a thing. You and your Commandos will have to obey orders like other people and that is all there is to be said about it. I am very sorry if you are not pleased. I do my best."[5]

It said much for Churchill's patience and understanding that, in spite of this violent contretemps, Keyes was encouraged to build up and train another Commando force. On March 4 they carried out a successful raid on the Lofoten Islands, destroying enemy supplies and shipping and taking two hundred German prisoners, but in the ensuing months no profitable tasks could be found for Combined Operations. This convinced the Admiral that there was a conspiracy to get rid of him, and once again he began to bombard the Prime Minister with complaints and exhortations. So violent became his criticisms of the Chiefs of Staff and their subordinates—"those marplots," he called them scornfully—that there could be only one outcome of it all. Sadly Churchill was forced to relieve Sir Roger Keyes of his command.

[5] Cecil Aspinall-Oglander, *Roger Keyes*, pp. 399–400.

10

The Greek Venture— and a Crisis in the Atlantic

THE decision to send an expeditionary force to Greece has been termed a gesture of quixotic chivalry which the Allies, with their straitened resources, could ill afford. And it has been suggested that they only became involved in this costly and unavailing venture as a result of Mr Churchill's short-sighted persistence. Neither charge can be substantiated.

The Prime Minister's reasons for supporting intervention in Greece were based on far more logical grounds than mere chivalry. By showing their determination to stand by their allies he considered that Britain might well persuade the whole Balkan bloc of Yugoslavia, Greece, and Turkey to remain firm, thereby dissuading Hitler from any immediate plans for pushing on to grasp the rich prize of the Middle East oilfields. Before the War Cabinet committed itself to any decision, however, Churchill was anxious for agreement to be reached on certain prerequisites.

Since the troops for Greece must be drawn from the Army of the Nile it was necessary to be certain that Wavell was left with sufficient strength to hold Cyrenaica; an advance into Greece at the cost of a substantial retreat in North Africa would serve no useful purpose. Equally he wished to be sure that, in the opinion of his military advisers on the spot, the Greek Army, given Allied stiffening, had a reasonable chance of holding back any German advance; unless from a purely military standpoint the venture offered a prospect of success it should not, he felt, be attempted. Churchill emphasized this by telegraphing to the Foreign Secretary: "Do not consider yourself obligated to a Greek enterprise if in your hearts you feel it will only be another Norwegian fiasco. If no good plan can be made, please say so."[1]

Eden, who had gone to Cairo with Dill to examine the situation in detail, reported that the C.I.G.S. and three Commanders-in-Chief in the Middle East all felt an effort should be made to help Greece as soon as possible; and they considered there was a fair chance of halting the Germans. Even when Admiral Cunningham had to point out that his existing naval resources were no longer sufficient to provide for the capture of Rhodes, which had been envisaged as the main air base, and serious differences arose with Papagos, the Greek Commander-in-Chief, over the rôle which the Allied force was to fulfil, the Prime Minister's advisers still recommended that the landings should go forward.

On March 5 the first troops began to disembark in Greece, watched with close interest by the staff of the German Embassy, who for a further month were free to observe and report on all the Allied preparations. In that month, and before the German invasion of Greece even began, the fate of the British expedition was sealed. On March 25 Yugoslavian envoys signed a pact with Germany.

Churchill thought it just possible that all was not yet lost, for he knew the Yugoslav people would repudiate such an agreement if they found a leader. He therefore urged the British Minister in Belgrade not to lose touch with Prince Paul, the Regent, and his Ministers. "Do not let any gap grow up between you. . . . Continue to pester, nag, and bite. Demand audiences. Don't take 'no' for an answer. . . . This is no time for reproaches or dignified farewells."[2] But although a rising against the traitor Government did indeed take place, Germany struck like lightning. Yugoslavia's ally, Hungary, through whose territory German troops would have to pass to quell the revolt, yielded to an ultimatum, and with Roumania and Bulgaria already in the Axis camp Yugoslavia was encircled.

On the day Germany marched into Greece she took terrible vengeance. The Yugoslav capital was razed to the ground, and the whole of the country on which Greek hopes had been pinned was quickly overrun.

* * * * *

Before the collapse of Yugoslavia so dramatically altered the whole aspect of the scene in Greece Churchill found himself faced with a situation far more disturbing in its way than any possibility of a Balkan setback. Allied losses at sea had now reached a critical stage.

In the middle of March the *Scharnhorst* and *Gneisenau* sank or captured over 80,000 tons of shipping in two days. U-boats, now hunting in 'wolf packs,' accounted for 142 Allied vessels in a period of twelve weeks, and over 2,600,000 tons of damaged shipping lay in British ports awaiting

[1] Churchill, Vol. III, p. 63. [2] *Ibid*, p. 142.

repair. "How willingly would I have exchanged a full-scale attempt at invasion for this shapeless, measureless peril, expressed in charts, curves, and statistics!" wrote Churchill later.[3]

Deciding that the enemy sea offensive must be treated as a specific operation the Prime Minister issued a "Battle of the Atlantic" directive. He then appointed a special committee, which included certain scientific advisers, to implement its recommendations, and at the start he took the chair himself. Soon afterwards he brought into the Government Frederick Leathers, who before the war had been chairman or director of more than fifty companies in the Cory group. A quiet but very determined man, the new Minister of War Transport did not find it easy at first to accustom himself to the working of the Civil Service machine, but he knew precisely what he wanted. By sound business methods he achieved striking results.

The Prime Minister's directive called for a determined counter-offensive against the U-boats and the long-range Focke-Wulf Condor aircraft, which were now reaching far out into the Atlantic to bomb Allied convoys or shadow them until the submarines could come up. The U-boats were to be attacked not only at sea, but while under construction or in dock. The Focke-Wulfs were to be tackled in two ways—by arming all merchant ships with better anti-aircraft weapons, and fitting some of the larger ones with catapult apparatus for launching Hurricane fighters from their decks.

The programme also demanded reorganization of the convoy system so that faster ships could proceed independently; a greater concentration of Coastal Command aircraft in the North-west Approaches—the main danger area for shipping proceeding to and from America; and drastic changes in the port organization to speed the turn-round of ships discharging their cargoes.

In a relatively short time these measures began to take effect, and as the Allied technique of hunting U-boats with special Escort groups improved the enemy lost several of their outstanding submarine commanders, including Prien, who had carried out the daring attack in Scapa Flow at the start of the war.[4] President Roosevelt's decision to extend the zone patrolled by American warships and aircraft came as an unpleasant shock to the German naval command, but even so the situation remained critical, for as the weather improved over the British Isles the West Coast ports came under terrific bombardment from the air. On Merseyside alone 76,000

[3] *Ibid.*, pp. 100–101.

[4] Krech, one of the U-boat aces constantly at sea in the North Atlantic during this period, had an aquarium in his boat. The fishes which swam in it were named after the crowned heads or Prime Ministers of all the countries at war with Germany. Churchill, a small but temperamental pirate fish made three patrols. When it died it was committed with full naval honours to a permanent resting-place in a glass tube which was hung under the lamp in the U-boat's wardroom. (Wolfgang Frank, *The Sea Wolves* (*Die Wolfe und der Admiral*), p. 75.)

people lost their homes; there were heavy attacks on Clydeside; and the Blitz spread to Manchester, Bristol, and Plymouth.

London too suffered again. When Mr Winant, the new United States Ambassador, and his wife dined with the Churchills for the first time in the Annexe the rain of metal from the anti-aircraft barrage was so heavy that the Prime Minister insisted on sending his guests back to Grosvenor Square in one of the bullet-proof cars which he now used. At first sight these Humber Snipe limousines looked like ordinary standard models, but the bodies were made of special steel and the windows were also proof against shell-splinters. Owing to their increased weight the cars had to be fitted with a more powerful braking system. At night Churchill's personal chauffeur was Sergeant Tribe, of the Royal Army Service Corps, who drove with great skill and apparent unconcern through the worst air raids. During the daytime his place was taken by a civilian named Hale, who used to complain to Tommy that the only hazard of his particular job was indigestion; "all this sitting about upsets my stomach," he would say lugubriously.

After that first dinner in the Annexe Gilbert Winant was a frequent visitor. Strangely enough for one who became an intimate friend of the Churchill family, he never overcame a certain sense of awe in the Prime Minister's presence. It was not that he suffered from an inferiority complex, but, being innately modest himself, he regarded Mr Churchill as a great and altogether unusual human being, and felt he could never measure up to him. The two men were, indeed, dissimilar, for the highly strung Winant was quiet and retiring and by nature somewhat introspective. Churchill, however, liked him immensely from the start and valued his complete sincerity.

At this time the Prime Minister was also seeing a good deal of two other visitors to this country—Averell Harriman and Robert Menzies. Harriman, who had come to England as the chief American adviser on Lease-Lend, had for some years headed the great Union Pacific Railroad Company. In Britain he was perhaps best known as an international polo-player. Although this was his first major post in public life, he soon showed himself to be a man of outstanding ability, a wise counsellor, and devoted to his job, which was in many ways complementary to that of Harry Hopkins. Physically the two could hardly have been more dissimilar. In contrast to the frail, ailing Hopkins—only kept alive by constant medical attention and his own boundless courage—Harriman was a tall, fine-looking man with the build of an athlete. His shrewdness and his immense capacity for work soon impressed Churchill; his unassuming charm made him a great favourite of the family, and he became a frequent member of the house-party at Chequers. On the rare occasions when it was possible to relax from the business of war he greatly enjoyed challenging Mrs Churchill at croquet or wresting the house record from her husband at Corinthian bagatelle. Harriman, Hopkins, and the Ambassador, Winant, made a notable trio, equally determined to find out and understand British needs and difficulties and render all the help they could. The knowledge that each in his different sphere was providing the President and the United States Government with full, sympathetic, and realistic reports meant much to the Prime Minister at this anxious time.

The relationship between Churchill and Menzies, the Prime Minister of Australia, was, perhaps inevitably, on a somewhat different plane from the intimate association which developed with Hopkins, Winant, and Harriman, but Menzies, a bluff, hearty, and refreshingly unpompous man, was always a welcome visitor—and a very staunch supporter in times of crisis.

Menzies attended Cabinet meetings and spent several week-ends at Chequers during the spring. It never ceased to astonish him that Churchill could maintain the working routine which he now followed. Hours seemed to mean nothing to him, and it never occurred to the Prime Minister that either he or anyone in his immediate circle were subjecting themselves to unusual strain. Ismay or one of his two deputies, Brigadier Hollis or Lieutenant-Colonel Jacob, would often be with him until three o'clock in the morning; they worked a fifteen-hour day seven days a week. For the secretariat it was just as arduous. When the Prime Minister was preparing an important speech the duty girl secretary would often be up till nearly 6.0 A.M. and back at her desk again by 10.0 the same morning.

Amid all his major preoccupations Mr Churchill still found time to fire his daily barrage of questions and suggestions which kept the various departments of State on their toes. After the Prime Minister had read in *The Times* that senior officers in a certain Army command were expected to take part in long cross-country runs the Secretary of State for War was taken to task. "Who is the General of this Division," asked Churchill, "and does he run the seven miles himself? If so he may be more useful for football than war. . . . In my experience, based on many years' observation, officers with high athletic qualifications are not usually successful in the higher ranks." The Lord President of the Council was directed to look into a complaint of high-handed action by a certain Government department: "When one is in office one has no idea how damnable things can feel to the ordinary rank and file of the public," was Churchill's human comment. There were searching queries about waste of manpower and waste of pig-food, the number of Japanese in British Columbia and the number of British Missions operating in America, the possibility of rich Americans leasing islands off the Kerry coast which could be used as radar bases and the desirability of continuing horse-racing. Being a stickler for style and the correct use of words, he waged gleeful war on official jargon. An invasion warning issued by the Ministry of Information gave him one good opening, for it included the phrase 'Stay put.' "First of all," he observed acidly, "it is American slang. Secondly it does not express the fact. The people have not been 'put' anywhere. What is the matter with 'Stand fast' or 'Stand firm'?" A favourite target was the Foreign Office, for he greatly disliked verbosity, and was delighted to remind that august body that "the zeal and efficiency of a diplomatic representative is measured by the quality and not the quantity of the information he supplies."[5] One morning he tossed a report across his desk to James Stuart, the Chief Government Whip. "Typical Foreign Office jargon," he said, with an angry snort. "It contains every cliché but 'Please adjust your dress before leaving!' "

* * * * *

At the beginning of April Churchill took Winant and Harriman with him on a memorable tour of inspection. After visiting Swansea and Aberporth, a rocket research station on the Cardiganshire coast where a new type of fuse was being developed for anti-aircraft shells, they spent the night in the train in a siding near the Severn Tunnel. From there they could see a heavy raid in progress on Bristol, where they were due on the following morning. As Chancellor of Bristol University Churchill was to confer degrees on Winant and Menzies.

Large areas of the city were still in flames when they arrived, and delayed-action bombs were exploding at intervals. As they drove through the streets, some half-blocked by rubble and others flooded by broken water-mains, women were busy cooking breakfast in half-demolished houses or over stoves in front gardens. "Almost every bombed house had a Union Jack stuck somewhere in the ruins," Tommy recalls. "The cheerfulness of every one seemed unbelievable. Crowds gathered round Mr Churchill, waving and cheering, and I never saw him more deeply moved. He kept murmuring to himself, 'Wonderful people . . . wonderful people.' We went to the Grand Hotel, where we were met by the Lord Mayor and Lady Mayoress, who had only just escaped by boat from their flooded home. Mr Churchill had intended to have a bath at the hotel, but he found that the water system was out of action. The staff, however, insisted on carrying up hot water in buckets from the kitchen, and he got his bath after all.

"The scene in the hall of the University was one I shall never forget, for no part of the normal ritual was omitted. There was the usual procession of University and civic officials, but under their academic robes was a

[5] Churchill, Vol. III, pp. 647–669.

remarkable variety of clothing. Many wore gum-boots and Civil Defence uniforms soaked and grimed by the night's work. Near-by buildings were still ablaze, and throughout the ceremony the acrid smell of burning kept drifting through the broken windows of the hall."

In a great speech that morning the Prime Minister referred to "this turning-point in the history of the world," and paid a moving tribute to the fortitude of the British people. The days which now followed were to test even his own buoyant optimism, for the savage air attacks on London and the home ports were accompanied by grave and unforeseen setbacks in the Mediterranean. By the end of the month not only were the Germans in Athens and the British Army expelled from Greece, but Axis forces, revitalized by the leadership of a little-known general named Rommel, had driven the Army of the Nile right back from the Tripolitanian border to Egypt.

II

The Last Outpost

Although the sudden collapse of Yugoslavia sounded a warning note to Churchill and the War Cabinet, the British public was completely unprepared for the series of disasters which now befell British Arms. The headlong retreat of the Italians across the Western Desert, the triumphant East African campaign, and a great naval victory off Cape Matapan at the end of March had bred an unreasoning optimism. The war was going well. Shackled to a demoralized ally, Germany would soon be forced on to the defensive, argued the amateur strategists. The shock of coming events was to cause disillusionment and anger.

Within a few days of the German invasion of Greece the Greek troops, already exhausted by months of hard fighting against the Italian Army, were swamped by superior air power and armour. On April 20 the armies on the Albanian front surrendered, and although Churchill still hoped a stand could be made at Thermopylae Papagos said he was no longer in a position to give any effective support to the British forces. Three days later Greece capitulated, and the Allies were left with the desperate task of evacuating 50,000 men in the face of complete German mastery in the air. Before this occurred disturbing reports began to arrive from Wavell on a different theme altogether. The weakened armoured forces which had been left to hold Cyrenaica were suddenly attacked at Agheila.

At first Wavell was not unduly anxious on this score. He believed the enemy offensive had been planned as a diversion with a strictly limited objective, timed to coincide with the attack in the Balkans. In this he was right, but he now faced an opponent of a very different calibre to Graziani —General Erwin Rommel, who had commanded the first German division to reach the Channel coast in the previous May.

Rommel had arrived in Tripoli in February. He soon became convinced that the British forward positions were lightly held, and without waiting for the main body of the German reinforcements promised to him he probed forward, found to his surprise that the British armour offered little resistance, and, ignoring his own considerable supply problem, he pressed on. Benghazi was soon evacuated, and by April 7 Churchill was urging Wavell to hold Tobruk at all costs. At the same time he called on Admiral Cunningham to cut the enemy supply line by attacking Tripoli and blocking the harbour with H.M.S. *Barham* and one of his few remaining cruisers.

This lead to a heated exchange of signals between the Admiralty and the Commander-in-Chief, Mediterranean, for Cunningham, who could never be accused of a lack of offensive spirit, considered that to attempt to block the harbour in the face of heavy enemy and air opposition was not only impracticable but suicidal. The Admiral stated that he would rather risk his entire fleet in a bombardment of the port, and the proposal to sacrifice *Barham* was abandoned. On April 21 he appeared off Tripoli with *Warspite*, *Barham*, *Valiant*, and *Gloucester* and for forty-five minutes shelled the shipping and harbour installations almost unopposed. Several enemy vessels were sunk, and the British squadron sustained no casualties either from mining or air attack. Nevertheless Admiral Cunningham felt strongly that to hazard his small fleet on a task which could be more effectively carried out by aircraft was an unacceptable risk. When, however, he reiterated this opinion he was sharply reminded by the Prime Minister that the first responsibility of the Mediterranean Fleet was to sever all communications between Italy and Africa. As at this time the Mediterranean Fleet was stretched to the limit in carrying out the evacuation from Greece and maintaining supplies to Malta, the tone of some of the messages Cunningham received from Whitehall—notably a signal from the First Sea Lord which included the phrase, "Failure . . . will be considered as having let the side down"—did nothing to lighten his burden.[1] It was, however, impossible for any senior officer in the field to realize the strain under which the Government, and the Prime Minister in particular, were labouring. Hard on the Greek evacuation it was learnt that the enemy were preparing a full-scale assault on Crete by sea and air; a new German armoured division appeared in the fighting line in the desert; and at the same time the luckless Wavell had to find troops for two new theatres, Iraq and Syria, where fresh trouble threatened.

It was evident that Crete would go the way of Greece, for the island was

[1] "Those of us who were on the receiving end abroad tended not to make sufficient allowances for the state of mind of politicians and the public at home. I had a much greater admiration for Mr Churchill when I found myself close to him as First Sea Lord."—Admiral Cunningham to the writer.

dominated by enemy air bases in both Greece and Rhodes. The German 11th Air Corps began a violent attack on the island on May 20 and soon captured Maleme, a vital airfield. The first attempt at a sea-borne invasion was wiped out by the Royal Navy on the following night, but the Mediterranean Fleet sustained heavy losses, and within a week the sheer weight of the air bombardment made further resistance impossible. In the brave defence of Crete the Allies lost 13,000 men, and at the end of yet another evacuation the Fleet was left with only two battleships, three cruisers, and seventeen destroyers. This was, however, no vain sacrifice, for Germany's only airborne division was so badly mauled by General Freyberg's troops that it never operated again.

* * * * *

In England the news of these reverses was received with stupefaction. Observers began to note a spreading despondency; "it has been as if living in a nightmare . . . the people are amazing . . . how long can they last out unless there continues real confidence in victory?"[2]

The heavy air raids went on. Over 2000 people were killed in attacks on London on April 16–17, and the House of Commons was destroyed. At Liverpool a blitz lasting a week caused 3000 casualties. Taking James Forrestal, the United States Secretary of the Navy, and Harriman with him, Churchill went to Merseyside and talked to great crowds of war factory workers. On his return he made one of his most stirring broadcasts.

"I was asked last week," he said, "whether I was aware of some uneasiness which, it was said, existed in the country on account of the gravity, as it was described, of the war situation. So I thought it would be a good thing to go and see for myself what this 'uneasiness' amounted to, and I went to some of the great cities and seaports which had been most heavily bombed, and to some of the places where the poorest people had got it worst. I have come back not only reassured but refreshed. To leave the offices in Whitehall with their ceaseless hum of activity and stress, and to go out to the front, by which I mean the streets and wharves of London and Liverpool, Manchester, Cardiff, Swansea or Bristol, is like going out of a hothouse on to the bridge of a fighting ship. It is a tonic which I should recommend any who are suffering from fretfulness to take in strong doses when they have need of it."[3]

He was not, however, under any illusions. The withdrawal from Greece and the ominous news from the desert had weakened confidence in the

[2] In a letter from Harriman to Hopkins, Sherwood says that Harriman's despondency was a reflection of the atmosphere prevailing in the upper levels of the British Government at this time. He adds that many people had expected America to enter the war in April 1941, but now they could see no signs of this happening. "To the average American Britain was a last outpost—seemingly as lonely and as exposed as Guam," and "certainly not worth risking one's salvation for." (Sherwood, *op. cit.*, Vol. I, p. 276.)

[3] Broadcast from Chequers on Sunday, April 27, 1941.

Government, and Mr Churchill took the opportunity of a debate on the war situation to make a spirited defence of the conduct of the Mediterranean operations. In the exchanges which followed he scored heavily off two persistent critics in the veteran Lloyd George and Leslie Hore-Belisha, a former Secretary of State for War, and a division produced a remarkable vote of confidence—by 447 to 3.

On the day the debate began an operation of great hazard was launched in the Mediterranean. Wavell had signalled the serious news that a fresh German armoured division had been identified and would shortly appear in the fighting line. Since our existing resources were entirely inadequate, and no reinforcements dispatched by the Cape route could meet this threat, the Prime Minister decided on a desperate course. A convoy carrying 300 tanks must fight its way through the Mediterranean, and despite Admiralty misgivings Operation *Tiger*—the passage of five 15-knot merchantmen from Gibraltar to Alexandria—was completed with the loss of only one ship. As a result 238 tanks and 43 Hurricane aircraft reached Egypt some forty days earlier than they could have done via the Cape.

Before Wavell launched his counter-attack in the desert two notable events occurred which call for a brief digression.

On the night of Saturday, May 10, London endured its greatest ordeal of the war. The enemy bombers pounded the capital all night, starting more than 2000 fires and killing or wounding 3000 people. At the height of the raid a lone Messerschmidt 110 was sighted by the Observer Corps over Jedburgh, in the Border country of Scotland, and shortly after midnight Sub-Lieutenant T. G. D. Galbraith, R.N.V.R., an assistant duty officer at the combined Naval and Air headquarters at Pitreavie, answered a telephone call from the police.[4] They reported that they had arrested a man in German uniform; he had parachuted from an aircraft which had crashed a few miles south-west of Glasgow. The prisoner was asking for the Duke of Hamilton and Brandon, so a call was put through to the R.A.F. Station at Turnhouse, not far away, where the Duke happened to be in command.

Churchill was at Ditchley that week-end, and on the following evening the Duke of Hamilton telephoned, asking to speak to him. Brendan Bracken went to the phone, and to him the Duke gave the astonishing news that the lone fighter pilot claimed to be Rudolf Hess, Deputy Leader of the Nazi Party. Summoned to Ditchley, the Duke of Hamilton explained that he had never known Hess personally; it was not, in fact, until Ivone Kirkpatrick, who had been First Secretary in Berlin before the

[4] Later the Hon. Thomas Galbraith, M.P., Civil Lord of the Admiralty, 1957–1959.

war, flew north to see the prisoner that Hess's identity was firmly established. The Duke of Hamilton had gathered, however, that Hess was labouring under a strange delusion. Anxious to put forward a peace plan of his own, he had found out that the Duke was Lord Steward of His Majesty's Household and had therefore assumed that part of his duties would be to wait on the King at dinner. He would therefore be well placed, Hess imagined, to urge upon the King the advice that Britain should capitulate. This greatly amused Churchill, who said to Tommy that evening, "I suppose he thinks that the Duke carves the chicken and consults the King as to whether he likes breast or leg!"

The Prime Minister himself attached little importance to this extraordinary happening. He was chiefly worried in case an impression should get abroad that the Government were for one moment considering the question of peace negotiations. Kirkpatrick had a series of exhaustive interviews with the unbalanced Hess, and as he kept reiterating that he had views of great importance to place before the Government Lord Simon was eventually asked to interview him in a house near Aldershot. By then, however, Hess was showing signs of a severe breakdown, and this final interrogation only confirmed his growing mental instability. For the rest of the war he was confined in a camp in Wales.

His erstwhile importance in the Nazi hierarchy, the dramatic flight alone across the North Sea, and the mystery which for so long surrounded his self-appointed mission gripped the imagination of the world, but Hess's flight from Germany was the act of a disordered mind and held no wider significance. Churchill was one of the first to place this bizarre incident in its true perspective.

Two week-ends later the Prime Minister was at Chequers. Before he left London reports were coming into the Admiralty that the *Bismarck* and her consort, the cruiser *Prinz Eugen*, were at sea and had been sighted in the Denmark Strait. The Home Fleet headed to intercept them, and in the early hours of the Saturday morning action was joined. When Mr Churchill woke he learnt that H.M.S. *Hood*, our biggest battle cruiser, had been sunk.

The rest of the week-end was spent in agonizing suspense, for far to the south steamed a large Allied troop convoy escorted only by destroyers, and other convoys were also within the *Bismarck*'s reach. The Prime Minister had taken a mass of papers to Chequers, but he found it difficult to concentrate on anything for long, and kept walking over to the large chart of the North Atlantic on which Tommy was trying to keep an up-to-date plot. The news which filtered through to the house was scrappy; time and again sighting reports were followed by signals that the shadowing cruisers had lost the *Bismarck* once more. It was not until half-way through the Monday morning that the German battleship was finally and firmly located from the air, steaming for Brest, some seven hundred miles away.

Torpedo attacks slowed her up considerably, and although the *Bismarck* signalled before midnight that she was no longer able to manœuvre, she stayed afloat for ten hours longer, surviving a terrific bombardment by *Rodney* and *King George V* at close range, before she was destroyed by torpedoes from the cruiser *Dorsetshire*.

On the Tuesday morning Churchill was able to give the welcome news to the Commons, now assembled in cramped and uncomfortable temporary quarters at Church House, Westminster, that the most powerful warship in the world had been sunk. Two thousand of her crew were lost.

* * * * *

One afternoon towards the end of May Tommy went with the Prime Minister to Luton to watch the trials of an ingenious device called the Beetle. Developed with much secrecy, this was a small, electrically driven caterpillar vehicle, filled with explosive, which could be dispatched from our forward positions to blow up advancing tanks. The demonstration was quite impressive until something went wrong with the remote control mechanism. The Beetle then scurried straight for General Dill, and although the C.I.G.S. made a rapid and agile retreat, it continued to pursue him for quite a distance.

This unrehearsed comedy was particularly appreciated by the Prime Minister, for he himself had been forced to take sudden evasive action during a rocket demonstration staged by Lindemann on an airfield near London. The day had been cold and cheerless, with a thin spring rain falling steadily. Only three rockets were available, and when the first failed to ignite at all Churchill showed signs of impatience.

The second rocket was placed in position. When the firing key was pressed it climbed straight into the air with a strange sobbing noise and exploded prematurely over the centre of the field. Mr Churchill still looked unimpressed, and the third and last rocket was prepared for its launching with special care. This one shot up to one hundred feet, and then, to every one's amazement it turned through ninety degrees and headed for the hangars on the edge of the airfield. The Prime Minister, removing his cigar, peered at the rocket with great interest, and he had just started to remark on its unexpected flight when the rocket changed direction altogether and came straight towards him. Casting discretion aside, Mr Churchill began to run for his life, but the rocket passed low overhead and buried itself in the ground some distance away. "Damn the man!" he said, when he had recovered his breath. . . . "I won't speak to him for a week"—but he continued to attend these trials of new weapons whenever he could spare the time. One research establishment in which he took a particular interest had its headquarters in a rambling Edwardian house called The Firs, on the outskirts of the Buckinghamshire village of Whitchurch. Here worked an experimental team under the leadership of Millis Jefferis, the Sapper officer who had greatly impressed Churchill with his plans for sowing fluvial mines into the Rhine in the winter of 1939.

With his flair for detecting the unconventional genius and giving him a free hand, Churchill had kept an eye on Jefferis from that moment, and in the summer of 1940 he had encouraged him to set up his own experimental establishment. It became known as MD 1.

At The Firs Jefferis gathered round him a small but brilliantly talented team who began to interest themselves in all manner of strange weapons and devices. His assistants included Ralph Farrant, a Gunner officer, and Norman Angier, former chief engineer of Radio Normandy, who were both carrying out important research in connexion with shaped charges for shells; Bobby Macrae, a scientific journalist who developed the limpet mine for shipping attacks; and James Tuck, one of the brightest of Lindemann's protégés at the Clarendon Laboratory. Tuck, the only pure scientist in the team, was later to be associated with the Polish mathematician Ulam in the solution of vital thermonuclear problems.

The Firs was an ideal base for the kind of work they were doing. The house and outbuildings were surrounded by a high brick wall. Beyond the garden the land sloped steeply to marshy ground in the valley below, and on the far side of this was an eighteen-acre field where many of the team's experiments were conducted. The people of Whitchurch could only guess at what was going on behind the high walls of The Firs, but they knew it must be important, for the house and grounds were guarded day and night by troops, and when some weapon was to be fired traffic was often halted on the main road from Aylesbury to Buckingham. These precautions were not infallible; on one occasion an R.A.F. truck arrived at Aylesbury Police Station to report that it had been heavily shelled just after passing through Whitchurch. There was therefore much conjecture in the White Swan, the small hostelry opposite the house, and some of the local worthies said it would not be long before they were all blown sky high.

Jefferis himself lived at Cublington, two miles away. If he got an idea for solving some problem in the middle of the night he would often dress and drive into the village. It amused him then to dodge the sentries, climb over the wall, and slip undetected into his office, where he would stay working at his drawing-board for the rest of the night.

In the garden he had his own facilities for filling projectiles, detonators, and fuses; a special electronic apparatus was available for measuring velocity; and there were large water-tanks where explosive charges could be detonated against submarine hulls. All manner of remarkable projects—bombs which jumped about on the ground, bombs which leapt in and out of the sea, and rockets which fired bridges over rivers—had their first secret trials there, and both Churchill and Lindemann gave Jefferis every encouragement.

The Prime Minister could not himself understand intricate technical detail, but "the Prof," as Lindemann was known in Churchill's inner circle, kept him in the picture. Lindemann's gift for reducing the most complicated scientific problems to simple terms has already been mentioned. It was of priceless value to the Prime Minister, and although other scientists disliked him, Jefferis found Lindemann a staunch supporter. He would arrive at The Firs at least once a fortnight and spend hours in the field watching trials. Jefferis never heard an impatient word from him, even when some experiment failed dismally—and there were some highly spectacular failures from time to time. Tuck was once trying to get the measurement of energy of a rocket, and omitted to clamp it firmly enough to its base. When ignited the rocket took off and went screaming across some of England's best hunting country in fine style, leaping walls and ditches as it disappeared from sight. The Prof, umbrella clasped in one hand and his bowler-hat rammed firmly on his head, accompanied the search-party, and eventually they found the rocket deeply embedded in the gateway to a field. Only a minute hole in the ground showed its whereabouts, and this was pointed out by a badly shaken farmer who had watched the missile come down.

Experiments with a bridge-carrying tank produced further surprises. The span of the bridge, which hinged over the nose of the tank, weighed five tons, and this had to be hurled vertically into the air by rockets. When the trials began they attached so many rockets to the framework of the bridge that the tank was blown on to its side.[5]

Such was the lighter side of MD 1. The team worked with great success on a wide variety of projects, among them anti-tank and personnel bombs, incendiaries and shaped explosive charges, and the Hedgehog, which revolutionized the whole technique of attacking U-boats. In the early stages, however, they had a struggle to preserve their independence, for the Ministry of Supply tried hard to bring MD 1 under their own control. This was the last thing that Jefferis, an inspired individualist, wanted to happen. He argued that Ministry control might be all right for mass-production problems, but research and development was a very different matter.

The controversy came to a head when a senior official from the Ministry was sent to Whitchurch to report on MD 1's activities. On his

[5] The manifold activities of MD 1 are described in greater detail in the author's book, *The Secret War, 1939–45*.

return to Whitehall he declared somewhat incautiously that the Bombard, which Jefferis was developing as an infantry support weapon, was quite useless, and recommended that work on it should cease forthwith.[6]

This reached the ears of the Prime Minister, who knew a good deal about the potentialities of the Bombard, and he immediately ordered a demonstration shoot at Chequers, with the Ministry's representatives in attendance. Mr Churchill announced that he himself would act as referee.

Ten pounds of high explosive detonated in the open makes an impressive noise—"the P.M.'s ears must have fairly rattled," said Jefferis afterwards—and the damage inflicted on an elderly tank was equally impressive. The Ministry observers were forced to admit that they had entirely underrated the new weapon, and so MD 1 were told to go ahead with it. After this there were no more attempts to deprive them of their independence.

Another brainchild of Jefferis which he demonstrated in the grounds of Chequers was a bomb designed for street-fighting and tank warfare. This looked more dangerous to the demonstrator than it really was, for its glass container turned to powder instantaneously and was unlikely to injure anyone close to it. Nevertheless, to the uninitiated it seemed highly spectacular, for it burst with a searing flash and a crack, and the young officer chosen to throw it had rehearsed an act requiring split-second timing. Standing in front of the target, he first saluted Mr Churchill, and then, turning smartly about, he hurled the bomb at the tank and saluted again as he threw himself flat on his face before the explosion.

The Prime Minister was delighted, and asked to be kept informed about the production of the bomb. When he discovered some time later that approval had not yet been given for its manufacture he sent a stern minute to Ismay demanding investigation of the delay. "Any chortling by officials who have been slothful in pushing this bomb . . . will be viewed with great disfavour by me," was his irate comment. To a critic at the War Office who retorted that this bomb was neither a safe missile nor, in his opinion, would it do any appreciable damage, the Prime Minister said sharply: "General, you had better make up your mind which horse you are going to back!"

Churchill's insistence that Jefferis should be given a free hand paid rewarding dividends, for in all this small team produced some twenty-five new weapons and devices which went into active service.

Scientific research brought many exciting developments at this time, for in May 1941 efforts to bend the enemy's directional radio beams met with striking success, completely thwarting a projected raid on the Rolls-Royce works at Derby. At last, too, came a notable advance in the technique of

[6] Originally developed as a Home Guard weapon, the Bombard was light and easy to handle and fired a 10-lb charge.

night-fighting by the R.A.F. This was due to the introduction of a new and ingenious piece of apparatus called the A.I. (Air Interception) Box, which provided the first direct link between the night-fighter and the enemy bomber.

By this new system night-fighter pilots patrolling over the Channel could be given the approximate height, range, and bearing of an approaching bomber when the latter was as much as fifty miles away from the coast. Then, when they were relatively close to it in the darkness, the A.I. box would reveal visually to the navigator the precise position of the enemy aircraft. From that moment it was essentially a team operation, demanding a high standard of intelligence, a knowledge of electronics, and complete sympathy between pilot and navigator.[7]

When the apparatus was first installed the results were very disappointing. This was partly due to the unreliability of the equipment itself, and when Group Captain William Elliot[8] arrived to take command of the R.A.F. station at Middle Wallop, in Hampshire, where 604 night-fighter squadron was based, he found that few of the air-crews put much faith in the new invention. They did not really understand it, and through operating it incorrectly they became even more distrustful of it. Elliot therefore cast around for some one who could 'put over' the A.I. box to its users. And immediately he thought of Derek Jackson.[9]

When the war broke out Jackson was Professor of Spectroscopy at Oxford—a brilliant, somewhat unconventional young man in his middle thirties. Leaving his work at the university, he became a civilian operator on the radar screen, but he was determined to get into the R.A.F. and asked Elliot, a friend of his then serving as Assistant Secretary to the War Cabinet, to help him. Elliot heard later that he had become a wireless operator/air gunner, and then he lost touch with him. When he made inquiries he found Jackson was just completing his training in Bomber Command.

With some difficulty he arranged for his transfer, and one morning in the spring of 1941 the unmilitary figure of Pilot Officer Jackson, cap askew, arrived at Middle Wallop.

Not only did Derek Jackson quickly master the intricacies of the A.I. apparatus, but he had a genius for imparting his knowledge and operating flair to others. Flying with the night-fighter pilots, he soon convinced them that the equipment could bring spectacular results. Before he descended on Middle Wallop 604 Squadron had brought down only five German

[7] The range of A.I. apparatus was roughly equal to the height of the fighter above the ground. At 15,000 feet the operator of the A.I. box could expect to contact an enemy aircraft three miles from him.

[8] Later Air Chief Marshal Sir William Elliot, G.C.V.O., K.C.B., K.B.E., D.F.C.

[9] Wing Commander Derek Ainslie Jackson, O.B.E., D.F.C., A.F.C., F.R.S.

aircraft in six months. In the next four months they made forty-eight kills, and soon they became the crack night-fighter squadron of the Royal Air Force, in which Group Captain John Cunningham greatly distinguished himself.[10] Jackson's task was then done, and he returned to Bomber Command to take part in the coming offensive against Germany.

Mr Churchill, fascinated by the uncanny way in which the night-fighter aces like Cunningham learnt to stalk their quarry through the dark night, coined his own name for the Air Interception equipment. "We're getting very good results from 'Mary Had A Little Lamb,' " he would say approvingly. He followed all these technical developments with close attention, and they provided some solace at a time of great anxiety. Apart from the achievements of the scientists, there was indeed little cause for rejoicing as the month of May ended, for hard on the evacuation of Crete came bitter news from the Western Desert.

[10] Cunningham's navigator, Squadron Leader C. F. Rawnsley, D.S.O., D.F.C., D.F.M., became another outstanding A.I. operator. An electrical engineer by profession, Rawnsley had flown with Cunningham for so long, both before and during the war, that pilot and navigator possessed a complete and instinctive understanding of each other's capabilities.

12

An Afternoon at Chartwell

THE situation in which General Wavell found himself as time drew near for the opening of his counter-attack in the desert was an unenviable one. Admittedly he had received substantial tank reinforcements as a result of the bold stroke in sending the Tiger convoy through the Mediterranean, but the need to strike at Rommel before the latter grew too strong meant that he would have to send these tanks into battle after only the sketchiest training.

This was a disquieting prospect, for his armoured division, which consisted of only two brigades, would have to operate with tanks of widely dissimilar calibre. The cruisers of the 7th Armoured Brigade had a speed of 20 m.p.h. and a radius of 100 miles, whereas the 4th Armoured had infantry tanks which could only travel at 5 m.p.h. To make matters worse, these infantry tanks had the absurdly limited range of 40 miles—a grave handicap seeing that they might have to cover at least a hundred miles during the battle. To quote an official historian, the two brigades resembled "badly matched partners in a three-legged race."[1] Since operation *Battleaxe* had been first proposed Wavell had also made the disturbing discovery that the British armoured cars were not only alarmingly vulnerable to air attack, but could be outpaced and outgunned by the heavy German cars.

When he signalled his misgivings on this score to Dill at the end of May Wavell did not consider that these drawbacks would ruin the chances of *Battleaxe*, but he was beginning to doubt whether the operation could possibly achieve all that the Prime Minister expected of it—an advance beyond Tobruk and the destruction of Rommel's force.

[1] Playfair, *op. cit.*, Vol. II, p. 172.

Over and above these practical difficulties Wavell had to shoulder another burden—intangible, perhaps, but none the less hard for a Commander-in-Chief to bear on the eve of a vital offensive. He was fully aware that for some time now he had not held the Prime Minister's confidence.

Even to those who knew him intimately General Wavell was something of an enigma. Mentally and physically fearless, he was at the same time extremely conscientious, and this side of his character made him reluctant to oppose a course of action urged upon him if he felt he was expected to give it a trial. In the case of *Battleaxe* his own judgment counselled that the operation should be delayed until his armour had been able to carry out at least an elementary programme of combined training, but Churchill was understandably anxious to strike as soon as possible at Rommel's supply-lines. This could only be done by gaining control of the forward air bases now in the hands of the enemy, and each day's delay irked the Prime Minister more. To him it suggested lack of energy and determination in the high command, and further confirmed a conviction which had grown in his mind since his discussions with Wavell in the previous summer.

Although a man of great intellect, Wavell was not a fluent or convincing talker. On paper he invariably expressed himself with complete clarity, but at the conference table he would often remain silent for an unconscionable period, apparently tongue-tied by indecision. In the circumstances it was hardly surprising that the Prime Minister, who liked to probe into the mind of a man and draw him out by verbal argument, formed an impression that these long, awkward silences of Wavell's indicated a decline in mental vigour and resolution.

From the outset he seems to have decided that the Commander-in-Chief in the Middle East needed prodding to get the best results out of him, and since, from England, he could not administer the prodding in person he achieved it by a barrage of signals. Too often these were concerned with relatively minor matters, and a case in point occurred after a Commando raid on Castelorizzo, a small Ægean island which had been captured and lost again within twenty-four hours during the previous February. On that occasion Wavell received a message from Churchill ordering him to report fully and at once the reason for what the Prime Minister considered a disgraceful affair.

Wavell showed the signal to Admiral Cunningham, who asked what his reply had been.

"I never report on patrol encounters," said Wavell evenly, and the demand for a full explanation went unanswered.

Outwardly the Commander-in-Chief could still show an obdurate disregard for such pinpricks, but he could hardly remain unaffected by the growing evidence of dissatisfaction in Whitehall. And the Prime Minister's lack of confidence had become more apparent from the signals which reached Cairo during the operations currently taking place in Iraq and Syria.

With Crete and the preparations for the Western Desert offensive already on his hands, Wavell had shown strong reluctance to involve himself in either of these new commitments, and on May 6 Churchill wrote, "I am deeply disturbed at General Wavell's attitude.... He gives me the impression of being tired out."[2] The readiness of General Auchinleck to make available troops from his own Indian command for the march on Baghdad which crushed German influence in Iraq at the end of May inevitably prompted comparisons. And when disagreement over Syria, which Churchill was anxious to remove from Vichy control, led Wavell to the point of offering his resignation Churchill began to fear that the same reluctance to act with vigour and purpose might also affect the attitude of his sorely tried Commander-in-Chief towards the desert battle on which so much depended. In fact, however, General Wavell acted with considerable energy.

Without waiting for the Tiger tank convoy to arrive he threw all his available armour into a preliminary attack designed to catch Rommel off balance before the latter could recover from his two unsuccessful bids to take Tobruk.[3] Brigadier Gott's instructions were to drive the enemy from the area of Sollum and Capuzzo. Although he was not successful, Halfaya Pass was captured and the losses inflicted on the enemy prompted the Prime Minister to send Wavell an encouraging message. On balance it had been a profitable enterprise, but in the days which followed Churchill became extremely critical of the delay in launching *Battleaxe*, the main offensive, which Wavell had now fixed to start on June 15. The date was governed by the time needed to unload the tanks from the Tiger convoy, overhaul and modify them for desert warfare, and give their crews the bare minimum of training, but the Prime Minister felt that too little imagination was being shown by G.H.Q. Middle East. Great risks had been run to ensure the safe arrival of the convoy, but not nearly enough thought had been given, it seemed to him, to the problem of speeding the delivery of the precious tanks to the troops who were to use them. He was further upset by the lack of any positive support from Wavell for his

[2] In a memorandum to the C.O.S. Committee urging determined opposition to the Iraqi Army despite Wavell's objections. Churchill's insistence on direct action, as opposed to Wavell's suggestion for seeking a "settlement," was quickly vindicated. Raschid Ali, the pro-German Prime Minister, fled to Persia as Allied troops entered Baghdad on May 30, and with the collapse of the rebel movement Germany was once and for all denied access to the oilfields. This swift and decisive campaign also removed the German threat to the line of communication between Turkey and the Middle East.

[2] Operation *Brevity*.

plan to send a second consignment of a hundred cruiser tanks through the Mediterranean. This was already being bitterly opposed by Dill, and Wavell did not press for the risk to be taken.

* * * * *

The course of the battle does not call for detailed description here. By the second day it was evident that little progress was being made against strong armoured opposition, and *Battleaxe* failed in the end for a variety of reasons, the most important being the lack of adequate training of the two Allied tank brigades. There was, too, a shortage of effective artillery, and the heavy Matilda tanks proved all too vulnerable to well-sited German 88-mm. anti-aircraft guns, enterprisingly used in an unfamiliar rôle. The need for a more powerful gun than the British 2-pounder had been foreseen as far back as April 1938, but no steps had been taken to rectify the deficiency.[4]

For weeks past all Churchill's hopes had been centred on this desert battle, and he found the prospect of failure almost unbearable. By noon on the second day it was not by any means certain that the offensive would be halted, but the news reaching Whitehall was ominous. Often in times of stress the Prime Minister preferred to be alone with his thoughts, and on this afternoon he sent for his car and drove down to his home at Chartwell.

The house itself was shuttered and empty, and so it was to remain until the end of the war. But Mr Churchill and Tommy often went there. In the valley below a cottage was kept ready for him next to his studio. When he was feeling worried or tired an hour or two there, looking at his pictures or walking in the gardens and the fields, with their chain of lakes and miniature waterfalls, soothed and refreshed him. On Tommy's first visit he was shown the kitchen garden, surrounded by the wall Churchill had built himself; one sunny corner of this garden was a sanctuary for butterflies, planted with all manner of flowers attractive to them. On the opposite side of the house was a shaded, secluded pond—the original Chart Well—in which swam golden orfe, some of them huge fish weighing four or five pounds. These were treasured possessions. Once some had been slain by an otter, but though the gardener found tracks leading to the edge of the pool, Mr Churchill remained inexplicably convinced that gipsies were responsible. And for some time afterwards he regarded any local gipsy encampment he came across with a very unfriendly eye.

He had extraordinary powers over birds and animals. Often when he entered the meadow he would make a strange honking call which Tommy found impossible to imitate, and from one of the lakes would emerge a

[4] See M. M. Postan, *History of the Second World War*: "British War Production," p. 194.

bar-headed Canadian goose known to the family as the Flag Lieutenant. Waddling hurriedly across the valley the goose would fall in two or three paces behind his master and march proudly round as he made his tour of the estate.

With animals Mr Churchill's affections were oddly selective. He was particularly attracted to creatures of an unusual kind or ones which possessed marked individual characteristics. Before the war he had a tame sheep, which maddened the rest of the family; later there was a baby badger; a fox; a small chocolate poodle named Rufus; and a succession of favoured cats. The most famous of these was a large ringed marmalade cat which lived permanently at Chartwell and had the distinction of having had its portrait painted by Sir William Nicholson.[5]

Mr Churchill adored the marmalade cat, and at meals it was often given a special chair next to him so that he could feed it with cream. Another favourite was Nelson, a black tom-cat of great ferocity which he found at the Admiralty and took with him to Downing Street. There Nelson waged bitter and unceasing war on a rival known as the Munich Mouser until, wounded in the Blitz, he was honourably evacuated to Buckinghamshire, his duties as "London cat" being taken over by a less belligerent creature named Smoky. Nelson fiercely resented his posting away from the front line, and in the country he became more and more ill-tempered, chasing and attacking every dog which showed its face at Chequers.

Chartwell gave Mr Churchill welcome scope for indulging in one of his favourite pastimes. Since there were the three lakes in the valley, and innumerable springs bubbling up all over the grounds, he could conduct fascinating experiments with water to his heart's content. He spent many happy hours damming or diverting the streams which ran down from the hillside, but it was a remark by Mrs Churchill which gave him the idea for his most ambitious operation.

Hearing her describe the beauty of some of the waterfalls she had seen on a visit to the Lake District, he immediately ordered three railway-truck-loads of Cumberland boulders. These he proceeded to place in position in the course of a small stream, thus forming a series of miniature cascades down the far side of the valley. After months of hard work the rivulet which trickled over the artificial waterfalls looked strangely unimpressive, but Mr Churchill refused to be discouraged. Sending for special machinery, he swelled the trickle to a torrent by pumping water back to the top of the valley from the lakes and using it again.

Next he decided to build a large swimming-pool. Although this would

[5] Rufus came to a sad end, being run over by a bus during the Tory Conference at Brighton after the war. The marmalade cat died on the day Tobruk fell in June 1942. The Prime Minister was then in America for the Second Washington Conference. For some time after his return to England no one dared to break the news to him.

be fed by a rill from the Chart Well, the spring water would first pass through a boiler house, where it would be warmed to the right temperature for bathing in all weathers. Unfortunately this did not prove an unqualified success, for although Mr Churchill finished up with a heating plant larger than that used to supply the whole of the Savoy Hotel, the water was invariably cold again by the time it had found its way through the open air to the pool. The enjoyment he got from planning such a project and directing its construction more than compensated, however, for any technical drawbacks of this kind.

Chartwell held so many happy memories for him that even when the house was closed, the gardens could be tended no longer, and Canadian troops stationed near by came and covered over the lakes with brushwood to hide them from the air, he found peace and contentment in even the briefest of visits there. On this anxious afternoon in June 1941, however, even Chartwell was not allowed to cast its spell for long. Soon after he arrived telephone calls to the cottage warned him that *Battleaxe* was doomed, and he returned unhappily to Downing Street.

Four days later he decided that a change must be made in the Middle East, and a signal was sent to General Wavell relieving him of his command. General Sir Claude Auchinleck, Commander-in-Chief in India, was appointed in his place.

Wavell accepted the decision with characteristic dignity. "The Prime Minister is quite right," he said, when the signal was brought to him. "There ought to be a new eye and a new hand in this theatre." At this very moment, however, came a dramatic development which for the time being banished all further thoughts of the desert scene. On Sunday, June 22, while the Prime Minister was at Chequers, he received a message which transformed the whole aspect of the war. The German invasion of Russia, her ally, had begun.

To the British Cabinet Hitler's move came as no surprise. For some weeks accurate intelligence of German intentions had been available, and Churchill had done his best to warn Stalin, through Sir Stafford Cripps, our Ambassador in Moscow. Similar warning came from other sources than Britain. According to Schellenberg, Richard Sorge, whom the Japanese eventually arrested for espionage, told the Russians the precise date for the German attack, but inexplicably all this evidence of German treachery went unheeded. No preparations whatever were made to meet the onslaught.

In the speech he broadcast on that momentous Sunday evening Mr Churchill said:

"No one has been a more consistent opponent of Communism than I have for the last twenty-five years. I will unsay no word I have spoken about it. But all this fades away before the spectacle which is now unfolding. The past, with its crimes, its follies, and its tragedies, flashes away. I see the Russian soldiers standing on the threshold of their native land, guarding the fields which their fathers have tilled from time immemorial. . . . I see the ten thousand villages of Russia where the means of existence was wrung so hardly from the soil, but where there are still primordial joys. . . . I see advancing on all this in hideous onslaught the Nazi war machine with its clanking, heel-clicking, dandified Prussian officers, its crafty expert agents fresh from the cowing and tying down of a dozen countries. I see also the dull, drilled, docile, brutish masses of the Hun soldiery, plodding on like a swarm of crawling locusts."

He warned that the invasion of Russia was no doubt only a prelude to invasion of the British Isles which Hitler—"this bloodthirsty guttersnipe," he called him—hoped to accomplish before the winter. And when he addressed the House of Commons he declared with characteristic realism, "Nothing that happened then, [in the previous war] nothing that we imagined in the interval, however alarming it seemed at the time, was comparable to the dangers and difficulties which now beset us."[6]

Announcing the decision to publish no more figures of shipping losses, he spoke of the desperate struggle still being waged in the Atlantic: 4,600,000 tons of Allied shipping had, he revealed, been lost in the past twelve months. The life of the country was "quivering in the balance of mortal peril," and he gave blunt warning that because the weight of the enemy war effort had suddenly been switched to the Russian front no one could afford to sit back and think that ultimate Allied victory was now a foregone conclusion.

Only too clearly Churchill saw that for long to come the invasion of Russia would be a hindrance rather than a help to the Allies. If she was to survive at all Russia would need from the West supplies of all kinds which could ill be spared. At the same time he was well aware that the whole outlook of the conflict had been altered by this one fateful stroke. It seemed almost unbelievable, but of her own volition Germany had committed herself—in defiance of all the lessons of history—to a major war on two fronts.

[6] Speech in Secret Session on June 25, 1941.

13

Voyage to Placentia

THE German attack on the Soviet Union brought a Russian Military Mission, headed by General Golikov and Rear-Admiral Kharlamov, hot-foot to London. They were warmly welcomed, but some of the warmth was soon dispelled by their truculent attitude and peremptory demands, which took no account of Britain's own precarious situation.[1] To meet even a proportion of their requirements for war supplies would obviously involve a recasting of the whole programme of American military aid to Britain, and the President sent Harry Hopkins back to London for urgent consultations with the Prime Minister.

Apart from the new situation which had now arisen over Lease-Lend supplies Roosevelt had other anxieties on his mind. Some of his advisers were already urging that it was profitless to continue to pour war material into Egypt—a theatre which, in their view, was unlikely to influence the course of major events. The vital sphere of decision, they proclaimed, was the North Atlantic; before long the Allies would in any case be driven right out of the Middle East. There were even suggestions that the forces now left in Britain were not strong enough to withstand invasion.

All these matters were discussed with considerable frankness when Hopkins met Churchill on July 24. On the following evening, as they drove down to Chequers for the week-end, Mr Churchill told Tommy that a plan was in the air for a meeting with the President. Since the Prime Minister was taking a large team of advisers with him, the journey would involve

[1] "They look like a lot of pigstickers," was Dill's terse comment to his Director of Military Operations after meeting the Russians for the first time (Major-General Sir John Kennedy, *The Business of War*, p. 149).

complicated security arrangements. "You'd better keep in close touch with Pug over this," added Mr Churchill.

It proved a memorable week-end at Chequers, for both the Prime Minister and Hopkins were preparing important speeches and the hard-pressed secretariat from No. 10 found their work doubled. Quentin Reynolds and Dorothy Thompson came down to help Hopkins; also in the house were Harriman, Winant, Lindemann, and three close friends of the Churchill family—Sir Maurice and Lady Violet Bonham Carter, and Miss Horatia Seymour. Miss Seymour, who had been one of Mrs Churchill's bridesmaids, lived in a cottage on the Chartwell estate which Mr Churchill had built himself. Like Violet Bonham Carter, she was an ardent Liberal, and to Hopkins at lunch she said what a pity it was that he had not so far met any representatives of the Liberal Party.

"Oh, yes, I have," said Hopkins mischievously, with a glance at the Bonham Carters. . . . "As a matter of fact, I've now met both of them!"

Word had come from the White House that he was to fly to Moscow next day to discuss American aid with Stalin, and this started a frantic search for M. Maisky, who alone could issue the necessary Russian visa. Hopkins was already dog-tired after his flight across the Atlantic and the conferences which had been going on ever since his arrival, but the feeling of being at the centre of great events always acted as a tonic to him. Although bedlam reigned in the house, he seemed surprisingly relaxed. He was to broadcast after the nine o'clock news on the Sunday night. When the last draft of his speech was ready he threw it on Tommy's desk and said, "Well, that's that. Any of you can alter it any way you like short of declaring war!"

The speech over, Hopkins and Churchill walked up and down the lawn at the back of the house in the gathering dusk until it was time for Hopkins to set off on his long journey. Churchill asked his guest to assure Stalin that Britain would give him all possible support.

While arrangements went ahead for the first meeting of Prime Minister and President off the shores of Newfoundland, General Auchinleck arrived in London. He came at Churchill's request, for signals which had passed between Cairo and London since Auchinleck reached the Middle East made it plain that the new Commander-in-Chief was no less determined than General Wavell had been to avoid launching a major offensive without adequate preparation. To the Prime Minister this reluctance to take advantage of Germany's preoccupation on the Russian front was extremely disturbing. Other differences, too, had arisen. One of Auchinleck's first actions had been to earmark the newly arrived 50th British Division for a holding rôle in Cyprus, instead of bringing them into his plan for the attack in the desert. This did not at all accord with the Prime

Minister's ideas, for he had become sensitive to criticism that the brunt of the desert fighting was being borne by Commonwealth troops. Active employment of the 50th Division would have gone some way towards stilling such complaints. In addition, Auchinleck had shown no disposition to accept repeated hints from Whitehall that command of the Army of the Nile should go to General Sir Henry Maitland Wilson.

After several exchanges during which the new C.-in-C. stuck firmly to his guns Churchill became incensed. "I could not help feeling at this time a stiffness in General Auchinleck's attitude, which would not be helpful to the interests we all served," he recorded later.[2]

The conversations which they had in London and, more informally, at Chequers did something to restore the Prime Minister's confidence. Auchinleck's strong and attractive personality, and the conviction with which he argued his case, commanded attention. As Auchinleck's biographer has pointed out, however, the good impression which the General made was seemingly confined to his personal qualities. He did not manage to convince the Prime Minister of his military ability, and from this stemmed a continuing lack of confidence in him which was to have unfortunate results later on.[3]

Auchinleck was insistent that before attacking Rommel he must be given time to re-equip, regroup, and reorganize his formations, improve the supply, movement, and repair organizations, and carry out proper training of his armoured forces.

In the end it was decided that the attack—Operation *Crusader*—would go in on November 1. For command of this Auchinleck was adamantly in favour of appointing Lieutenant-General Sir Alan Cunningham, who was younger than Wilson, and had handled his forces with great distinction in the Abyssinian campaign. And again he got his own way.

* * * * *

To spirit the Prime Minister and his large party out of the country at such a time without a word reaching enemy ears presented a formidable problem. Arrangements for the journey to Placentia Bay, more than 2000 miles away, involved the issue of hundreds of orders—to staffs in Whitehall, where papers had to be prepared for the Prime Minister's guidance; to naval depots, for additional cooks and stewards had to be drafted to the ship taking Mr Churchill to his rendezvous with the President; and fragments of information, any of which could interest an enemy agent, had to be passed to troops, police, railway staff, and shops. It was one thing for

[2] Churchill, Vol. III, p. 360.

[3] "It was not enough that he should be impressed by the General's demeanour and personality: he had to be convinced of the rightness of the General's arguments, and of his professional skill. He [Churchill] never established this conviction." (John Connell, *Auchinleck*, pp. 268–269.)

the Government Hospitality Fund to approve the purchase of a supply of unrationed 'extras' so that Mr Roosevelt could be offered an adequate meal, but quite another matter, as Tommy found, to buy these and arrange for their delivery to the ship without exciting any comment or conjecture.

Many of the party bound for Placentia obeyed a summons to London in some bewilderment. Among them were two well-known authors, Howard Spring and H. V. Morton. When Brendan Bracken rang up late one night Spring was at his home in the little Cornish village of Mylor, and the last thing he wanted was to journey anywhere, even as far as neighbouring Falmouth. He had just had all his teeth out, and the prospect of this mysterious assignment which Bracken was offering him seemed singularly unattractive. He had no idea of its duration or even what clothes he would need.

"I can tell you nothing," said the rasping voice. "If you are willing to come you must report to me at the earliest possible moment."

Deciding to travel light, Spring packed one suit and an overcoat. Comparing notes with H. V. Morton when they met at the Admiralty, he found to his dismay that Morton's luggage contained clothes for every clime and occasion; he had even brought a dinner jacket and his Home Guard uniform. "He seemed to have thought of everything except a kilt," said Spring ruefully.

They were shepherded to a special train which left from Addison Road —a station then closed to ordinary passenger traffic. On the platform they recognized many of their fellow-passengers, and when the train halted at Wendover the Prime Minister, wearing a yachting cap, was already waiting with Dill, Pound, Air Chief Marshal Sir Wilfrid Freeman, Vice-Chief of the Air Staff, Lindemann, and Sir Alexander Cadogan.[4]

"We must be joining a ship," said Morton; "there are sleeping-cars on the train. For a journey starting at midday we wouldn't need sleepers unless we were bound for the far north." Not until they had crossed the Scottish border were they told that they would reach a seaport next morning.

At breakfast-time on Monday, August 4, the special train pulled into Thurso, and a little boat called *Morning Glory* took them out to a waiting destroyer. It was a grey, cheerless day, with a thick sea fret, and the surrounding hills were blanketed in cloud.

The destroyer *Oribi* carried them swiftly to Scapa Flow, and there they found Britain's latest battleship, H.M.S. *Prince of Wales*. Harry Hopkins was already on board. He had arrived back from Russia on the previous day, and those who saw him come off to the ship were alarmed at his appearance; he looked desperately ill. In his haste to leave for Moscow he

[4] Cadogan was Permanent Under-Secretary of State for Foreign Affairs.

had not taken the injections which alone kept his illness at bay, and for some days his condition caused great anxiety.

The spacious Admiral's quarters in *Prince of Wales*, which had been set aside for the Prime Minister, were situated over the propellers. As the battleship headed into a rising gale her stern shuddered and shook so severely that Mr Churchill was soon forced to move to the Admiral's sea cabin on the bridge. Howard Spring, who by now had discovered that he and Morton were to represent the British Press at the forthcoming meeting with the President, also found the shattering vibration aft more than he could stand. To his relief he was transferred to the Sick Bay, which he shared with the Prime Minister's detective. There they were given special cots slung on gimbals—a great luxury—and were waited on hand and foot by a zealous sick berth attendant who spent much of his time polishing Spring's shoes with surgical lint.

On the second day at sea a drastic alteration of course was necessary. A U-boat disguised as a ketch had been sighted far ahead on the intended route. By now *Prince of Wales* had left her escorts, who were unable to keep pace with her in the heavy seas, and she was driving on alone at top speed. As the rough weather continued Mr Churchill spent most of each day in his quarters on the bridge.

For the first time in almost two years he found himself isolated from direct responsibility, for strict wireless silence was maintained, and he could send no signals. A little to his surprise, he found the enforced inaction very agreeable. "All this ozone is making me lazy," he remarked to one of his party. . . . "I used to want to see red boxes all the time. Now I have difficulty in driving myself to two hours' work a day."

In spite of this, he produced a steady flow of memoranda, including one important directive for the Chiefs of Staff on the desert war. He had, however, to work without his usual secretariat, and when on the first morning at sea he rang the bell in his cabin an Army sergeant named Kinna arrived to take his dictation.

A highly skilled shorthand-writer, Patrick Kinna had served with Colonel Redman's French liaison unit in Paris in the early days of the war, and later he had been attached to the British Embassy in Washington. But he had never worked for the Prime Minister, and when Mr Churchill, without looking up, began, "This is indeed a melancholy story . . ." Sergeant Kinna laid down his pencil and remarked sympathetically, "Oh, dear! How unfortunate . . ." To his alarm this interjection brought a glare of baleful surprise, directed first at the unnerved sergeant and then at the idle notebook on his lap. It was an unpromising start, but the Prime Minister soon became favourably impressed, and by the end of this first voyage Patrick Kinna found himself an accepted member of the

Downing Street team. This was the first of many such journeys he was to make to all parts of the world.

Each evening after dinner the Prime Minister came down to the Wardroom to see one of the films which Tommy had brought for the voyage. Among them was *Lady Hamilton*, which never failed to move him, although he had seen it many times before.

To those around him Mr Churchill's addiction to films was a never-ending source of interest. While the humour of the Marx Brothers remained beyond his comprehension, he seemed in all other respects completely uncritical. He preferred stories with vigorous action, but he could become easily engrossed in the most trivial comedy or romance. Early in the voyage he sat through one particularly banal film about love in a New York department store with evident enjoyment. And he was delighted by an extravaganza featuring Laurel and Hardy.

In this particular picture the two comedians, resting exhausted by the roadside, were passed by a St Bernard dog with the inevitable barrel round its neck. Their frantic efforts to persuade the dog to let them drink from the barrel were unavailing until Hardy tore up a mass of paper which he hurled into the air to represent a snowstorm.

"A bright if inconsequential performance," said the Prime Minister with a beaming smile as he left the Wardroom that night.

The projection of the films invariably introduced its own element of comedy, for there was no skilled cinema operator on board, and when a reel was changed familiar characters would often reappear upside down, or in rapid reverse. During these breaks Mr Churchill called for gramophone music. His favourite records during the journey were Noel Coward's *Mad Dogs and Englishmen* and a popular dance tune of the moment, *Franklin D. Roosevelt Jones*. To the surprise of the ship's officers he appeared to know every verse of both by heart.

When dawn came on August 9 they were close to the Newfoundland shore. On the starboard beam they could see densely wooded valleys filled with grey mist, and an occasional peak jutting from the swirling cloud. Apart from the winking beam of a lighthouse there was no sign of life, but overhead they could hear aircraft circling.

About nine o'clock *Prince of Wales* dropped anchor in Placentia Bay, close to the United States cruiser *Augusta*. Near by were other American warships, including the old battleships *Arkansas* and the cruiser *Tuscaloosa*. On the deck of the *Augusta* they could see the President waving a greeting to them, and as soon as the Admiral's barge could be lowered Churchill set off to pay his first formal call. They had, in fact, met once before—at a dinner in London in the First World War, when Roosevelt was Assistant Secretary of the U.S. Navy—but although Roosevelt remembered the meeting well, Churchill himself had no recollection of it, an admission which slightly piqued the President whenever he recalled it.

Roosevelt was at the head of the gangway, leaning on the arm of his son Elliott, when the barge drew alongside the American cruiser, and as he shook hands with the British party Tommy was impressed by his skill at putting strangers at their ease. "I had never met a person of the President's distinction who showed such apparently real interest in one's own replies to his questions. Not until much later did I realize what a tremendous physical ordeal it was for him to stand for a period even as long as he did that morning. The irons and complicated braces which he was forced to wear on his legs were uncomfortable and even painful."

The next day was a Sunday. The President, who was to come on board *Prince of Wales* for church, announced that he would walk from the destroyer bringing him over, and would stand while the usual naval honours were accorded to him. With one hand on the rail of the gangway, and supported on the other side by his son, Mr Roosevelt made his way slowly across from the after structure of the destroyer to *Prince of Wales*' quarter-deck and stood motionless while the National Anthem was played. Only the tenseness of his grip on the rail betrayed the strain he was undergoing. Howard Spring, one of the many who were seeing the President for the first time, was shocked to notice how crippled he was. "I shall always remember the look on his face. Every muscle seemed to express his determination to complete that short walk on his own, and when he reached his chair he beamed with triumph."

The service on the quarter-deck, attended by hundreds of British and American sailors, was a simple and intensely moving occasion. Mr Churchill chose the hymns himself, ending with *O God, Our Help in Ages Past*. "None who took part in it will forget the spectacle presented that sunlit morning . . .—the symbolism of the Union Jack and the Stars and Stripes draped side by side on the pulpit; the American and British chaplains sharing in the reading of the prayers. . . . Every word seemed to stir the heart," he wrote afterwards. "It was a great hour to live."[5]

Only when the service was over would Roosevelt use his wheeled chair. In it he was pushed to the Wardroom for a lunch-party attended by Prime Minister and President, the British Chiefs of Staff and their opposite numbers, General Marshall, Admiral King, and General Arnold, and as many of the ship's officers as could be fitted in. As a surprise for the President the menu included grouse. Fortunately the opening of the grouse-shooting season in Britain had been advanced to August 1, and on the way north the Chief Steward had secured a dozen brace at Inverness.

From the start of the joint talks there was an air of easy informality. No

[5] Churchill, Vol. III, p. 384.

agenda had been prepared, and although Churchill was chiefly anxious to reach agreement on a common policy of resistance to Japanese aggression the discussions ranged over a wide field. The possibility of a German move into Spain and Portugal led to consideration of the Azores, already offered by President Salazar, as an Allied base of operations; useful progress was made in determining Lend-Lease priorities; and the United States Navy undertook additional responsibilities for patrolling the Allied convoy routes across the North Atlantic. There was even some discussion, initiated by the British team, of an operation with the provisional title of *Round Up*, which envisaged a future Allied landing in Europe. The American Chiefs of Staff pointed out, however, that they had no authority to deal with major strategic problems. Neither would Roosevelt commit himself to any hard-and-fast declaration of American intentions regarding Japan. He agreed, however, to give a warning in general terms to Nomura, the Japanese envoy in Washington.

While the talks continued the Wardroom of *Prince of Wales* was the focal point of a strenuous social programme. For security reasons there was no general shore leave—indeed, there was little to encourage a visit to the barren wilderness which fringed the great bay—but when one of the ship's officers went in to collect stores Churchill himself gave permission for Spring and Morton to go as well. Alone of those on board the ship they found that, after all, they had no active part to play. The President's party included no representatives of the American Press, and Churchill had therefore agreed that no eyewitness accounts of the meeting would appear in British newspapers on their return.[6] The two authors found the small harbour of Placentia silent and deserted apart from a few old men who sat staring at the idle fishing-boats. A vast American air base was being built near by at Argentia, and all the able-bodied young men of the village had left their usual jobs to work at rates of pay hitherto undreamed of by fishermen. "They will never come back," said the old men gloomily; . . . "this place will die."

Although they had hopefully changed English money for Canadian dollars, they found little they could buy in the few ramshackle shops, but on their walk Spring dug up some iris bulbs for his Cornish garden. Unhappily they did not survive the homeward voyage; the well-meaning sick berth attendant stowed them on top of a boiler, where the bulbs shrivelled to parched fragments.

When they got back to the ship they heard there was to be a Guest Night in the Wardroom to bid farewell to a large number of American officers. And dinner jackets would be worn. This dismayed Howard

[6] H. V. Morton has since described the journey to Placentia in his book *Atlantic Meeting*.

Spring, but his offer to withdraw was brushed aside, and a collection on his behalf yielded a weird and wonderful assortment of coats, trousers, shirts, and collars, none of which fitted him. Nevertheless he thoroughly enjoyed an evening which began amid traditional naval ceremony and decorum, and ended uproariously with teams of British and American officers carrying the smallest midshipmen on stretchers at breakneck speed over an improvised obstacle course in the anteroom.

As the Conference drew to its close Lord Beaverbrook arrived on board *Prince of Wales* after a hazardous flight from England. He took an active part in the final discussions over the draft of the official communiqué, and next day he joined the farewell lunch-party which the President gave for Mr Churchill. Hopkins' biographer, Robert Sherwood, describes this as "the most satisfactory session of all. There was no business to be transacted. Both Roosevelt and Churchill were relaxed and amusing and amused." Hopkins was anxious to show the President that it was possible for him to feel completely at ease with Churchill, and "Beaverbrook, whom Roosevelt had known of old, helped considerably in this process."[7]

At five o'clock on the afternoon of August 12 *Prince of Wales* sailed for home. Mr Churchill walked aft and stood waving his cap to each American ship in turn, remaining on deck until they were almost out of sight. The British escort was now increased by two American destroyers, in one of which the President's younger son, Franklin Roosevelt junior, was serving.

Until Iceland was reached the Prime Minister spent much of the time resting in bed. Clambering up and down ladders and over the many obstructions encountered in a modern fighting ship, he had injured his leg, and was also suffering from a heavy cold. He was much cheered, however, when he learnt that a slight alteration of course would bring *Prince of Wales* in sight of a great Allied convoy homeward bound from Halifax, Nova Scotia. It consisted of seventy-two ships, disposed in twelve columns some five hundred yards apart.

As they sailed through the midst of this vast concourse of merchantmen the Prime Minister asked Tommy to send them his wishes for a safe journey home. In the International Code it was easy enough to make 'Good Voyage,' but the Chief Yeoman pointed out that 'Churchill' was not in the signal book. Earlier in the war Tommy had always used the words *église* and *colline* when referring to Mr Churchill in telephone conversations with the French liaison officers at the Admiralty. The suggestion of signalling 'Church' and 'Hill' in two separate hoists, however, horrified the Chief Yeoman, who insisted on spelling out the Prime Minister's name letter by letter.

Steaming at over twenty knots, *Prince of Wales* made two runs through

[7] Sherwood, *op. cit.*, Vol. I, p. 364.

the convoy and the men lining the decks cheered wildly. On the bridge of the battleship they could see an unmistakable figure, giving the V-sign which was soon to become as closely identified with him as his cigars.

Early next day the coast of Iceland appeared, and a Canadian destroyer took Mr Churchill and his party fifteen miles up the fjord to Reykjavik. There he called on the Icelandic Prime Minister and took the salute at a parade of British and American troops. He also visited a market garden, where he was much intrigued to see masses of carnations grown in glass-houses warmed by the abundant hot springs. He was told of a plan for heating the whole of Iceland's capital with these springs. So far nothing had come of it, for with the outbreak of war they had been unable to obtain the supply of special piping they had ordered from Britain.

On the day of Mr Churchill's visit the weather was glorious, and the British party noticed that many of the population were sun-bathing in the nude on balconies running round the large baths in the centre of the city.

Howard Spring, for one, found his previous conceptions of Iceland far wide of the mark. The leading hotel in Reykjavik, with its smartly uniformed bell-hops, had an atmosphere indistinguishable from the Savoy; many of the women they saw were dressed in the height of Paris fashion; fine modern stores were crammed with luxury goods long forgotten in England; and there were bookshops well stocked with the latest novels in many languages, English predominating.

Soon after *Prince of Wales* put to sea again that evening she ran into a full gale. In some ways this was providential, for the low visibility reduced the danger from enemy U-boats and aircraft, but by the time they entered Scapa Flow at nine o'clock on the morning of Monday, August 18, the skies had cleared and there was brilliant sunshine. It was exactly a fortnight since they had arrived in the special train at Thurso.

Soon they were travelling south, and next morning, when they drew into King's Cross, Mrs Churchill and members of the Cabinet were waiting on the platform to welcome them home.

The Atlantic Charter, which the Prime Minister and the President had drawn up at the conclusion of their meeting, and which had been broadcast to the world while *Prince of Wales* was still at sea, established "certain common principles" on which hopes might be based for securing a better future for the world. It proclaimed the joint desire of Great Britain and her allies and the great nation still at peace to work together for freedom—freedom of government for all peoples of the world, freedom of trade, freedom from fear and want, and the outlawing of force as a means of settling future problems.

To many who confidently expected a meeting between Churchill and Roosevelt to portend America's declaration of war the Atlantic Charter seemed at first sight a disheartening nebulous profession of good intentions. But Roosevelt's endorsement of this declaration had a significance far greater than was at first apparent to anyone lacking an understanding of the American political scene. The tone of the communiqué he had signed —in particular a passage in it which referred to "the final destruction of Nazi tyranny"—was uncompromisingly forthright, and in a broadcast a few days after his return Mr Churchill underlined the real significance of their joint manifesto.

"It symbolizes in a form and manner which every one can understand in every land and clime the deep underlying unities which stir, and at decisive moments rule, the English-speaking peoples throughout the world. . . . It symbolizes something even more majestic, namely the marshalling of the good forces of the world against the evil forces which are now so formidable and triumphant."

In fact the transatlantic journey produced much more than this declaration of principles. Robert Sherwood, who knew the President intimately, was to write later, "It would be an exaggeration to say that Roosevelt and Churchill became chums at this conference or at any subsequent time"; but it was at Placentia that they established "an easy intimacy, a joking informality, and a moratorium on pomposity and cant—and also a degree of frankness in intercourse which, if not quite complete, was remarkably close to it."[8]

Coming events were to show that the foundation of that intimacy and mutual understanding between the two leaders of the English-speaking world was perhaps the most important outcome of all that happened in Placentia Bay.

[8] Sherwood, *op. cit.*, p. 364.

14

The Shadow of the Bomb

After Placentia came anticlimax. Satisfaction at the outcome of operations which freed Persia of German influence and secured an important supply-line to Russia was tempered by the news of an Australian political crisis. Mr Menzies resigned. Both Mr Fadden and Mr Curtin, who followed him into office with a Labour Government, presented uncompromising demands that the Australian troops in Tobruk should be withdrawn and placed under a separate Australian command.

This stemmed from a growing impression in the Commonwealth, fostered by isolationist factions, that the Australian forces were bearing more than their fair share of the burden in the Middle East, and although Mr Churchill pointed to the grievous harm which this move would cause to the preparations for the *Crusader* offensive the Australian Government remained obdurate.

On top of this the Prime Minister had to contend with increasingly unrealistic demands from Stalin, one of which called for the immediate landing of thirty British divisions at Archangel. Allied shipping losses continued to cause deep anxiety, and although in public the Prime Minister maintained his usual confident bearing—"To-day we may say aloud before an awestruck world: 'We are still masters of our fate,' " he assured the Commons—he was aware of a growing disillusionment as the weeks went by and still there came no sign of America abandoning her neutrality. If anything, she seemed to be drawing farther away from active alliance, for Roosevelt—under heavy fire himself from isolationists—repeatedly emphasized in public that the Atlantic meeting had brought the United States no closer to war. He was in an unenviable position. On one hand he had men like Stimson counselling greater firmness towards Germany. At the same time he was confronted by almost hysterical appeals for caution. Few in Britain understood his predicament.

On returning to London Mr Churchill resumed his tours of inspection whenever he could get away from Whitehall. To war-workers in the Midlands and the North of England he explained the part they were playing, and told them frankly of the difficulties ahead. Every one who heard him was heartened by his sturdy defiance.

To his Flag Commander the extraordinary feature of these speeches was that every one of them would be intensely interesting even to those people, like himself, who listened to them all.

"They would contain precisely the same sort of material, but each time this was presented in a different order, and with different phrasing. I asked him one day, when we were touring the Birmingham area, how he managed to make three or four long speeches in succession without using a single note, for his broadcasts and his major speeches were always meticulously prepared and then typed out in what he called 'Speechform'—pages of subject headings to which he could refer. He looked at me in some surprise, and said, 'It isn't nearly as difficult as you think. I just start my mouth off talking and leave it.' "

"Because Mr Churchill wanted to cause as little dislocation as possible to the war effort he insisted that there should be no enormous organized crowds on these provincial tours. At some factories he would give a talk over the loudspeaker system, and then walk round chatting informally to the men and women at the benches. When we got back to the train Royal Marine couriers were always waiting with fresh batches of papers sent up from Downing Street for his attention. Having dealt with these he would go carefully through the latest editions of the local newspapers. Mr Churchill was always an avid reader of newspapers, but for some time he was content to see these when they arrived at breakfast. One evening, however, Brendan Bracken sent out for an early copy of *The Times*, which used to reach the Ministry of Information a few minutes after the first edition came off the presses. When he saw this the P.M. immediately wanted to know where Bracken had obtained it. 'I want the whole lot sent round here in future,' he said. Whenever these early editions of the national newspapers failed to turn up at the expected time there was a considerable commotion."

Shortly after Placentia *The Times* published a leading article entitled "Looking Ahead." It was the last leader written by Geoffrey Dawson, who had edited the paper for more than a quarter of a century, and in it, after praising Churchill's handling of the Persian situation and reviewing other current topics, Dawson turned to "the problem—constantly debated in private but never, it may be hoped, to call for an answer while the war lasts—of a successor to the Prime Minister if a successor were suddenly required."

The editor then went on, "Like no one else in sight he has the courage, the imagination, the power of leadership which are the attributes of a great War Minister. England is fortunate indeed, as she has so often been fortunate in the past, in having produced the man to fit the emergency."[1]

These reflections were not prompted by any widespread criticism of Churchill's leadership at this time, but national anxiety led to a certain amount of sniping at the Government. This eventually drew from the Prime Minister a characteristic retort to his critics. "Nothing is more dangerous in war-time," he said, "than to live in the temperamental atmosphere of a Gallup Poll, always feeling one's pulse and taking one's temperature. I see it said that leaders should keep their ears to the ground. All I can say is that the British nation will find it very hard to look up to the leaders who are detected in that somewhat ungainly posture."[2]

In addition to touring the industrial areas Mr Churchill renewed his inspections of those parts of the coast most vulnerable to invasion. On September 25 he went to Margate and Walmer, near Deal. He had just been made Lord Warden of the Cinque Ports—an office endowed with an official residence at Walmer Castle, where the great Duke of Wellington had died ninety years before. Now the Castle, built by Henry VIII, was within range of the German guns. After visiting it the Prime Minister told the Minister of Works that it would be better if it was used, for the time being, at any rate, for some public purpose. He doubted whether he himself would ever be in a position to occupy it—"or, indeed, whether anybody will be able to live in such fine houses after the war."[3]

The possibility of invasion had obviously been lessened by the German attack on Russia, but the Prime Minister was by no means convinced that the existing intelligence organizations had a true picture of this danger. An inter-Service committee was therefore told to examine the problem from the German angle, and make a plan for an invasion of Britain in the spring of 1942.

Their report envisaged many possibilities, including the widespread employment of saboteurs to cause disruption and confusion in advance of the main landings, and the dropping of a large force on the night of D minus 2 to attack telecommunications. The main assault should, they suggested, take place on four beaches between Reculver, in Kent, and Littlehampton, in Sussex, with diversionary attacks on the Falmouth area and East Anglia, the latter being supported by a feint by the *Tirpitz* and a

[1] Wrench, *op. cit.*, p. 445.
[2] House of Commons, September 30, 1941.
[3] Churchill, Vol. III, p. 737.

convoy of empty transports towards the Yorkshire coast. Eight thousand airborne troops, with a hundred light tanks, would be dropped to take the defenders in the rear. And they planned to smash the R.A.F. in one massive onslaught by medium bombers, dive-bombers, and fighters flying over 7000 sorties on D-Day alone.[4]

The actual enemy plan approved by Hitler at the time when Operation *Sealion* was first conceived was much less imaginative, particularly over the use of airborne troops and the staging of diversionary assaults. And even in the summer of 1940, when the R.A.F. was relatively weak, the German High Command were not prepared to set the invasion attempt in motion until the British air forces had been completely eliminated. Now, more than a year later, their prospects of achieving this preliminary stroke were infinitely more remote.

* * * * *

At the very time when Mr Churchill's Invasion Committee were hotly debating whether they should use poison gas, a sinister relic of earlier warfare, in their imaginary attack on Britain a weapon more fearful than any in the history of mankind was slowly taking shape in English laboratories.

The possibility of atomic warfare had long cast its shadow across the world, but few could read the signs—the scraps of evidence which filtered from research centres to technical journals and the lay Press. The ultimate significance of discoveries made by Rutherford in England, Niels Bohr in Denmark, and leading physicists of many other countries after the First World War was beyond the comprehension of untrained minds. Even the scientists themselves were often unaware of the full import of their own achievements, and when chain reaction in uranium first took place in Rome in 1934 it was incorrectly interpreted.[5]

A year later, however, Professor Joliot-Curie gave a clear warning that "scientists who can construct and demolish elements at will may also be capable of causing nuclear transformations of an explosive character." In a German scientific journal Hahn and Strassmann revealed that uranium fission was something different from normal radioactive decay, and by the end of 1938 it was widely recognized by scientists from work done in England, the United States, and several European countries that the release of atomic energy was a scientific possibility. Even so many still doubted whether the discovery would be exploited. They could point to

[4] The report of the Inter-Service Committee on Invasion is referred to at greater length by Marshal of the R.A.F. Sir John Slessor, one of its three members, in his book, *The Central Blue* (pp. 391–393).

[5] In his absorbing account of the development of atomic energy Dr Robert Jungk mentions that the physicist Emilio Segré, who had taken part in the experiments in Rome, said twenty years later, at the funeral of his teacher, Enrico Fermi, "God, for His own inscrutable reasons, made every one blind at that time to the phenomenon of nuclear fission" (*Brighter than a Thousand Suns*, p. 60).

the views of Bohr, the distinguished disciple of Rutherford, who as late as the start of 1939 was advancing an array of reasons why the fission process would never be developed; and of Einstein, who was announcing that he did not believe in "the release of atomic power."[6] But Einstein, it would appear, was speaking only from a limited technical viewpoint, and Bohr, not being an industrialist, could be forgiven for doubting whether any country in the world could or would want to initiate a project of such immensity.

Up to this stage research into the release of atomic energy had been carried on in the full floodlight of scientific publicity. With the threat of war the work went underground. In England it was continued mainly in the university laboratories of Oxford and Cambridge, Liverpool and Birmingham. When, however, it was realized that the scientists were on the brink of success the whole complex undertaking was co-ordinated under the Ministry of Aircraft Production.

Guided by a committee headed by Sir George Thomson, the Ministry exercised a sensibly elastic control which in no way interfered with the scientists' working routine, but they took over responsibility for the growing administrative and financial problems involved. The atomic research project had become a major operation; in addition to the teams working at the various universities, many leading industrial firms like Imperial Chemical Industries, Metropolitan Vickers, and Mond Nickel were concerned with its development.

Throughout 1940 the work was pressed forward. By this time groups at Liverpool and Birmingham had independently expressed the view that it would be possible to create a military weapon of terrifying power.

What was happening in Germany? Strangely enough, very little. Jungk records that a meeting of nuclear physicists took place in the Army Weapons Department in Berlin on September 26, 1939. A detailed programme of work was drawn up, but for some time after that little progress was made because a specialist chosen to carry out certain important chemical tests was away on military service. In the summer of 1940 Carl Von Weizsacker wrote an important paper explaining that an entirely new substance ("which could be used as an explosive") might arise in a uranium pile, but this was not apparently circulated outside a group calling themselves the Uranium Society. Even when Speer, the Minister most closely concerned, eventually learnt of the availability of atomic energy he was only interested in its development as a prime mover, and research work continued on the same limited scale as before.

In England the liaison between the scientists and the war machine was from the outset very much closer, and for this Lindemann was largely responsible. At every stage he had kept in touch with the teams at the

[6] Jungk, *op. cit.*, p. 78.

universities, and Churchill himself was therefore fully aware of what was happening. The reports he read on his return from Placentia showed that a critical stage had been reached. If full advantage was to be taken of the progress already made the project must be given even higher priority. Plant for producing the material had to be designed and built; methods of assembly and fusing had to be investigated; and some means of effectively controlling the energy released had to be discovered. Two French physicists, Dr Halban and Dr Kowarski, were already working on this last problem at the Cavendish Laboratory at Cambridge.

The whole undertaking, which now bore the cover title of "Tube Alloys," was therefore brought under the wing of the Department of Scientific and Industrial Research (D.S.I.R.), and the Lord President of the Council, Sir John Anderson, was made directly responsible to the Cabinet for its future progress. This was a particularly happy choice, for Anderson, a wise, patient man and a brilliant administrator, had had a really competent scientific training in his youth at Leipzig University. It was he who invented the cover title for the atomic energy project—but not for the reason which he afterwards came to believe.

In later years Anderson was under the impression that he had chosen the name of Tube Alloys because the isotope separation process envisaged in 1941 involved the use of apparatus with a great deal of tubing in it. What actually happened was that Wallace Akers, a senior member of the staff of I.C.I., who had been appointed Director of Atomic Energy Research, and Michael Perrin, his deputy, suggested that the title should be *Tank Alloys*—a satisfactorily meaningless name in itself, but one which embraced a top priority word, for tanks were then very much to the fore.[7] With characteristic foresight, however, Anderson pointed out that tanks might not retain their high priority. Instead he suggested a piece of equipment to be found in almost every weapon or device connected with the war—and *Tube Alloys* the atom project became.

By now Sir George Thomson's committee had produced the definite estimate that it would be possible to manufacture an atom bomb with the explosive power of 8000 tons of T.N.T. For Mr Churchill here was the dramatic fulfilment of a prediction he himself had made long years before:

> May there not be methods of using explosive energy incomparably more intense than anything heretofore discovered? Might not a bomb no bigger than an orange be found to possess a secret power to destroy a whole block of buildings—nay, to concentrate a force of thousands of tons of cordite and blast a township at a stroke?

[7] Akers was knighted for his services in 1946; Mr M. W. Perrin, C.B.E., also a senior executive of I.C.I. when he joined Tube Alloys, has been Chairman of the Wellcome Foundation since 1953.

With prophetic insight he had written those words as far back as 1925. Now, by the strange working of fate, it had fallen to him to launch atomic research on the last decisive phase.

*   *   *   *   *

Crusader remained the linch-pin of Churchill's hopes for the immediate future, and he awaited Auchinleck's offensive with undisguised anxiety. The nagging conviction that his Commander-in-Chief in the Middle East was squandering precious time refused to be stilled, for the Russian armies were now fighting desperately in front of Moscow itself and von Bock's new offensive had compelled the Government to move to Kuibishyev. At all costs the Allies must strike in the West while Russian resistance remained alive.

This was already an obsession when Auchinleck signalled that he would need a further fortnight's preparation before launching his attack. In his disappointment the Prime Minister "turned frantically to all kinds of other possibilities for offensive action."[8] Among these were an attack on Trondheim and a plan for invading Sicily (Operation *Whipcord*).

For a time the Trondheim project dominated his thoughts, and the Chiefs of Staff, who thoroughly disliked the idea of yet another landing doomed to be carried out with little or no air support, were angrily accused of conspiring to place difficulties in his way. During one meeting at Downing Street the Prime Minister remarked bitterly, "I sometimes think some of my generals do not want to fight the Germans."[9] And he elaborated on this theme with some indignation to Lord Louis Mountbatten when the latter came to see him early in October.

Mountbatten had been waiting in America to take command of an aircraft carrier refitting at San Francisco when he received orders to return immediately for an interview with the Prime Minister. His air passage was given top priority, but although he reached London in a matter of hours, Mr Churchill demanded to know why he had taken so long. The Prime Minister then said with some asperity that far too many people were concentrating on defence. He had therefore decided to set up a body whose sole aim it would be to train for attack. The enemy must be demoralized by constant displays of aggression and the threat of offensive action at any point on their long coastline. He spoke for some time in this strain and then informed Mountbatten that his posting had been cancelled. He was to take up a different appointment.

The background to this conversation, which took place at Chequers, provided another example of the difficulties which the Prime Minister had to face during this period. In recent weeks had occurred the unhappy renewal of the friction between Sir Roger Keyes and "the Inter-Service

[8] Kennedy, *op. cit.*, p. 173. [9] Bryant, *op.cit.*, p. 262.

committees of comparatively junior officers without practical war experience" whose dictation the Admiral so bitterly resented, and once again Keyes had started bombarding the Prime Minister with complaints.[10] A final effort to persuade his old friend to compose his differences had only provoked further violent argument on eight sheets of foolscap, and after that Churchill realized he could do no more. On October 4 he wrote to Keyes:

> MY DEAR ROGER,
>
> I am sorry that you do not feel able to fall in with the proposal all the Chiefs of Staff have made to you. I have really done my best to meet your wishes. I have to consider first my duty to the State, which ranks above personal friendship. In all the circumstances I have no choice but to arrange for your relief.
>
> Yours very sincerely,
> WINSTON S. CHURCHILL[11]

On October 19 Mountbatten, then a Captain of only four years' seniority, took charge of Combined Operations.

The conversation he had with the Prime Minister on the eve of his new appointment made a great impression on him, for Churchill's discourse on "Thinking Offensively" was delivered at a time when we were cruelly hardpressed on land and at sea and our only effective ally, Russia, seemed on the verge of collapse. It reflected Churchill's astonishing resilience and far-sighted optimism. Nothing dismayed him, and although he could be criticized for intervening too frequently and in too great detail with Auchinleck's preparations he gave him the staunchest support from the moment the desert battle was joined. John Connell has recorded that "his courage and his calmness in the face of apparently imminent disaster were of immeasurable importance to the Commander-in-Chief."[12]

In the wake of a violent storm, which flooded all the enemy airfields and kept their reconnaissance planes on the ground throughout the day, Auchinleck's attack was launched at dawn on November 18.

The main aim of *Crusader* was the recapture of Cyrenaica and the destruction of the Axis armour. For the first time in the war Allied strength matched that of the enemy ground forces, and in the air the Allies held a marked advantage; Rommel could only muster 120 serviceable aircraft of his own and 200 Italian planes, against a force of over a thousand.

General Cunningham achieved complete tactical surprise, and for a time the enemy were under the impression that the Allied advance was no more than a reconnaissance in strength. It was not long, however, before

[10] Aspinall-Oglander, *op. cit.*, pp. 408–409. [11] *Ibid.* [12] *Op. cit.*, p. 400.

Rommel regained control of the situation, and by the afternoon of November 19 the two armoured forces had come together in fierce battle at Sidi Rezegh.

From that moment Allied fortunes were in the balance, and when Rommel staked everything on a break-through by the Afrika Corps towards the Egyptian frontier only the personal intervention of Auchinleck, who flew from Cairo and took over control of the battle, prevented disaster. Even then it was touch and go, but Rommel's race for the frontier had dangerously exposed his supply-lines, and the flower of his army was now at the mercy of Tedder's air forces, ranging unopposed. By November 27 the bold thrust had spent itself, and frantic calls for help were reaching Rommel from the Axis formations still locked in battle at Sidi Rezegh. He therefore turned and headed back towards the west.

The vital throw had failed, but much stern fighting still lay ahead. It was not until December 10, after three weeks of bitter conflict, that the enemy were in full retreat. They lost 33,000 men and 300 tanks.

* * * * *

The outcome of the desert battle was still undecided when Churchill went to Chequers for the last week-end of November. Before he left London Brendan Bracken had asked him to meet a party of American Congressmen, and on November 28 they came to Chequers for lunch. Convinced isolationists, they had arrived in England on a fact-finding tour, and although they were politely non-committal, Tommy gathered that they thought Britain's chance of survival was slender. A few days earlier an American military observer, General Embick, had reported that a German invasion attempt might well succeed now that the Allies were so heavily involved in the Middle East, and it was plain that the Congressmen agreed with this view.

During lunch they listened with critical attention while the Prime Minister ranged over the whole field of the war, and outlined possible enemy moves. Then one of the visitors asked the question which was obviously on all their minds: "What will happen if the Germans gain a foothold in this country and you are overrun?"

"With dying hands we shall pass on the torch to you," said Mr Churchill gravely.

For a moment there was dead silence, and then the Prime Minister began speaking again—and demolishing in vivid phrases all ideas of an Allied defeat. If the worst happened, he pointed out, the British Fleet would form a rallying force for carrying on the fight from new bases overseas, but Tommy doubts whether the Congressmen heard him. They were all too busy jotting down for posterity that memorable and characteristically Churchillian reply.

15

Christmas at the White House

WHILE the eyes of the Western world were still focused on the battle in the desert a series of messages which reached the Prime Minister from Washington made it ominously clear that Japan was on the brink of some major move.

Ever since the signing of the Tripartite Pact with Germany and Italy in the summer of 1940 the rôle of the Japanese had been an enigma. They possessed few resources for waging a modern war, and since the embargoes imposed by the United States, Britain, and Holland had cut off all their supplies of oil their position had become even more precarious. But to a warrior race this was no time for reason. Men of moderation like Prince Konoye were viewed by the powerful Army clique as little better than traitors, depriving the nation of her rightful place in the New World Order which German victories were doing so much to create.

Konoye was ousted from the Premiership, and although General Tojo, who succeeded him in October, continued diplomatic negotiations with the United States "to settle outstanding differences" the discussions in Washington no longer held any significance. Japan was bent on war, and before her envoys had even seen the State Department's reply to her "final demands" the Japanese Fleet had already sailed for Pearl Harbour.

On the last day of November the Japanese Government sent a warning to Berlin that war in the Far East might break out "quicker than anyone dreams."[1] This was intercepted in the United States, for the Americans had broken the secret Japanese ciphers a year earlier, and had been regularly decoding their signals, but there was still no indication where the blow might fall.

[1] Churchill, Vol. III, p. 553.

In a speech at the Mansion House on November 10 Churchill had said, "Should the United States become involved in war with Japan the British declaration will follow within the hour." He saw all too clearly, however, that if the attack was made on British or Dutch possessions alone Roosevelt's hands might well be tied.

This agonizing possibility was uppermost in his mind when he went to Chequers for the first week-end of December. Winant drove down to spend Sunday with him, and he asked the Ambassador if he thought America would come in. Winant could only reply that the responsibility for declaring war rested solely with Congress.

Tommy recalls that the dinner-party that night was a far from cheerful affair. "Mrs Churchill had not been feeling well, and had gone to bed. The P.M. looked unusually worried and hardly spoke. Just before nine o'clock Sawyers came in and put the portable radio on the table at his elbow. At first Mr Churchill did not seem to notice it was there, and when eventually he switched it on Alvar Liddell had already begun to read the summary of the 'headlines.' We heard him say something about air attacks on the Hawaiian Islands. Before it had dawned on us what this meant he was already talking about a tank battle south of Tobruk, but the P.M. sat bolt upright in his chair and asked, 'Didn't he say there has been an attack on American bases?' Sawyers, who had been standing near the radio, said he had heard it too, but no one else was quite sure, and by now the summary was dealing with a new German thrust towards Moscow and daylight raids by the R.A.F. We were still staring at each other and wondering whether we had been imagining it, when Liddell began again: 'The news has just been given that Japanese aircraft have raided Pearl Harbour, the American naval base in Hawaii. The announcement of the attack was made in a brief statement by President Roosevelt. Naval and military targets on the principal Hawaiian island of Oahu have also been attacked. No further details are yet available.' At this the P.M. jumped up and said, 'We will declare war on Japan.' I heard Mr Winant suggest that it would be better to wait for confirmation, but Mr Churchill told me to get a call through to the President. Within five minutes the White House was on the line. Then Mr Eden rang up from Scotland. He was on his way to Moscow for talks with Stalin and had just heard the news. Next day war was declared on Japan; within a week we were at sea in the *Duke of York*, bound for America."

* * * * *

The Prime Minister lost no time in suggesting a meeting with the President, for at a stroke the whole outlook of the war had been violently changed. The United States were active allies at last, but from the British point of view the immediate situation was grave. Simultaneously with the seaborne onslaught on Pearl Harbour Japan had begun an invasion of Malaya, and it was in a vain attempt to intercept one of their transport fleets that the Royal Navy's most powerful battleship, *Prince of Wales*, and the battle-cruiser *Repulse*, operating without air cover, were sunk by overwhelming air attack on the morning of December 10. Among more than eight hundred officers and men who lost their lives was Admiral Sir Tom Phillips, Commander-in-Chief designate of the new British Far Eastern Fleet, which it had been hoped to form in the spring of 1942.

This was a great personal shock to the Prime Minister. Mr Churchill had played an important part in sending the ships to Singapore—a decision supported by the Foreign Office, who had considered that their presence there might well deter Japan from entering the war, but strongly opposed by the First Sea Lord. The shock was all the greater because the Prime Minister had come to know Admiral Phillips well during his spell as Vice-Chief of the Naval Staff and had greatly admired him.

To the Royal Navy it was a crippling blow. The battleship *Barham* and *Ark Royal* had already been lost in the Mediterranean, where further disasters now befell Admiral Cunningham's depleted forces. H.M.S. *Neptune* was sunk, and two more cruisers, *Penelope* and *Aurora*, were badly damaged in a minefield; *Galatea* was sunk by a U-boat, and *Queen Elizabeth* and *Valiant* were put out of action by Italian frogmen while lying in harbour at Alexandria. By Christmas all that remained of the Mediterranean Fleet was three cruisers and a handful of destroyers; in the whole of the Far East there was no Allied capital ship. To complicate the Admiralty's task substantial German submarine reinforcements had now reached the Mediterranean, and an air fleet under Kesselring had been transferred there from the Eastern front to strike at Malta. When the Prime Minister reviewed the war situation in the House of Commons on the eve of his departure he was heard in gloomy silence.

* * * * *

Since the whole outline of Anglo-American strategy had to be agreed at the forthcoming discussions in Washington, the party which travelled north to board the *Duke of York* for the journey to America included a large team of military advisers. Among them was General Dill, but he was no longer C.I.G.S.; Sir Alan Brooke had been appointed in his place.

For all his brilliant gifts Dill had never been able to establish a *modus operandi* in his contacts with the Prime Minister. Gentle, almost diffident by nature, he had a far from forceful manner when challenged, and inevitably this gave an impression of indecisiveness which grew more pronounced as the strain of his responsibilities told on him. He was unable to stand up to Churchill, and the Prime Minister was well aware of this.

To a lesser man than Mr Churchill this ability to dominate a subordinate of Dill's calibre and undoubted intellect by sheer force of personality and power of exposition might have seemed gratifying. But although the Prime Minister liked to have his own way, and was often greatly put out when he could not get it, he seemed intuitively to realize that he must have people around him who could offer firm checks to his own exuberance. Dill wore himself out in his efforts to hold his own in argument with the Prime Minister, whereas the other Chiefs of Staff developed their own effective tactics for restraining him. Portal, the Chief of the Air Staff, seemed to understand him better than anyone, and handled him with subtlety and skill; Pound would often get his own way by a process of masterly inactivity. Dill, however, found the Prime Minister's fierce eloquence in support of some project on which he had set his heart, and his somewhat peremptory manner when opposed, intensely disconcerting, and he would often relapse into tongue-tied silence. In the days to come Brooke was to face storms just as fierce, but by temperament he was far better equipped to deal with Churchill when the latter was in one of his most obstinate and seemingly intransigent moods.

* * * * *

Of all the journeys which the Prime Minister was destined to make during the war few rivalled this first voyage to America for sheer discomfort. Hardly had *Duke of York* left the Clyde before she ran into a full gale. Captain Cecil Harcourt, who had recently left the Admiralty to command the new battleship, had an unenviable responsibility, for his ship was not fully worked up; while the First Sea Lord kept counselling him not to run any risk of damaging her in the heavy seas, the Prime Minister was all for pressing on at top speed.

For most of the trip *Duke of York* could make only twelve knots. All watertight doors were closed, and with the ship battened down no one could take any exercise on deck. Lord Beaverbrook, a sufferer from asthma, found the lack of ventilation a sore trial. "This is worse than being imprisoned in a submarine," he complained, and the stifling atmosphere below decks made many other people short-tempered. On his way to dinner one night Tommy met Major Macdonald-Buchanan, Dill's Military Assistant. "He was barefooted and his trousers were rolled up to his knees. A scuttle right aft had not been tightly screwed down, and as that particular compartment was sealed off by the watertight doors the first anyone knew of this was when the sea reached a ventilator and flooded forward into the cabins occupied by our staff officers. The Army soon realized that life afloat was not all it was cracked up to be!"

U-boats were constantly reported in the vicinity, and the Prime Minister spoke hopefully of ramming one. The possibility of taking part in a naval action delighted him, and when news came that the *Tirpitz* was missing from her base he eagerly discussed the chances of engaging her.

As on the voyage to Placentia, strict wireless silence was maintained. The ship could receive messages, but transmitting was a laborious process, long groups of cipher numbers being signalled visually to an escorting cruiser. These would be repeated to the Admiralty when the ship was several hundred miles away on her return journey.

Each forenoon the Prime Minister visited the navigating bridge for a while, but he spent most of the day in bed, holding court with his advisers and working on his papers. He drafted several important memoranda on the future course of the war, one outlining a suggested sequence of operations in the Mediterranean theatre during 1942, while another, looking much farther ahead, discussed the employment of Anglo-American forces in the liberation of Europe.

Although lack of exercise usually worried him less than most people, he too found the unnatural living conditions increasingly trying. One morning he threw down the notes from which he was dictating to Patrick Kinna and said angrily, "Go out and tell those sailors to stop whistling!" Kinna was used to this particular foible, for at Downing Street the Prime Minister was always ringing the bell and ordering the Royal Marine pensioner on duty to dash out into the street and "stop that confounded noise." As the culprit was often a boy on a bicycle he would be well out of range by the time the front door opened, but when the diminutive Kinna emerged from the cabin on this occasion he was confronted by two massive Able Seamen who stopped swabbing down the passageway and surveyed him with interest. As the whistling had ceased abruptly Kinna's nerve failed him, and instead of passing on the Prime Minister's message he asked them what the time was and beat a hasty retreat.

Captain Harcourt also became acquainted with the Prime Minister's idiosyncrasies. One morning Sawyers arrived on the bridge with an urgent request. Could the Captain come to Mr Churchill's aid? "The Prime Minister doesn't like the ship's water, and I've run out of white wine!"

On the afternoon of December 22 *Duke of York* arrived off Hampton Roads, the bleak anchorage at the mouth of Chesapeake Bay. When the pilot came on board and recognized the Prime Minister his astonishment was so obvious that every one knew there had been no major breach of security during the voyage.

Churchill was impatient to reach Washington, and while the rest of the party boarded a special train he went on ahead in a U.S. Navy plane. After the darkness of England under threat of air attack it seemed almost unbelievable to be flying over a countryside ablaze with light. From the air

Washington, with its myriad dancing neon signs, looked to British eyes like a fairy city.

On landing the Prime Minister went straight to the White House, which was to be his base for the next three weeks. He was given a suite on the same floor as the President—the North-east Suite, which had been used by the Queen during the royal visit to America just before the war and was decorated with beautiful prints of scenes in Victorian England. He was to occupy these rooms during all his subsequent visits. Opposite was the Monroe Room, which Roosevelt had set aside as the Prime Minister's Map Room, and next door to this was the suite occupied by Harry Hopkins. Mr Roosevelt's own rooms were at the end of the gallery which ran the length of the house and contained pictures, relics, and mementoes of past Presidents. Hopkins had an office attached to the White House, but he never seemed to use it. He did all his work sitting on the huge four-poster bed in his room.

John Martin, Churchill's Private Secretary, and Tommy had rooms opposite the President's study. Within a few hours of their arrival they were faced with a problem they had not foreseen. "The White House became inundated with fan mail for Mr Churchill, and it soon became impossible to deal with it on our own. In addition to letters from men and women well known in public life there were thousands of welcoming messages from every part of America, and a special staff had to be recruited to answer them. At the same time arrived hundreds of gifts of every conceivable kind. Eventually they filled two entire rooms in the British Embassy. It was clearly impossible to take home more than a fraction of these presents, and they were distributed to hospitals and charitable organizations. One tribute which found its way into the P.M.'s bedroom was a gigantic V sign composed of lilies, carnations, and irises, and standing fully six feet high. No parcel was allowed into the White House without close examination, and the Secret Service were kept busy opening hundreds of boxes of cigars."[2]

The cigars which reached the Prime Minister from admirers all over the world were to remain something of a problem throughout the war, for they arrived in their thousands. From time to time the Government of Cuba sent him huge presentation cabinets; he was often asked to accept cigars of all kinds and sizes when he toured war factories; and from every quarter of Britain boxes were continually reaching Downing Street, often with no clue to the identity of the sender.

Churchill had smoked cigars all his life. At the age of twenty he had been warned by a doctor that unless he gave up cigars and champagne he would be dead in five years. He had cheerfully ignored this advice at the

[2] C. R. Thompson, Notes.

time, and now, nearly half a century later, he had no intention of denying himself either luxury as long as it remained available. It was obvious, however, that some risk attached to accepting cigars from unknown sources, and early in the war friends of his consulted Lord Rothschild, who was carrying out secret experimental work for the War Office. Would it be possible, they asked, to check the composition of cigars in such a way that Churchill's safety would be ensured?

Rothschild reported that there was no means of doing this, for although X-rays could detect tampering of a certain kind they would not necessarily reveal poison injected with a syringe. The only safe course was to burn the contents. During the Prime Minister's stay in America the Secret Service X-rayed every parcel addressed to him. And the only cigars he was allowed to smoke were those sent by people specially 'cleared' for security.

* * * * *

The daily routine at the White House was very different from that at Downing Street. Each morning the President worked with his Service Aides, General 'Pa' Watson and Rear-Admiral Wilson Brown; Stephen Early, the Press Secretary; and his personal private secretary, Grace Tully. He then received a stream of callers, and after lunch he would spend some time in the office block connected to the main building. Later on in the day, however, he appeared to have no personal staff at his disposal. Several times Tommy was summoned to his room, to find him busy writing. Looking up, Roosevelt would say, "Be a good fellow and take these down to the office for me." There was not a soul on duty in the house to carry out any task for the President.

In marked contrast the Prime Minister had six secretaries at Downing Street, of whom four dealt with all current operational matters. One of these—and a confidential shorthand typist—was always on duty during Churchill's waking hours. In addition he had three Personal Assistants—Professor Lindemann (by this time Lord Cherwell), Major Desmond Morton, and Tommy.

As a young Gunner officer Desmond Morton had first met Churchill in the trenches in 1916. When Churchill revisited France as Minister of Munitions their paths crossed again. By that time Morton had won a Military Cross, and, having miraculously survived a shot through the heart, he was serving as A.D.C. to Haig. Churchill was much impressed with Morton's linguistic ability, for he spoke fluent French, German, Italian, and Russian, and it was on his recommendation that Morton afterwards entered the Foreign Office. Between the wars their friendship had continued, and on becoming Prime Minister Churchill had brought him on to his own staff from the Ministry of Economic Warfare. Now he was the Prime Minister's liaison officer with the foreign Governments in exile in London.[3]

On Churchill's journeys abroad he was always accompanied by one, if not two, of his 'operational' Private Secretaries. In Washington on this occasion he had with him John Martin, who had come to Downing Street from the Colonial Office, and Francis Brown, of the Foreign Office.[4]

Another contrast between the routine of Prime Minister and President was immediately noticeable when Churchill went to Capitol Hill to address both Houses of Congress four days after his arrival. The Washington City Police provided a spectacular cavalcade of cars and escorting motor-cycles, with sirens screaming as they drove through the densely packed streets. Moved by the tremendous welcome he received from the waiting crowd as he left the building after delivering his speech the Prime Minister walked across to speak to some of the onlookers. Instantly he was surrounded by a posse of Secret Service agents, who did their best to hustle him away. This greatly surprised him, but he was soon to find out that security regulations were altogether different from the pattern in England.

Mr Churchill had a strong dislike of ostentatious precautions for his safety. If he walked anywhere in London plain-clothes detectives were always closely but unobtrusively at hand. Travelling by road he was accompanied only by one police car, following behind, for the system of guarding him relied on surprise in the sense that it was never advertised in advance where he was going, and a planned interception was therefore unlikely.

Wherever Mr Roosevelt moved, however, he was escorted by a squadron of motor-cycle police and followed by an enormous car known irreverently as the Queen Mary. This was crammed with Secret Service agents, armed to the teeth. Others stood on the running-boards, and whenever the procession slowed down these men would jump off and surround the President.

The streets through which he passed were lined with plain-clothes police, all armed. They stood with their backs to the road, scanning the crowds and the buildings overlooking the route. At any cross-roads not already guarded two police-cars would accelerate past the President and stop broadside on across the roadways of the intersection.

When Tommy asked Mike Reilly, chief of the President's personal bodyguard, why such elaborate precautions were considered necessary, Reilly remarked, "It's different for you. We've had three of these guys

[3] Now Sir Desmond Morton, K.C.B., C.M.G.

[4] Martin, one of three Principal Private Secretaries to serve the Prime Minister during the war, was knighted in 1952, and became a Deputy Under-Secretary of State in 1956.

bumped off, and you haven't had any. One out of every five of our Presidents has been shot at. We'd be crazy to take any risks."[5]

What chiefly worried the Secret Servicemen was President Roosevelt's immobility. The greatest danger they had to face was an attack by a lunatic who did not care if he got away or not. The President himself never seemed unduly worried by this hazard, but he told Tommy of an attack made on him in Miami years before. A man had leaped from the crowd and fired a shot before the guards pounced on him. The bullet missed Roosevelt, but hit the Mayor of Chicago, who was standing beside him.

Immediately a section of the crowd closed in on the assailant, but the Secret Servicemen reached him first. "When the car moved off I asked what they had done with him," said the President. "I received the surprising reply that at that very moment he was lying on the luggage grid behind me, with two agents sitting on top of him!"

* * * * *

The staff talks and Churchill's own conferences with Roosevelt and his advisers had begun straight away. In addition the Prime Minister got through an immense amount of other work, including the preparation of his speeches to Congress and to the Canadian Parliament, for he had decided to pay a short visit to Ottawa after Christmas. As in England, his working day began at breakfast-time. Often he would continue to dictate a stream of directives and memoranda as he lay in his bath.

The morning bath was often quite a spectacular event. He would fling himself under the water, and then surface again, blowing like a whale. When he emerged from the bath Sawyers would be standing with an enormous towel, and, draped in this, the Prime Minister would pace to and fro, followed by Kinna with notebook and pencil.

Kinna was with him on the morning when Mr Roosevelt entered the bathroom to discuss the draft declaration of the United Nations Pact which set the seal on this first Washington Conference, and heard his famous remark—often considered apocryphal—to his host. Naked and unashamed, Mr Churchill declared, "I have nothing to conceal from the President of the United States!"

The President had told him to treat the White House as his own. If he wanted anyone to call on him he had merely to give their names to one of the Ushers, without reference to him. The Ushers, of whom there were four, were in charge of all the domestic arrangements at the White House. They appeared to know every one and everything; like magicians, they

[5] President Lincoln (1865) was shot in his box at the theatre by a mad actor, John Wilkes Booth; President Garfield (1881) was shot by a man named Guiteau on a Washington railway platform; and a known anarchist, Leon Czolgosz, concealed a revolver in a fake bandage and shot President McKinlay (1901) at point-blank range in a Buffalo park as he was about to shake hands.

seemed able to meet any request of the British party, from a tube of toothpaste to a motor-car, at a moment's notice.

Every evening there was a pleasant ritual in Roosevelt's study. Half an hour before dinner he would seat himself at his desk, with a tray of Gordon's gin, vermouth, and ice before him and mix extremely potent dry Martinis for his guests. He knew that Churchill disliked cocktails, and it was therefore understood that the Prime Minister himself would not appear until just before dinner. Then Tommy would push the President in his wheeled chair along the passage to the lift.

Normally Roosevelt went to bed early, but he had been warned by Harry Hopkins that Churchill liked to talk till the small hours. As a result he rarely took any notice when the Prime Minister tactfully suggested that it was time he himself retired, and they would all stay on chatting until long after the President's usual bedtime. This was not viewed with any favour by Mrs Roosevelt, anxious to see that her husband did not overtire himself, and one night when they were later than usual she arrived in the Map Room and asked Harry MacMullen, the R.N.V.R. lieutenant on duty, to go in and tell the Prime Minister it was time for the President to go to bed. MacMullen opened the door leading into the study for her, thinking it would be better if she gave him the message herself, but when he turned round she had fled rather than face the Prime Minister.

The work of the Conference went on with hardly a break throughout the Christmas period, but on Christmas Eve there was a traditional ceremony in the grounds of the White House. A huge Christmas-tree was illuminated on the lawn, and a crowd of several thousand gathered to hear speeches from Roosevelt and Churchill. Afterwards there was carol-singing. That evening was something of an ordeal for Tommy, for before the house-party assembled Hopkins invited him to come to his room. "A kind friend from Chesapeake Bay has sent me some oysters," he said, pointing to a barrel on the floor. "Come and help me eat them."

They had got through a large number of these when it was time to go to the President's study for their evening cocktail. As they entered the room Mr Roosevelt said, "I have a nice surprise for you all. A friend of mine from Chesapeake Bay has sent me a barrel of oysters, and we're going to have them for dinner to-night." Harry Hopkins and Tommy, who had not the heart to disclose that they had already been eating oysters for the past hour, made heavy weather of this unwelcome addition to the menu.

On the afternoon of December 28 Churchill left by train for Ottawa to stay with the Governor-General of Canada, Lord Athlone. By this time his discussions with the President had given the Chiefs of Staff plenty to deal with, and for the time being there was little more he could do in

Washington. Two days later he addressed the Canadian House of Commons.

He had worked particularly hard on his two major speeches, but, having completed the outline of the Ottawa speech, he had put it aside. "He was in one of his relaxed moods, and showed great disinclination to tackle the final draft—so much so, in fact, that on the evening before he had to deliver it not a word was on paper. Superhuman efforts by Kinna and two of the Governor-General's typists produced the final version in time, but then, at the very last minute, the P.M. decided to scrap one entire page and dictate a fresh passage. When we set off Francis Brown was left behind to deal with this, and we had to hope that he would arrive before the speech started. Mr Churchill had already begun his address when the mising sheet was slipped into his hand."[6]

In one memorable passage of that speech the Prime Minister said:

"In this strange, terrible world war there is a place for every one, man and woman, old and young, hale and halt; service in a thousand forms is open.... The mine, the factory, the dockyard, the salt sea waves, the fields to till, the home, the hospital, the chair of the scientist, the pulpit of the preacher—from the highest to the humblest tasks, all are of equal honour . . . all have their part to play."

He described his last visit to France—for the meeting at Tours just before the country was overrun. "When I warned them that Britain would fight on alone . . . their chiefs told their Prime Minister . . . that in three weeks England would have her neck wrung like a chicken. Some chicken! Some neck!" Oddly enough the *double entendre* of the word 'neck'—translated by his audience as 'cheek'—had not occurred to him when he drafted the phrase, and he was momentarily puzzled by the roar of delighted applause which greeted this remark.

Before he left Ottawa Mr Churchill had an unexpected meeting with an old friend. At a small informal dinner-party given for him by the Canadian Premier, Mr Mackenzie King, he heard that Air Vice-Marshal Billy Bishop, V.C., who had brought down seventy-two enemy aircraft while serving with the Royal Flying Corps in the First World War, was living near by. Bishop was invited round to join the party, and as the two were still busily swapping stories when the time came to leave the guest of honour, who was greatly enjoying himself, got into Bishop's car, which set off at high speed for the Air Marshal's own home, with a surprised police escort in hot pursuit.

On New Year's Eve Churchill boarded the President's special train to return to Washington. A vast army of Press correspondents travelled on the train, and as it passed through the State of Vermont at midnight that

[6] C. R. Thompson, Notes.

night they sent a message asking if the Prime Minister would visit them to see the New Year in.

Tommy told the Secret Servicemen that Mr Churchill would do this on the strict understanding that any remarks he made must be off the record, and that he did not wish to pose for photographers. Hardly had he entered the Press coach, however, before a woman journalist jumped up on to a seat at the back of the compartment and there was a flash as she took a picture. Before the Prime Minister could say a word the rest of the correspondents had turned on her and torn the film from her camera.

Churchill, who took a very real pride in his own long and active connexion with journalism, had the happiest relations with the Press during this first war-time visit to America, and this was to continue as long as the war lasted. It was easy to see why. He trusted the Press, and even when he was not in a position to comment freely the manner of his replies, and the spontaneous humour with which he parried the most awkward questions, always made good 'copy.'

At a lunch given for him by the Press corps in Washington he was at the top of his form. Tommy took a note of his answers to the barrage of questions fired at him on this occasion; one which brought a roar of laughter was his comment on the dilemma facing Italy. "Signor Mussolini's position is indeed unenviable," said the Prime Minister: "the organgrinder has got his head in the monkey's collar."

The action of the Free French in seizing the small Vichy-controlled islands of St Pierre and Miquelon, off the coast of Newfoundland, on Christmas Eve, without reference to the British or American Government had brought violent criticism of De Gaulle from the U.S. State Department. When Churchill was asked why Canada had not expelled the Vichy Minister there he said urbanely that "a courtyard likes to have a window."

There were questions about the Hess incident ("He tells us that Hitler loves England and his heart would bleed for us if Germany had to invade Great Britain"), and the Prime Minister fenced skilfully with attempts to draw him into discussions of Ireland's neutrality. When, however, a correspondent asked if he considered it vital to the war effort that Roosevelt should remain President for the duration the chairman ruled the question out of order. "Not at all," said Churchill cheerfully. "I'll answer that."

He paused, and then said warily, "After a long experience of public life I have come to the conclusion that very few understand the politics of their own country—and none the politics of other countries."

* * * * *

Throughout his fortnight at the White House the Prime Minister had been working at high pressure. Inevitably the strain of public appearances, speeches, and the constant meetings—there were eight major conferences with the President and the Joint Chiefs of Staff—now began to tell on him.

He had intended to stay for only a week at the White House and then, after the visit to Canada, to start for home on New Year's Day, but on his return to Washington he was feeling far from well. When Edward Stettinius, one of the President's special assistants, suggested a few days' rest at the seaside house he owned on the coast of Florida Mr Churchill gratefully accepted.

16

Interlude in Florida

POMPANO, where the Prime Minister was to spend his first real holiday for nearly three years, lies on a narrow neck of land flanked by the Atlantic and the great swamp of the Everglades some thirty miles to the south of Palm Beach. The Stettinius villa was conveniently secluded, and apart from the couriers who arrived from time to time with papers from Washington there was no contact with the outside world. The vigilant Secret Servicemen saw to that.

In the mornings Mr Churchill worked in bed, getting up for a swim before lunch. He had only to cross a small lawn of coarse grass to reach the shore. Although the skies remained overcast the sea was calm as a millpond and he bathed several times a day, rolling and plunging in the warm water like a contented dolphin.

In the evenings he would sit on the veranda watching the ships—mostly tankers plying to and from the Gulf—pass slowly across the horizon. Tommy noticed that they seemed to be following their normal peace-time routine, the north-bound ships coming quite close inshore to gain the full advantage of the Gulf Stream, while the south-bound vessels steered an undeviating course farther out, taking no precautions against submarine attack.

"The President had sent down a staff from the White House to look after us, but apparently the cook had not been warned of the P.M.'s somewhat rigid preference for simple meals. He liked plain English cooking, and enjoyed roast beef or steak so much that, with rationing in force at home, he often saved half his portion at dinner-time and had it for breakfast next morning. I think he would have been perfectly happy to lunch off cold roast beef every day of his life, but our new cook felt he was on his mettle, and on our first day there he provided an elaborately prepared clam chowder. The coloured butler was mystified when the P.M. politely declined this—and he was completely nonplussed when Mr Churchill said firmly, 'If you haven't any clear soup, please bring me a plate of Bovril, double strength.'

"As the butler had never heard of Bovril (which the P.M. pronounced 'Boe-vril') the request caused some consternation in the kitchen."[1]

Throughout his holiday Churchill was able to keep in close touch with the work of the Conference, for a scrambler telephone connected the villa to the White House. The switchboard operator there could quickly obtain any number he required, and one day the Prime Minister decided he would like to have a word with Wendell Willkie. The fact that he had been able to spare so little time to see Roosevelt's Republican opponent during Willkie's visit to England after the Presidential election had long been on his mind, but he had not liked to suggest a meeting while he himself was under the President's roof. Now, however, he asked Francis Brown, who had remained on duty at the White House, to find out where Willkie was and get him on the line.

Brown had a list of code names for various important people whom the Prime Minister was likely to contact in the United States, but when the call came through from Pompano the line was indistinct, and, thinking that the Prime Minister wanted to speak to the President, he put him straight through to Roosevelt's study. A very confused conversation followed, with Churchill trying to persuade the President (whom he took to be Willkie) to join his train for a few hours on the return journey, and Roosevelt vainly endeavouring to discover what he was talking about. When Churchill found he was speaking to the President he was much embarrassed, but happily Roosevelt himself realized that this was only a friendly gesture, and no more was thought or said of the matter.

Churchill's rest by the sea lasted five days. Greatly refreshed, he left Florida on January 10 to return to Washington. Before joining the special train he decided to lunch with old friends, Colonel Jacques Balsan and his wife, with whom he had spent his last holiday in France in August 1939.[2] The war had driven them from their château near Ivry; now they were living in a new home just inland from West Palm Beach.

As it happened, the Balsans had a guest staying with them, and, knowing the Prime Minister would prefer to lunch with them alone, they suggested to her that she might like to spend this particular day with friends. The guest was, however, none other than Elsa Maxwell, high priestess of

[1] C. R. Thompson, Notes.
[2] Madame Balsan had formerly been married to Mr Churchill's first cousin, the ninth Duke of Marlborough.

international Society and, moreover, a newspaper columnist. Although she readily agreed to the plan, Miss Maxwell was far too astute not to notice the Balsans' anxiety to have the house to themselves, and, deciding that something of unusual interest must be afoot, she returned with all speed—but only in time to exchange a parting word with the Prime Minister in the hall.

By the time Churchill arrived back in Washington many major problems concerning the future direction of the war had been thrashed out. The entire military and economic resources of Britain and America were to be pooled, and agreement had been reached for the creation of a combined Chiefs of Staff Organization, which was henceforward to assume the main responsibility for the conduct of all operations. Perhaps most important of all, however, was the decision that the first aim of the Allies must be the defeat of the Axis in Europe; settlement of America's score in the Pacific would come later. Against the instincts of Churchill, who foresaw the difficulty of any unified control of such a vast area as the Far East, General Wavell was appointed Commander-in-Chief of all the Allied forces in that region.[3] At the final session of the Conference agreement was reached on the composition of a Joint Munitions Assignment Board, which Harry Hopkins and Lord Beaverbrook were to head in their respective countries.

* * * * *

When, just before midnight on January 14, the Prime Minister set out on the first leg of the long journey home he intended to fly from Norfolk, Virginia, to Bermuda and there rejoin *Duke of York*, but before he went to bed in the train that night he asked if it was feasible to fly all the way home. Tommy replied that if Captain Kelly-Rogers, the senior pilot of the B.O.A.C. flying-boats, saw no objection from the load and range point of view it would be easy enough to alert ships along the route as an additional safety measure.

The idea of cutting out the long sea voyage was strengthened in the Prime Minister's mind when he discovered the comfort offered by the great Boeing flying-boat—the biggest aircraft in the world at that time—on the flight to Bermuda next day. He was impressed, too, by the obvious capabilities of its captain. Kelly-Rogers, a big, bluff Irishman, thirty-six years of age, had come to America in the previous year to take delivery of these Boeing Clippers which the British Government had purchased. With them he had inaugurated an all-the-year-round Transatlantic service.[4]

Churchill cross-examined him about the problems of flying direct to England, and when he reached Bermuda the Prime Minister returned to

[3] Wavell did not, in fact, ever take up this appointment.

[4] At the end of the war Kelly-Rogers launched the first British land-plane service between London and New York with Constellation aircraft. He is now Deputy General Manager of Ireland's national airline, Aer Lingus.

the subject. "It is a war-time convenience that I should reach home as soon as possible," he said. "I would like you to work out with Sir Charles Portal whether we can make this flight to-morrow."

Kelly-Rogers saw no difficulties, provided that he was asked to take no more than ten passengers. Up to this point Tommy had been an enthusiastic supporter of the plan, but when they began to go into details it suddenly dawned on him that there might not be room for him after all. Some one pointed out that Brigadier Hollis, who had to take back all the Cabinet papers, had been left off the passenger list, and although the Prime Minister suggested that Tommy could toss up with John Martin for the last place if they could persuade the captain of the aircraft to take eleven Kelly-Rogers firmly refused to increase the load. He was still adamant when Tommy woke him up in the middle of the night to ask if he could take the place of the steward. It was firmly pointed out that the steward had certain flying duties to perform as well as serving the meals.

Churchill himself has described the departure from Bermuda next day, and Tommy's chagrin at being left behind:

> He explained how deeply wounded he was at the idea of going home by sea. I reminded him of his devotion to the naval service, and of the pleasures to a hardy sailor of a life on the ocean wave. I dwelt upon the undeniable hazards from the U-boats. He was quite inconsolable. . . . We taxied out to the far end of the harbour, leaving Tommy lamenting as bitterly as Lord Ullin in the poem. . . . Never before and never afterwards were we separated in these excursions.[5]

The flight was uneventful, and when the Prime Minister, who had a large and comfortable suite in the rear of the aircraft, retired to bed he slept soundly. By the time he awoke and went forward to find out the estimated position at dawn, however, the Clipper had for some hours been flying through a grey wilderness of cloud, and soon Churchill appears to have become convinced that they were off course:

> Presently Portal, who had been studying the position, had a word with the captain, and then said to me, "We are going to turn north at once." This was done, and after another half-hour in and out of the clouds we sighted England. . . . Later on I learnt that if we had held on our course for another five or six minutes before turning northwards we should have been over the German batteries in Brest.[6]

From consideration of the evidence available it seems doubtful that the Clipper and its passengers were in the hazardous position that the Prime Minister imagined. Kelly-Rogers and his co-pilots, Loraine and Shakespeare, were admittedly navigating by a combination of astronomical

[5] Churchill, Vol. III, pp. 627–628. [6] *Ibid.*, p. 629.

observations and dead reckoning which, in the cloud conditions prevailing over much of the route, could well have produced a possibility of error. But although wireless silence was otherwise maintained the Boeing was transmitting a three-letter code signal at regular intervals. By taking bearings on this the flight control organization in Britain could keep its course under observation. As the Clipper neared England the Wing Commander on duty at the flight control centre was able to follow the movements of the aircraft more closely. He for one strenuously asserts that at no time was the plane within ninety miles of Brest.

The flight plan led to Milford Haven, where a special train was waiting, but the weather deteriorated, and when still west of Ireland Kelly-Rogers decided to divert to Poole. Before reaching Land's End, however, he was informed that the weather had closed in over Poole as well, and he therefore decided to make for Plymouth Sound, which was still open and nearest to hand.

He altered course to the southward, but his only concern was whether the alteration had been big enough. He therefore asked Land's End for a bearing, and on checking this he changed course again to pass just south of the Lizard. At the moment when he did this he had reached his farthest distance to the south. Soon the Clipper was using its automatic direction-finder in conjunction with the transmitter at Plympton, and after a few minutes Shakespeare, the Chief Officer, pointed downward. Through a gap in the fog Kelly-Rogers saw the Mewstone, and then the R.A.F. station at Mount Batten, for which they were heading. The final approach was made from the seaward side to avoid any risk of collision with the balloon barrage over Plymouth.

The Prime Minister's transatlantic crossing had taken only eighteen hours twenty-three minutes. He was delighted with his first long journey by air, and if his misapprehension over the Clipper's position caused him any anxiety at the time he soon dismissed it from his mind. A few hours after he arrived back at Downing Street a signal reached *Duke of York*, still far out in the Eastern Atlantic:

Following for Commander Thompson from Prime Minister

MISSED YOU VERY MUCH ON TRIP WHICH WAS GREAT SUCCESS. BETTER LUCK NEXT TIME.

Not long afterwards Kelly-Rogers was summoned to Number Ten. There the Prime Minister presented him with a beautifully inscribed silver tray as a personal memento of the flight from Bermuda.

17

An Unhappy Homecoming

IT WAS not a happy homecoming. Messages from Wavell had already indicated that resistance in Malaya might be shortlived. Now he revealed that even Singapore—hitherto regarded as a fortress capable of withstanding prolonged siege—was in point of fact dangerously vulnerable to assault on its landward side. Since the Australian Government was already protesting bitterly at British policy in the Far East, which, they claimed, had paved the way for the swift successes so far achieved by the Japanese, this was an unpleasant shock, but worse was to come. In the desert, where all had promised so well and Auchinleck's forces had reached the Libyan frontier, Rommel suddenly launched a violent counter-attack. Before the War Cabinet realized what was happening the evacuation of Benghazi was imminent, just when the Royal Navy had got the port in working order again and had landed 3000 tons of petrol. At a stroke all Auchinleck's plans for staging his next major offensive—the advance into Tripoli due to start in February—were brought to naught.

The full implications of this setback were not at this stage recognized by the Press or the public in England, but already there was widespread confusion and dismay at the news from the Far East. And from Parliament and the newspapers came blunt criticism of the conduct of affairs on the home front. Declaring that "production is now the major problem of the war," *The Spectator* called for a thorough overhaul of the machinery in Whitehall and cited disturbing examples of the overlapping of Government departments and general inefficiency. "There is much public uneasiness and it must not be smothered," said the *Manchester Guardian* in a leading article. On the eve of the full-dress debate which Churchill was to open with a review of the war situation Sir William Beveridge crystallized this prevailing uneasiness in a letter to *The Times*:

> The whole people, with exceptions probably still insignificant, want Mr Churchill as Prime Minister to lead them through the war to victory. A growing, and by now, I believe, a considerable proportion of the people feel that they need a different Government.

After questioning the calibre of some of the country's leaders, the disposition of Allied resources, and Mr Churchill's wisdom in combining the rôle of Prime Minister and Minister of Defence he went on to say:

> These comments are not meant to shift by a hair the conviction that Mr Churchill is the right war leader and one for whose existence the British peoples and all free peoples should be thankful. They do lead to the suggestion that Mr Churchill should be willing to resolve, as he alone can resolve, the dilemma of the British nation by remaining Prime Minister but revising some of his views and deciding to change both the structure and some of the personnel of his Government.

A deep-rooted loyalty to those who shared his burden made it difficult for the Prime Minister to view these demands for new blood in the Government with complete detachment. Unjustifiably but not unnaturally he felt a sense of personal affront. He was, too, undeniably sensitive to any proposal that his powers as Minister of Defence should be curtailed.

> The Press was full of suggestions that I should remain Prime Minister and make the speeches but cede the actual control of the war to some one else. I resolved to yield nothing to any quarter, to take the prime and direct personal responsibility upon myself, and to demand a Vote of Confidence from the House of Commons,

he wrote afterwards.[1] This tactic was, however, to bring further criticism upon him.

> He makes a mistake in waving Votes of Confidence about, and in asserting the indivisibility of the Government. His loyalty is admirable, but since no one wants to turn the Government out, and since every one wants only to improve its efficiency the securing of overwhelming votes is a manœuvre that has no virtue. The public disquiet about our lamentable failures in the East and about the pace of our war production needs to be met with frankness and without respect of persons.[2]

On this point of procedure Mr Churchill remained adamant. Realizing the steadying effect that it would have on opinion throughout the world, and particularly in countries where the British political system was not

[1] Churchill, Vol. IV, p. 54.
[2] *Manchester Guardian*, January 19, 1942.

fully understood, he regarded a Vote of Confidence as essential.[3] And there was never any doubt that the crowded House which listened to his long and candid survey of the whole war scene—a survey in which he spoke frankly of the difficulties confronting the Allies, with their straitened resources, in the Far East—would give him the support which he demanded.

In the speeches which followed Sir Herbert Williams, the Conservative Member for South Croydon, ridiculed the idea that a Vote of Confidence was in any way necessary. "It is like going into Church on Sunday and the parson starting the service by proposing a Vote of Confidence in the Almighty"—and then went on to attack the "deplorable" inefficiency of the Civil Service; Lord Winterton, one of several speakers who complained that the Prime Minister took too great a burden on his own shoulders, compared him with Dr W. G. Grace, "who went in first, invariably remained in until the last wicket fell, and bowled the whole of the time." And charges of blundering, mismanagement, misjudgment, and lack of foresight were bandied about with considerable freedom and imprecision.

On the whole, however, it was a surprisingly good-humoured debate, conducted with more restraint than had been generally expected. The Prime Minister's own convincing speech had done much to quieten the more irresponsible and hot-headed critics. When it came to a division the vote for the Government was 464 to one, the solitary dissenter being James Maxton, who laughed gaily at his own discomfiture.

To meet the demands for a strengthening of his Government the Prime Minister made several changes and created one important new post—Minister of Production. This was offered to Lord Beaverbrook. When ill-health compelled his resignation his place was taken by Oliver Lyttelton, hitherto Minister of State in the Middle East. Sir Kingsley Wood and Arthur Greenwood retired from the War Cabinet, to which a new recruit was Sir Stafford Cripps, lately Ambassador in Moscow, who now assumed the joint rôle of Lord Privy Seal and Leader of the House of Commons.

The loss of Lord Beaverbrook, who for some time had been suffering grievously from the asthma which had plagued him so long, was keenly felt by the Prime Minister, who had had great difficulty in persuading him to undertake the new task in the first place. Despite many personal disagreements there was a close bond between the two men, founded on their association during the First World War and strengthened by a mutual regard for each other's qualities. An antipathy which had latterly developed between Beaverbrook and Ernest Bevin, the Minister of

[3] Goebbels, for one, took a realistic view. Before the debate opened he noted, "In London things look none too good. Even though in my opinion the recurring rumours of a Government crisis are grossly exaggerated, nevertheless one cannot overlook the fact that the English people are very restive and apprehensive. . . . Churchill must work very hard to dispel this unrest and worry. But I suppose he will succeed once again, all the more so since England has nobody to put in his place." (*The Goebbels Diaries*, p. 9.)

Labour, had sorely tried the Prime Minister's patience, but Beaverbrook's departure at this stage deprived Churchill of a comrade whose support meant much more to him than most people realized.

* * * * *

In the weeks to come Winston Churchill, still outwardly the proud, defiant, and indomitable leader of a Government reinforced in power, was to feel the need for personal support and encouragement to a greater extent, perhaps, than at any time in his life. A quarter of a century earlier the bitter failure in the Dardanelles had been hard enough to endure. But now he bore the responsibility for everything, and as blow after blow continued to fall the chorus of criticism swelled once more.

By the end of January the whole of Western Cyrenaica was again in enemy hands; over-confidence, faulty tactical leadership, and the inexperience of an untried Armoured Division in facing Rommel's tanks had all played a part in the debacle. Everywhere the enemy seemed to be seizing the initiative. Churchill's reaction to the passage of the *Scharnhorst* and the *Gneisenau* through the English Channel was one of utter incredulity, although the Admiralty, who could muster no adequate surface forces to prevent such an attempt, had warned that this shortest route back to their home waters from Brest was the most likely one to be taken by the German squadron. Three days later Singapore fell, and in the shadow of "the worst disaster and largest capitulation in British history," as he termed it, the Prime Minister broadcast to the world.

He sounded desperately tired, and his voice as he prophesied "hard, adverse war for many months ahead" lacked its usual vibrant and challenging ring. When, however, he spoke of the fierce Soviet resistance, and dwelt for a moment on the prospect facing the German armies—"disaster, failure, the shame of unspeakable crimes . . . and the icy winds that blow across the Russian snows"—there was a note of exultation. After an appeal for unity he ended with the simple, stirring call for fortitude: "Let us move forward steadfastly into the storm . . . and through the storm."

The brave words he spoke that night concealed an increasing sense of frustration and depression. To some of those closest to him he hinted that he was seriously thinking of handing over his responsibilities. Underestimating the solid support which he could count on from the nation as a whole, he was distressed by the sniping at him from certain governing circles and sections of the Press. Tired and dispirited, he no longer felt certain that the man in the street was not echoing the strictures so freely passed upon his leadership in the West End clubs, and one day in the Map Room he asked a senior naval officer point-blank what he considered were the views of the rank and file of the country. Did they accept what they read in the Press, or were they really prepared to support him in the bad days? He continued to talk dejectedly in this strain for some time. When on a motion by Lord Addison the loss of Singapore was debated in the House of Lords the Prime Minister was attacked by both Lord Hankey and Admiral of the Fleet Lord Chatfield for concentrating so much power in his own hands; the constitution and functions of the Defence Committee were strongly criticized.

Churchill was stung to retaliation. In a speech shortly afterwards he said ironically:

"When one is burdened by the very hard labour of the task and its cares, sorrows, and responsibilities there may sometimes steal across the mind a feeling of impatience at the airy and jaunty detachment of some of those critics who feel so confident of their knowledge, and feel so sure of their ability to put things right. If I should be forced, as I hope I shall not be, to yield to such a temptation I hope you will remember how difficult it is to combine the attitude of proper meekness and humility towards assailants at home with those combative and pugnacious qualities, with the spirit of offensive and counter-attack, which we feel were never more needful than now against the common enemy."

During the debate in the Lords the Prime Minister had also been reproached for what Chatfield called the "perfectly intolerable" working hours which he imposed on his subordinates. To-day such a charge, levelled as it was at the height of war, may smack of triviality and a lack of proportion, but to the long-suffering Chiefs of Staff and others who were dragged from their beds to attend meetings in the middle of the night this was, in fact, far from a trivial matter.

"At the hour when most men, exhausted by the day's labour, were seeking recreation or sleep," writes Brooke's biographer, the Prime Minister "awoke to full and volcano-like activity ten times greater than that of any ordinary being."[4] He would then gather his jaded advisers around him and bombard them with plans and projects, facts and figures. Although they had been working without rest since the previous morn this was not a factor to which Churchill ever managed to attach importance. His extraordinary routine was the one that suited him best, and since he had to bear the chief burden he saw no reason to alter his habits.

If he had spent his mornings less industriously it would have eased the strain, but he had always been loth to sleep for long at any one time. Soon after eight o'clock in the morning he was already sitting up in bed ready to resume work.

The first person he usually saw when he rang his bell was Charles Barker, an imperturbable, bespectacled Civil Servant who brought him the telegrams which had come in overnight. Often the Prime Minister would

[4] Bryant, *op. cit.*, Vol. I, p. 302.

begin dictating before Sawyers, his valet, had even removed his breakfast tray. He had brought dictation to a fine art, rarely going back on anything he had already said, but to the shorthand writers this morning session was always an ordeal. The Prime Minister worked at high pressure, and they could not afford to relax for a moment; but the atmosphere in the small room soon became so heavy with cigar-smoke that they had difficulty in breathing and there were constant distractions—phone calls to Mr Eden, who invariably had to be fetched from his bath; the comings and goings of Sawyers; interruptions from secretaries and staff officers; and the arrival of the "C" boxes containing the latest Top Secret messages.

There was a special ritual over the "C" boxes, the Prime Minister locking and unlocking them personally with a silver key which the King had given him. The boxes had locks of a unique design, which supposedly made them proof against any unauthorized attempt to open them, but one day Charles Barker, who was an expert on locks—as well as a great authority on old English silver—was idly examining one when he made an interesting discovery. He told Desmond Morton, who offered to show the Prime Minister that it was perfectly easy to abstract the contents of the "C" boxes without using a key at all. Barker was promptly invited to give Mr Churchill a demonstration. Ignoring the lock altogether, he merely undid four screws on the underside, whereupon the bottom of the box fell out!

In addition to Barker or Kinna one of the Private Secretaries always visited the Prime Minister before he had finished breakfast. At this time the Principal Private Secretary was John Martin, who has already been mentioned. Under him worked Leslie Rowan, a former Private Secretary to the Chancellor of the Exchequer, and captain of England at hockey; John Peck, who had been with Churchill at the Admiralty; and Francis Brown and Jock Colville, from the Foreign Office.

For long periods Colville and Brown alternated as a member of the team, for each was determined to join up. Colville volunteered for the R.A.F. and was rejected for defective eyesight. He had contact lenses fitted, and tried again. To the Prime Minister's annoyance—for Colville had become almost indispensable to him—he succeeded at this second attempt and went off to serve as a fighter pilot. Brown, temporarily unfit for military service at the time, eventually became restive, and when he persuaded Churchill to let him rejoin his regiment Colville was recalled. He managed to escape again, however, and went back to his squadron when Francis Brown, wounded and partially disabled, returned unwillingly to Whitehall.

The Prime Minister had two other senior secretaries, but they did not normally concern themselves with current operational matters. Anthony

Bevir, who remained with him throughout the war, dealt mainly with Patronage work, and Miss Watson looked after the Parliamentary and political side.[5]

The 'operational' secretaries remained on call for twelve days at a time and then had forty-eight hours off, but no one in the inner circle at Downing Street, from the Chiefs of Staff, the Joint Planners, and Ismay and his deputies, to the Prime Minister's immediate entourage, which included his own personal secretary, Mrs Hill, and the girl shorthand-typists, took account of their hours of duty.

In this context two devoted servants of the Churchill family also deserve mention. Mrs Landemare, the Churchills' cook, had worked for the family off and on at Chartwell before the war. On the day war broke out she wrote offering her services as a permanent member of the household staff, and stayed for fifteen years. Short and very stout, she was married to a celebrated French chef. At Downing Street she produced superb meals, often under most difficult conditions. When later in the war Mr Churchill fell gravely ill abroad one of the first anxious messages he received was a telegram from his cook. "Dear Mrs Landemare . . . how very nice of her to worry about me," he said. "Please send her a special signal saying that I'm much better."

Frank Sawyers, the butler-valet, was a little, baldish Cumbrian with a round, florid face, piercing blue eyes, and a pronounced lisp. He seemed to work all hours of the day and night, and long after every one else had gone to bed Tommy would find him still busily pressing suits; yet he was always up and about soon after dawn.

Something of a wag, he had a way with Mr Churchill that no one else dared to emulate. He would chide him on his choice of a waistcoat or jacket, remonstrate with him when he looked like being late for an appointment, and would often tell him sharply that it was high time he was in bed. Mr Churchill took these admonitions in surprisingly good part. Even when —on one of the journeys by sea across the Atlantic—Sawyers absent-mindedly squeezed a strip of liquid shoe polish on to the Prime Minister's toothbrush and induced him to clean his teeth with it Mr Churchill bore the shock with remarkable stoicism. Sawyers worshipped him, and every year one of the birthday presents which delighted the Prime Minister most

[5] In addition to Martin, mentioned earlier, the Prime Minister's secretarial team have subsequently had distinguished careers. Sir Leslie Rowan, K.C.B., C.V.O., left Government service in 1958 to become Director of Finance, Vickers Ltd; Sir Anthony Bevir, K.C.V.O., C.B.E., was Secretary for Appointments to the Prime Minister, 1947–56; J. H. Peck, C.M.G., became the United Kingdom's representative on the Council of Europe in 1959; Francis Brown has held a number of important diplomatic posts and was created C.M.G. in 1959; and J. R. Colville, C.B., C.V.O., who became Joint Principal Private Secretary to the Prime Minister (1951–55) is now a director of the merchant banking firm of Philip Hill, Higginson, and Co.

was the flowering plant—usually a cineraria or an azalea—which his valet bought for him.

* * * * *

Writing to Smuts at the end of March, Churchill said, "Just now I am having a very rough time, but we must remember how much better things are than a year ago, when we were all alone. We must not lose our faculty to dare, particularly in dark days."[6] In the spring of 1942, however, the dark days which had started with the desert retreat and Singapore's surrender stretched on and on.

By early March Japan had completed the conquest of the Dutch East Indies; soon Rangoon fell, and with the loss of Burma came the threat of Japanese attacks on Ceylon and the Indian mainland. India's leaders began to agitate for their country's independence. Australia, also fearing invasion renewed their demands for the return of their fighting men from the Middle East. In the desert there was stalemate, with Auchinleck firmly resisting the Prime Minister's calls for a renewal of his offensive, and it seemed doubtful whether Malta could survive much longer.

Wherever one looked for an opportunity to dare a limiting factor was the desperate shortage of shipping. War supplies for Russia were piling up at the ports, but lack of escorts made every Murmansk convoy a reckless gamble. The United States could give little effective aid, for a mere handful of U-boats were inflicting shattering losses off the American coast. In March alone nearly half a million tons of shipping were lost, the German submarines picking off their victims at will, for it was many months before an effective American convoy system came into operation. The German surface raiders could have taken terrible toll, but Hitler forbade them to leave home waters. After the Vaagsö operations in the previous December, when Combined Operations assault forces were put ashore for a short time at various points in the approaches to Vestfjord, he became convinced that Norway was the "zone of decision." So Raeder was ordered to keep his heavy warships and a large U-boat force close at hand.

Norway was, in fact, much in Churchill's mind. All through the spring and early summer he urged the planning of an operation—given the code name of *Jupiter*—which involved an amphibious assault on the Norwegian coast. And for a time it seemed possible that *Jupiter* might well become part of a joint Anglo-American strategic scheme. The President, too, had been studying ways and means of taking the offensive, and early in April he sent Harry Hopkins and Marshall to England to explain what was in his mind.

The Americans brought with them outline plans for a major cross-Channel assault, to take place in 1943. To give some relief to the hard-

[6] Churchill, Vol. IV, p. 202.

pressed Russian armies while this was in preparation they proposed that a mainly British operation, more limited in scope, should be carried out in the coming autumn. They had in mind the seizing of a bridgehead at Cherbourg or Brest; the Prime Minister, feeling that any Allied force put ashore on the Cherbourg Peninsula could be all too easily bottled up without drawing off an appreciable number of German troops or aircraft from the Russian front, was in favour of attempting either *Jupiter* or *Gymnast*, the long-debated descent on the North African coast to link up with the desert army. In the end *Gymnast* was to gain the day.

Before General Marshall left England the Prime Minister took him on one of his inspection tours. He wanted him to see British troops training in the Salisbury area, and Fighter Command had also laid on a demonstration of low-level strafing by Spitfires on the downs near Warminster. On the previous day a rehearsal for this was staged in misty weather, and, breasting a slope on the downs, one of the Spitfire pilots mistook the markers laid for him. Instead of attacking dummy vehicles, he opened fire on the spectators lining the course and many were killed. The Prime Minister was therefore asked if he would like the Fighter Command demonstration to be cancelled in view of the risk, but he vehemently refused. General Marshall carried out his inspection, and the calibre and bearing of a Guards battalion he visited made a great impression on him.

Next day, jubilant at having reached agreement on the main points they had raised with the Prime Minister and the British Chiefs of Staff, he and Hopkins left for Northern Ireland to see American troops training there. Tommy, who saw them off, was later given a hilarious account by Harry Hopkins of their subsequent misadventures, which included a night of appalling discomfort in a draughty Irish castle and a narrow escape from being arrested as spies in a village on the Scottish coast.

The first Tommy knew of this was a call from Scotland Yard. The police at Portpatrick had reported that two suspicious characters calling themselves Mr A. H. Hones and Mr C. G. Mell were trying to ring up the President of the United States from a local inn. Police reinforcements were already hastening to Portpatrick when Tommy, who recognized the cover names which Hopkins and Marshall were using, got through to the number Scotland Yard had given. A few moments later a rather agitated Hopkins—alias Mr Hones—was speaking from the little Scottish fishing village to Mr Roosevelt in the White House.

Soon after Hopkins and Marshall left Stranraer by flying-boat on their journey home a Russian bomber landed near Peterhead, and it fell to Tommy to act as host to the strangest visitors who ever stayed at Chequers during the war.

18

Molotov Comes to Stay

THE new arrivals were the Soviet Foreign Minister, Molotov, and a Russian delegation. Russia were anxious to conclude a Treaty of Alliance, but since they proposed that this should embody recognition of certain territorial claims—among them the right to permanent occupation of the Baltic States overrun in 1940—it was clear that an Anglo-Soviet agreement could not be reached without more detailed discussions than Mr Eden had been able to hold during his visit to Moscow. Stalin's offer to send his Foreign Minister to London had therefore been welcomed.

In the message to Churchill proposing the visit Stalin had also stressed his desire to learn what plans Britain had in mind for opening a Second Front in Europe in 1942.

As Molotov had asked that he and his immediate entourage should be accommodated somewhere outside London, Churchill put Chequers at his disposal, and decided to remain himself at Storey's Gate.

"For some reason unknown to us Molotov's departure from Moscow was repeatedly delayed, and the reception committee, headed by Cadogan, who went to Scotland to meet him were left kicking their heels day after day. The Russians also sent a party north from the London Embassy; they flew in one of the Flamingos we had used ourselves from time to time, and the plane crashed, killing the Russian Air Attache and three companions. When Molotov's own aircraft finally appeared it made a landfall many miles south of the expected point, but fortunately the A.A. defences did not open fire.

"As there was a lot to do at Chequers I stayed there and met the party for the first time when they arrived in the P.M.'s special train at Wendover.

We had been told that only six of the Russians—Molotov himself; Pavlov, later the interpreter for Stalin at many Allied conferences; and two secretaries, a personal bodyguard, and a woman typist—would be staying in the house. At the station we therefore showed the rest into cars which were to take them to London. To our surprise they all followed us back to Chequers. And they flatly refused to leave.

"We were expecting twelve for dinner, for Molotov had asked Maisky and one or two of the senior officials from the Russian Embassy to stay on and return to London later. Instead, we now had twenty to feed, and all of them seemed to be insisting on taking up residence at Chequers. While I was trying to sort out this muddle Geoffrey Wilson, who had been sent down by the Foreign Office to act as interpreter, was also in trouble. When he took the Russians already on our list to their rooms they refused to enter them until Molotov had given permission. So the baggage remained in the waiting cars, and there were heated arguments until Maisky appeared and ordered fourteen of the party to go back with him after dinner."[1]

The discussions which began in London next day between the Prime Minister, Attlee, Eden, and the British Chiefs of Staff on the one side, and Molotov, Maisky, Rear-Admiral Kharlamov, and Major-General Asseyev on the other, were conducted in a much more friendly atmosphere than the British representatives had expected. The Russians seemed genuinely anxious to reach agreement; the chief stumbling-block was their desire for official recognition of their occupation of Eastern Poland, and claims on Roumania. It was Eden who eventually produced a workable solution, suggesting that, although Britain's own diplomatic commitments made any such recognition out of the question, there was no reason why a treaty of friendship should not be signed. The territorial questions were therefore left in abeyance.

While the talks continued life at Chequers followed a strange pattern. "When Molotov left in the morning we never knew what time he would arrive back, or how many people he would bring with him. The Embassy would ring up to say he would like to dine at 9.0 P.M. As the day wore on there would be further messages to say the party would be returning at 10.0 P.M., and then 11.0. Finally, when the food had been ruined beyond salvation, they would arrive about midnight. At breakfast there was a strange ritual. The secretaries would come down first, but the moment Molotov entered the room they would dash for the door and disappear, regardless of whether they had had anything to eat or not. This odd behaviour happened at no other meal, and we never discovered the reason for it."[2]

For the household staff life was full of surprises. To her dismay the head

[1] C. R. Thompson, Notes. [2] *Ibid.*

housemaid found a loaded revolver in Molotov's bed on the first morning. Afterwards she was never allowed by the Russians to enter the room until the bodyguard or the typist had been sent for; they would then sit there, watching everything she did. The housekeeper, Mrs Lamont, also had a disconcerting experience.

In view of the isolated position of the house a strict black-out was necessary. Although this was carefully explained to the Russians, it was not long before a sentry reported that a bright light was shining from one of the bedrooms. In her dressing-gown Mrs Lamont went out into the garden to identify the room, and then, climbing the stairs, she knocked and called out several times without getting any reply. Suddenly the door was flung open, and a figure leapt at her. It was Molotov himself, revolver in hand.

Each day one or two of the party would remain at the house. To kill time in the afternoons Tommy and Geoffrey Wilson tried to teach them golf croquet. One of the secretaries always insisted on bringing his brief-case with him, and they could never persuade him to let go of it for more than a few seconds. He would place it on the lawn close to him while he played a shot, and then snatch it up hurriedly as if he expected some one to make off with it.

The typist rarely emerged from the room allocated to her as an office, but though she sat at her desk for hour after hour, she appeared to do no work. If she thought anyone was within earshot she would start striking the keys of her typewriter in a desultory way, but it was evident that she did not know how to use the machine she had brought with her. Her precise rôle puzzled Tommy. Much later he learnt that the bodyguard too was not what he seemed. As Stalin left the Kremlin one day during Mr Churchill's first visit to Moscow he was accompanied by six Russian generals. To his astonishment Tommy saw that one of them was Molotov's watch-dog. His rank and status concealed, on his visit to England he had been regarded as no more than a personal servant throughout his stay at Chequers.

Twice during the week Mr Churchill drove out to Chequers for the evening. With Molotov, who was going to Washington for further discussions on the Second Front, he spent much time explaining the problems of a large-scale amphibious assault. On the Russians' final night at Chequers the Prime Minister gave a formal dinner-party for them.

Rationing, and the erratic hours which the Russians themselves kept, had prevented them from being entertained on anything like the scale provided for the Prime Minister and his party when they later visited Moscow, but on this occasion a special effort was made to produce an impressive menu. The *pièce de résistance* was quail. Where these birds had come from was a mystery, but the quail had obviously been a long time in the refrigerator. They were dry and tasteless, and Mr Churchill was extremely displeased. Catching Tommy's eye he said gruffly, "Tell Crankshaw that these miserable mice should never have been removed from Tutankhamen's tomb!"[3]

By this time, however, the Russians, who had dined nearly every night on soup and sandwiches owing to their late return from London, were clearly resigned to the odd feeding habits of their hosts, and the evening passed pleasantly enough. There were many toasts to the Anglo-Soviet Pact, which had been signed that afternoon. Next day Molotov left by air for Washington, and life at Chequers returned to a more peaceful routine.

* * * * *

By the end of May there were, for a welcome change, some fresh entries on the credit side of the Allied account. A combined operation to secure Madagascar, which had begun with the swift capture of the naval base at Diego Suarez from the Vichy French, was making encouraging headway; so encouraging, in fact, that Goebbels, who had not long before been speculating whether Churchill could survive as leader of the nation, now likened him to "a victorious Field Marshal."[4] The first thousand-bomber raid had been launched, on Cologne, and far away in the Pacific the United States Navy had gained a major success in the Battle of the Coral Sea.

In North Africa, however, events once more took an unhappy turn. On the night when the Prime Minister was bidding farewell to his Russian visitors Rommel opened a new offensive, and after heavy fighting his armour gained command of a vital area—the higher ground between El Adem and Knightsbridge. With this German success it became unpleasantly apparent that Tobruk—the key to any enemy advance on Egypt—could well be menaced.

At this moment the Prime Minister was preparing to leave for Washington. Already a decision on many pressing strategic problems was overdue, and he hesitated to postpone his visit. He therefore signalled to General Auchinleck emphasizing the importance of holding Tobruk at all costs. The reply he received was reassuring. Pointing out that his troops held far stronger positions than they had occupied in the previous year, Auchinleck declared that he had no intention whatever of giving up Tobruk. With this Churchill had to be content. On the night of June 16 he set out from Stranraer on his second war-time journey to America.

[3] Lieutenant-Colonel Sir Eric Crankshaw, K.C.M.G., as Secretary of the Government Hospitality Fund, was responsible for the catering during the Russians' stay at Chequers.

[4] "This man is a real ogre . . . brimful of lies and bumptiousness. The British Empire will owe its collapse to him." (*Diaries*, p. 155.)

There was much to discuss with the President, for although a statement —mainly intended for enemy consumption—had already hinted at the creation of a Second Front in Europe before the end of the year it was still difficult to see how this could be achieved. At the same time there was obviously a danger that if no landing was made on enemy territory in the near future the United States might well switch their main effort to the Pacific.

Another important item on the joint agenda was Tube Alloys. The American atomic research effort was now forging ahead fast; soon a start would have to be made on building the production plants. With the shortage of physicists in Britain, and industrial resources already stretched to the limit, it seemed likely that this would become an American responsibility.

As the Prime Minister was anxious to be away for the shortest possible time he decided against travelling by sea. Some time previously Kelly-Rogers had been warned to stand by. When the April days passed and no summons reached him at his cottage in the New Forest he wrote a plaintive note to John Martin. "The Prime Minister told me I was still held by the leg until he said otherwise. Maybe he has taken the manacles off, but how am I to know?" Now at last he received his orders, and the flying-boat *Bristol* was made ready for a non-stop journey of well over 3000 miles to the Potomac River.

The Prime Minister took with him only a small party this time—the C.I.G.S., Brigadier Stewart (Director of Plans, War Office), and Ismay; Sir Charles Wilson, his doctor; and John Martin and Tommy. In order to avoid the Focke-Wulf bombers which prowled over the Western Approaches the take-off was delayed until just after dark. Twenty-seven hours later the Clipper came to rest on the waters of the Potomac off Anacostia. It had been a peaceful, uneventful flight, and every one apart from Mr Churchill seemed glad of the brief rest. Ismay, for one, was so exhausted that he slept for twelve hours on end. The Prime Minister, however, was his usual energetic self. He worked on his papers, went forward from time to time to talk to the crew, and at regular intervals he ate a hearty meal.

In vain Tommy pointed out that if meal-times were not specially adjusted they would find themselves in difficulties at the end of the journey. "The P.M. would have none of this. Ignoring Greenwich Mean Time and Local Time alike, he announced that he intended to go by Stomach Time. And he was relaxing with a whisky and soda and a cigar after a large dinner when we taxied to our moorings in the Potomac. By Mr Churchill's calculations it was then 11.0 P.M. (Stomach Time), but in Washington it was only 6.0 P.M., and sure enough Lord Halifax, who knew nothing about Stomach Time, had arranged a dinner-party at the

British Embassy. An hour after our arrival in America we began eating again. The P.M. took this second dinner in his stride, and afterwards he sat on the veranda and talked till 6.0 A.M. (Stomach Time). It seemed a very exhausting arrangement to me, but it evidently suited Mr Churchill."

* * * * *

The President was at Hyde Park, and when Churchill landed at New Hackensack, the nearest airfield, next day Roosevelt and his son James were there to meet him. The President had a Ford V8 convertible which had been specially adapted so that all the normal foot-controls could be operated by hand. After reaching Hyde Park—one of many large houses in a magnificent setting on the bank of the Hudson, with heavily wooded grounds running right down to the river's edge—he took the Prime Minister and Tommy for a drive round the estate.

"This was a hair-raising performance, for the President took a boyish delight in trying to outwit the Secret Servicemen following him in another car. Their job was never to let him out of their sight; *his* aim was to give them the slip, but he rarely succeeded for long, for although he knew the woodland tracks much better than they did they countered by posting several cars equipped with radio at strategic points. If one lost touch they hoped to alert another which would pick him up as soon as he emerged from cover. On this particular day the game went to him, for we were driving along quite a good track with the Secret Service in hot pursuit when he suddenly swerved to the left and crashed through some dense foliage on to a narrow, rutted path just passable for a car. The Secret Servicemen plunged through the gap after us, but this fitted in with Mr Roosevelt's scheme, for he told us that not far ahead there was a hairpin bend which he knew the larger Secret Service car would not negotiate. The ruse worked beautifully and when we last caught a glimpse of our escorts they were charging backwards and forwards on the hairpin without making any headway at all. The President kept to the woods and we never saw another Secret Service car till we broke cover close to the house."[5]

On their tour of the grounds Roosevelt took them round the building which he called the "Library"; crammed with souvenirs he had gathered from all parts of the world, it was more like a museum. The President was very proud of it—and he was greatly touched when Churchill told him he had brought a personal contribution to the collection. This was a complete set of his own books, which he had had magnificently bound in red leather by the London firm of Sangorski and Sutcliffe.

Only one night was spent at Hyde Park. Then the President and the Prime Minister travelled together to Washington. Hardly had they reached the White House before grave news arrived. Tobruk had fallen; 25,000

[5] C. R. Thompson, Notes.

Allied troops had been taken prisoner; and Admiral Harwood warned that in view of the growing enemy air threat to Alexandria he was sending the Mediterranean Fleet to greater safety south of the Suez Canal. Reports from American observers suggested that Rommel would be in Cairo within a week.

Churchill was dumbfounded. Once again a large Allied force had surrendered, it seemed, with humiliating readiness. Equally astonished was Admiral Sir Andrew Cunningham, who had only recently handed over command of the Mediterranean Fleet to Harwood in order to take up an important new post in Washington. With his Chief of Staff, Rear-Admiral Edelsten, he had some time earlier drawn up a secret plan for the evacuation of Alexandria if extreme danger threatened. But he had not for one moment envisaged such a plan being put into operation until the enemy reached the anti-tank ditch some ten miles from the city. Now, apparently, the Navy were preparing to leave Alexandria before Rommel had even arrived at El Alamein, eighty miles away.

The American reaction to the desert reverse was generous and unquestioning. They stripped their own 1st Armoured Division of three hundred Sherman tanks and a hundred self-propelled guns, and offered them for immediate shipment to the Middle East. Inevitably, however, the staff talks on the wider scene of the war opened in an atmosphere of chill foreboding, and there were bitter arguments on the subject of the Second Front. Churchill repeatedly counselled caution over the staging of a major cross-Channel landing, but in the end it was decided to press on with plans for invading Northern France in 1943, and this operation was given the code-name of *Bolero*. It was also agreed that a subsidiary landing must be attempted at an earlier date; if France or the Low Countries offered no reasonable prospect of success here it might be necessary to look more closely again at alternatives like *Jupiter* or *Gymnast*.

While all these operations were being examined in greater detail General Marshall suggested that Churchill and Brooke should visit Fort Jackson, in South Carolina, where a young general named Mark Clark was toughening up thousands of raw recruits to America's citizen army. A mass paratroop drop was staged for them, and the scale and intensity of the training programme at this vast camp made a deep impression on the British party.

This day in the field helped to take the Prime Minister's mind off ill news from home. Already the American Press was stridently reporting a political revolt in England. There were predictions that the fall of Tobruk would bring down the Government, and on the day Churchill arrived back in Washington a motion was tabled in the Commons in the name of Sir John Wardlaw-Milne, M.P. for Kidderminster. It asserted that the House "has no confidence in the central direction of the war."

This challenge to the Government was made more formidable by the identity of its sponsor. Sir John Wardlaw-Milne was no political adventurer, intent on seeking notoriety; he was an experienced and able backbencher, much liked and respected by all parties in the House where he had served for two decades. At this time he was chairman both of the Select Committee on National Expenditure and the Conservative Committee on Foreign Affairs. Many years before he had come into conflict with Churchill on the question of Government policy towards India. The rift had never been repaired, but though a suspicion seems to have formed in the Prime Minister's mind that Wardlaw-Milne was over-ready to embarrass the Government with captious criticism, this did less than justice to Wardlaw-Milne's sincerity and sense of responsibility. Prominent among the supporters of his motion were Churchill's old friend, Admiral of the Fleet Sir Roger Keyes, and the former Secretary of State for War, Leslie Hore-Belisha.

That night, after dining with Roosevelt and Hopkins, the Prime Minister left Washington to face the music. The flying-boat was waiting at Baltimore, and when they arrived there Tommy found Mike Reilly, the President's chief Secret Service agent, in a state of some excitement. A few minutes earlier his men had arrested an Irish-American employee of B.O.A.C. who had been standing close to the aircraft. Some one had heard him muttering Churchill's name over and over again. When the Secret Service pounced on him they found in his pocket a fully loaded revolver.

Characteristically Mr Churchill seemed quite unmoved by this alarming incident, and before the Clipper reached Botwood on the first leg of the flight home he ate a hearty breakfast. Once again, however, his fellow-passengers were forcibly reminded of the rigours of Stomach Time, for at the Newfoundland air base where the Clipper put down to refuel they found a veritable banquet of lobster and other shell-fish had been prepared for them.

At dawn thirteen hours later they sighted the Scottish coast, and the special train was waiting at Stranraer to carry them south.

19

Churchill and his Critics

IN SPITE of the personal implication in Sir John Wardlaw-Milne's motion of censure, the flood of criticism which filled the daily newspapers after the fall of Tobruk was directed mainly against "defective military leadership" and the shortcomings of the supply organizations.

The Times devoted most of a first leader, and an article entitled "Lessons of the Libyan Campaign," to the deficiencies of British tanks; the *Manchester Guardian* spoke of "painful weakness" in the system which "should unite the men who design, the men who choose, and the men who produce our weapons of war"; and the *Daily Mail*, basing their charges on a full-page article by their able war-correspondent, Alexander Clifford—headed "Our Army was not rightly handled"—declared that British generalship was "too slow, too cautious, and too easily led into traps." In the same newspaper Liddell Hart complained that British Army doctrine had always shown a preference for "soundness" rather than "subtly conceived surprise"; our older officers, he considered, were unable to adjust themselves to the "immense change in operating pace from slow-time to tank-time."

With the announcement of a two-day debate, to take place in the week following the Prime Minister's return, the emphasis of criticism shifted, however, to a closer examination of Churchill's own responsibility. In many quarters the debate was condemned as a "political manœuvre"—an over-astute move to discourage further rocking of the Government boat. "They know that their critics won't support [Wardlaw-Milne] in the lobbies, however high their feelings may be against the Government," said the *Daily Mirror*; "the strategy here seems decidedly better than that employed in Libya." And on the day Churchill reached Stranraer *The Times*, which carried news of a heavy defeat for the Government in a by-election at Maldon, declared that both Commons and country were "still strongly against this Vote of Confidence." Taking the same line, the *Manchester Guardian* spoke of

> the harm that . . . the personal angle does at the present critical stage of the war. It compels the Government to be combative in reply, and though the fireworks may make a pretty Parliamentary display they are not good for dispassionate searching; . . . they confuse and annoy the country which, unlike the critics, does not attribute every failure we have to the Prime Minister.

In this they were undoubtedly right. The public mood was one of uneasy perplexity, but Churchill's position as leader of the nation was unchallenged; in the country as a whole there was no disposition to blame the Prime Minister for the recent disasters. Oddly enough, however, Churchill himself still underestimated the support which he commanded.

The House of Commons was his god. And an unfavourable reaction from even a small section of its members was often enough to convince him of a widespread opposition. The desire for a full-dress debate on the conduct of the war, which some saw as a move of Machiavellian cunning, was in fact prompted by his deep-rooted veneration for the will of Parliament. It was only in the House of Commons, he felt, that the damage to British prestige abroad caused by the recent criticism could be repaired; only an overwhelming vote of confidence, freely expressed in Parliament, could put matters right in the eyes of the world. Providentially Wardlaw-Milne's censure motion had supplied the means by which this could be secured. When the Member for Kidderminster offered to withdraw it on the grounds that the debate might be harmful at such a critical time the Prime Minister firmly declined:

> *Mr Churchill to Sir John Wardlaw-Milne* *30th June [19]42*
>
> I brought your letter of June 30 before the War Cabinet this morning, and they desired me to inform you that in view of the challenge to the competence and authority of the Government, which has now for some days been spread throughout the world, it is imperative that the matter should go forward to an immediate issue, and for this all arrangements have been made.[1]

While Churchill tended to exaggerate the extent of the opposition to his leadership, undoubtedly there was, however, a hard core of men, influential both inside and outside the House, who would have welcomed his removal from office. He was the subject of much malicious gossip, and

[1] Churchill, Vol. IV, p. 353.

although his complete pre-occupation with the task in hand made him normally impervious to this he was far from unaware of its existence. At times such as this, when he paused to reflect on the strange, apparently unreasoning resentment which he seemed to inspire in certain circles he was puzzled and distressed by it. Many years before Admiral Fisher had said to him, "It is really curious why they hate you so." But perhaps it was not so curious after all, for Churchill had never courted popularity, or taken the trouble to establish a warmth in his personal relationships with more than a small handful of his fellow-men. Absorbed in his own affairs, he seemed to many people brusque, vain, intolerant, and overbearing. He "gave the *impression*—for this was not wholly true—of being untellable, intransigent, obstinately sticking to his own point of view; . . . what was lacking was some intuitive tactile sense to tell him what others were thinking and (especially) feeling."[2] And because he lacked any such understanding—indeed, he rarely attached more than momentary importance to the humouring of people outside his own close circle—he was all the more perplexed and hurt by malicious rumours and innuendoes when they were reported to him.

He had very few intimate friends in the normally accepted sense of the word—few close acquaintances unconnected with his working life. To a slightly lesser extent this was true, too, of Mrs Churchill, who had never led a social life, choosing to concentrate all her interest and energy on her husband.

The only men who really belonged to the inner circle were the "Prof," Brendan Bracken, and Lord Beaverbrook. Among women there were Venetia Montagu (the talented widow of the Liberal, Edwin Montagu), Horatia Seymour, beautiful and intelligent, who had been one of Mrs Churchill's bridesmaids, and Freda Casa Maury.

The war had, admittedly, brought others very close to Churchill, in particular "Pug" Ismay, Jock Colville, and Leslie Rowan, but these were men with whom he worked day in and day out. In a sense they were too closely associated with events to fill the rôle of counsellor and confidant in the predicament which faced him now.

* * * * *

When the debate opened on July 1 Sir John Wardlaw-Milne developed his attack with some skill. Contending that no one person could successfully combine control of the entire military and political field, and that owing to his preoccupations as Minister of Defence the Prime Minister had been forced to neglect many important matters which should have engaged his attention on the home front, he called for a "strong and independent man" to take command of the Armed Forces. He dealt in some

[2] A. L. Rowse, *The Later Churchills*, p. 454.

detail with Allied weaknesses in guns and tanks; "in my view we are not yet getting the full production of which this country is capable. . . . Production, the mainstay of the Army, is suffering badly from the want of a single head. We want some one to cut the red tape, to inaugurate new methods, and to put an end to the interminable delays in getting decisions."

Unfortunately for his case, however, some of his suggestions for bringing new and vital leadership to the military scene were not as convincing as his recital of the Government's failings. The Supreme Commander he had in mind must, he declared, reign unchallenged over the three Services, appointing his own Admirals, Generals, and Air Marshals. But he must be ready to resign immediately if he did not get what he wanted. The House was still weighing the implications of this military dictatorship when Wardlaw-Milne made an even more surprising proposal.

He called for the appointment of a Commander-in-Chief of the British Army, and here he was unexpectedly specific. It was "very desirable," he urged, that this post should be filled by the Duke of Gloucester.

This suggestion was received with unfeigned astonishment. It embarrassed the House by involving the Royal Family in a matter of controversy. At a stroke it destroyed much of the force of a speech which had so far commanded close and respectful attention. Mr McGovern, for one, waxed so sarcastic that the Speaker was forced to intervene.

Wardlaw-Milne's case lost further ground with the very next speech, for Sir Roger Keyes, who had only agreed to second the motion in the quaint belief that it involved no personal attack on the Prime Minister, was so intent on belabouring his old enemies, the Chiefs of Staff, that he quickly lost the thread of the main argument he was supposed to be putting forward.

Keyes was a muddled speaker—passionately sincere, but unable to pursue a logical train of thought. Seeking to expose the baleful influence imposed on the war effort by the Whitehall machine, he now demanded that the Prime Minister should be given not less but far wider freedom of action, which was not at all what his companions in opposition had in mind. He went on to attack "the pusillanimous and short-sighted policy" of the Admiralty in two world wars; he castigated the First Lord, the Home Secretary, and the Ministry of Labour; and he demanded the retention of Churchill "at the head of a real National Government." Long before he had finished it was almost impossible to determine whether he was speaking for or against the motion, and most of the stuffing had been knocked out of it.

Even so, many of the speeches that followed were surprisingly half-hearted. Plainly there was widespread feeling that the structure of the War Cabinet had its defects, and that the Prime Minister was trying to do too much. At the same time few felt like entering the lists against him; he was so obviously the only man to lead the country. The critics did their best over some of the other Ministers, and there was a full-blooded attack on Oliver Lyttelton, who delivered a long and immensely ponderous speech, full of facts and figures, and was barracked almost continuously. In a laboured way Arthur Greenwood expressed something of the genuine bewilderment of the man in the street at the recent reverses, and his anxiety to have the facts honestly presented to him, and heavy fire was directed on a number of ancillary targets like the Ministry of Information, the Ministry of Supply, the War Office, and the Air Ministry.

Collectively the Government came in for a good deal of abuse—its members were variously described as "nincompoops," "incompetents," and "the greatest friends Hitler ever had"—but many speakers unfriendly to it went out of their way to exclude Churchill himself from blame. Only Lord Winterton was uncompromisingly severe.

"No one dares to put the blame where it should be put constitutionally—on the Prime Minister," he said. "During the thirty-seven years which I have been in the House I have never seen such attempts to absolve a Prime Minister from Ministerial responsibility as are going on at the moment." Mr Churchill was not in his seat when this broadside was delivered. He had somewhat pointedly left the Chamber, for Winterton and Emmanuel Shinwell were acid and inveterate critics; for some time now they had been known in the House as "Arsenic and Old Lace."

Later Mr Silverman spoke aggrievedly of the Prime Minister's "lecturing, hectoring, and sermonizing tone." He sadly prophesied, however, that Churchill would continue to get votes, "not on his merits, or on the merits of the Government, but *faute de mieux* . . . anything else might be worse." And before the House was counted out in the early hours of the following morning Mr Gallacher was even ruder at the expense of Wardlaw-Milne and his supporters. "It would be a complete disaster if in place of the Prime Minister and the Government we had the Hon. Member for Kidderminster and the tatterdemalion group that gather round him," he said scornfully.

On the second day came the only really effective Opposition speech. It was made by Mr Aneurin Bevan, who claimed that far more people supported the motion outside the House than were represented on the Order Paper. He objected to Churchill winding up the debate rather than opening it, though he admitted that the latter was a better move tactically. "The Prime Minister wins debate after debate, and loses battle after battle. The country is beginning to say that he fights debates like a war, and the war like a debate."

Referring to the morale of the troops, he expressed the view that it was not what was said in the House that mattered, but what they themselves experienced in battle. Three things were wrong. "First, the main strategy of the war has been wrong. Second, the wrong weapons have been produced. And third, those weapons are being managed by men who are not trained in the use of them."

Ignoring jeers at his own resistance to rearmament he added that even if our rearmament had been quantitatively lacking that was no excuse for its being qualitatively inefficient, which showed lack of brains. He complained that the Army had no text-book on the co-ordination of land and air forces, and suggested that a foreign general—a Pole, a Czech, or a Frenchman—trained in German techniques should be put in command of the Allied forces until our own leaders had learnt their lessons.

Not even his characteristic emotionalism over the question of a Second Front robbed this speech of a certain effect, and Mr Hore-Belisha made a number of trenchant points (some of which rebounded on him later). The House as a whole, however, did not really trust either Hore-Belisha or Bevan. It was therefore beyond the power of either to retrieve the damage done by the opening speeches.

Churchill's reply, which filled twenty-six columns of Hansard, was masterly in its range, its logic, its frank admission of difficulties, and the powerful conviction with which he demanded a renewal of support for the Government.

"Everything that could be thought of or raked up has been used to weaken confidence in the Government, has been used to prove that Ministers are incompetent, and to weaken their confidence in themselves; to make the Army distrust the backing it is getting from the civil power, to make the workmen lose confidence in the weapons they are striving so hard to make, to represent the Government as a set of nonentities over whom the Prime Minister towers—and then to undermine him in his own heart and, if possible, before the eyes of the nation. All this poured out by cable and radio to all parts of the world, to the distress of all our friends and to the delight of all our foes."

After reviewing "the military misfortunes of the last fortnight" he told of the shock of hearing about these reverses while in America, and then having to face the flood of speculation and criticism broadcast by the Press. "I do not think," he said, "that any public man charged with a high mission from this country ever seemed to be barracked from his homeland in his absence to the extent that befell me on this visit to the United States."

He dealt devastatingly with Hore-Belisha, reminding him that many of the shortcomings of our armour dated from lack of preparations put into effect at the War Office during his time as Secretary of State for War. And while accepting what Lord Winterton had termed "the constitutional responsibility" for what had gone wrong in the desert, he spoke of the need for commanders in the field to feel they were free to take risks, free to fight their battles without over-frequent admonitions from Whitehall . . . "and you will not, I may add, get a *Government* to run risks unless they feel that they have got behind them a loyal, solid majority."

He continued:

"I ask no favours for myself or for His Majesty's Government. I undertook the office of Prime Minister and Minister of Defence, after defending my predecessor to the best of my ability, in times when the life of the nation hung upon a thread. I am your servant, and you have the right to dismiss me when you please. What you have no right to do is to ask me to bear responsibilities without the power of effective action. . . . If to-day, or at any future time, the House were to exercise its undoubted right, I could walk out with a good conscience and the feeling that I have done my duty according to such light as has been granted to me. There is only one thing I would ask of you in that event. It would be to give my successor the modest powers which would have been denied to me."

He went on to criticize Wardlaw-Milne's proposal for the appointment of "some military figure or some other unnamed personage" as Supreme Commander of all the fighting Services. This would, he presumed, reduce the Prime Minister to "an appendage," charged with making "the necessary explanations, excuses, and apologies to Parliament when things go wrong, as they often do and often will."

He pointed out that to vest this unspecified individual with such powers meant that by threatening resignation he would be in a position to pit himself against his political colleagues; "it is a system very different from the Parliamentary system under which we live. It might easily amount to, or be converted into, a dictatorship."

At one point Hore-Belisha challenged him about the Churchill tank. His reply convulsed the House. "This tank, the A 22, was ordered off the drawing-board and large numbers went into production quickly. As might be expected it had many defects and teething troubles, and when these became apparent it was appropriately rechristened the Churchill," he said blandly. "These defects have now been largely overcome. I am sure that this tank will prove in the end a powerful, massive, and serviceable weapon of war."

By now he had the House in his hand. An overwhelming gesture of confidence was certain, but he was determined to drive home his advantage. He ended a speech which had lasted an hour and a half with these words:

"The setting down of this Vote of Censure by Members of all parties is a considerable event. Do not, I beg of you, let the House underrate the gravity of what has been done. It has been trumpeted all round the world to our disparagement, and when every nation, friend and foe, is waiting to see what is the true resolve and conviction of the House of Commons it must go forward to the end. . . . Every vote counts. If those who have assailed us are reduced to contemptible proportions, and their Vote of Censure on the National Government is converted to a Vote of Censure upon its authors, make no mistake, a cheer will go up from every friend of Britain, and every faithful servant of our cause, and the knell of disappointment will ring in the ears of the tyrants we are striving to overthrow."

A handful of Members, among them Winterton, Shinwell, Sir Archibald Southby, and Lady Megan Lloyd-George, abstained from voting. A smaller handful still, including Sir Herbert Williams, W. J. Brown, Hore-Belisha, Aneurin Bevan, Richard Stokes, Cunningham-Reid; the Liberals, Clement Davies and T. L. Horabin; and a militant trio of I.L.P. Members, followed Sir John Wardlaw-Milne. In all they numbered only twenty-five, and the Motion of Censure was crushingly defeated by a Government vote of four hundred and seventy-five.

In its way this was a turning-point in the war, both politically and militarily. Churchill had won his mandate. Soon it was to be reinforced and proudly sustained by a dramatic change in Allied fortunes.

20

Flight to Cairo

ON THE day the Censure debate opened Rommel's Afrika Corps reached El Alamein, the last position which offered any real defensive advantage before the Nile Delta. At that point the desert front narrowed to a gap of thirty-five miles between the sea and the Qattara Depression. From there the Allied flank was guarded by the great salt-water marsh stretching far to the south.

By now General Auchinleck had taken personal command of the Eighth Army, and when the debate was over Churchill sent him an encouraging signal. To those around him, however, it was clear that the Prime Minister had no real confidence in the direction of the desert campaign. He spoke with great bitterness of Auchinleck's lack of offensive spirit, the ineptitude of British tactics, and the misuse of manpower in the Middle East. While still in America he had come to the conclusion that General Ritchie must be relieved. Now it was equally plain that, whatever Auchinleck might do to retrieve Ritchie's blunders, the Commander-in-Chief himself was tarred with the same brush. The Prime Minister no longer believed in his capacity as a leader.

Undoubtedly Auchinleck's task had been complicated by criticism and advice from Whitehall, which too often counselled action no longer desirable in the light of subsequent developments. Tobruk was a case in point. Here, as the Prime Minister saw, was the one place where Rommel could have been destroyed, but when Ritchie failed to recognize this fact and embody it in his initial plan the damage was done and no amount of directives from Whitehall could rectify it.

Neglect to strengthen the garrison and its defences in the first place made the Tobruk enclave untenable as soon as things began to go wrong, but this Churchill did not appreciate. His later demands for the holding of Tobruk should in all the circumstances have been ignored; mistakenly Auchinleck tried to meet them by issuing orders which only increased the confusion. Like Ritchie, he had lost his grip on the situation.

With his forces spread all over the desert, Ritchie was trying to hold linear defensive positions—a policy doomed from the outset by the relative weakness of his mobile arm—instead of concentrating his available resources for one decisive blow. For his part Auchinleck sensed that the initiative was passing to Rommel; his letters and signals to Ritchie showed that he realized far more clearly than his Army Commander the mistakes the latter was making, and the dangers he faced. But still he kept Ritchie in command. Why?

The reasons were twofold. In the first place it was not for a considerable time that Auchinleck realized the *extent* to which Ritchie had lost control. And then, when it began to dawn on him, the strange diffidence which had long marked his dealings with individuals made him reluctant to take any decisive step. Morally courageous, he nevertheless shrank from an act which might have been construed as showing a lack of loyalty to a trusted subordinate.

John Connell throws a revealing light on this attitude of mind. A week before Tobruk fell Sir Reginald Dorman-Smith, the Governor of Burma, passed through Cairo and was invited to lunch with the Commander-in-Chief, to whom his brother, Major-General Eric Dorman-Smith, was D.C.G.S. After lunch General Dorman-Smith, who was obviously worried at the way the battle was going, remarked that Rommel had imposed his mind on Ritchie to such an extent that Rommel would always come out on top.

Greatly surprised, his brother asked why, in that case, Ritchie had not been removed. He received the astonishing reply that "the Auk was not very partial to sacking people; he had sacked Cunningham, and that was about the end of his sacking ration."[1]

As a serious reason for retaining an unsuccessful commander this seemed hardly credible, but General Dorman-Smith was evidently not far wide of the mark. Shortly afterwards Ritchie flatly disobeyed a direct order from his Commander-in-Chief, preferring to act on the advice of Gott, one of his own subordinates. Even then Auchinleck took no immediate action. When he finally relieved Ritchie of his command and took over himself Auchinleck handled a difficult situation with the greatest resolution and skill, but by then Churchill's mind was made up. The Censure Debate was hardly over when he announced he would fly to Cairo to see for himself what

[1] Connell, *op. cit.*, p. 571.

changes were necessary. Only with great difficulty was he dissuaded from starting immediately.

* * * * *

What chiefly influenced his decision to defer his visit to the Middle East was the need for reaching final agreement with the Americans over the operations discussed in Washington. General Marshall and the U.S. Chiefs of Staff were strongly in favour of *Sledgehammer*—the lodgement at Brest or Cherbourg—but the more closely this was examined by the British planners the more obvious it became that such a venture posed grave problems. To mount it would inevitably delay the greater cross-Channel operation (*Bolero*); the need to hold the bridgehead would weaken the Allied bombing offensive on Germany; and to British minds it still seemed more sensible to concentrate in 1942 on an objective less heavily defended than the coast of Northern France. Churchill himself still pressed the claims of *Jupiter*, but opinion in general was veering in favour of *Gymnast*, the Allied landing in North Africa.

On July 18 Harry Hopkins, Marshall, and King arrived for final discussions. They had been told by the President that agreement must be reached within a week. Taking Averell Harriman with him, Tommy flew to Prestwick to meet them—a bumpy, unpleasant trip dodging through the Welsh mountains in low cloud—and brought the visitors back in the Prime Minister's train. He told them that Mr Churchill was expecting them to join him at Chequers, and the train would therefore be stopping at Wendover, but Hopkins firmly pointed out that their first duty was to call on their own Ambassador. In point of fact, the more pressing reason for declining the Prime Minister's invitation was their anxiety to confer first of all with General Eisenhower, now hard at work in London with his own planning staff, and the train therefore proceeded straight to Euston.

Mr Churchill, who had wanted to present the British case against *Sledgehammer* at the earliest possible moment, did not take at all kindly to this change of plan, and he had a somewhat heated telephone conversation with Hopkins when the Americans reached Claridge's. He fully recognized, however, that his visitors were quite within their rights, and the highly coloured description which Eisenhower's naval aide has given of a scene between Hopkins and the Prime Minister, who read him a lecture from "a British book of war laws" and, tearing out each successive page of this imaginary work, threw it on the floor, remains an engaging flight of fiction.[2] When the joint talks began two days later the reasoned British objections to *Sledgehammer* prevailed, and *Gymnast* took its place. It was decided that the invasion of North-west Africa would be launched before the end of October, and the whole operation was given the new

[2] Harry C. Butcher, *Three Years with Eisenhower*, p. 20.

code-name of *Torch*. *Jupiter*, Churchill's own favourite project, was quietly interred, and on July 25 the President's envoys flew home.

* * * * *

Rommel's confident belief that he would be in Cairo by the end of July was shaken and finally destroyed by a series of sharp engagements which cost him casualties in men and equipment, and the expenditure of virtually all his heavy ammunition. On July 18, in one of the letters he wrote almost daily to "Dearest Lu," his wife, he said:

> Yesterday was a particularly hard and critical day. We pulled through again. But it can't go on like it for long, otherwise the front will crack. Militarily this is the most difficult period I've ever been through. There's help in sight, of course, but whether we will live to see it is a question. You know what an incurable optimist I am. But there are situations where everything is dark.[3]

Rommel had, in fact, decided to retire to the frontier if Auchinleck resumed the attack put in on the 26th, but this last fierce battle of two months' desert fighting convinced the British Commander-in-Chief that he too had reached the end of his resources. He needed time to rest and reorganize his formations, and he therefore signalled that he would not be in a position to mount a further offensive before the middle of September. This message was passed to Brooke, who was already on his way to Cairo, the Prime Minister adding drily that it showed "how necessary it is for us to get to the Middle East at once."[4] A few hours later the Prime Minister himself was on his way to the battle-front.

A visit to the Middle East and the possibility of flying on to Moscow for a conference with Stalin had long been in Mr Churchill's mind, and several months earlier Tommy had asked Kelly-Rogers for a survey of the alternative routes. To reach Cairo by flying-boat Kelly-Rogers proposed a journey of 7000 miles from Calshot via Bathurst and Lagos, and then across French Equatorial Africa and the Sudan to Khartoum.

Using the Clipper plainly had its drawbacks. The outward journey would take nearly three days, and there was a distinct possibility that the return route might involve a double transatlantic crossing from Bathurst to Trinidad, Bermuda, and the United States, and then a flight via Botwood to Stranraer, lasting in all the best part of a week. In addition, such a route would involve the passengers in a series of inoculations which Sir Charles Wilson, the Prime Minister's doctor, strongly opposed.

In the end the plan was shelved, but when July came, and with it the crisis in the desert, Tommy was told to look into the whole question of a long-distance flight once again. Not only was the Prime Minister deter-

[3] *The Rommel Papers*, (ed. Liddell Hart), p. 257. [4] Churchill, Vol. IV, p. 411.

mined to examine the Middle East situation at first hand, but the rejection of *Sledgehammer* in favour of the landing in North Africa meant that there could now be no Second Front in Europe in 1942. And some one had to break the unpleasant news to Stalin.

Tommy went upstairs to Portal's room and put the problem to him. When Portal summoned him to a meeting in the Air Ministry a few hours later he was introduced to a short, sturdy, fair-haired American named Vanderkloot, who had been flying Liberators with a Ferry Command crew.

Vanderkloot explained that he had already made the flight to Cairo over a far shorter route than the Clipper could follow. It involved only one stop, at Gibraltar. Then, leaving the Rock at dusk, they would cross the North African coast near the boundary of French and Spanish territory, and head south-west across the Sahara to Wadi Halfa. From that point they would fly up the Nile to Cairo.

Admittedly they would have to pass over a stretch of Spanish territory, but this could be done under cover of darkness, and Spanish fighters had shown no interest in any previous flights made along this route. By first light next morning the Liberator would be well clear of the danger area, and too far south for any encounter with German or Italian aircraft.

Mr Churchill liked the new plan, and Vanderkloot was told to make the necessary arrangements as soon as possible. He was given an R.A.F. navigator, Squadron Leader C. T. Kimber, but the rest of his aircrew were drawn from Ferry Command. The second pilot, John Ruggles, was an American, and the radio officer, Russell Holmes, was a Canadian.

The stop at Gibraltar raised security problems, and discussion of possible cover-plans put an impish idea into Mr Churchill's mind. Without telling anyone on his staff he rang up M I 5, and next day a mysterious box was delivered to him by special messenger.

A few minutes later one of his Personal Assistants was surprised to hear loud chuckles coming from the Prime Minister's room. His curiosity aroused, he knocked and went in. Standing in front of the mirror was a figure which might have stepped straight from the world of Walt Disney, for above the black coat and striped trousers was a round, smiling face almost entirely hidden by a long bright red beard and luxuriant side-whiskers.

"A very effective disguise, you will agree?" said the Prime Minister, pulling droll faces at himself in the glass; "I think I shall go and see the King in this this afternoon."

On the night of Sunday, August 2, they took off from Lyneham. The Liberator, which was named *Commando*, was a far cry from the specially fitted aircraft which Churchill was to use later in the war. In the unheated bomb bay it was bitterly cold and deafeningly noisy, and the sleeping accommodation—roughly rigged canvas bunks or mattresses laid on the bare steel deck—was primitive in the extreme. When Averell Harriman, who joined the Liberator for the onward flight from Cairo to Moscow, climbed into one of the top bunks his weight stretched the canvas so much that Tommy, already asleep in the berth below, was squashed flat and nearly suffocated.

At dawn they were far out over the Atlantic, making a wide sweep to avoid enemy aircraft. Picnic baskets and Thermos flasks of hot coffee were produced, and Mr Churchill munched happily at the cold beef sandwiches he had brought with him. This was one of his favourite meals on a journey, but he was very particular about the way his sandwiches were prepared. "The bread must be wafer-thin," he insisted; "it is nothing more than a vehicle to convey the filling to the stomach."

They were only in Gibraltar for a few hours, and Mr Churchill did not wear his red beard after all. It might well have proved useful during the short journey he made to inspect the defences of the Upper Rock, for the security precautions were unexpectedly defeated by a temperamental Spanish donkey. The cortège of cars was taking a short cut through a narrow back street when it came to a sudden halt. The way ahead was completely blocked by a cart laden with vegetables from La Linea.

While the Prime Minister's party shouted at the driver, and the driver shouted unavailingly at the donkey, which refused to move in any direction, a stream of passers-by peered into the cars. Many recognized Mr Churchill, and bowed and smiled—but for generations the Spanish of the Campo area have been loyal to Britain, and not a word of his presence in Gibraltar that day reached the enemy agents in La Linea and Algeciras.

At six o'clock that evening *Commando* took off from the dangerously short runway at North Front, and with an escort of Beaufighters headed for the African coast. Before dawn the Liberator crossed the Egyptian frontier, and soon Churchill sighted the great river which held such stirring memories for him.

It was August the fourth. Forty-four years earlier, to the day, he had traversed the selfsame stretch of the Nile in the paddle-steamer which carried his troop of the 21st Lancers to fight in the battle of Omdurman.

Elaborate precautions had been taken to ensure that the Prime Minister's arrival in Egypt was not widely known, but as Mr Churchill was driven into the capital from the great military airfield at Cairo West he could not resist giving the V-sign to groups of Allied troops they passed on the Mena Road. There was, in fact, an air of unreality about the security arrangements for many of the Prime Minister's journeys abroad, for although he invariably travelled under an assumed name—Colonel Warden was his favourite pseudonym—the steps taken to guard the routes over which he was to pass could hardly be concealed, and he was too well-known a figure not to be instantly recognized whenever he appeared, however fleetingly, in public.

Admittedly Cairo, hotbed of espionage, intrigue, and rumour, posed singular security problems, but there seemed at times to be some confusion, too, over official Allied censorship policy. Tommy was astonished to see a picture of himself in a daily paper soon after their arrival. It was captioned "Commander C. R. Thompson, Personal Assistant to the Prime Minister, greets an Army officer at Cairo West." As the Army officer was easily recognizable as General Alexander, hurriedly and secretly summoned from England to replace Auchinleck as Commander-in-Chief, Middle East, this must have been a welcome offering to enemy intelligence.

On the morning he reached Egypt Churchill went straight to the British Embassy, where he remained for more than a week as guest of the Ambassador, Sir Miles Lampson. Brooke was already there, and Smuts soon joined them. That afternoon the Prime Minister had a long talk with Auchinleck; for the next forty-eight hours there were frequent and anxious conferences while Churchill gradually built up a picture of the military situation and formed his own judgments of the principal officers serving under the Commander-in-Chief. Subsequently he visited Alamein and a number of the great Army camps outside Cairo. In the sweltering August heat he seemed inexhaustible, and he spent one particularly arduous day with the Yeomanry Division, moving from brigade to brigade and explaining to large gatherings of officers the steps being taken to re-equip the Division with new American tanks.

In the Embassy he was able to do most of his work in the Ambassador's air-conditioned office, where an impressive portrait of Lord Kitchener, the victor of Omdurman, gazed down on him at his desk. At night he slept soundly in a large cool bedroom looking out over the lawn to the Nile, which flowed along the end of the garden.

By the evening of August 6 he and Brooke had agreed on the principal changes to be made in the Middle East command. Mr Churchill himself has described at length the reasons which influenced these changes. He has also paid tribute to the "soldierly dignity" with which General Auchinleck received the news of his dismissal, and their subsequent meeting in the Embassy on the eve of the Prime Minister's departure.[5] The main decisions submitted for the approval of the Cabinet can therefore be briefly summarized. They involved the appointment of General Alexander as the new Commander-in-Chief, Middle East, and General Gott, who had

[5] Churchill, Vol. IV, pp. 412–424.

much impressed Churchill at their first meeting in the desert on August 5, as Commander of the Eighth Army. When Gott met his death—his plane was shot down two days later as he flew to Cairo for further talks with the Prime Minister—the choice fell on General Montgomery, who had only just been named as Alexander's successor in command of the British First Army for the Torch landings.

On the night of August 10 the Prime Minister set off for Moscow. Vanderkloot had decided to delay the take-off for Teheran, on the first leg of the long journey, so that *Commando* could make a daylight passage of the great mountain range which guards the approach to the Persian capital. There was therefore time for a farewell dinner with the Lampsons at the Embassy, and then, shortly after midnight, Mr Churchill drove out past the Pyramids to the airfield.

21

On to Moscow

THE conference party had grown considerably and two more Liberators followed *Commando*. Among the newcomers was General Wavell, a qualified Russian interpreter who had first visited Moscow before the 1914–18 war.

By the time they all landed at Teheran it was obvious that they would not reach Moscow before dark. The British Minister, Sir Reader Bullard, suggested that Mr Churchill should stay the night in the Legation, but the great heat, the pandemonium of street cries, and the continuous hooting of car horns soon convinced him that he would get little rest if he remained in the city. The Prime Minister and his personal staff therefore moved to the Summer Legation at Gulhek, high in the hills outside the capital, where Tommy and Leslie Rowan camped out in a magnificent Persian tent in the garden.

"Next morning we were on the airfield by 6.0 A.M., and soon we were flying north towards a gap in the mountains bordering the Caspian Sea. Away to the east we could see the snow-capped peak of Mount Demavend, looking staggeringly majestic in the morning sun. Until we passed through the gap the country below us was parched and bare. Then, to our amazement, the scene changed dramatically and we saw green, fertile slopes, almost tropical in their luxuriance, stretching away to the shores of the Caspian. Altering course, we kept to the east of the Caspian Sea, for the German armies were close at hand and the direct route over Stalingrad was barred to us. For a time we followed the line of the Ural River, and then flew over Kuibishyev. Only when we reached Moscow did we learn that the Russians had intended us to land at Kuibishyev and a welcoming committee headed by the President of the Soviet Republic had waited there throughout the afternoon. A gigantic lunch had been made ready; twenty-four hours later the same food, by then considerably less appetizing, was tackled by Brooke and his fellow-passengers, whose plane had been delayed by engine trouble.

"We landed at Moscow in the early evening and were met by Stalin, Molotov and a galaxy of Commissars and Generals. Stalin, closely attended by a security guard of half a dozen men, was dressed with striking simplicity—a khaki bush shirt, and blue trousers tucked into half-length boots. He led the P.M. over to inspect a very smart Guard of Honour and then we were driven off to a country house some eight miles outside the city. Known as State Villa Number 7, it was, in fact, a bungalow consisting of one large suite, which Mr Churchill used, and three small bedrooms. Linked to it by a covered passageway was another building where the household staff lived, and this contained the only spare bathroom. Whenever we wanted a bath we had first to ring for the interpreter, and then N.K.V.D. guards would be summoned to unlock the doors at either end of the corridor to the adjoining house.

"The garden had one unusual feature; the grounds were surrounded by an inner and outer wall. Between these the soil had been stripped of every scrap of vegetation, and not even a mouse could have hidden from the guards who manned a series of platforms commanding each section of the perimeter. This was not the only safety measure. Ninety feet below ground in the garden was the most luxurious Air Raid Shelter I had ever seen—a suite of expensively furnished rooms reached by two electric lifts. The rooms had elaborate marquetry ceilings, inlaid with wood of varying colours.

"Right from the start we were entertained with a lavishness which made me think uncomfortably of the reception we had given to Molotov and his party at Chequers. At any hour of the day or night we could sit down to a twenty-course meal. This was served in two sections. We would start with caviar, vodka, hors d'œuvres of every imaginable kind, and sucking pig. Then we had to go through a supplementary menu of soup, fish, chicken, beef or mutton, ice-cream, fruit and cheese. Unfortunately the two elderly English-speaking waiters who looked after us seemed to regard this as the standard fare for every occasion, morning, noon, or midnight.

"On our first morning there we did not get back from the Kremlin till the small hours, and I could not face a breakfast starting with caviar and vodka. I therefore asked if I could have eggs, bacon and coffee. A few moments later a plate bearing four eggs and nine rashers of bacon was placed in front of me! When I remarked to Pavlov, Stalin's interpreter, how wonderfully we were being fed in spite of the food shortage he looked surprised and said rather pointedly, 'In Russia we do not ration our guests.' "[1]

On the evening of their arrival Churchill and Harriman went to the Kremlin for their first conference with Stalin. In the dark they could see little of the Kremlin buildings, but they noticed that the rooms through which they passed on their way to Stalin's office were furnished in the faded scarlet and gold magnificence of Czarist days. While the meeting was in progress Tommy and Colonel Kutznetzov, who had been attached to Mr Churchill as A.D.C. and bodyguard, whiled away the time in the anteroom playing chess with members of Stalin's staff. All of them munched apples and pears continually to counteract the effects of the vodka which the Russians drank with unflagging enthusiasm.

In the inner room Churchill and Harriman strove patiently to overcome the cold hostility which met their revelation of the Allied change of plan. When the conference broke up they sensed with relief that some progress had been made, for Stalin had been surprisingly quick to grasp the potentialities of *Torch* and his mood as the long discussion ended seemed almost friendly. By the time the talks were resumed twenty-four hours later, however, his attitude had undergone one of those swift changes which were to become a predictable part of Allied negotiations with the Russian leader.

Alone, or with the silent Molotov at his side, Stalin would often give the impression of being open to reason; he would accept without reservation some unpalatable Allied proposal and seem genuinely convinced by the need for it. And yet a few hours later he would appear entirely oblivious of the points he had conceded, and the same ground would have to be covered all over again, the same taunts and recriminations endured.

By the end of a stormy meeting on the second day in Moscow it seemed that the talks might well founder there and then, for Stalin spoke contemptuously of British reluctance to face the enemy, and accused the Prime Minister bluntly of breaking his word over *Sledgehammer*. Happily the whole atmosphere was changed for the better by two events—a dinner-party which the Russians gave for the British delegation at the Kremlin on the following evening, and a long and convivial private meeting between Churchill and Stalin at the latter's house after the final talks on the night of August 15.

The official banquet lasted more than four hours. "In time we got used to these extraordinary affairs," Tommy recalls; "it was quite common to have between forty and fifty toasts during the course of one dinner, embracing almost every one connected with the war from the King and President Roosevelt to Egyptian N.A.A.F.I. Canteen Assistants in the Western

[1] C. R. Thompson, Notes.

Desert. On one occasion Stalin himself proposed the health of Sawyers, the P.M.'s valet."

On this particular evening at the Kremlin Stalin's mood was quite different again from the night before, and with Pavlov interpreting he chatted away with great animation to Mr Churchill. The Prime Minister had spent part of that afternoon walking round the grounds of the villa, and had much admired some goldfish which swam in a large stone font in the garden. They reminded him of his own golden orfe in the pond at Chartwell. He mentioned that he was very fond of goldfish, and Stalin, anxious to appear hospitable, promptly remarked, "If you like, you are very welcome to take some for your breakfast."

"After dinner we all went down to an underground cinema. Next to each person's armchair was a small table piled high with fruit and bottles of wine, and we saw two rather dull films—one a Russian documentary and the other an indifferent American comedy. I found it more interesting to watch the behaviour of Marshal Voroshilov, who had drunk so much yellow vodka at dinner that he had hardly been able to rise from the table. During the film show he continued to drink, but oddly enough he became more and more sober, while Marshal Timoshenko, who had arrived in the cinema apparently sober, became rapidly so intoxicated that he had to be helped from the room."[2]

The military talks ended on the following day, and at seven o'clock that evening Churchill went to the Kremlin to say good-bye. General Anders, the Polish leader, had arrived to discuss with the Prime Minister the repatriation of Polish prisoners of war from Russia, and Churchill, who said he would be back for dinner, asked him to wait at the villa; they could have their talk afterwards. But the hours went by, and eventually Anders, Tommy, and Leslie Rowan all fell asleep on sofas in the Prime Minister's drawing-room.

Not until three o'clock did Mr Churchill appear. Stalin had invited him back to his house for a farewell drink while the official communique was being drafted. An array of snacks had been provided, and, after midnight, a full dinner, at which Stalin had distinguished himself by tackling a whole sucking-pig single-handed.

During the evening Stalin had recounted with much amusement the now familiar story of Molotov's visit to Berlin while the Russo-German alliance was still in force. A conference with Ribbentrop had been rudely interrupted by a British air raid, and Ribbentrop had hurried his guest into the nearest and deepest shelter. In a tone of mock reproach Stalin added, "I believe you knew perfectly well Molotov was there, and bombed him on purpose!" Only Molotov himself seemed unamused.

[2] *Ibid.*

The Liberator was due to take off in little more than two hours, and even Mr Churchill's stamina was not equal to starting the long-delayed discussions with General Anders so late in the night. He therefore suggested that Anders, who had already flown from Tashkent to Moscow, should make his way to Cairo and have his talk there. As the grey dawn was breaking they drove to the airfield, where an exhausted Molotov was waiting with the inevitable Guard of Honour. *Commando*'s passengers slept soundly for most of the flight back to Teheran.

* * * * *

After the strenuous days and nights in Moscow it was a relief to return to the peace and quiet of the Summer Legation. The blazing sunshine of the late afternoon tempted several of the Prime Minister's party to bathe in the blue-tiled pool in the garden, but most of them immediately re-emerged gasping for breath, for the swimming-bath was fed by a mountain stream which flowed straight from the snowline. One of the hardier spirits was General Wavell. As he dived into the icy water Churchill remarked admiringly "There goes my Roman Cæsar!"

Wavell had spent much of the journey back to Teheran composing a poetic commentary on the Russian talks. Each of its four verses ended with the words "No Second Front in 1942!" At dinner that night he was called upon to recite this, but next morning the Prime Minister warned every one present to forget what they had heard; even a light-hearted poem on such a subject carried a security risk.

As it happened, Sir Reader Bullard's staff needed no reminders about security. The presence of the Prime Minister in a country where there were still many German sympathizers had already provided enough headaches, and even in the isolation of Gulhek stringent precautions had been taken for Churchill's own safety. The servants had been banished from the upper rooms, and General Sir Edward Quinan, the G.O.C., Persia and Iraq, had been pressed into service to make the Prime Minister's bed. As an added safeguard Sawyers slept that night on the balcony across the open window of the bedroom.

* * * * *

At times Mr Churchill was an exacting and somewhat exasperating master to serve. He was apt to take little account of the difficulties under which people might be working, and Patrick Kinna had a trying afternoon when they all got back to Cairo. At the hottest period of the day the Prime Minister rang for him, and as soon as Kinna entered the room he began dictating at top speed.

Nonplussed at finding no desk to sit at, Kinna first tried to write his shorthand standing up and resting his notebook on a chest of drawers. This was at an awkward height, however, and as the Prime Minister was speaking very fast Kinna soon had to confess that he was unable to keep up with him. The only apparent alternative was to kneel on the floor and balance the book on a very rickety table.

With the sweat pouring off him he wrote slower and slower, and the Prime Minister became more and more irate. Finally the long-suffering Kinna was banished in temporary disgrace.

On such occasions Mr Churchill would remain blissfully ignorant that he had in any way behaved heartlessly. His whole mind was concentrated on the work in hand; anything which hindered his task was inexcusable. But if anyone suggested that he had been inconsiderate he would at once be filled with remorse.

One day General Ismay found Mrs Hill, the Prime Minister's personal secretary, standing obviously distressed in the corridor outside the Cabinet Room at No. 10. When he entered the room he asked Mr Churchill whether he had been bullying his staff.

"Why do you say that?" inquired the Prime Minister, with a puzzled frown. Ismay told him he had just seen Mrs Hill in tears.

"Oh, dear!" said Mr Churchill, much concerned. "I must put that right."

He rang the bell, and when Mrs Hill entered he said to her gently, "Please take this letter." Then, more slowly and clearly than usual, he dictated:

"My dear Ambassador,
I fully agree with you . . .

"That is all," he said. "Please take that away and type it for me immediately, will you?"

When Mrs Hill brought it back a minute later the Prime Minister took the letter and studied it closely. Then, quite seriously, he said to her, "That is a very good piece of typing. It is beautifully done. Thank you very much!"

And when the astonished Mrs Hill left the room he turned to Ismay with the air of a conjuror demonstrating just how easily a difficult feat could be accomplished!

* * * * *

During the Prime Minister's absence in Moscow General Montgomery had assumed command of the Eighth Army under Alexander, the new Commander-in-Chief. Alexander now took Mr Churchill and Brooke to visit Montgomery's headquarters on the edge of the Mediterranean, near Burg-el-Arab.

"The new regime had only been established a few days, but it was making its presence felt. We noticed a change in the attitude of the officers we talked to. They seemed far more cheerful, confident, and alert, and I gathered that not only the officers were aware of a change in the atmosphere. On one of his first visits to the desert Alexander's car, with flag flying, had passed a group of British soldiers lounging at the side of the road who paid no attention to him. Alex had stopped the car, walked up to them, and introduced himself as their new Commander-in-Chief—'and in future you will salute the Union flag when you see it!'

"We arrived at Montgomery's H.Q. in time for dinner, and the P.M. slept that night in the General's caravan. The rest of us had tents in a little camp pitched right on the edge of the shore. Before breakfast next morning Mr Churchill was splashing about in the sea, happy as a schoolboy. All day he went round talking to the troops, including his old regiment, the Fourth Hussars. Later during this return visit to Cairo he saw the 51st Highland Division and went to the Toura Caves, where the stone for the Pyramids had been quarried. The caves had been cleared of rubble and turned into fine workshops for the repair of aircraft engines. This was a notable enterprise; previously any major repair jobs had necessitated the engines being sent back to England. The Air Officer-in-Charge was aware that Averell Harriman would be accompanying the P.M., and prominently displayed were a large number of Pratt and Whitney engines which were unserviceable. These were laid out in rows, and tickets attached to them proclaimed "AWAITING SPARE PARTS FROM AMERICA." Averell took the hint!"[3]

On August 23 Churchill reluctantly decided it was time to return home. Since every one sensed that Rommel's next thrust was imminent he longed for an excuse to remain close to the scene of operations, but daily there were reports of anxious developments in India, where the Congress Party leaders had launched a programme of sabotage and mob violence; the harsh lessons of the Dieppe Raid, which took place on the day he spent with Montgomery in the desert, called for urgent examination; and the planning of the *Torch* landings kept raising major points of Allied policy which were difficult to decide satisfactorily with both the Prime Minister and the C.I.G.S. out of close contact with Eisenhower and his American deputy, General Mark Clark.

Since Mr Churchill's presence in Cairo was now well known to the enemy it was not easy to organize his departure unobserved and unreported by the many agents in the city still in contact with the Italians. A cover plan was therefore devised, and he drove out to Mena about tea-time, ostensibly to pay a social call on Mr Casey, the Minister of State, at his home, the Villa Bleu. The baggage was sent on separately to the airfield, and at seven o'clock that evening *Commando* took off in a sandstorm from Cairo West.

[3] *Ibid.*

Until Algeria was reached Vanderkloot followed much the same route as he had flown on the outward journey. He then continued along the North African coast, crossing Spanish Morocco in the darkness, and flew on until it was possible to swing round and come in towards Gibraltar from the Atlantic. It was hoped that any unfriendly observer sighting the plane from Spanish territory at first light would report merely another routine arrival from England.

Undeterred by a dense morning mist, Vanderkloot approached the Rock low over the water—a tactic which alarmed Mr Churchill—but he made a perfect landfall, and when *Commando* came to rest at North Front, the air-strip built out into the sea on the narrow neck of land joining Gibraltar to the Spanish shore, a plain van with no windows was backed up to the door. A great show was then made of loading baggage into it, and while this was going on the Prime Minister was persuaded with some difficulty to crawl into the van himself. The doors were closed, and he was driven to the Convent, the Governor's residence in the main street, where he remained unwillingly in hiding till the time came for the flight to England.

It had been planned to wait until nightfall, but as the weather reports showed cloud cover over the whole route the departure was brought forward. Soon after lunch the Liberator took off again, and eight hours later they landed safely in Wiltshire, where Mrs Churchill was waiting with Randolph and Averell Harriman's daughter, Kathleen, to welcome them home.

22

The Lighting of the Torch

THE Prime Minister's homecoming gave a much needed impetus to the *Torch* planning. By the end of August the American Chiefs of Staff had become firmly convinced that their only hope of putting the *Torch* forces ashore in North Africa without heavy casualties depended on the degree to which they could restrict British participation in the invasion. They pointed out that since the fall of France the American Government had maintained diplomatic contact with Vichy, and American troops had not been directly involved in any conflict with Frenchmen. British relations with France, on the other hand, had been compromised by the memory of Oran and Dakar.

By now, too, a fundamental difference of opinion had also arisen over the scope of the landings. Churchill's strategic sense told him that the farther east the Allies could gain a foothold inside the Mediterranean the better chance they would have of dictating subsequent events. He therefore stressed the importance of seizing Algiers, and, if possible, the ports of Philippeville and Bone. Marshall, however, wanted to confine the landings to Casablanca and Oran.

While the arguments raged Eisenhower, in London, could make little headway. It was impossible for him to decide on the allocation of his forces or put forward his shipping requirements, but with Churchill's return disagreements were soon resolved. He convinced the President of the need to include Algiers in the plan; a swift advance from there could well deny Tunisia to the Germans and expose Italy to heavy attack from North African bases. The final pattern of *Torch* emerged as a three-pronged assault, with a joint British and American force descending on

Algiers, and all-American landings at Casablanca and Oran. Eisenhower was chosen as overall commander of the operation, and D-Day was fixed for November 8.

The Prime Minister's grasp of every problem relating to the operation, his resilience, and his inexhaustible energy made a lasting impression on Eisenhower and Clark, who saw him almost daily at this time. He seemed the only person completely confident about *Torch* during this anxious period when the staffs in London and Washington were involved in what Eisenhower wryly termed the "Transatlantic Essay Competition," with proposals and counterproposals being cabled daily, and Clark has described a typical evening at No. 10.[1] After dinner they discussed transport difficulties at great length, and Pound and Mountbatten were summoned from their beds to answer questions. The Prime Minister pressed the First Sea Lord on his estimate of the time needed for the convoy from Britain to reach the African coast, and when Pound had been persuaded that it was feasible to reduce this he said triumphantly, "See, I've saved you eight precious days. . . . Now, Sir Dudley, you can turn in!" But the rest of them were kept there until after two o'clock in the morning.

The Eighth Army, awaiting Rommel's counter-attack, was much in his thoughts. "We've chosen a new general," he told a gathering of Junior Ministers, to whom he gave a brilliant survey of the war situation on his arrival back from Egypt; "I don't think any of you would like the fellow." But he himself had been enormously encouraged by Montgomery's self-assurance and drive. When Rommel's attack, which began on August 30, was firmly repulsed with few casualties he knew his confidence had not been misplaced.

Despite the welcome success in the desert this was a period of great anxiety for the Prime Minister. The vital need for secrecy about both *Torch* and the major offensive to be launched from El Alamein made it impossible to give even senior members of the Government an inkling of what was afoot, and the Commons again grew restive. Sir Stafford Cripps, the Lord Privy Seal, and Leader of the House, threatened to resign on the grounds that the war was not being prosecuted with the necessary vigour and imagination, and messages from Moscow once more assumed a critical and unfriendly tone. Since it was now plain that the launching and sustaining of the *Torch* landings would absorb most of the Royal Navy's efforts, there was no alternative but to suspend for the time being the convoys bearing war supplies to Murmansk. There were simply not enough warships available to protect them. It was equally certain that this news would provoke more violent recriminations from Stalin.

Amid all these worrying preoccupations the flow of directives from

[1] *Calculated Risk*, p. 56.

Downing Street on every conceivable aspect of the war continued without interruption. Discovering an attempt to remove General Hobart—an expert on tank warfare whom he had brought from retirement earlier in the war to command one of the new Armoured Divisions—from his post on the grounds of alleged medical unfitness, Mr Churchill minuted angrily to the Secretary of State for War:

> He is a man of quite exceptional mental attainments, with great strength of character, and although he does not work easily with others it is a great pity we have not more of his like in the Service. I have been shocked at the persecution to which he has been subjected. . . .
>
> The High Commands of the Army are not a club. It is my duty and that of His Majesty's Government to make sure that exceptionally able men, even though not popular with their military contemporaries, should not be prevented from giving their services to the Crown.[2]

Two days after this he was indignantly drawing the attention of the Lord President of the Council to the action of the Metropolitan Water Board in

> giving better treatment to a conscientious objector than to a young man who volunteered for the Army. This is a disgrace to any body of Englishmen, and is on a par with the same miserable sentiments which degraded our country before the war and played a recognizable part in bringing these miseries upon the world.
>
> Your remark about "stealing a march on their colleagues," to be just, requires amplification as follows: "Stealing a march *towards the enemy* on their colleagues."[3]

The Prime Minister also applied himself energetically to such varied matters as fog dispersal on airfields, bus services for businessmen, the seemingly over-rapid expansion of the R.A.F. Regiment, and the quality of food in public restaurants. He rarely forgot anything he heard, and a minute which he dictated to the Minister of Food on the subject of ice cream was prompted by a conversation with his old friend, Santorelli, the *maître d'hôtel* at the Savoy.

Mr Churchill had asked him how war-time food could be made more attractive without an increase in the ration. Santorelli promptly gave him an example. Government regulations prevented hotels and restaurants from serving ices, and yet they were allowed to present the same ingredients in the form of a mousse. There was no reason, Santorelli argued, why this mixture should not be placed in the hotel refrigerator and frozen. Mr Churchill looked into the matter. He found that the Government embargo

[2] Minute of September 4, 1942. (See Churchill, Vol. IV, pp. 790–791.)
[3] Minute of September 6, 1942. (*Ibid.*)

had not, in fact, been intended to apply to hotels at all. It had been aimed at the big ice-cream factories. Soon afterwards the order was amended.

Nothing which had any bearing on the war, either in the military or civil sphere, seemed to escape him. And every useful fact he learnt was filed away in an appropriate compartment of his mind, from which he would produce it instantly, months or years later. The range of his military knowledge was astonishing, and hardly any technical point which cropped up at a Service meeting had to be translated for him. Without effort he could recall the potentialities of every weapon in current use, the calibre of shells, the performance of aircraft, and the detailed construction of warships.

Some people—often those with an axe to grind—accused him of being a bad listener. He was, in fact, a selective listener, and he would pay close attention to anyone with a genuine case to put forward, but he disliked verbosity and was quick to analyse the weak points in an argument. For ever in search of the truth, he grew rapidly impatient with some one who attempted to mislead him and therefore wasted his time.

With his own staff he was wonderfully good-tempered and considerate during this agonizing period of waiting, and Tommy marvelled that his responsibilities appeared to sit so lightly upon him.

One haunting and constantly recurring fear was the possibility of a leakage of the *Torch* plans to the enemy. Although for security reasons the Free French had not been put in the picture about the operation, there were indications early in September that their suspicions had been aroused. Later in the month the U.S. War Department intercepted a message in plain language from the news editor of an international news agency in London to his office in Washington stating that American forces were about to strike at Casablanca.

The scares continued. A letter from Mark Clark to General Mason-Macfarlane, the Governor of Gibraltar, giving vital details of the invasion plans fell into Spanish hands. It had been found in the pocket of a naval Paymaster Lieutenant whose body was washed ashore at Cadiz after the aircraft carrying him to Gibraltar had been lost at sea. Although the letter was handed over to the British authorities in Madrid there was no means of telling whether its contents had been photographed and passed to the Germans, who maintained a large Secret Service organization in the Spanish capital. The military section of their Embassy staff, which alone numbered nearly a hundred, was accommodated in a building which also housed a short-wave listening and decoding post, and a meteorological office with sub-stations in Portugal, the Canaries, and North and South Africa.

At home, too, there were other alarms. A newly enlisted Aircraftman who had just arrived in London on leave saw a sealed envelope lying in the gutter near the pillar-box at the end of King Charles Street, outside

Illustrations

Colonel Warden

Flag Commander.

Continue to clean up all these small points, making sure nothing drops to the ground unheeded.

Let me have the report of the proceedings which is expected, and draft a Minute for me to send to all Departments concerned.

Done 16/3.

14.3.40

Memorandum for Tommy from Mr Churchill when First Lord of the Admiralty, in March 1940

Mr Churchill with members of his Persona
Staff. Front (L. to R.): J. R. Colville, th
Prime Minister, J. M. Martin, Anthony Bevi
Back: Leslie Rowan, J. H. Peck, Miss Watsor
Tommy, Charles Barker

Captain Richard Pim, R.N.V.R., head of the Prime Minister's Map Room

With Admiral Darlan at Marceau—November 1939

'White Rabbit'' undergoing trials at Clumber, n the Dukeries. ''At the end of its run the great machine emerged with perfect precision on to the surface of the Park, leaving behind it a clean, well-formed trench along which Mr Churchill slowly walked'' (see Chapter 3)

Imperial War Museum

THE PLACENTIA CONFERENCE

Mr Churchill greets President Roosevelt on his arrival on board H.M.S. *Prince of Wales*. On the President's left is his son, Elliott

Imperial War Museum photographs

Lord Beaverbrook and Averell Harriman

The President has a word with Tommy on the quarter-deck

ary Churchill served at home and in North-West Europe with an anti-aircraft battery

Imperial War Museum

Sarah Churchill, who accompanied her father on several of his war-time journeys, receiving gunnery instruction on board H.M.S. *King George V* on the homeward voyage from Gibraltar in January 1944

Admiralty

Major Randolph Churchill held a commission in the 4th Hussars. After fighting with a Commando unit in the desert he was attached to the British Mission to the Jugo-Slav Army

Imperial War Museum

The blinding floodlights of a C.D.L. tank illuminate a farm building in the wild fell country of the Lake District when secret training was carried out to test this device in the winter of 1941–42 (see Chapter 23)

Mrs Churchill

Marshal Stalin and Mr Churchill have both signed this photograph, taken at their first meeting, in Moscow, in August 1942

Mr Churchill waves to the rowds waiting outside the Capitol after addressing Congress during the *Trident* Conference in May 1943. Second from the right is Mike Reilly, head of the President's personal bodyguard. On the Prime Minister's right is his own senior detective, Det.-Inspector Thompson

Imperial War Museum

In the Middle East before Alamein. The Prime Minister with (L. to R.): General Sir Alan Brooke, General Sir Henry Maitland Wilson and General Sir Harold Alexander

n the garden of the British Embassy in Cairo, Mr Churchill and Field Marshal Smuts with the infant son of he British Ambassador to Egypt, Lord Killearn

Imperial War Museum

IN CASABLANCA

VERGEBLICHER KREUZUNGSVERSUCH

Kladderadatsch

A German commentary on one aspect of the Casablanca Conference. This cartoon, which reached a British intelligence unit soon after the Conference in January 1943, greatly amused the King and Mr Churchill

To see

Prime Minister
This refers to the Pantellaria Pension bet.
CRT 5/7

ALLIED FORCE HEADQUARTERS
Office of the Commander-in-Chief

29 June, 1943

My dear Thompson:

I thank you for your letter enclosing 65 francs taken from the purse of the Prime Minister. It is only natural that I should be pleased at winning from such a gallant opponent.

Is it possible to make a wager covering the next operation - or would Mr. Churchill insist on odds?

Please convey my respects to the Prime Minister, and kindest regards to yourself.

Sincerely
Dwight D. Eisenhower

Commander C. R. Thompson,
10 Downing Street,
Whitehall,
London, England.

Letter to Tommy from General Eisenhower acknowledging the settlement of a wager by the Prime Minister on the outcome of the attack on Pantelleria (see Chapter 25)

Stalin at Teheran

TEHERAN AND CARTHAGE, 1943

Christmas morning at Carthage, 1943. Mr Churchill, just recovered from his serious illness, is standing on the steps of General Eisenhower's villa with Eisenhower and General Maitland Wilson. Also in the group are Major-General "Jock" Whiteley (extreme L.), Air Chief Marshal Sir Arthur Tedder, Admiral Sir John Cunningham, General Alexander, Captain M. L. Power, R.N., Lieut-General Sir Humfrey Gale, Brigadier L. C. Hollis, R.M., and (extreme R.) Lieut-General Walter Bedell Smith, Eisenhower's Chief of Staff

Imperial War Museum photographs

Mulberry Harbour units being towed across the Channel—an artist's impression by the late Charles Pears, R.O.I.

MR CHURCHILL RETURNS TO FRANCE

Field Marshal Montgomery talking to Admiral Sir Philip Vian, Tommy, and the Prime Minister during Mr Churchill's visit to the Normandy beach-head—June 12, 1944

Imperial War Museum photographs

Outside Montgomery's mobile map room in the grounds of a château at Creully. Watching from a hiding place in a rhododendron bush a few yards away as this picture was taken were two fully armed German paratroopers (see Chapter 31)

Imperial War Mus

Admiral Sir John Cunningham, the Allied Naval Commander-in-Chief for the invasion of the South of France, on the bridge of H.M.S. *Kimberley* with the Army Commander, General Sir Henry Maitland Wilson. On Admiral Cunningham's left are the author and Lieutenant-Commander J. W. Rylands, the destroyer's captain

XV

THE DRAGOON LANDINGS

An enemy air attack is met by flak from the invasion fleet

Chief of Bureau of Aeronautics, U.S.A.

IN ITALY—AUGUST 1944

The Prime Minister with Marshal Tito (R.) during their talks at the Villa Rivalta in Naples. Also in the group are Brigadier Fitzroy Maclean (2nd from left) and Mme Olga Homo, Tito's interpreter

Imperial War Museum

Visiting Allied troops with General Alexander

Imperial War Museum

With General Mark Clark he inspects an American unit

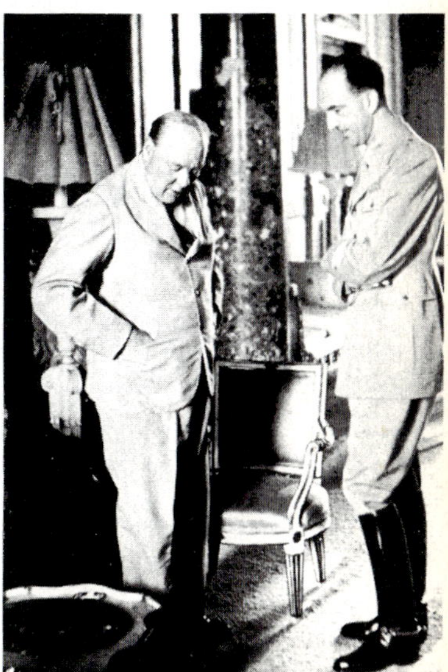

During his visit to Rome Mr Churchill met King Umberto at the British Embassy

Imperial War Museum

THE GREEK CRISIS—DECEMBER 1944

The Prime Minister on the airfield at Athens with (L. to R.): Lieutenant-General R. M. Scobie, Mr Reginald Leeper the British Ambassador, Mr Harold Macmillan (behind), and Mr Eden

On the bridge of H.M *Ajax*. Next to the Pri Minister is Rear-Admi J. M. Mansfield, comma ing the 15th Cruiser Squ ron

Imperial War Museum photograp

The scene at the "Can light Conference" with rebel (ELAS) leaders in Greek Foreign Office Chapter 35)

rris and Ewing

Franklin D. Roosevelt—the portrait which the President inscribed for Tommy

The picturesque setting the Yalta Conference– view from the garden of t Livadia Palace, scene of t Plenary sessions

U.S. Navy

With Mr Eden and Archbishop Damaskinos, Regent of Greece, on Mr Churchill's triumphal return to Athens after Yalta

Imperial War Museum photographs

Talking to Ibn Saud, whom he entertained at Fayoum before flying back to England

IN GERMANY—
MARCH 1945

Watching the crossing of the Rhine

Imperial War Museum photographs

At Wesel the Prime Minister came under shell-fire while inspecting a damaged bridge

With Tommy and Field Marshal Montgomery at the latter's headquarters camp

Imperial War Museum

The Prime Minister waves to the huge crowd in Whitehall on VE Day

VICTORY IN EUROPE

With leading members of the war-time Coalition Government at the farewell reception at No. 10 Downing Street

Universal News X

The Prime Minister painting at St Jean de Luz during his brief holiday before the Potsdam Conference in July 1945—an impression by Margaret Nairn, which Mr Churchill has signed

THE POTSDAM
CONFERENCE

Colonel Warden with F
Marshal Montgomery
Air Chief Marshal Sir Sh
Douglas, on his arriva
Berlin

Imperial War Museum photograp

President Truman insp
the British Guard of Ho
before paying his off
call on the Prime Min

A visit to Hitler's rui
Chancellery

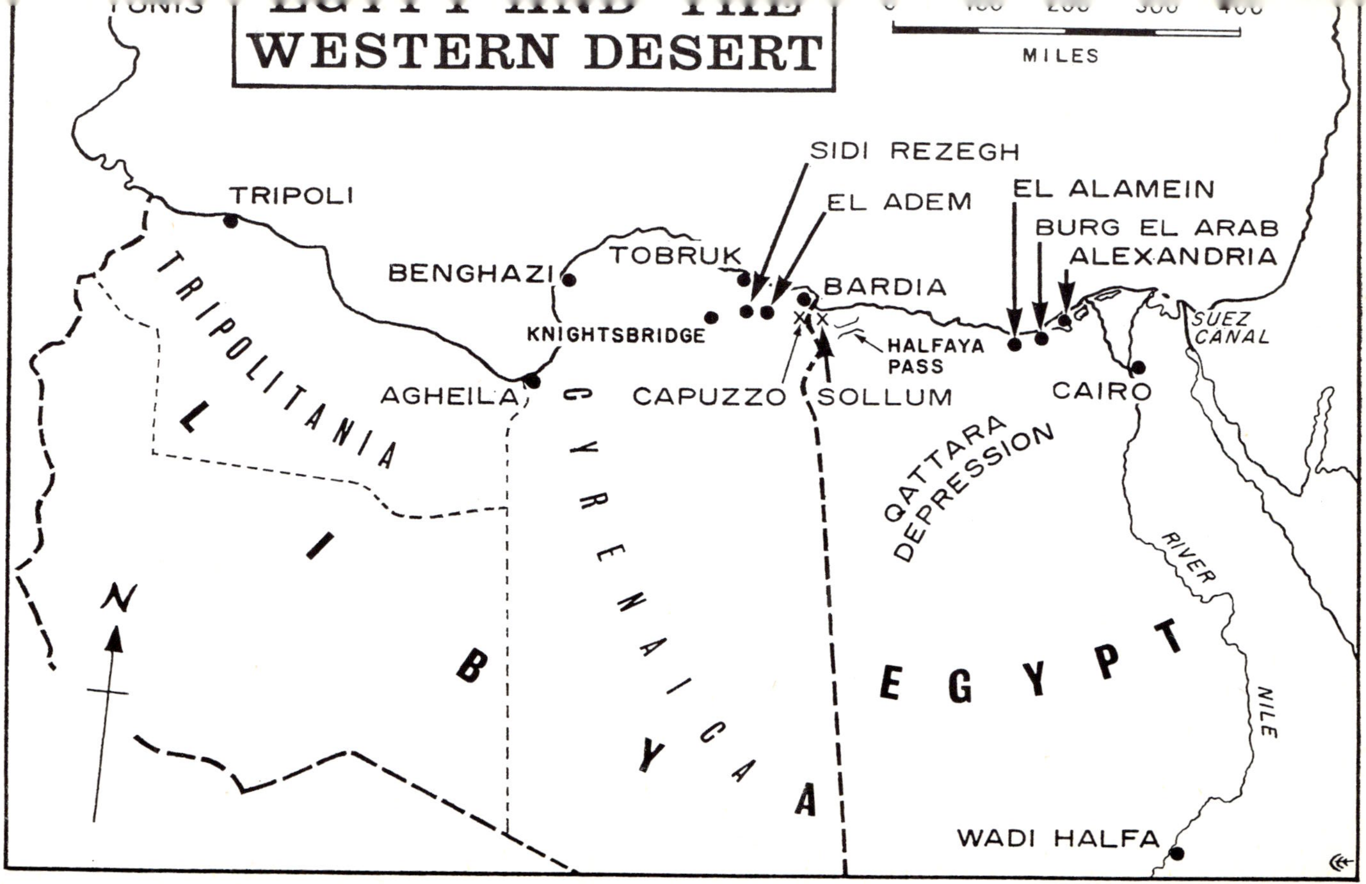
EGYPT AND THE
WESTERN DESERT
MILES
TRIPOLI
BENGHAZI
TOBRUK
SIDI REZEGH
EL ADEM
BARDIA
KNIGHTSBRIDGE
AGHEILA
CAPUZZO
SOLLUM
HALFAYA PASS
EL ALAMEIN
BURG EL ARAB
ALEXANDRIA
SUEZ CANAL
CAIRO
QATTARA DEPRESSION
TRIPOLITANIA
CYRENAICA
LIBYA
EGYPT
RIVER NILE
WADI HALFA
N

the Air Ministry. He picked it up intending to post it, but as it bore no address he put it in his pocket, thinking he would examine it and return it to the sender when he reached home.

One look at the contents of the envelope that evening showed him to his dismay that he was in possession of a TOP SECRET document; it appeared to be a communication from the Prime Minister to the Chief of the Air Staff giving full information of an Allied attack on North Africa. It seemed all too likely that if he tried to return this to the proper quarter he might well find himself in serious trouble for having the document in his possession at all, but his mother persuaded him to go to the Air Ministry early next morning and show it to no one but the Chief of the Air Staff himself.

The young Aircraftman therefore went apprehensively to Whitehall and asked to see Sir Charles Portal. Firmly resisting every attempt to persuade him to hand over the envelope to officials ranging from junior civilian clerks to senior Air Officers, he was at last shown into the presence of the C.A.S., still clutching the precious document. For his courage and persistence he was recommended for immediate promotion. And for many months afterwards the Prime Minister himself tried—unavailingly, as it happened—to secure some fitting award for the Aircraftman's mother, a Hampstead charwoman.

* * * * *

On the night of October 23, by the light of a full moon, the Battle of Alamein opened with the greatest artillery barrage in the history of warfare. General Montgomery held an advantage in men and equipment which his predecessors had never been able to command. He had a two-to-one superiority in numbers, he had over a thousand tanks and 1200 serviceable aircraft at his disposal. His plans were confidently laid, and carried through with relentless determination. The course of the battle which marked the turning-point in Allied fortunes calls for no detailed description here, but by November 2 the final stage of the attack—Operation *Supercharge*, designed to force the decisive break-through—was launched with the New Zealand Division and the 9th British Armoured Brigade in the van, the 1st British Armoured Division hurling back the last despairing counter-thrusts by Rommel's tanks, and the 5th Indian Brigade completing the enemy rout. Four days before the invasion of North Africa began from the west General Alexander was able to report an overwhelming victory in the desert and the capture of 30,000 prisoners.

* * * * *

Politically, *Torch* was the most hazardous and unpredictable venture attempted by the Allies. None could foretell the reaction of the French; none could be certain that landings in North Africa would not prompt

Spain to abandon her uneasy neutrality and allow a German drive southward to the Straits to seal off the Mediterranean. Militarily, it was a tremendous undertaking, with an armada of 650 ships advancing on the African shore from the Clyde and American ports.

The nerve-centre of the whole vast project was Gibraltar, where Eisenhower established his headquarters and where the ships and aircraft massed. Preparations on such a scale could not possibly be concealed. Much, therefore, depended on the success of Allied deception plans and on the reaction of the local Spanish commanders. If they sent panic-stricken reports to Madrid that an invasion of Spain appeared imminent it might well precipitate a German move.

In the vicinity of Gibraltar the Axis had an extensive intelligence network. German officers occupied two houses in Algeciras, both of which commanded a good view of the Rock. They busied themselves with cloak-and-dagger operations, and garnered what information they could from agents working in Gibraltar dockyard. From a comfortable vantage-point on the flat roof of a house in La Linea a Luftwaffe observer kept regular observation on the Allied planes taking off and landing at North Front, only a few hundred yards away.

There were other Germans who arrived on special missions lasting two or three days. They stayed at the British-owned Reina Cristina Hotel at Algeciras, where an entire wing housed yet another enemy intelligence staff. This was an Italian party headed by their local consul, a retired naval officer. They had a powerful telescope trained on the Rock, and one room, which the hotel maids were never allowed to enter, contained a radio transmitter.

The British Vice-Consul, Mr Edward Cottrell, also had a room in the Reina Cristina. In the darkest days of the war, when England was undergoing heavy air raids and existing on scanty rations, he found it particularly galling to watch the German visitors guzzling prodigious quantities of the best white bread and English marmalade, and monopolizing the most comfortable chairs in the lounge while they pored over the current copies of the *Illustrated London News*.[4]

At the start of the war in the Mediterranean there had been fairly extensive collaboration between the Spanish and the Italians and Germans. Axis frogmen, setting off from Algeciras, carried out frequent operations in the Bay. Their mission completed, they would make for the nearest stretch of deserted coast outside La Linea, and, once ashore, they would head for a secret hide-out in a villa between the village of Campomento

[4] Sir Edward Cottrell, C.B.E., J.P., knighted in 1957, was vice-consul at Algeciras from 1941 to 1956, and has been consul since 1956. He was Chairman of the Gibraltar City Council, 1940–45.

and San Roque hill, overlooking the Rock. Occasionally, when the British made particularly strong protests at this barefaced contravention of Spanish neutrality, the Spanish military patrols would arrest the frogmen as they came ashore. They would then announce that the prisoners had been sent for trial. In fact, they were merely taken to Seville and there released to find their way back to Algeciras.

The Spanish military commander in the area, General Barron, had been trained in Germany, and to begin with his sympathies were not unnaturally pro-German. Whether from a sense of expediency, or because he came to resent the attitude of the German officers who moved so freely about the Campo area, his attitude gradually changed, however, and when, late one night, the British Vice-Consul rang up to ask if he could come and see him urgently the General readily agreed.

A violent gale was raging, and a British lighter which had broken away from its moorings had drifted on to the Spanish coast. It was vitally important that no German or Italian agents should examine the lighter's cargo, for it consisted of two Mosquito aircraft, the design of which was then unknown to the enemy. The aircraft had been sent to Gibraltar for assembly before they were flown to Malta.

When General Barron received him the Vice-Consul came straight to the point. "I will be frank with you," he said. "These are secret aircraft, and while we have no objection to your own men seeing them we do not want Germans or Italians with technical knowledge to examine them."

It was then eleven o'clock at night, and the General immediately ordered a Spanish guard to be placed on the stranded lighter. "You must send out your most powerful tugs and pull the lighter off before day breaks," he said. "If she has vanished by dawn I shall know nothing about her."

He was as good as his word. No one, not even the Colonel of the Spanish Civil Guard, was allowed on board. When dawn came the lighter was safely back in Gibraltar.

On the eve of D-Day for *Torch* Edward Cottrell saw from his hotel room at Algeciras that several large troopships were anchored in full view of the shore. He was hurriedly shaving when he received an urgent message that General Barron wanted to see him immediately. When the Vice-Consul reached the General's residence Barron led him to the window.

"I have been trying to emulate your famous Admiral Lord Nelson," he said; "but if I was blind in both eyes I could hardly fail to see those ships lying off our coast. Tell your Admiral to get them away before I have to report their presence to Madrid." The ships were hastily moved to a less conspicuous anchorage, and no report was made.

On November 8 the landings in North Africa began. Early reports reaching the underground Operations Room in the Rock presented a confusing picture, for there was fierce fighting at sea off Casablanca and some resistance ashore at Port Lyautey. Algiers surrendered after brief resistance, but there was more fighting at Oran. Within two days, however, Darlan, who was in Algiers when the landings took place, ordered all his fellow-countrymen throughout North Africa to lay down their arms.

For some time to come Allied expediency in negotiating with Darlan was to provoke bitter controversy. And, to the embarrassment of the Americans who had brought him from occupied France to rally support to the Allies, General Giraud found himself cast in a rôle beyond his capabilities. But whatever political and administrative problems remained to be solved a firm foothold had been gained along hundreds of miles of the Mediterranean shore.

On the day the Cease Fire sounded in North Africa Churchill spoke at the Mansion House. "The bright gleam has caught the helmets of our soldiers, and warmed and cheered all our hearts," he said. "This is not the end. It is not even the beginning of the end. But it is, perhaps, the end of the beginning."

* * * * *

When he got back to Downing Street that afternoon Churchill had a long discussion with Eden, Winant, and Eisenhower's Chief of Staff, Major-General Walter Bedell Smith, about future plans. Bedell Smith got the impression that the Prime Minister was "cooling on the *Round-Up* plan for Northern France except as an ultimate death-blow against an opponent tottering and reeling from blows struck elsewhere," but this was incorrect.[5] Admittedly Churchill was anxious that the Americans should not fail to recognize the strategic opportunities which the occupation of North Africa presented, but at this stage he saw no reason to defer the cross-Channel operation. Indeed, he was soon pointing out to the President that this would be a "most grievous decision."

A few days later another long conference, this time on future Mediterranean strategy, took place at Chequers, where the Prime Minister spent nearly every week-end. The Churchill family had become very fond of Chequers. With Chartwell closed it was their only real home, the only place where they could relax at all. Although there was often little noticeable difference in the tempo of work from the routine of a weekday in Downing Street, and a Private Secretary and two confidential shorthand typists were always on duty there, Mr Churchill did not stick so rigidly to a set programme. There was an air of greater informality, uniforms were discarded, and the talk was not solely of war, for though politicians and

[5] See Sherwood, *op. cit.*, p. 653. *Round-Up* (afterwards known as *Overlord*) was the plan for the liberation of France.

senior officers of the Services were the most frequent guests Chequers had many other visitors.

Staying there on his week-end of the Mediterranean conference were the distinguished pianist, M. Benno Moiseiwitsch, and his wife. M. Moiseiwitsch had been a tireless supporter of Mrs Churchill's Aid to Russia Fund, which had just passed its first anniversary. On the piano in the Great Hall he played several times for his fellow-guests, and greatly intrigued the Prime Minister by his versatility. After a recital of classical music he asked for two oranges, and, rolling them up and down the keyboard, he played a succession of popular tunes without his fingers ever touching the keys at all.

Because it formed a memorable part of Mr Churchill's weekly routine life at Chequers deserves more than a passing mention. The house itself stands in a large park bounded on its north and west by the Icknield Way, the earliest known road made by the British before the Roman occupation. Lord Lee of Fareham had presented it to the nation after the First World War in the hope that it would be an inducement to "our rulers" to spend two days a week "in the high and pure air of the Chiltern hills and woods," and he had endowed it so that the Prime Minister of the day would be able to live there even if he had no other income than his salary. Lloyd George, in 1921, had been the first Premier to use it.

A mellow red brick mansion, Chequers had not changed hands except by inheritance for more than eight hundred years until Lord Lee went to live there in 1909. The North Front remained as William Hawtrey left it in the sixteenth century—the Hawtrey family occupied Chequers for three hundred and fifty years—but the rest of the building had undergone many changes, and Lord Lee himself roofed over the central courtyard to form the Great Hall which is now the main feature of the ground floor.

As a war-time residence the house had decided drawbacks. There was no effective central heating, and the Great Hall, with its lofty roof, was a draughty meeting-place in the depths of winter. Harry Hopkins was not the only one who found it difficult to sleep at night on account of the icy cold; more than once Tommy had to stuff sheets into the warped window-frames of his bedroom to keep out the snow.

On the first floor the whole of the north side of the house was taken up by a long gallery. As most of the west side was occupied by a large drawing-room this left little space for bedrooms and bathrooms, and accommodation was woefully cramped. There were, in fact, only four spare bedrooms and one bathroom available for guests in addition to the master suite generally reserved for the most distinguished visitor. On one occasion Tommy, walking in the garden, was astonished to see the American Ambassador emerging furtively from the window of the downstairs cloakroom. He had been in the inner part of the only bathroom when he heard some one enter to take a bath. Fearing this was the Lady Curator, whose rooms were in the same passage, Mr Winant escaped as rapidly as possible by the only remaining route—through the window!

Churchill did most of his work in the Hawtrey Room, on the right of the main entrance. A secret stairway led from it to a small garret on the top floor where Lady Mary Grey, sister of the beautiful and ill-fated Lady Jane, had been kept prisoner for a year by Queen Elizabeth. The Hawtrey Room had two exhibits which the Prime Minister greatly prized. One was a huge globe of the world which General Marshall had presented to him; the other was an epidiascope—an apparatus for projecting and magnifying small objects—which was used to interpret the reconnaissance photographs brought to Chequers once a week by an officer from Air Marshal Harris's headquarters near by.

To Chequers came a constant stream of callers, some to stay, some invited down for a meal and a talk. One member of the Churchill family who was always a welcome guest was the Prime Minister's younger brother Jack.

A London stockbroker, Jack Churchill had never been in the public eye, and had taken little active part in politics, but he had travelled widely, was a discerning student of foreign affairs, and an entertaining *raconteur*. Tall and good-looking, with a neatly trimmed moustache, he looked very much the retired Army officer and had, in fact, won the D.S.O. in the First World War. One son, Major John Churchill, was in charge of a camouflage organization carrying out work for Combined Operations; his daughter Clarissa was later to marry Anthony Eden.

Jack Churchill had a shrewd financial brain, and when his wife, a daughter of the Earl of Abingdon, died early in the war he was given a room in Downing Street and devoted all his time to helping his brother, taking over management of all his private affairs. Soon he became an accepted member of Winston Churchill's inner circle—his *famille militaire*—and although he remained in the background, he was, in his quiet way, a very real source of strength to his brother.

At Chequers the Prime Minister rarely appeared before lunch. He would work in his bedroom throughout the morning, and perhaps hold meetings there. Anyone who received a summons to Chequers had to be prepared for ruthless cross-examination at any hour of the day or night. A senior member of the naval planning staff who went there often has a vivid recollection of those week-ends:

"If you argued on policy or strategy with the P.M. you had to be straightforward, but one fatal mistake was to *volunteer* information, for unless you were very sure of your facts you were likely to be harried remorselessly. This became a standing joke among staff officers invited to Chequers, and we would remind each other, "For God's sake, no volunteering!" Winston was a charming host, and after going at a problem hammer and tongs all morning he would shepherd us into lunch and be thoroughly relaxed, amusing and entertaining. Then back we would go to more violent argument, with no holds barred."

At some point in every afternoon Churchill would retire to bed. After a brief sleep he would resume work until it was time for dinner. Sometimes he would take his papers into the garden, and he liked to dictate from a rustic seat sheltered by a semicircular yew hedge on the border of the North Lawn. Occasionally he would sit out on the terrace overlooking the rose garden, where an ancient sundial bore the legend:

Ye houres doe flie
Full soon we die
In age secure
Ye house and hills
Alone endure.

To many who arrived straight from the maelstrom of the London Blitz, or some far-away battlefront, the writing on the sundial seemed to convey perfectly, in those few words, the ageless tranquillity of Chequers and its surroundings.

Indoors the focal point of life was the Great Hall, which contained a variety of good and excruciatingly bad pictures, and a strange assortment of furniture. Under the window was a great leather-covered chest with brass studs. This bore the royal cipher, and had belonged to James II, who had kept his papers in it when, as Duke of York, he had served at the Admiralty.

Mr Churchill himself always sat in a high-backed armchair by the open fireplace. When something was particularly on his mind he would often say to Tommy, "Play the gramophone!" Then, to a background of American military marches or Gilbert and Sullivan, he would pace up and down, thinking aloud. In addition to comic opera and Sousa marches he had some unexpected favourites. One scratched and ancient record which he demanded time and again was of Eddie Cantor singing "Build a little home" and "Keep Young and Beautiful," from the pre-war film *Roman Scandals.*

He had a prodigious memory for Victorian music-hall songs, and could recite dozens of them without apparent effort. Two of his star turns were a comic song called "Poultry" and a heroic ballad entitled "Who's in charge of the clattering train?"

After dinner there would frequently be a film show in the Long Gallery, to which the officers and men of the Guard quartered at Chequers had a standing invitation. As time went on the task of providing new films for the Prime Minister to see became increasingly difficult, and often Jack Beddington, the Director of the M.O.I. Films Division, was at his wits' end. Happily Mr Churchill never grew tired of seeing certain old films again and again, the most popular of these being *The Mikado* and Korda's *Lady Hamilton*.

The evening film show over, the Prime Minister would start a conference with his military advisers, or the house party would return to the Great Hall for more gramophone music. Mr Churchill had few other diversions. He enjoyed an occasional game of five-pack bezique, but the only other amusement which seemed to take his mind off the war in times of crisis was Corinthian Bagatelle, the pin-table game which he encouraged every one to play. On his instructions a book was kept, in which every score of over a thousand was meticulously entered. Averell Harriman was the most successful performer, and the Prime Minister never gave up trying to beat his record.

It was a sheer waste of time for his staff to drop hints about the need for him to get some rest. Until he was ready to go to bed no one could persuade him to do so. Although he disregarded it himself, he had a favourite aphorism about sleep. "The older you get the more sleep you need. Finally you sleep all the time. In life there are many avenues, but all lead finally to kindly, all-embracing death," he was fond of observing. But though he was now nearing his seventieth year, he seemed to grow less and less inclined to retire early. The gramophone in the Great Hall would play on, and even when Tommy hopefully changed the record to Brahms' "Lullaby" or "Goodnight, Sweetheart," Mr Churchill paid not the slightest attention.

It was equally difficult to persuade him to leave Chequers when the week-end was over, and it was time to return to London. If he had a meeting to attend in Downing Street the journey by road was often done at breakneck speed, for although at first he allowed seventy-five minutes there came a day when there was little traffic on the road and the driver arrived at No. 10 with a few minutes in hand. Mr Churchill promptly decreed that in future it was quite unnecessary to allow more than sixty-five minutes. Finally this was reduced even further. Considering the problem mathematically, Mr Churchill obviously thought he was erring on the side of caution in allowing an hour for the forty odd miles to the heart of London. If the traffic happened to be heavier than usual then that was an obstacle which skill and determination could plainly overcome.

Unconcerned by any possible hazards of the road, he would settle down to concentrate on some current problem of the war. His companions, however, often found these journeys to Downing Street a little nerve-racking!

23

Stalemate in Tunisia—and a Secret Weapon

In his anxiety to reach a firm decision on future Allied strategy with all possible speed Mr Churchill was not alone. Before November ended the President was urging an early conference between Britain, the United States, and Russia. "Our own Combined Chiefs of Staff will, I believe, have a recommendation for us within a few days as to what the next steps should be, but I feel very strongly that we have got to sit down at the table with the Russians."[1] For a welcome change Stalin approved of the Allied proposal, but he explained that he himself would be unable to leave the Soviet Union. "I think that in spite of [this] you and I should get together," wrote Roosevelt to Churchill, and with Stalin's concurrence plans were made for a British-American military conference at Casablanca early in the New Year.

On the evening of Sunday, November 29, Churchill broadcast one of his periodic reports to the nation. After reviewing the stirring events in Africa he warned the Italian nation of "prolonged, scientific, and shattering attack" on their cities and military bases. "Africa is no halting place. It is not a seat but a springboard," he said. He paid tribute to the determination with which the Russians were pressing home their attacks in the Stalingrad area. "The Germans have at least the consolation of knowing that they have been led, not by the German General Staff but by the military genius of Corporal Hitler," he added.

Turning to the sinking of the French fleet, he said very movingly, "From the flame and smoke of the explosions at Toulon France will rise again." He ended on a characteristically realistic note, warning that bitter and

[1] Churchill, Vol. IV, p. 594.

bloody years might lie ahead, and that if the war in Europe should end before the conquest of Japan we should go to the aid of the Americans in the Pacific. He also warned against too much bickering about academic post-war planning problems.

"The dawn of 1943 will soon loom red before us, and we must brace ourselves to cope with the trials and problems of what must be a stern and terrible year. We do so with the assurance of ever-growing strength, and we do so as a nation with a strong will, a bold heart, and a good conscience."

There was indeed a surprising amount of petty bickering in high places now that the tide had turned in Africa, and a strangely unrealistic preoccupation with peace-time planning. The leader of the Parliamentary Labour Party girded at the Government for its reluctance to concentrate on the difficulties which peace would bring. Mr Greenwood and his supporters ignored the fact that from Norway to the Mediterranean Europe was still firmly gripped by the enemy and appalling losses were being suffered at sea.[2] The Government were, in point of fact, far from unmindful of the need for social reform, and on December 4 the Beveridge Report was published.[3] Churchill refused, however, to be stampeded into making extravagant promises which it might well prove difficult to fulfil. "Nothing would be more dangerous than for people to feel cheated because they had been led to expect attractive schemes which turn out to be economically impossible."[4]

Feeling continued to run high over the negotiations with Admiral Darlan, but the climate changed abruptly after the Prime Minister had addressed the House in Secret Session. In one of the most able speeches he had ever made he convinced a critical House by sheer logic that there was no alternative to the Clark-Darlan Agreement.

"The question which we must ask ourselves is not whether we like or do not like what is going on, but what we are going to do about it. In war it is not always possible to have everything go exactly as one likes. In working with allies it sometimes happens that they develop opinions of their own. . . .

"I hold no brief for Admiral Darlan. . . . But it is necessary for the House to realize that the Government and to a large extent the people of the United States do not feel the same way about Darlan as we do."

After pointing out that it was "only through Darlan's help that we are now fighting the Boche in Tunisia instead of somewhere in the vicinity of

[2] Over the whole year Allied shipping losses amounted to 1664 ships, totalling 7,790,697 tons.

[3] Many years earlier Sir William Beveridge had been closely associated with Churchill over the launching of unemployment insurance.

[4] In a memorandum to the Chancellor of the Exchequer on December 17, 1942.

Bone or even west of that," he emphasized the enduring French belief in the principle of *droit administratif.*

"Much therefore turns in the minds of French officers upon whether there is a direct, unbroken chain of lawful command. . . . Many Frenchmen who admire General de Gaulle and envy him in his rôle nevertheless regard him as a man who has rebelled against the authority of the French State, which in their prostration they conceive to be vested in the person of the antique defeatist who to them is the illustrious and venerable Marshal Pétain, the hero of Verdun. . . . Darlan was the only authority plainly derived from Marshal Pétain. General Giraud does not claim that authority. . . . He was quite convinced that he had no power whatever to influence the decision, and, more than that, he seems to have felt himself at a disadvantage compared with those other Frenchmen who could prove that they had obeyed the orders emanating legally from the Head of the State. . . . Giraud quickly gave up trying to help us."

He ended on a note of scorn. "I must say I think he is a poor creature with a jaundiced outlook and disorganized loyalties who in all this tremendous African episode, West and East alike, can find no point to excite his interest except the arrangements made between General Eisenhower and Admiral Darlan."[5]

Fate decreed that Darlan was not long to survive as a figure of contention on the African scene. On Christmas Eve he was assassinated in Algiers by a twenty-year-old youth believed to hold monarchist sympathies. His death paved the way for a *rapprochement* between the followers of De Gaulle and the Frenchmen who had hitherto taken their orders from Pétain. Giraud, an uninspiring figurehead but an honest man and the only logical choice in the existing circumstances, took over the reins.

* * * * *

Before long it became evident that the Germans were prepared to fight every inch for Tunisia. With the Axis forces in rapid retreat across Libya it was more important than ever for them to hold this bridgehead, and the scale of their airborne reinforcements soon ruled out any possibility of a swift advance on Tunis by General Anderson's Army. American and British troops got within twelve miles of Tunis itself, but then the rains set in and roads and airfields became impassable. There was nothing for it but to hold the ground already gained and wait for the brief winter to end.

Although the forthcoming Conference was much on his mind, Churchill watched developments in North Africa with close attention. When the rainy season opened Anderson, waiting for the 11th Armoured Division to reach him from Britain, signalled that its Sherman tanks would not be heavy enough for the Tunisian mud. Weighing the suggestion that this

[5] *Secret Session Speeches,* pp. 76–96.

Division should be held back and the 25th Tank Brigade, equipped with heavy Churchill tanks, should be sent in its place, the Prime Minister inquired on what day the 25th Brigade would be in a position to fire its first shot in North Africa if the plan was carried out.

The change would obviously involve a tremendous reshuffle, and the time it would take was difficult to calculate in a matter of hours, for the 25th Brigade had not been expected to leave the United Kingdom for three months. Before it could depart ships and escorts had to be made available; men had to be brought back from courses; the routes to various West Country ports had to be examined so that the big loads could negotiate obstructions on the roads; embarkation leave had to be granted, and security problems investigated. The Prime Minister's question therefore caused something of an upheaval in the War Office, and ten Major-Generals and many other staff officers sat up all night. By five o'clock in the morning they were in a position to supply the answer in a single sentence, and to make their reply more impressive the C.I.G.S. even gave the exact minute when the first shot would be fired. Churchill was delighted with this concise reply, but his memory was so phenomenal that the War Office knew he might well make inquiries later. The Commanding Officer of the North Irish Horse was therefore summoned, and specially briefed to open fire on the stroke of 4.30 P.M. on the day in question. This was duly done.

To the young staff officers in the War Office who frequently came in contact with the Prime Minister Churchill seemed a galvanic figure. Recalling this period, an officer on the Military Operations staff remarked to the writer, "We never regarded him as the instigator of crazy schemes, who wasted precious time with unnecessary questions. Every intervention was very much to the point. He inspired a sense of awe, even fright! It was leadership exercised to the very highest degree. All of us had the feeling that he was constantly at our right hand. We could not afford to make a single mistake."

One Saturday at the end of November the same officer went to Downing Street to bring the maps up to date. It was a task which fell to him once a week, and he chose Saturday as Mr Churchill was usually at Chequers.

On this particular morning he was lying full length on the floor, marking alterations to the British front line on the Algerian border. His tunic was unbuttoned, and beside him on the floor he had placed his cap and Sam Browne belt.

Suddenly he heard the door open, and into the Map Room came the Prime Minister and the American General Simpson. Ignoring the silent figure on the floor, they talked for a few minutes, and then left the room.

A second later the door opened once more. To his astonishment the recumbent artist, still busily drawing his chalk lines, heard the chink of coins landing in his upturned cap. He looked round just in time to see Mr Churchill stealthily retreating, a beaming smile on his face. Not a word had been spoken!

At night the Prime Minister had a disconcerting habit of coming through on the scrambler telephone to quite junior officers on duty in the War Office. Without any preamble he would begin firing questions, and woe betide the officer who did not have the current operational situation at his fingertips.

He generally rang up soon after the midnight news broadcast, but one evening when all was quiet the duty officer, a captain in the Dorset Regiment, decided it was safe to slip out for a breather. Unfortunately for him, the Prime Minister came through on the phone a few minutes later, and was highly displeased to find a Warrant Officer left in charge. Next day one of his Private Secretaries rang up. The Prime Minister, he said, considered it unforgivable that no commissioned officer had been on duty.

The Gunner Major who answered the telephone on this occasion ventured to disagree. "After all," he pointed out, "when the P.M. goes away he leaves Mr Attlee in charge." Unable to think of any suitable reply to this profound observation the Private Secretary rang off!

* * * * *

Apart from a journey to Dover with Smuts Mr Churchill had not for some weeks been able to leave Whitehall, but early in December he went north on one of his inspection tours, taking with him the Secretary of State for Air (Sir Archibald Sinclair), Averell Harriman, Ernest Bevin, Subaltern Mary Churchill, and Tommy.

On a freezingly cold afternoon he drove round the Bradford area for nearly an hour, sitting perched up in the back of an open car and waving to the crowds who flocked to see him pass. Ten thousand assembled in front of the Town Hall to hear him speak. "He looks champion," said a man in the crowd: "you'd never think he had all the cares of the world on his shoulders."

He watched troops undergoing a toughening course in remote Teesdale. He also went to Lowther Castle, near Penrith, where in great secrecy units of the 79th Armoured Division, commanded by General Hobart, were training to use C.D.L. tanks.

The story of the C.D.L. tank is little known even to-day. It was destined to make only a fleeting appearance on the battlefield, for it took many months to perfect a very complicated apparatus and train men to use it. Then, for a frustratingly long time, there was no suitable opportunity for bringing it into action, for it introduced an entirely new technique into tank warfare.

The men of the Royal Armoured Corps who operated these C.D.L. tanks were never quite sure what the initials signified. It was hinted that they represented the code words "Canal Defence Line," but no one was encouraged to ask unnecessary questions; rumour had it that a soldier who talked about C.D.L. tanks in a bar while on leave in Cairo had been imprisoned for a long term. When an officer first arrived at Lowther Castle he signed an oath of secrecy. No one would speak to him about the work he had come to do. He was told he would find out in due course.

On the following night he would be taken out into the training area on the wild moorland overlooking Lake Ullswater. In the distance he would hear the roar of approaching tanks, and suddenly he would be bathed in a searing white glare. Then the light would go out. Close at hand he would hear movements, the sound of engines, and the voices of men, but, temporarily blinded, he would see nothing in the black darkness which surrounded him.

The basis of the whole idea was that by mounting powerful floodlights, developing millions of candlepower, on the front of each tank, and oscillating this light by the manipulation of a steel shutter, you could defeat the critical vision of the eye. It was believed that as a result enemy fire directed against a formation of these tanks would tend to be aimed too high and the tanks would be able to advance unscathed.

In each troop there would be eight C.D.L. tanks, with one Sherman gun tank in the centre. The zones of light from each C.D.L. tank would overlap to form one huge moving curtain of glare. Behind this men and machines were invisible.

The technique of operating a C.D.L. tank demanded a high standard of driving skill, for the tanks had to be closed down, and kept in perfect formation. Wearing asbestos gloves, the tank crews had to change the carbon arcs in the lamps every thirty minutes. In the Matilda tanks used early on the power for the floodlights came from the engines of the tanks themselves. Later, when Grants took their place, a special generator was incorporated.

The first men to come to Lowther were a mechanized detachment of the Durham Light Infantry. The Geordie miners soon became highly expert in their new rôle, continually setting up fresh records for the time taken to change the white-hot carbons, but it was hard and heartbreaking work to keep the tanks in service, for the tracks broke easily on the Cumbrian stone walls whenever the drivers charged them at an angle, and the weather they had to contend with during this first bitter winter of 1942–43 was appalling. Officers and men alike lived under canvas in a sea of mud;

several times all the tents were uprooted by gales. As the Matildas churned their way across the sodden moorland falling snow froze on their steel hulls, and the tank park—an expanse of bare ground with no concrete hard-standings—was often an impassable swamp.

Civilians were kept well away from the training area by a ring of sentry posts, but the strange activities on the moors could hardly remain unnoticed. The great white glare of the floodlamps lit up the night sky for miles around, and the local police had to answer anxious inquiries from as far afield as Newcastle, over sixty miles away.

Sometimes, when the tired tank crews were having a night off and drinking their ale in a pub in Penrith, there would be a hush in the conversation as the walls of the bar were suddenly and fiercely illuminated through the drawn blinds, but the soldiers who came into the town on a night's leave were rarely questioned about what they were doing. The men and women of the Lake District sensed that something of vital importance was being attempted. And it became an accepted, unspoken rule that they should not discuss it in public, either among themselves or with inquisitive strangers.

A favourite haunt of the young C.D.L. officers was the ancient George Hotel, in Penrith's main street, where some extremely pretty girls served behind the bar. To their regret, however, the officers never made much headway with the barmaids, because, as all training took place at night, they could rarely spend an evening in the town. When they did get an evening off duty they would walk into the bar, pale and haggard after many nights without sleep, only to find more fortunate rivals in firm possesssion.

On the night when Mr Churchill went to Lowther a special marquee was erected for the visitors, and a C.D.L. attack was staged with this as the target. It was, as usual, bitterly cold, but Tommy for one found the climax of the exercise an unforgettable experience—the sound of the tanks roaring towards them through the darkness and the sudden perfectly synchronized transition from starless night to synthetic day as the power was switched on and the shimmering curtain of light enveloped them.

For the officers and men engaged on this Top Secret project the Prime Minister's visit was a welcome break in the monotony. After Mr Churchill had gone the intensive training continued in the same conditions of stringent secrecy, but as the months went by and still there was no news of the tanks going into action a feeling of frustration set in. Some of the officers even volunteered for a transfer to the Palestine Police. They were sharply told to get on with the task in hand.

The end of the C.D.L. story belongs to a later chapter, but one strange and unexplained incident on the moors deserves recording here. Security on every aspect of the C.D.L. project was rigidly enforced, and the whole training area was heavily guarded. It was therefore difficult for any unauthorized person to approach the perimeter unobserved, much less penetrate into the training ground.

One night, however, when the tanks were out on an exercise and the order was given to switch on the lights, all the tank crews saw quite clearly a tall, motionless figure standing watching them from a small plantation on high ground near Emperor's Lodge, one part of the estate which was particularly closely guarded.

The tanks had halted. For a few seconds the crews stared in amazement. Then the man suddenly vanished. The tanks charged headlong for the spot, but when they reached the belt of trees there was no sign of a living soul.

A few nights later the lone watcher reappeared—to vanish once again just as swiftly and mysteriously as soon as the pursuit started. For some time after that the tanks went into the training area at night with armed men lying on top ready to leap down and search the plantation. But the elusive intruder was never captured.

24

Return to the Mediterranean

THE closing hours of 1942 brought news of a naval engagement off the North Cape which was to have far-reaching consequences. A powerful German force which included the pocket battleship *Lutzow* and the heavy cruiser *Hipper* sailed to intercept an Allied convoy bound for Russia with war supplies, but the convoy got through almost unscathed, Captain Robert St Vincent Sherbrooke fighting a most gallant destroyer action to hold off the *Hipper*, and Rear-Admiral R. L. Burnett, with the cruisers *Sheffield* and *Jamaica*, driving off the *Lutzow*.[1]

The failure of the German heavy ships to press home their attack infuriated Hitler, and Goering, who had long and bitterly complained of the wastefulness of maintaining capital ships which achieved such meagre results, at last had his way. A month later Admiral Doenitz, arch-protagonist of the U-boat, took over command of the Navy. With Raeder's departure the German surface fleet was never again destined to challenge the Royal Navy effectively at sea.[2]

The successful passage of these supply ships earned little recognition from Moscow. In message after message Stalin continued to complain of the inadequate scale of the Allied convoy effort. He seemed to have no understanding of the hazards and difficulties involved. "Maisky should be told that I am getting to the end of my tether with these repeated Russian naggings, and that it is not the slightest use trying to knock me about any

[1] Captain (later Rear-Admiral) Sherbrooke, severely wounded on the bridge of H.M.S. *Onslow* during the action, was awarded the Victoria Cross.

[2] A year later the *Scharnhorst* sailed from Alten Fjord to attack another Russian-bound convoy. She was engaged by units of the Home Fleet under the command of Vice-Admiral Sir Bruce Fraser, and sunk with the loss of nearly 2000 officers and men.

more," wrote the Prime Minister shortly before he left for Casablanca.[3] At such a critical stage in the war Russia's attitude towards her Allies seemed bereft of rhyme or reason. While demanding extravagant sacrifices from them on the one hand, she deliberately sought every opportunity for inflicting petty pinpricks. One example will suffice. During the past year vast consignments of medical supplies had been sent to Russia by Mrs Churchill's Fund, but even this provoked an official complaint. Claiming that this British charitable organization had no right to spend its money on aid of this kind, Maisky presented a formal demand that all medical stores should be provided under the Lease-Lend agreement.

On the night of January 12 Churchill set out in *Commando* for his North African rendezvous with the President. Tommy sensed that they were in for a trying journey, for the Prime Minister, who had one of the only two beds in the aircraft, soon complained that it was cold and uncomfortable. He spent most of the night sitting up; when he was finally persuaded to retire he noticed the glow of a heater which had been installed for the trip and became instantly convinced that the Liberator was about to catch fire. He therefore ordered the crew to switch off the apparatus altogether. After that his frozen fellow-passengers waited miserably for dawn to break.

"As the sun rose we sighted the African coast. What a contrast to the chill, wet England we had left a few hours before. Above us was a cloudless blue sky; below, the brilliant line of the coast, shimmering in the hot sun.

"The P.M. was supposed to be travelling strictly incognito. When we landed we were met by a major in the American Security organization who took one look at him and then said scornfully to Averell Harriman, 'Fancy dressing up a little guy like that in R.A.F. uniform and expecting us to believe he's Winston Churchill. The British certainly get some crazy ideas.' "[4]

The scene of the Conference was not, in fact, Casablanca but Anfa, a small holiday resort four miles to the south, where a number of picturesque villas were grouped round a hill-top hotel. One of these, the Villa Mirador, had been allocated to Mr Churchill; another, two hundred yards away and owned by a film star, had been set aside for the President. The whole Conference area, which had been cleared of civilians and surrounded by barbed wire, was heavily guarded by American troops under the command of General George Patton, whose headquarters lay just outside the perimeter. Not satisfied with the barbed wire, the Americans had brought in

[3] Minute to Foreign Secretary and First Sea Lord, January 9, 1943. (See Churchill, Vol. IV, p. 825.)
[4] C. R. Thompson, Notes.

a number of guard dogs which prowled around biting every one impartially.

"As soon as we reached our villa the P.M. decided to take a bath. This produced a minor crisis, for the staff sent out from England were mystified by the heating system. They stoked the fire until it was white-hot, but only a trickle of cold water reached Mr Churchill's bathroom. As the united efforts of our own cook and stewards, the French housekeeper, and six Sappers continued to meet with no success, a local plumber was sent for. He discovered that some one had connected up the small *chauffage d'été* direct to the main boiler and cut out the bath. As a result the two boilers were almost at bursting-point, for the water was being driven from one to the other, getting hotter and hotter!"[5]

On the following day the President arrived. His long journey by air via Trinidad, Belem (Brazil), and Bathurst had taken him over Freetown and in the harbour there he had noticed a new Norwegian tanker lying apparently idle. "Surely we should be making some use of her," he remarked to the Prime Minister when they met. Lord Leathers, who was present, promptly explained that the tanker was there because we were still waiting for steel from America to build oil-tanks ashore at Freetown. Until these were completed some means had to be provided for storing the oil needed for refuelling Allied ships which called at the port. To Roosevelt's astonishment, Leathers, who had no notes with him, then gave him the name of the tanker he had seen, its precise tonnage, and the exact length of time it had been at Freetown.

Another member of the British party who made an instant impression on the President was General Alexander, who had flown from his headquarters to report on the Eighth Army's progress. Although it was now the eve of a major attack on Tripoli, Alexander, gay and debonair, looked as if he had not a care in the world. Tommy asked him if the sudden summons to the Conference had upset his calculations. "Not at all," said Alexander; "I've been over all the plans, and there's really nothing for me to do now but leave things to Monty. Anyway, I can always get back quickly if he wants me."

The staff talks were spread over eight days. The chief issue was whether the Allied effort in 1943 should be concentrated on Germany or Japan. Once it was decided to throw the main weight of the Anglo-American forces against the mainland of Europe it was agreed to press on with preparations for *Bolero*; plans were approved for an early assault on Sicily, the obvious stepping-stone to the Italian mainland; and Alexander was chosen as Eisenhower's Deputy Commander-in-Chief in the Mediterranean theatre. The talks then ranged over a wider field—the outline

[5] *Ibid.*

of future operations in the Pacific and Burma theatres, the Russian convoy programme, the reinforcement of General Chennault's forces in China, and the air offensive against the Ruhr. There was much anxious discussion, too, about the shortage of landing-craft, which already threatened to become a limiting factor in Allied plans.

Neither the Prime Minister nor the President attended these staff conferences. Every day they worked with their own advisers, and problems were referred to them as they cropped up. On most evenings Churchill and Roosevelt dined together, and there was often the atmosphere of a family party, for Elliott Roosevelt and Franklin Roosevelt junior had joined their father; Randolph Churchill had flown across from the Tunisian front; and Harry Hopkins's son, a private in the American Army, had also been given leave for the occasion. After dinner one night a group of American coloured troops sang spirituals in the President's drawing-room, and Mr Churchill was much moved by a negro soloist's rendering of "The Londonderry Air."

Another evening the Prime Minister dined with General Patton. As he never drank cocktails he decided to delay his arrival until a few minutes before the time mentioned for dinner, but when he and Tommy entered the house they found Patton—two pearl-handled revolvers in his belt—sitting in the lounge hall with his staff and drinking what the General termed 'cog-nak.' Tumblers of neat brandy being more than even Mr Churchill's iron constitution could stomach before dinner he declined to follow his host's example. It was just as well, for when they all went into dinner an hour later every one but the guest of the evening had iced water. In front of Mr Churchill, however, was a bottle of champagne, which Patton, who had gone to great trouble to procure it, obviously expected him to drink without assistance.

An important item on the Conference agenda was the question of French leadership in North Africa. General Giraud, seemingly unaware of his invidious position as the American-sponsored rival to de Gaulle, was already at Anfa, but de Gaulle only consented to join in the discussions after considerable pressure had been brought to bear on him by Eden in London. When Tommy met him two days before the Conference ended he found de Gaulle "glum as usual, and rather pompous and vinegary." He was incensed to find himself on French soil and yet heavily guarded by American troops; he was incensed to find Giraud, with the backing of the Americans, claiming an equality with him in the future ordering of French affairs.

It was some time before he could be persuaded to meet Giraud at all, but at the Press conference held at the conclusion of the talks the two French generals were persuaded to shake hands in public. The occasion was enlivened by some of Mr Churchill's best French. Speaking to Giraud of one person, he observed, "Il a la racine de la matier dans lui." The phrase "pulling his punches" was translated with even greater directness as "minimisant ses punches"!

It was during this Press conference that the President used the much criticized phrase about "unconditional surrender" in defining Allied aims. It did not, in fact, appear in the draft of the official communiqué, but was brought up by Roosevelt when talking to the Press. Writing to Hopkins's biographer after the war, Churchill said, "I would not myself have used these words, but I immediately stood by the President and have frequently defended the decision. It is false to suggest that it prolonged the war. Negotiation with Hitler was impossible. He was a maniac with supreme power to play his hand out to the end, which he did; and so did we."[6]

* * * * *

When the Conference broke up the Prime Minister, who was still uncertain about his next move, decided to drive to Marrakesh with the President, who was leaving from the airfield there next morning. Tommy organized a picnic lunch for twenty-eight, and a convoy of cars set off across the desert. Even by war-time standards it was an unusual picnic. They halted on a stretch of exposed, stony ground, round which a screen of armoured scout cars patrolled, and they ate their lunch watched by a posse of Secret Servicemen with tommy-guns at the ready. The isolation and the cordon of guards did not, however, prevent a group of Arab children appearing mysteriously from nowhere to beg for food.

The President was greatly attracted by Marrakesh, the lovely capital of Southern Morocco, set in its oasis of trees and green fields and dominated by the Atlas Mountains. In the clear light the snow-capped range, fully forty miles distant, seemed to hover just over the walls of the city.

The Villa Taylor, where they spent that night, was an unusual and luxurious house built some five years earlier by a wealthy American, Mrs Moses Taylor. From its Berber tower it commanded a magnificent view over the rooftops of Marrakesh to the plain and the mountains beyond. The house and garden had been created in native style, with a central courtyard, orange-trees, and fountains, and the interior decoration, with its lavish use of native painted wood, mosaics, and rich furnishings, was exotic in the extreme. Perhaps the Villa's most striking feature, however, was its tiled bathrooms. The baths themselves, sunk deep in the floor, were like small swimming-pools, and were fed by water gushing from the mouths of marble lions.

[6] Sherwood, *op. cit.*, p. 693.

The Villa Taylor had only one drawback. Its owner had installed a somewhat eccentric central heating system, which discharged showers of black snow on the surprised newcomers sitting out in the courtyard.

* * * * *

Seen off by the Prime Minister, who went out to the airfield in his dressing-gown and bedroom slippers, Roosevelt and Hopkins set out early next morning on their flight home. When he got back to the villa Churchill set up his easel in the tower, and spent most of the morning painting while he awaited word from England which would decide his immediate plans. The Foreign Office were urging him to return to London, but the Prime Minister himself had other ideas. He was anxious to revisit the Middle East and encourage Turkey to abandon her neutrality—a move which the Foreign Office, fearing a diplomatic rebuff, regarded with some apprehension. He also wanted to see something of Alexander's victorious troops in the desert.

Knowing by now that the Prime Minister generally got his own way, Tommy had a hunch that Cairo would be their next stop. He therefore arranged with Vanderkloot to take the Liberator up on a test flight and have a look at the pass through the Atlas Mountains while it was still light. That same evening they were in the air again, and heading for Egypt.

"We kept level with the snow-line for a time. Below us the land seemed barren and uninhabited, but as dusk fell hundreds of little fires blazed out all along our route. Once we were over the summit the ground fell sheer away for several thousand feet until it reached the Sahara. We flew east till daybreak, when we picked up the Nile and followed it to Cairo. As usual the P.M. seemed intensely stimulated by the journey and the prospect of conducting negotiations in a fresh sphere. When he reached the Embassy he had a long talk with Admiral Harwood about the French squadron still lying at Alexandria. Next day came a message from the Turks saying they would meet us at Adana, on the coast near the Syrian border.

"This started a frantic search for plain clothes as we couldn't wear uniform in a neutral country. The only suit I could buy which anywhere near fitted me was a startling affair in electric blue. We all thought that Jumbo Wilson, for one, would never find any plain clothes he could get into, but to our astonishment he eventually appeared in a suit which was too *large* for him. It belonged to the Ambassador. In our civilian disguises we looked like a band of gangsters."[7]

The site of the Adana Conference was a railway-siding in desolate open country. All around was ploughed land churned to an impassable morass by torrential rain. The Turks had provided two trains which were coupled

[7] C. R. Thompson, Notes.

together. In them the Prime Minister's party and the entire Turkish Government worked and slept.

"It was known that many Germans were living and working in the neighbourhood. In the circumstances the arrangements for guarding us seemed a little casual, and Randolph suggested that we might do some patrolling ourselves when night fell. Admittedly there were guards on the line, but they spent most of the time sheltering from the bitter weather in the lee of the railway coaches. In the end, however, we came to the conclusion that as anyone who could not speak Turkish would almost certainly be shot if he ventured out after dark it would be more sensible to remain on board the train and place additional sentries inside the P.M.'s coach.

"That night we all dined with President Inönü. Mr Churchill was at the top of his form, although I doubt whether Inönü understood any of the stories he told him in very free French. We sat at small tables in the dining-car. My own companion was a Turkish major who announced that his favourite drink was "the English whisky." He drank half a tumbler at a time with only a splash of soda, but although he got through the best part of a bottle it had no apparent effect on him!"[8]

After two days in the train the Conference ended. The Turkish Government were not prepared to enter the war at this stage, but the discussions left no doubt where their sympathies lay. An agreement was therefore drawn up covering the reinforcement of their troops and equipment from Allied sources if Turkish neutrality was threatened.

The Prime Minister's large aircraft had landed at Adana without undue difficulty, but taking off again was a very different matter. When *Commando* began to taxi round the apron of the track the starboard wheel sank right through the tarmac. The Liberator was stuck fast, and no amount of pulling and pushing by dozens of helpers had the slightest effect. The Prime Minister and his party therefore transferred to General Brooke's aircraft.

Churchill had said earlier that he intended to return straight to Cairo. Tommy passed on the information, but just as they manœuvred on to the runway the Prime Minister asked the pilot where he was going. "Cairo? Oh, no, I want to go to Cyprus," he announced.

There he paid a visit to his old regiment, the Fourth Hussars, and spent a night at Government House, Nicosia. The old Government House had been burnt to the ground during riots in Sir Ronald Storrs' day. In its place had risen a fine modern building with one feature which greatly intrigued the Prime Minister. At the touch of a button the partitioning walls in the main rooms of the ground floor disappeared up into the ceiling to make additional space for large official gatherings.

[8] *Ibid.*

Two days later Churchill flew from Cairo to Tripoli. The Eighth Army were about to cross into Tunisia, but little more than a week before the city had been in enemy hands, and as *Commando* circled over Castel Benito its passengers could see the efforts which the Germans had made to put the airfield out of action. The entire landing area had been deeply ploughed in gigantic circles, but already an emergency runway was in use.

The Prime Minister went straight to Montgomery's headquarters, where one of the General's caravans had been allotted to him. Tommy, who slept under a canvas lean-to alongside the caravan, put on a monkey jacket and trousers over his pyjamas, but still found it freezingly cold in the night air of the desert.

"Next morning the P.M. drove into the city to watch the ceremonial entry of the Eighth Army. I was worried about this as the route was overlooked by houses which could not, as yet, have been thoroughly searched. Montgomery seemed quite satisfied that everything would be alright but I spent a very uncomfortable forenoon. On the seafront the greater part of the 51st Highland Division were lined up. They looked magnificent. We had last seen them on their arrival in Egypt, pink as lobsters from their first painful days in the African sun. Now they were bronzed and fit. Men and vehicles were turned out as though there had been a month to prepare for the parade. There was one superb touch of showmanship. Silhouetted against the clear blue sky, a lone kilted soldier stood motionless on top of Mussolini's triumphal arch as the troops marched past with pipes playing. It was a sight I shall never forget. Nor will the P.M., who was in tears."[9]

All that afternoon Churchill went round visiting units. He addressed thousands of officers and men, inspected Freyberg's New Zealanders, and paid calls on the R.A.F. and the Royal Navy, who were busy clearing Tripoli harbour. Everywhere he was cheered to the echo.

During dinner that night Tommy was handed a signal. It was from General Alexander to the Prime Minister and ran:

> The orders you gave me on August 10 1942 have been fulfilled. His Majesty's enemies, together with their impedimenta, have been completely eliminated from Egypt, Cyrenaica, Libya, and Tripolitania. I now await your further instructions.

* * * * *

A memorable tour of over 10,000 miles was nearing its end, but before flying home Churchill was anxious to call at Algiers. His staff heard this with mixed feelings, for a report had come in that a prominent German agent was known to be in the vicinity and that an attempt on the Prime

[9] *Ibid.*

Minister's life was imminent. Churchill, however, flatly refused to alter his mind.[10]

When he landed at Maison Blanche he was driven by a roundabout route into Algiers in a bullet-proof car, its windows smeared with mud. For the next two days he remained at the Villa Klene, Admiral Cunningham's residence on the hillside overlooking the harbour. It was a convenient *pied à terre*, for Eisenhower lived only a few yards away in another house in the same grounds. There were political talks with Harold Macmillan, the newly appointed British Minister of State in North-west Africa, and his American counterpart, Robert Murphy; with the French Governors-General of Algeria and Morocco, Peyrouton and Noguès; and long discussions with Eisenhower and Cunningham about future operations. On the following night they set out for the airfield.

By now Eisenhower was extremely uneasy. He was certain that the Prime Minister's presence was well known to the enemy, and in an attempt to divert attention from the night flight he had earlier in the day ordered his own B 17 aircraft to be ostentatiously prepared for a special journey. He had then sent his naval aide, Captain Butcher, and Tommy out to Maison Blanche in an armoured convoy with a full motor-cycle escort and they had taken part in an elaborate piece of deception, pretending to smuggle people into the plane which took off with only the crew on board while onlookers stood at the salute.

The heavily protected convoy in which the Prime Minister and his party travelled to the airfield that night reached Maison Blanche safely, and they went on board the plane. While he was running up *Commando*'s engines, however, Vanderkloot discovered that one of the magnetos was faulty. There was nothing for it but a return to Villa Klene, and every one disembarked from the aircraft except Sir Charles Wilson, already asleep and unnoticed in the darkness. He was not discovered and released from the locked cabin until several hours later.

As most of the cars had already left the airfield the return journey to Algiers was made without any escort at all, but, strangely enough, the only incident which caused any alarm during this eventful day occurred in the grounds so closely guarded by Eisenhower's troops. Firing a short burst from his tommy-gun to check that it was in working order, Colonel "Tex" Lee, the General's Military Aide, put three bullets into the wall of Admiral Cunningham's villa!

An extraordinary story about the postponement of the Prime Minister's flight from Algiers was later to gain wide currency. It was suggested that

[10] General Lahousen, the German Chief of Secret Operations, confirmed in 1950 that Hitler had ordered an attempt to be made to assassinate the Prime Minister during his visit to North Africa. (See Colvin, *Flight* 777, p. 13.)

Churchill, anxious to prolong his stay in North Africa, had ordered his own aircraft to be sabotaged. In an account which he published of his service on Eisenhower's staff Captain Butcher referred to the Prime Minister sending "one of his detectives" secretly to Maison Blanche to remove a magneto wire. The allegation is, of course, preposterous. Had he wished to stay a further day in Algiers Churchill would have done so. He had no need to resort to a clumsy subterfuge such as Butcher has suggested.[11] And since he was always mindful of his safety in the air the idea of the Prime Minister sending Detective Inspector Thompson—the only detective who accompanied him on this visit to the Mediterranean—to tamper with aircraft engines, which he knew nothing whatever about is so grotesque that it is surprising to find a senior member of Eisenhower's staff spreading it abroad.

The engine fault was soon rectified and on Sunday, February 7, the Prime Minister flew direct from Algiers to Lyneham. It was the last journey Churchill ever made in *Commando*. Soon afterwards the Liberator, with a different crew, crashed with the loss of every one on board.

By the time the Prime Minister's party reached London every one but Mr Churchill himself was dead tired, but Brendan Bracken announced that he had arranged a film show for them. It was, he said, a newsreel taken during the Casablanca Conference. Mr Churchill was delighted, and at ten o'clock that night they all trooped into the Ministry of Information's private cinema.

No sooner had the credit titles appeared on the screen than Bracken realized that some one had made a dreadful mistake. The film was admittedly entitled *Casablanca*, but there all connexion with the Conference ended, and the exhausted travellers sat wearily through an American spy story featuring Humphrey Bogart and Ingrid Bergman.

[11] Writing of Butcher at a later date, Eisenhower said, "He used the confidential position he had with me to form his own conclusions about a great number of things, including personalities and operations, and does not hesitate to give his views with an air of the greatest authority." (Montgomery, *op. cit.*, p. 350.)

25

Discord in Washington and Agreement in Algiers

For nearly a month now, without a break, Mr Churchill had been carrying out a daily programme which would have taxed the powers of a man half his age. Travelling thousands of miles in extremes of heat and cold, he had slept in aircraft, trains, and caravans; he had rarely been able to obtain the plain food which agreed with him best; and mentally and physically he had driven himself to the limit of his endurance. When he addressed the Commons on February 11 he was feeling far from well, with a heavy cold and a sore throat. A few days later the watchful Sir Charles Wilson diagnosed pneumonia, and he retired rebelliously to bed.

Since he regarded even temporary capitulation to any ailment as a sign of weakness he was an impossible patient. In a high fever he would sit up in bed reading State papers and drafting memoranda. Wilson was as firm as he dared to be, and the flow of documents which reached the Prime Minister's bedside was drastically curtailed, but not a day passed when the invalid did not put in several hours' work. At the height of his illness he was cabling Harry Hopkins about the progress of *Tube Alloys*, dictating far-sighted minutes on post-war planning, and keeping a watchful eye on developments in North Africa, where General Anderson's First Army had just sustained a severe mauling. From his sick bed he sought to placate Stalin, now complaining about the delay in launching *Husky*, the Sicilian invasion.

By February 22 he was protesting that his temperature was only 100 degrees and that he really felt very much better, but Brooke, who had not seen him for a week, thought he still looked very ill. It was not until the beginning of March that the Prime Minister was his old vigorous self again.

Although few in England realized it at the time, March 1943 was a fateful month. It was the last time that Germany came within sight of inflicting a mortal blow on her enemies in the west. While public attention had been riveted on the land fighting the Battle of the Atlantic had taken a grave turn. In the first three weeks of March over half a million tons of Allied shipping was sunk.

Providentially the U-boat packs could not sustain this offensive. New radar equipment and very long-range aircraft were coming into service on the Allied side, and Doenitz was soon warning Hitler of an alarming improvement in British anti-submarine technique. The German High Command never knew how close they had come to cutting the Atlantic lifeline. "Even our submarine warfare is not as successful as we really expected," wrote Goebbels in his diary, adding dejectedly, "I sometimes feel that we lack the necessary initiative for fighting the war, . . . the enemy has had the upper hand almost everywhere. He is defeating us in the air; he is inflicting heavy wounds on us in the East; he is beating us in North Africa."[1]

The North African campaign was, indeed, nearing its end. Early in April the Desert Army joined hands with the troops who had gone ashore at Casablanca and Algiers five months earlier. Fighting all the way, the enemy were driven back towards the northern tip of Tunisia. There they were harried remorselessly from the air and pounded by the Allied artillery. There was no escape for them; the Royal Navy barred the way to Sicily. "Sink, burn, and destroy," signalled Admiral Cunningham to the ships of the Mediterranean Fleet patrolling the Sicilian Channel; "let nothing pass!" By May 13 all enemy resistance had ceased, and General Alexander could proudly proclaim, "We are masters of the North African shores."

When the news reached England and the church bells rang out for the first time in four long years Churchill was not there to join in the celebration. On May 5 the Prime Minister, accompanied by the largest team of advisers to take part in any Allied deliberations hitherto, had set out for the Third Washington Conference.[2]

Although much progress had been made at Casablanca, the swift end of the African campaign and the possibility of a rapid conquest of Sicily called for a further reappraisal of Allied strategy. To Churchill it seemed unthinkable that all action in the Mediterranean theatre should be halted while forces were transported and regrouped for a cross-Channel attack which might not take place for a further year.

He was anxious, too, to find some means of harassing the Japanese.

[1] May 14, 1943 (see *Diaries*, p. 298).
[2] The Conference was given the code name of *Trident*.

Lack of resources seemed likely to rule out any hope of staging Operation *Anakim* (the reconquest of Burma) in the near future, but ample forces were available to launch an amphibious operation against some other point on the perimeter of Japanese-held territory, such as Sumatra or the Andaman Islands. Both in the Mediterranean and the Indian Ocean continued action of some kind, however limited, seemed immensely preferable to doing nothing at all, but an obsession with China—consistently overrated as a military force—coloured American views of the pattern of Eastern strategy, and the Prime Minister sensed that any suggestion of committing Anglo-American forces to a full-scale attack on the Italian mainland would be viewed with little favour. The United States Chiefs of Staff were convinced that such a move would inevitably hamper plans for the build-up of the assault on Northern France.

These and many other pressing problems could not be resolved by transatlantic cable. A further meeting with the President was imperative, but Churchill's doctors, still anxious about him after his recent illness, sternly vetoed a journey by air. In any case the size of the Conference party—one hundred and twenty-five in all—would have called for a major airlift. It was therefore decided that the *Trident* party would cross the Atlantic in the *Queen Mary*, shortly leaving the Clyde to bring American troops to England. On her westward runs she sailed comparatively empty, and there was no difficulty in accommodating the Conference team, but much work had to be done before the Prime Minister arrived on board.

The great ship had been stripped of most of her original furnishings before she began ferrying troops. Now she regularly transported 14,000 men at a time. They took it in turns to use the available sleeping accommodation, and as many as eight officers shared a cabin. Talking to the Chief Cook Tommy learnt that more than 30,000 eggs were served at breakfast each morning. For the coming trip some of the temporary bunks had to be stripped from the cabins. Cabin doors, which had been removed as a safety measure, had to be replaced, and for security reasons a section of the main deck had to be partitioned off as, in addition to Churchill and his party, the ship was to carry 5000 German prisoners to America.

While this work was being done it was discovered that the *Queen Mary* was infested by bugs which had burrowed their way into the baggage of Australian troops during storage in Suez warehouses. This put back the date of departure by several days, for the ship had to be sealed and flooded with poison gas. The gas dealt satisfactorily with the active bugs, but it did no harm to those about to hatch out. The *Trident* passengers were therefore warned that they would only be reasonably safe for the few days of the incubation period. Fortunately this gave just enough time for the crossing, and the only man to be attacked by the dazed bugs was Sir William Beveridge.

The security problem proved a bigger headache than usual. It was known that the German Legation in Dublin had contacts with merchant seamen visiting British ports, and a cover plan was devised, the *Queen Mary* being placarded with notices in Dutch to suggest that Queen Wilhelmina and members of her Court would be among the passengers.

On the afternoon of May 5 the *Queen Mary* sailed from the Clyde, and soon after passing the north coast of Ireland she worked up to her average speed of twenty-nine knots. Escorted by the cruisers *Scylla*, *Glasgow*, *Charybdis*, and *Uganda*, she headed south to avoid the most likely concentrations of U-boats. Half-way across the Atlantic the United States cruisers *Augusta* and *Tuscaloosa*—old friends from the meeting in Placentia Bay—took over escort duties.

Early on May 11—a grey, misty day which hid the New York skyline from view—they picked up a pilot at the Ambrose Light, and soon afterwards the *Queen Mary* anchored off Staten Island. Harry Hopkins was there to meet them, and a special train carried the party to Washington.

Churchill went straight to the White House. The familiar flood of messages and gifts from well-wishers began almost immediately. One parcel addressed to the Prime Minister contained what appeared to be a partially eaten biscuit. The accompanying letter explained that it was a prized heirloom—an eighty-year-old fragment of Army rations from the knapsack of a soldier who had fought in the American Civil War.

"That week-end Mr Roosevelt announced that he was taking us out to Shangri-La, his camp in the Catoctin Hills, in Maryland, to relax and get some mountain air. As we neared Fredericktown on the drive out we noticed advertisements for Barbara Frietchie Candy on all the telegraph poles. Mr Churchill remarked that the name seemed familiar, and the President reminded him that Barbara Frietchie ('Shoot if you must this old grey head, But spare your country's flag, she said') had been the 70-year old heroine of an incident in the Civil War. To the astonishment of us all the P.M., who told me afterwards that he hadn't read the ballad for at least forty years, then recited the whole of it with hardly a pause. As no one else in the car could remember anything but the first two lines it was an extraordinary feat; Harry Hopkins talked about it for days. But Mr Churchill's memory was phenomenal. Later in the war, when we were lying in the harbour at Ajaccio in H.M.S. *Largs* before the South of France landings he surprised another American audience including Mr Forrestal, the Secretary of the Navy, by reciting the Lays of Ancient Rome with great fervour in the middle of dinner."[3]

[3] C. R. Thompson, Notes.

By now there was a close and still growing bond of intimacy between Churchill and Roosevelt, but the joint staff talks made slow progress. The final report, drafted after six plenary sessions, indicated that broad agreement had been reached on most of the matters under consideration. In the main, however, its recommendations consisted of little more than vague generalities. The Italian theatre was a case in point, for it was agreed "to plan such operations in exploitation of *Husky* as are best calculated to eliminate Italy from the war," but—the sentence continued—"which of the various specific operations should be adopted, and thereafter mounted, is a decision which will be reserved to the Combined Chiefs of Staff."[4]

Throughout the fortnight in Washington the British and American delegations never really established mutual confidence. Like boxers in the ring they circled warily round, each team waiting for the other to make a move and then stepping in to counter it as forcefully as possible.

The Americans, with Admiral King as their most trenchant spokesman, made it plain from the outset that their views on global strategy were altogether different from those of the British. They regarded the invasion of Northern France as the only worth-while operation in Europe. If this could not be carried out in the near future the main weight of American strength would be more profitably employed in the Pacific. The Mediterranean they considered a subsidiary theatre of little significance. They had only become involved there against their judgment, and the sooner Allied operations were suspended in that area the better it would be. At all events, argued the extremists, it would be fatal to become embroiled on the Italian mainland. To Churchill, who saw so clearly that the collapse of Italy could undermine the whole foundation of the Reich, and that the means for achieving this were now at hand, it was an agonizing impasse.

In all the long and heated discussions Sir John Dill proved an invaluable mediator. Since becoming Head of the British Joint Staff Mission in Washington in the previous year he had gained the affection and respect of every American who worked with him. A senior Army officer present at most of the main *Trident* meetings recalls his genius at smoothing over apparently irreconcilable disagreements. "It was impressive to see the regard in which the Field Marshal was held by our opposite numbers. They invariably called him by his Christian name, and although other officers of the same rank were there the phrase—'You must talk to the Field Marshal,' referred to Dill alone if an American said it. He was a wonderful man for keeping people happy, and his friendship with General Marshall helped enormously to hold the balance. The Americans, who liked to consider an operation from the broadest possible point of view, plainly thought we were far too cautious. For our part we became perhaps too

[4] Churchill, Vol. IV, p. 724.

easily exasperated by American reluctance to get down to brass tacks. In the end the broad sweep of American thought, coupled with British attention to detail, generally produced a satisfactory answer. This Conference at Washington was not, however, a very happy one, and King and Stilwell went out of their way to oppose us on nearly every point."

General "Vinegar Joe" Stilwell, who commanded the Chinese troops in Burma, took little trouble to conceal his dislike of the British. King's opposition, however, sprang more from his genuine conviction that a Pacific strategy was the correct one for his country to follow. Certainly he was harsh-spoken, often blatantly rude. To some he gave an impression of toughness verging on inhumanity. And yet, when Field Marshal Dill was lying seriously ill and alone in the Walter Reed Hospital not a day passed without a call from the American Admiral. King never arrived empty-handed. He would bring a book, some little present like pencils and paper, or just an amusing story to cheer up the patient. Often King himself was tired out, but he would sit by the hospital bed for at least half an hour, trying to take Dill's mind off the illness which was tragically soon to end his life.

After one of the *Trident* meetings an R.A.F. officer complained angrily to the Field Marshal of King's "anti-British" attitude. Dill shook his head. "The Admiral is pro-American, but never anti-British," he said. "He more than anyone else made me want to get well."

* * * * *

After his week-end at Shangri-La the Prime Minister moved to the British Embassy. The Hon. Richard Wood, the Ambassador's third son, who had been gravely wounded in the desert fighting, had just arrived to join his parents, and Mr Churchill, who had sent regular bulletins on his progress to Lady Halifax while the young subaltern lay in hospital in Egypt, was greatly impressed by his determination to triumph over his appalling injuries. He had lost both legs, and now, holding on to a rail which had been fitted in one of the corridors, he was just learning to walk again on his artificial limbs. Most of the time, however, he spent in a wheeled chair in which he propelled himself at breakneck speed up and down the passages, gleefully pursued by the Halifax's small dog.

Richard Wood's courage was an inspiration. As soon as he could walk with reasonable safety he toured American war hospitals helping to rehabilitate others who had been badly wounded. On one particular day when an ice-storm hit Washington the roads were so glassy that the car taking him to talk to some crippled Servicemen was unable to climb the steep gradient to the hospital. Rather than disappoint the men he had promised to visit he insisted on getting out, and in the freezing cold he somehow managed to stagger the last quarter of a mile on his artificial legs.

When the Prime Minister addressed Congress for the second time in the war on May 19 there was a deeply moving scene as the tall, stooping figure of the British Ambassador wheeled his injured son on to the floor of the House to hear Churchill's speech.[5]

* * * * *

When the *Trident* Conference broke up a B.O.A.C. Clipper was waiting to take Churchill on to North Africa. Some days before he had sounded Tommy about flying non-stop to Gibraltar, for he knew that if he returned to England people would urge him not to undertake another strenuous journey straight away. But time was growing short. A strategic plan to take full advantage of the victory in Africa must be hammered out before the Sicily landing. Little headway had been made in Washington, but Churchill felt that all was not yet lost. If he could take General Marshall with him to Algiers and hold further talks with the Allied Commanders on the spot Marshall's own doubts about the policy to pursue after *Husky* might well be dispelled.

Roosevelt offered no objection, and after Tommy had made some calculations with a globe and a piece of string in the President's map room he was able to assure the Prime Minister that a direct flight to the Mediterranean was perfectly feasible. By Great Circle track it was not, in fact, much farther to Gibraltar than the normal return trip to Stranraer, and already there were several warships at sea which could be disposed along the route in case of emergency.

On the morning of May 26, in pouring rain, they took off from the Potomac River. They reached the Rock on the following afternoon, and next day they were in Algiers.

"Although I accompanied the Prime Minister on many further journeys, this week in North Africa was the happiest and most successful of all our missions abroad. After Washington, where one had heard senior officers and politicians referring to the North African theatre as a mere sideshow, the atmosphere in Algiers was exhilaratingly different. Every one we talked to seemed full of confidence that *Husky* would pave the way for the first major landing in Europe, and when Eisenhower went over the detailed plans with Marshall he strongly urged that we should lose no time in advancing into Italy.

"Once again we were staying in Admiral Cunningham's villa, only two minutes away from the Allied H.Q. in the Hotel St George. Our next-door neighbours in Eisenhower's household were much interested in Mr Churchill's daily routine, and I was asked by one of the General's staff if it was really true that the P.M. habitually had nothing but white wine for

[5] Richard Wood became Conservative M.P. for the East Riding (Bridlington Division) of Yorkshire in 1950. He was appointed Minister of Power in 1959.

breakfast; for some strange reason the Americans seemed to think he rarely ate food like anyone else! In point of fact, Mr Churchill liked a perfectly normal breakfast, but in the Mediterranean, where tea had to be made with tinned milk (which he loathed), he preferred to drink a light white wine.

"So many odd stories have circulated about the Prime Minister's alleged eccentricities in this direction that the truth deserves to be put on record. At home he usually drank a glass of white wine at lunch, champagne at dinner, and then a glass of port or brandy afterwards. As a meal he disliked afternoon tea, and if he had anything at all at that time he would ask for a whisky heavily diluted with ice and water. Cocktails he avoided altogether. He liked to provide champagne for his guests, but as the war went on champagne became more and more difficult to obtain. I therefore suggested that since champagne agreed with him and our stock was running low he might have half a bottle with his meals while his guests were given something more easily obtainable. This was brushed aside. 'What happens if we run out?' I asked. 'Get some more!' he said. He obviously thought the question was slightly ridiculous."[6]

* * * * *

After examining the operation orders for *Husky* Churchill and Marshall held a series of meetings at which future operations—the invasion of Northern France, the possible occupation of Corsica and Sardinia, and the advance across the Straits of Messina into Southern Italy—were reviewed. It was during one of these discussions that Eden, who had flown out from England to confer with de Gaulle and Giraud, made a passing reference to the possibility of bringing Turkey into the war if and when our troops reached "the Balkan area." Later this remark was to be quoted as evidence of Churchill's "Balkan ambitions." According to Eisenhower, however, Mr Churchill "did not propose in my hearing any campaign on a major scale with the Balkans or even northern Italy as a minimum objective. He seemed honestly concerned in the quick capture of southern Italy."[7]

Macmillan and Eden made unexpected headway with de Gaulle, and as soon as the French Committee of National Liberation—the marriage at long last of the de Gaulle and Giraud factions—was formed both the French leaders came to lunch at Villa Klene. Churchill also saw a good deal of his old friend General Georges, who had just escaped from occupied France.

They spent two days in the field, flying first to Tunis, where the Prime Minister attended the briefing of an American squadron about to attack

[6] C. R. Thompson, Notes.
[7] Dwight Eisenhower, *Crusade in Europe*, p. 185.

Pantelleria, the small island in the Sicilian Channel which Keyes had been so anxious to capture with his Commandos two years before. Now a full-scale assault on it was imminent. They then drove over part of the recent battlefield, cluttered with burnt-out tanks, guns, and aircraft. Tommy examined one German plane with particular interest. It was a troop-carrying Messerschmidt with six quite small engines and no undercarriage, the landing being made on a series of tiny wheels projecting from the side of the fuselage. "It looked just like a huge mechanical centipede."

They stayed the night at Eisenhower's forward headquarters camp, and during dinner the Prime Minister questioned the Supreme Commander about the Pantelleria operation.

"Mr Churchill was convinced that there were no more than 3000 Italians on the island, and offered to pay Ike five centimes for every one captured above that number. This wager eventually cost him 65 francs."[8]

On the following day they flew back to Algiers in a new aircraft, which had just come out from England. This was a York transport plane which had been taken over by the R.A.F. and specially fitted out for the use of the Prime Minister. After the comfortless austerity of the Liberator it was almost luxurious. Mr Churchill had a private cabin, there were comfortable bunks for the rest of the passengers, and at long last proper meals could be prepared in a small galley. The Prime Minister was so impressed with his new plane that he decided to return to England in it instead of using the Clipper which had brought him from America. At the time he was unaware of the tragic prelude to this flight home.

On the day Churchill went to Tunis Leslie Howard, the film star, whom he greatly admired, left Portela Airport, at Lisbon, to return to England after carrying out a lecture tour for the British Council. Howard was travelling in the normal civilian aircraft which for the past three years had flown between Lisbon and Bristol with prisoner-of-war mail and newspapers, diplomatic couriers and other civilian passengers. The daily service, which benefited enemy intelligence organizations as well as our own, had been allowed to function unchallenged for three years, but on this first morning of June 1943 the B.O.A.C. Dakota was intercepted by a Ju 88 from Germany's crack shipping reconnaissance squadron, KG 40, halfway across the Bay of Biscay, and shot down in flames. There were no survivors.[9]

Hitherto the incident has always been coupled with Churchill's presence

[8] See facsimile of General Eisenhower's letter to Tommy at p. 192. The attack on Pantelleria was carried out on June 11 after a heavy bombardment from sea and air. Eleven thousand prisoners were taken. One British soldier was alleged to have been bitten by an Italian mule, but otherwise there were no Allied casualties. Another Italian island, Lampedusa, hastily surrendered to one Allied aircraft!

[9] See Colvin, *op. cit.*

in North Africa. The explanation most widely accepted for the cold-blooded attack on the defenceless airliner is that Alfred Chenhalls, Howard's accountant, who resembled the Prime Minister, had been seen to board the plane. This theory, however, does not bear close scrutiny. With Howard, Chenhalls had been in Lisbon or Madrid for over a month, and had been much in the public eye. It is inconceivable that the German agents in either city would have been still unaware of his identity. A further point arises. The likelihood of the Prime Minister returning from North Africa at the height of the war in an unarmed civilian aircraft, flying to a regular schedule in broad daylight, was remote enough. But if he *had* done so he would certainly have been accompanied by some of his personal staff. To make room for them would have entailed a drastic pruning of the original passenger list.

Now the Germans knew perfectly well who was on that list, for by devious means they had access to such information in advance. Had there been any significant last-minute changes they would have been readily apparent when the group of men and women assembled to board the plane. If, therefore, Chenhalls *was* initially mistaken for Churchill the fact that his only close companion that morning was the film actor would surely have made the most credulous observer think again.

So the mystery remains. If the tragic end of the lone Dakota had, as now seems likely, no connexion with any report about Churchill, this still, admittedly, leaves at least one major problem unsolved. Why was it that for nearly a week up to June 2, 1943, there was a general Luftwaffe alert over the whole Biscay area?

There are grounds for thinking that the intensified patrols flown by the squadrons of KG 40 during this period may well have had a different purpose altogether from any attempt to intercept the Prime Minister. Churchill's inward route from Botwood to Gibraltar took him nowhere near the Bay, but on May 31 two Hudsons with V.I.P.'s on board *did* cross the Bay of Biscay, flying south. The leading plane carried the Foreign Secretary and his staff; in the second Hudson was Admiral Sir John Cunningham, shortly to succeed his namesake as Allied Naval Commander-in-Chief, Mediterranean. They had intended to leave Portreath, in Cornwall, twenty-four hours earlier, but Mr Eden's aircraft caught fire just before take-off, and one of the emergency exits was damaged.

In the early hours of May 31, when enemy air activity in the Bay was at its height, both Hudsons took off for Algiers. There was little cloud cover, but they reached Gibraltar safely. It would appear that they had a fortunate escape.

26

Planning for Overlord

IN THE face of a north-westerly gale the assault force for *Husky* put to sea on the afternoon of July 9. It was still blowing hard when darkness fell, but the wild weather proved an unexpected ally. After many nights continuously on the alert the enemy relaxed their vigil. A firm foothold was secured over a wide arc extending from Licata in the west to Syracuse, the Americans fighting off a powerful German counter-attack in the western sector. Augusta soon fell to the Eighth Army, and although the Germans hastily dispatched reinforcements from the mainland, including some of their crack parachute troops, the fate of the island was decided within a week of the landings. By that time the Allies had the use of a dozen airfields and completely controlled the skies over Sicily. Palermo, in the north, yielded to Patton's Seventh Army on July 22, and with the capture of Messina on August 16 the whole island was in Allied hands. The campaign lasted only thirty-eight days.

In the meantime a dramatic development had occurred in Rome. At a meeting of the Fascist Grand Council on June 24 Dino Grandi, once Italy's Foreign Minister, demanded that Mussolini should hand over command of the armed forces to the King and allow the formation of a National Government. He was supported by Ciano, the Duce's son-in-law, and a clear majority. On the following afternoon Mussolini was arrested and sent, a closely guarded captive, to the island of Ponza. His long reign was over, and with his going the whole fragile fabric of Italian resistance began to crumble. While none could predict the immediate consequences of Mussolini's downfall, it seemed inevitable that the King and Marshal Badoglio, who now took over the leadership of the Government, would seek a separate peace.

Writing to Roosevelt, Churchill urged the need for exploiting this new situation to the full. Apart from the obvious benefits of an Italian surrender in terms of captured territory, he emphasized the effect which such a capitulation might well have on Greece, Bulgaria, Roumania, and Hungary, and the encouragement it would offer to Turkey to enter the war against the Axis. The strategic implications of an Italian collapse were, in fact, profound, and they called for urgent examination. Although only two months had passed since the *Trident* Conference the rapid march of events had already overtaken Allied planning and a further meeting with the President and his advisers was imperative. Not only was it vital to hammer out agreement on the policy to be pursued if Italy sought armistice terms. The planning of *Overlord* had now reached a stage where the problems of landing in Northern France could be reviewed in detail. And to give impetus to operations against the Japanese the Prime Minister wanted approval for the establishment of an independent South-east Asia Command.

At the President's suggestion Quebec was chosen as the venue of this hurriedly convened Conference. Once again it was decided to transport the British team in the *Queen Mary*, and on August 4 the Prime Minister left London for the Clyde.

For the Churchill family it had been a particularly busy day. Lord Burghley, the newly appointed Governor of Bermuda, came to lunch at Downing Street with his wife. Mrs Churchill, whose Aid to Russia Fund was holding a flag day, had to hurry off immediately afterwards to direct operations, and although the family had arranged that whatever happened they would have dinner alone before setting off for the north, she and Mary returned to find an unexpected guest—Brigadier Wingate, who had arrived in London only that afternoon and was still wearing the crumpled tropical uniform he had put on for the flight from Burma, where he had earned a legendary name in the jungle.

Wingate stayed to dinner. The Churchills thought he looked strained and ill, but his strong personality and the forceful way in which he presented his theories about jungle fighting cast a spell on them all. When eventually the Prime Minister said to him "You must come with me to-night and tell all this to the President," Wingate, who had known nothing about Churchill's imminent departure from London when he arrived at No. 10, showed not a flicker of surprise. He merely asked in a diffident aside if a message of explanation could be sent to his wife, who was on her way from Scotland to see him.

Just before midnight they drove to Addison Road station, and Mr Churchill, elated as usual by the prospect of a war-time journey, marched up the platform singing, "I go away this very day to sail across the sea, Matilda!"

The party for Quebec was over two hundred strong. In addition to Mrs Churchill and Mary, who had been given special leave from her Anti-aircraft battery to act as A.D.C. to her father, it included Wing Commander Guy Gibson, who had just won the Victoria Cross for his leadership of the attack which had breached the Ruhr dams. The Prime Minister knew Roosevelt would like to hear about this remarkable exploit at first hand. He had also been told by Air Marshal Harris, the Commander-in-Chief of Bomber Command, that Gibson badly needed a rest from operations, but was strongly resisting all attempts to transfer him to a less active rôle. Harris therefore proposed that he should give a number of lectures on the work of his squadron to American and Canadian Service audiences after accompanying the Prime Minister to Quebec. For Guy Gibson it did not prove the happiest of experiences. He was restless at being removed from operations, he intensely disliked being 'exhibited' as a war hero, and the Churchills could not help thinking of the young submarine commander who had so violently resisted all attempts to rest him from operational patrols in the first winter of the war.

Mrs Lorna Wingate joined the party when the special train reached Scotland. The RTO who had removed her from the London train on the previous evening had not been able to give her any inkling of the reason for intercepting her, and she had spent a miserable night wondering if her husband had met with an accident. Now, to her delight, she found that all was well, and learnt that on Churchill's orders she was to go with them to Canada.

Soon after lunch they went on board the *Queen Mary*, at anchor in the Clyde off the Tail of the Bank. It was a blustery afternoon, with a strong east wind, and soon the escorts were struggling to keep station in the rising seas. For two days the bad weather continued. The Prime Minister spent most of the time in his quarters on the port side of the main deck, preparing for the Conference. With officers of General Morgan's planning staff he went over the whole co-ordinated plan for *Overlord*, and the intricate design of the Mulberry Harbours, with their outer breakwaters, their floating piers, and all the fascinating array of impedimenta—the Corn Cobs, Gooseberries, Phœnix units, Beetles, and Whales—was explained to him.

On the third morning at sea he called a meeting to discuss a project for invading Northern Sumatra and cutting the Japanese sea communications between Singapore and Rangoon. "When can this operation be carried out?" he demanded. It was explained that this would not be possible until the end of the monsoon season. "No good!" said the Prime Minister. "Make another plan."

For the last thirty-six hours before the ship reached the Canadian shore she was enveloped in thick banks of swirling mist, with visibility never more than a few hundred yards. When the *Queen Mary* arrived off Halifax the pilot cutter, unable to come alongside owing to the heavy swell, lowered a small boat, but the engine refused to start, and the unfortunate crew had no option but to row their dinghy frantically in pursuit of the still moving 84,000-ton liner.

The usual elaborate security arrangements had been made before the journey began—on this trip the Prime Minister was once more travelling as Colonel Warden—but Mr Churchill's imminent arrival was evidently well known to the people of Halifax, who turned out in strength to give him a tremendous welcome at the railway station. When he reached Quebec he went to the residence of the Governor-General of Canada, high on the cliff overlooking the St Lawrence River. The rest of the British and American missions were accommodated in the Château Frontenac Hotel. The Americans were not, however, due to arrive in Quebec for several days, and the President, who was at Hyde Park, suggested that Churchill might like to go there until it was time for the Conference to begin. The President of the Canadian National Railways offered him the use of his own private rail-car, and in this they left Quebec on the evening of August 11.

The Prime Minister had decided to show his daughter the Niagara Falls on the way, and by breakfast-time next morning they were at Victoria Park. They spent some time looking at the Falls and the whirlpools, and then they drove over the bridge to the American side to rejoin the train. When they arrived in the siding below the President's house that evening Roosevelt and Harry Hopkins were there to meet them. Mrs Churchill, who had not been feeling very well when the time came to leave Quebec, had not accompanied the Prime Minister. It was probably fortunate that she decided to remain in Canada and rest, for the heat throughout the stay at Hyde Park was almost unbearable. One night Mr Churchill, unable to sleep, left the house and sat for a time watching the dawn come up over the Hudson River. His sudden appearance in the garden in his night attire greatly surprised the Secret Servicemen patrolling the grounds.

The Conference at Quebec consisted in the main of staff meetings, and there were only two plenary sessions in which the Prime Minister and the President took part. A target date of May 1, 1944, was set for the *Overlord* landings on open beaches in the Cotentin Peninsula; a proposal for an ancillary attack in the South of France was discussed; and it was agreed to form the South-east Asia Command on which Churchill had set his heart, with Mountbatten as Supreme Commander in this theatre, where Wingate's Chindits were now to be employed in a new attempt to reopen land communications with China. The joint missions had many other problems to consider—the pros and cons of recognizing the French Committee of National Liberation, the progress of the *Tube Alloy* project, and the rôle of British forces in the war against Japan when the fighting ended in Europe.

The Prime Minister had originally envisaged a British commander for *Overlord* and had, in fact, already offered the post to Brooke. He now changed his mind, for in view of the preponderance of American troops who would be taking part in the invasion of France it seemed more fitting that the Supreme Commander should be an American. The name of General Marshall was therefore put forward. This was a bitter blow to Brooke, who spent an unhappy time at Quebec, much of it devoted to efforts at heading off the Prime Minister from two new goals which were already becoming something of an obsession with him. The first was Operation *Culverin*, the attack on Sumatra; the second was a plan for capturing Rhodes and certain other enemy-held islands in the Ægean. To Brooke's relief—for British resources were strained enough as it was—*Culverin* made little headway.

One of the basic problems which beset these major Allied Conferences was the unwieldy nature of the meetings. The Joint Chiefs of Staff were attended by a formidable array of subordinate staff officers whose very presence often made a senior officer reluctant to concede a point for fear of being criticized by his own delegation. Early in the Quebec talks the disagreements between the British and the U.S. Chiefs of Staff became so acrimonious that complete deadlock threatened. Happily common sense prevailed. Abandoning their teams of advisers, they went into private session, and, as one of the British officers said later, "we really let our hair down." After that the air was cleared.

It was, incidentally, on this particular day that Mountbatten provided welcome light relief by demonstrating the possibilities of *Habbakuk*, a fantastic project conceived by a member of his own Combined Operations Staff, Geoffrey Pyke. *Habbakuk*, two million tons in weight and built mainly of ice, was to provide an unsinkable platform for aircraft supporting the invasion. Initially it was planned to take an existing iceberg, level off the upper part to provide a vast landing area, install engines, and propel this huge floating island like a ship. No enemy attack could have any lasting effect on it, Pyke declared, for damage by bombs or torpedoes would be made good by filling the cavities with water and allowing it to freeze.

This bizarre idea received further impetus when it was discovered that ordinary ice could be given additional strength by the incorporation of wood pulp. Unfortunately, its designers overlooked the fact that the equipment needed to drive a mass of this size through the water and at the same time prevent it from melting away was so enormous that it would have been far quicker and more economical to construct orthodox warships. To equip one of these mechanically propelled icebergs called for tens of thousands of tons of cork insulation, thousands of miles of steel tubes for water-circulation and reinforcement, not to mention four complete power-stations.

Habbakuk, in which Churchill took a keen interest, was to prove a spectacular failure, but Mountbatten's demonstration to the Joint Chiefs of Staff, coming as it did immediately following hours of bitter argument, did much to ease the tension. Producing a revolver and a hatchet, the new Commander of S.E.A.C. carried out tests, first on a block of ordinary ice and then on a lump of Pykrete—the frozen wood pulp. As they listened to the fusillade of shots those outside the room concluded with wry satisfaction that the Chiefs of Staff were settling their differences once and for all.

At this time any diversion came as a relief. The two Staffs were decidedly on edge, and even the Prime Minister was not his usual resilient self. He was, indeed, feeling far from well. As a result he took each setback more than usually to heart, and the arrival of Major-General "Jock" Whiteley with unwelcome news from Algiers put him in a particularly bad humour. If he was to gain his way over Italy and prevent the Americans from losing all interest in the Mediterranean theatre it was vital that Eisenhower's force, now poised to attack the mainland, should make the maximum progress before German reinforcements from the north slowed up the Allied advance. Whiteley's report made it clear, however, that no appreciable Allied force was now expected to enter Naples before December.

"The constant disagreements had produced such a strained atmosphere and the staffs had been working at such pressure that it was decided to have a brief let-up in the middle of the Conference. The Canadian Government provided a steamer to take the members of the two missions on a trip up the Saguenay River. The P.M. and the President also decided to take the day off and go fishing, so we drove to a lake twenty miles from Quebec. There we were given a boat and a boatman each. As usual the Secret Servicemen were much in evidence. Three of them went afloat with a walkie-talkie radio and cruised round with Mr Roosevelt. I had Inspector Thompson with me, and we tried to show the Americans that we too were on the job, but every time we came within a hundred yards of the P.M. we were violently denounced for disturbing his fish.

"During lunch Harry Hopkins suggested a competition to see who could catch the most fish in the afternoon. The lake was heavily overstocked, and I found that by fishing with a very short line, with the fly just under the surface, I could get a catch about every other minute. The others, using more orthodox methods, weren't nearly so successful, and at tea I was rewarded with a huge sum of dollars for my twenty-eight fish."[1]

When the Conference broke up on August 24 the Prime Minister, who was travelling to Washington a week later for further talks with the President, and then going to Harvard to receive an Honorary Degree, accepted an invitation from Colonel Frank Clark, head of one of Canada's biggest firms producing wood pulp for newsprint, to spend a few days at his fishing lodge on the Snow River. Brooke and Portal had already gone ahead to the Lac des Neiges, a large lake higher up the mountains, but Pound had made excuses for not joining them. Knowing the Admiral's passion for fishing Tommy realized for the first time that the First Sea Lord, who had not looked well throughout the trip, must be more seriously ill than anyone had imagined. A few days later Admiral Pound had a stroke which partially paralysed him, and he asked to be relieved of his post there and then.

In the party which set off with Colonel Clark for a sixty-mile drive through the mountains were Mrs Churchill and Mary, Sir Charles Wilson (now Lord Moran), and John Martin and Tommy. After a night at the Lodge they went up to the Snow Lake. Several miles long and at least a mile wide, it was the centre of the logging area. They were met by canoes with outboard motors and taken to a camp which consisted of several luxurious cabins heated by huge log fires.

After the stress and strain of the Conference the peace of the Snow Lake seemed almost unbelievable. Bears roamed in the woods which ran down to the edge of the water. Brooke, with his passionate interest in birds, reported delightedly that he had seen an osprey and a Great Northern Diver. And the keen anglers were in their element, for the lake had plenty of brown trout. Tommy noted with interest that those off the south shore, where peaty water came down from the mountains, were a bright pink—a different colour altogether from those caught in other parts of the lake.

Mr Churchill was no expert angler, but he enjoyed himself enormously. Attired rather quaintly in his siren suit, a shapeless old hat, and a tweed overcoat, he spent many hours on the water, but each day he got through a tremendous amount of work as well. The first Royal Marine orderly to arrive with official papers for him fell into the lake on the journey across, but sturdily kept a grip on his brief-case as he went under. No sooner had he been rescued, dried, and returned to Quebec than Patrick Kinna, who brought some TOP SECRET reports on the *Tube Alloy* project, all but shared the same fate.

Brooke and Portal, both expert and fanatical fishermen, wisely took a

[1] C. R. Thompson, Notes.

thorough rest. They were out on the lake from dawn to dusk, and one blazing summer day when Mary Churchill had only managed to land one small fish they arrived back at the Lodge with such a vast catch that she could hardly believe her eyes. The wild life of the lakeside yielded constant surprises. Returning to camp one evening the Churchills' car was held up by a skunk which refused to move from the road. Since they were warned that they would have to burn their clothes if it released its cloud of suffocating and evil-smelling fluid at them they treated it with the greatest respect. At the camp the only discordant note was sounded by a loon, whose wild, tormented cries often echoed eerily across the water.

The time to set out for Quebec and Washington came all too soon. On September 1 Churchill arrived at the White House. For the last fortnight of his stay he was once more the President's guest, and when Roosevelt left for Hyde Park he invited the Prime Minister to remain and hold any meetings he chose there. So it was that he came to preside over a conference of the Combined Chiefs of Staff in the Council Room of the White House—a singular distinction for a British Premier.

During this visit to Washington Churchill greatly missed the company and wise counsel of Harry Hopkins, who had been ordered to enter the Naval Hospital at Bethesda for a complete rest. The Prime Minister drove out to see him there. He also visited another patient—Richard Pim, of his own staff, who had just undergone an operation.

In the next room to Pim was a U-boat commander, Lieutenant Friederich Guggenberger. One of only seven survivors when his submarine was sunk off the Brazilian coast, Guggenberger had broken his leg. When the Prime Minister discovered that he had been captain of the U-boat which had sunk the *Ark Royal* in the Mediterranean two years earlier he was greatly intrigued and asked if he could see him. He was persuaded, however, that this might not be diplomatic.

Before the President left for Hyde Park he gave a lunch-party with an amusing sequel. One of the very few subjects on which Roosevelt and Churchill never saw eye to eye was British policy in India. Roosevelt was never averse to criticizing British imperialism, and probably with his tongue in his cheek he suggested one day that much good might come from a meeting between the Prime Minister and Mrs Helen Ogden Mills Reid, who, he said, was particularly interested in Indian affairs. A sister of the redoubtable Colonel McCormick, the editor and publisher of the *Chicago Tribune*, Mrs Reid—herself a vice-president of the *New York Herald Tribune*—was an important figure in the American newspaper world, and as Mr Churchill gathered that she considered the people of India had been brutally oppressed by the British he agreed to see her.

She came to lunch at the White House, and afterwards, as they sat on the veranda, the question of India was brought up. At once Churchill sai firmly, "Before we proceed further let us get one thing clear. Are we talk ing about the brown Indians in India, who have multiplied alarmingl under the benevolent British rule? Or are we speaking of the red Indian in America who, I understand, are almost extinct?"

This brilliant opening so disconcerted Mrs Ogden Mills Reid that sh never began her peroration at all and the topic was instantly dropped. Th President laughed so much that Tommy thought he would have a seizure

* * * * *

By now momentous news was arriving almost hourly from Eisenhower' headquarters. The invasion of Italy had begun; on September 8 Badogli accepted the Allied surrender terms; and on the following morning Allie assault convoys entered the Gulf of Salerno.

Operation *Avalanche*, designed to leapfrog ahead of the forces advan cing up from the toe of Italy, met with fierce resistance. While the fate o the landings was in the balance the Prime Minister was anxious to remai in touch with Roosevelt and his advisers, and it was not until the nigh of September 11 that he set out for home. He broke his journey to bi farewell to the President at Hyde Park, and there the Churchills cele brated their 35th wedding anniversary. Unhappily the news from Salern was grave, and although H.M.S. *Renown* was waiting at Halifax Chur chill seriously considered cancelling his plans to return by sea and flyin to England instead.

By now many of the Conference party had already left and the last o the British team were embarked in *Renown* when the Prime Ministe arrived on board. At three o'clock on the afternoon of September 14 *Renown* drew away from the jetty and headed slowly for the channel t the open sea. It was a lovely day, with clear skies, bright sunshine, and a soft breeze. As Mr Churchill stood on the bridge hundreds of shipyar workers, men and women, waved their farewells, and across the wate came the strains of "O Canada" and "Will ye no come back again?"

H.M.S. *Renown*, commanded by Captain W. E. Parry, a tall, quie torpedoman who had been captain of the *Achilles* in the River Plate battle had once flown Dudley Pound's flag. Now the Admiral was taking passage in her for the last time. On the five-day voyage he rarely emerged from his quarters. He was a stricken man with less than a month to live, but he told the Surgeon Commander who had flown out from England to accompany him home how moved he was to be sailing in his old flagship once again.

Of all the Prime Minister's party no one felt the departure from Canada more keenly than Mary, his youngest daughter, who was to have her twenty-first birthday on the voyage home. For her the journey with her father had been an unforgettable experience. Both she and Mrs Churchill had made broadcasts during their stay, and at General Marshall's invitation Mary had carried out a tour of American Women's Army Corps training camps. Her natural charm and good looks had made her immensely popular, and Tommy had found her a great help in organizing the countless official functions at Quebec.

Mr Churchill, who was deeply fond of her, sensed how sad she was that the trip was nearing its end. Before dinner that night he sent for her to walk with him on the quarter-deck, and they paced up and down discussing the events of the past month. That evening established a pattern for the rest of the voyage. The Churchills were joined at dinner by John Martin, Leslie Rowan, General Ismay, Lord Moran, Brendan Bracken, and Tommy. After proposing "The King" the Prime Minister gave one of Wellington's Peninsula toasts—"Our Men, Our Swords, Our Religion, Ourselves, Our Women, Absent Friends"—a ritual which he repeated each night.

After dinner they all went up on to the quarter-deck, and the Prime Minister made them carry out Cavalry Drill. When they returned to the Admirals' cabin he took a box of matches and, arranging them on the table, he demonstrated the disposition of Kitchener's forces at the battle of Omdurman. Mr Churchill remarked that he was under fire for the first time in his life on his twenty-first birthday. Mary, whose own twenty-first birthday it was next day, pointed out excitedly that she had beaten her father by just over a year.

It proved an eventful birthday for her, for she nearly lost her life. In the afternoon *Renown* was driving on fast, unescorted, in a following swell when the time came for her to execute a zigzag—the normal precaution against U-boat attack. The quarter-deck had been cleared of men, but just as the ship was about to alter course one of her young officers, Lieutenant David Williams, saw to his horror that Mary Churchill had appeared and was walking up and down with "Schoolie"—the Instructor Lieutenant-Commander—entirely oblivious to what was about to happen.

Before he could shout a warning the ship violently changed course and the quarter-deck was submerged in what to Mary Churchill seemed "a pale emerald-green wall." At that moment she was quite certain she was about to be washed overboard and drowned, but she and her companion were swept up against a stanchion and, clutching this, she just managed to save herself. A very shaken Commander arrived and took her below. He gave her a stiff brandy, followed, curiously, by an equally stiff Scotch. She was soaked to the skin, and as she had no spare uniform she arrived for dinner in the Admirals' cabin that night wearing a cocktail dress.

The news of her misadventure had been carefully kept from Mr Churchill, and he looked at her with some surprise. "I did not give you permission to wear plain clothes," he said severely, but he asked no questions, and the secret was kept until the end of the voyage. From that time on, however, Miss Churchill was a great deal more circumspect on her visits to the quarter-deck.

By a happy coincidence one of *Renown*'s escorts, H.M.S. *Orwell*, had as passengers Petty Officer A. P. Herbert, M.P., and another Member of Parliament, Major Sir Derrick Gunston, returning to England after a Parliamentary Mission to Newfoundland. When the destroyer made her rendezvous with the battle cruiser Herbert decided to let the Prime Minister know that he had a Parliamentary as well as a naval escort. So he set to work to compose a greeting in verse.

He could not use the word "Churchill" for security reasons—"but what about Ulysses returning to his island after many toils and dangers?" Eventually the following signal was made from *Orwell* to *Renown*:

> From Derrick Gunston and A. P. Herbert—Respectful salutes and greetings. Return, Ulysses, soon to show the secrets of your splendid bow. Return and make all riddles plain to anxious Ithaca again. And you, Penelope the true, who have begun to wander too, we're glad to meet you on the foam and hope to see you safely home.

On board *Renown* this provoked much discussion, and the Prime Minister decreed that a reply must be sent in similar vein. Every one in his party was put to work, and in the end Mary supplied the winning effort, her father adding the last two lines. This ran:

> Ulysses, and Pempy too,
> Return their compliments to you.
> They, too, are glad to wend their way
> Homewards to Ithaca after a stay
> With friends from where the land is bright
> And spangled stars gleam all the night.
> And when he's mastered basic Greek
> Ulysses to the world can speak
> About the plots and plans and bases
> Conferred upon in foreign places.
> We thank you from our hearts to-day
> For guarding us upon our way.
> To chide these simple rhymes be chary!
> They are the first attempts of Mary.

Petty Officer Herbert was not allowed by his shipmates to rest on his laurels. He agreed that Miss Churchill deserved an ode to herself for this creditable effort, but he could not remember if Ulysses had a daughter. He did recall, however, that Telemachos was the son of Ulysses and Penelope, and he therefore decided on a compromise. Just before *Orwell* broke off contact with *Renown* on September 17 the following signal was passed to the Prime Minister's daughter:

> Telemacha, the sailors send
> Their greetings to a fighting friend.
> The Major adds a smart salute
> To any lady who can shoot!
> And I, poor scribbler, must give place
> To one who writes with such a grace.
> Why not (when Mr Masefield's passed)
> A Lady Laureate at last?

* * * * *

At 9.30 on the morning of Sunday, September 19, as H.M.S. *Renown* anchored off Greenock Mr Churchill sent for the chaplain.

"We will have Divine Service, and I will speak to the ship's company," he announced. "Do your sailors sing?"

The chaplain, Henry Lloyd, who had won the D.S.O. while serving in the aircraft carrier *Illustrious* in the Mediterranean, assured him that the ship's company had a well-deserved reputation for singing hymns.[2]

"In that case," said the Prime Minister, "we will sing 'Onward, Christian Soldiers.'"

"Surely not?" protested Lloyd. "After all, sir, this is the Royal Navy!"

"You are quite right," said Churchill ruefully. "I think you had better choose the hymns after all."

And so, as a weak autumn sun struggled to pierce the morning mist the ship's company assembled on the quarter-deck beneath the great guns of *Renown* and sang "Eternal Father, Strong to Save." The Prime Minister gave a short address, and then the Conference party went ashore to board the special train.

When it reached London that night an ambulance was waiting to take Admiral of the Fleet Sir Dudley Pound to the Royal Masonic Hospital. There Churchill visited him soon afterwards, and at the special request of the King he placed in the Admiral's hands the insignia of the Order of Merit. Pound was unable to speak, for he had had another severe stroke, but he recognized the Prime Minister and grasped his hand.

Churchill had often remarked that the First Sea Lord was one of three men whose companionship meant most to him, the others being Smuts and Beaverbrook. Admiral Pound's death on the anniversary of Trafalgar greatly distressed him.

[2] The Very Rev. H. M. Lloyd, D.S.O., O.B.E., M.A., now Dean of Truro.

27

Rifts on the Road to Teheran

BY THE time the Prime Minister reached England the crisis at Salerno wa over. After six days of fierce fighting Kesselring's forces were driven fron the high ground dominating the landing area, and the way to Naples la open. But it had been touch and go. Operation *Avalanche* had shown th hazards of attacking an enemy coast at a range which denied adequat air cover for the invading troops; and it had shown, too, the need for rapi reinforcement of men and material once the initial lodgement had bee made.

In Sicily the Germans were not able to concentrate their forces wit sufficient speed to jeopardize Allied operations at any stage. At Salerno i was a very different matter, and in the end it was mainly the weight o naval gun support which turned the scales.

When Churchill addressed the Commons two days after his return h deplored suggestions that the bitter fighting at Salerno could have bee avoided if there had not been undue delay in mounting the operation "When I hear people talking in an airy way of throwing modern armie ashore here and there as if they were bales of goods to be dumped on beach and forgotten I really marvel at the lack of knowledge which sti prevails of the conditions of modern war," was his bitter retort.[1]

He had expected criticism of the Government for accepting the Italian as co-belligerents and dealt with it trenchantly. "I wish to make it per fectly clear," he said, "that we are endeavouring to rally the stronges forces together in Italy to make head against the Germans and the Mussc lini-Quisling-Fascist combination."[2]

[1] Churchill, Vol. V. p. 139. [2] *Ibid.*, p. 143.

Mussolini's escape from captivity had, indeed, added further to the confusion of the Italian scene. At the beginning of August Hitler had decided that an attempt must be made to rescue the Duce. He had, however, no idea where Mussolini was imprisoned. The steps he took to trace him show how readily his mind was influenced by primitive superstitions, for he summoned a number of dabblers in occult science, locked them up in a lakeside house near Berlin, and told them to divine Mussolini's whereabouts. The oddest feature of this extraordinary experiment was its success, for it was not long before one of these magicians—a self-styled "Master of the Sidereal Pendulum"—announced that the Duce would be found on an island west of Naples.[3]

Mussolini had, in fact, been transferred from Ponza to Maddalena by the time the German agents got on to his track. Before they had time to put a rescue plan into operation there he was moved once again—to the mountain camp in the Appenines where Skorzeny and his glider troops made their perilous landing to release him. Shortly afterwards the rescued Dictator found himself the reluctant figurehead of a puppet Italian Government—the Repubblica Sociale Italiana—at Gargnano, on the shore of Lake Garda. Now there were at least three Italian factions all exercising a measure of control—the Badoglio Government at Brindisi; Mussolini's Republic of Salo, as it became known; and an underground organization directing Partisan activities from Rome.

By the first week of October both Corsica and Sardinia had fallen, the great port of Naples and its near-by airfields had been captured, and Allied forces were pressing on towards the Volturno River.

For Germany the outlook was bleak indeed, and Goebbels began pleading with his master to come to an arrangement "with one side or the other." "I am rather inclined to regard Stalin as more approachable," he wrote in his diary. "Churchill is a romantic adventurer with whom one cannot talk sensibly."

At the very time when Goebbels was recording this opinion in Berlin a somewhat similar charge was being levelled at Churchill by his own allies. Even before the position on the Italian mainland had been stabilized the Prime Minister was seeking support for a new operation designed to drive the enemy from the Eastern Mediterranean.[4] This was the capture of Rhodes—Operation *Hercules*—for which he had campaigned so vigorously at Quebec. From the airfields of this large island the enemy fortresses of Cos and Leros could be subdued. With the command of the Ægean secure Turkey might well become an active partner of the Allies, and the Dardanelles would then offer a new sea line to Russia.

Strategically this far-sighted view had much to commend it, but to

[3] See Schellenberg, *op. cit.*, p. 386.

[4] Churchill, Vol. V, p. 189.

American eyes any operation against Rhodes could hardly fail to hamper the two main tasks which lay before them—the reinforcement of the Italian front and the need to prepare for *Overlord*. They were frankly suspicious that the Prime Minister might well embroil them in a costly sideshow which, if all did not go according to plan, would commit troops and landing-craft for an unpredictable period. "As I see it," wrote Roosevelt in reply to an urgent appeal from Churchill on October 8, "it is not merely the capture of Rhodes [which is entailed], but it must mean of necessity, and it must be apparent to the Germans, that we intend to go farther. Otherwise Rhodes will be under the guns of both Cos and Crete."[5]

From this position neither Eisenhower nor Roosevelt and his advisers in Washington would shift, and although Cos, Leros, and Samos and a number of other Ægean islands were occupied by small detachments of British troops, they were unable to remain for long in the face of determined German counter-attacks. The attack on Rhodes was never mounted, for although Churchill persuaded the President to allow a final discussion of the project at Eisenhower's headquarters early in October, the unwelcome news that German troops were being strongly reinforced south of Rome ruled out further consideration of Operation *Hercules* for the time being.

Churchill was greatly upset by this incident. Unhappily, it was the prelude to a steadily progressive weakening of the close relationship and understanding he had hitherto enjoyed with the President. As plans went forward for the first meeting between Churchill, Roosevelt, and Stalin—a meeting which was to review not only the plans for *Overlord* and decide finally on its commander, but was to settle the whole future Allied policy for conducting the war—the Prime Minister detected a growing tendency on Roosevelt's part to take an independent line in his communications with Stalin.[6] Very soon this led to practical difficulties.

In the middle of October Eden and Cordell Hull flew to Moscow for a Foreign Secretaries Conference, convened to pave the way for the Big Three meeting. It soon became plain to them that Stalin was prepared to travel to Teheran for the major conference, and nowhere else. Churchill therefore suggested to the President that as there were many purely British-American matters to discuss beforehand, particularly those concerning the invasion of France, they should meet first in Cairo and thrash these problems out before proceeding to join Stalin.

To his dismay he then learnt from the British Ambassador in Moscow that Roosevelt, on his own initiative, had invited Molotov to attend these

[5] *Ibid.*, p. 190.

[6] By now it was evident that opinion in America was veering against the choice of Marshall as Supreme Allied Commander on the grounds that this would be demotion for him.

preliminary British-American discussions. At a stroke this threatened to jeopardize the whole success of these talks, for if Russian observers were present an immense amount of time would be wasted in interpreting all the proceedings. Churchill was convinced, too, that the Chiefs of Staff would make little headway if Russian officers with no previous knowledge of the technical problems of *Overlord* were allowed to take part in detailed discussion of them.

As it happened, all was well, for the President's invitation was hastily declined as soon as Stalin found out that Chiang Kai-shek had also been invited by Roosevelt to attend the preliminary conference. It was, however, a somewhat disturbing sign of a change of front by the President. At the same time Stalin's own attitude towards Britain once again became dictatorial and even abusive. He demanded an immediate resumption of the Murmansk convoys, and yet sought to impose a host of petty restrictions on the personnel of the British base organization charged with handling the convoys at the terminal ports. And so, as the Allies began at long last to dominate the battlefield, the shadows of dissension which were to obscure so many future victories loomed ominously over their joint councils.

* * * * *

While preparations were being made for the conference at Teheran Churchill received an important visitor. Early in October the distinguished Danish physicist, Niels Bohr, escaped in a fishing-boat to Sweden, where a British Mosquito picked him up and flew him to Aberdeen. His arrival in the Allied camp came at an opportune moment.

Due largely to Churchill's efforts agreement had recently been reached for improving co-operation between the teams working in the United States and Britain on the Atomic Development programme (*Tube Alloys*). Between 1941 and the Quebec Conference the American research programme had made immense strides, but the scientists working in Britain had found it more and more difficult to secure any exchange of information. By now it was widely recognized that the development of an atomic bomb might well prove a decisive factor in the war. It was not known, however, if Germany was making similar progress.

Disturbing fragments of intelligence filtered to England—it became known that Otto Hahn had discovered the principle of atomic fission—and it seemed vital that Allied research should not be hindered by national jealousies.[7] For a long time now, however, the Americans had tended to belittle the British effort. The arrival of Bohr, one of Rutherford's greatest disciples, strengthened the British team at a crucial moment.

[7] In fact, the American scientific mission which entered Germany in November 1944 discovered that the Germans had made only as much progress by that date as the British had done four years earlier.

When he first reached England it was important that his precise whereabouts should remain unknown to the enemy. A man of striking appearance, with his massive head, long white hair, and bushy eyebrows, he was already well known in British scientific circles, and he was persuaded that it would be safer for the time being if he stayed incognito in a small hotel off St James's Park.

Bohr was extremely anxious to put certain views about the atom bomb to the Prime Minister, and when a date had been fixed for them to meet he went to immense trouble to prepare his remarks. Among those from whom he sought assistance was Sir Henry Dale, President of the Royal Society.

One Sunday morning Bohr walked round to the Royal Institution to collect his friend, and he suggested to Dale that no one would be likely to pay any attention to them if they held their talk in Hyde Park. To make doubly sure that no eavesdropper could steal upon them unobserved he insisted on carrying two chairs into the middle of the Park, and there they sat close together, conversing in low tones.

Possibly Bohr could not have chosen any setting where the two of them presented a more incongruous and arresting sight. As far as eavesdroppers were concerned, however, it was highly unlikely that they would have been able to make head or tail of anything they heard. Bohr always talked in a low, indistinct tone, and his habit of speaking with his pipe in his mouth made him even more inaudible.

Churchill found him extremely difficult to understand, and their talk was not a conspicuous success. The Danish physicist was intent on discussing the global implications of atomic development while the Prime Minister's own concern at this stage was naturally concentrated upon the possible use of an atomic weapon by the enemy. At the end of a long and somewhat confusing discourse Churchill was far from certain whether he had been listening to an address on physics or politics, but Bohr, who was given a British passport, was destined to carry out highly important work for the Allies for the rest of the war.

A large atomic establishment had been set up in Montreal earlier in 1943, and almost the whole of the Cambridge research team under Dr Halban moved to Canada to continue their study of slow neutron research. After Churchill and Roosevelt had reviewed the atom project at Quebec a combined Policy committee for dealing with atomic research and development was established in Washington, and many of the scientists still engaged on *Tube Alloy* work in England went to America. Among them was Niels Bohr, his identity concealed under the prosaic pseudonym of Mr Nicholas Baker.

* * * * *

As it happened Germany's atomic programme was at this time subordinated to efforts in another sphere of scientific research altogether. She was planning an entirely different form of attack on Britain.

For more than a year now reports had been reaching England of increasing German activity in rocket research. The centre of this activity appeared to be Peenemunde, on the Baltic coast, and by the middle of 1943 reconnaissance flights revealed that a number of rocket-launching sites were already under construction in Northern France. There was also evidence that some form of attack by pilotless aircraft was in preparation.

A heavy air attack was made on Peenemunde in mid-August, and the sites in Northern France were also bombed. The Prime Minister's scientific advisers were unable to forecast with any certainty when the attack might begin, and what damage the missiles could cause. Since some reports suggested that this new Blitz might be launched as early as the middle of November the Prime Minister gave public warning of this when he spoke at the Mansion House just before his departure for the Middle East.

"We cannot . . . exclude the possibility of new fronts of attack upon this island," he said. "We have been vigilantly watching for many months past every sign of preparation for such attacks. Whatever happens they will not be of a nature to affect the final course of the war. But should they come they will certainly call for the utmost efficiency and devotion in our fire-watchers and Home Guard. . . . This is no time for persons who have practical war work to do to dream easy dreams of brave new worlds."

* * * * *

The organization of the forthcoming two-part conference provided more headaches for the joint staffs than any other Allied meeting. At one time or another a whole series of possible meeting-places for either the Big Three or the preliminary British-American talks were put forward, including Asmara (in Eritrea), Habbaniya, Baghdad, Khartoum, Basra, Alexandria, Oran, and even over-crowded Malta. But Stalin flatly refused to consider any other venue than Teheran for the major conference, and for communication and security purposes Cairo offered obvious advantages as the scene of the preliminary discussions. On October 31 the Prime Minister signalled hopefully to Washington, "Everything will be ready for Operation *Sextant* from [November] 20th onwards, and Colonel Warden will await Admiral Q and Celestes at rendezvous."[8]

Once again the Prime Minister and his party were to take passage in H.M.S. *Renown*. Before the special train left London there was an unexpected contretemps. Although the train was always searched as a matter

[8] Churchill, Vol. V, p. 281. "Admiral Q" was one of Roosevelt's code-names. "Celestes" referred to Chiang Kai-shek.

of course before it left its siding at Watford M I 5 decided on this occasion to examine the train crew's baggage. This was bitterly resented, for the crew regularly manned both the Prime Minister's and the Royal Train, and for an anxious hour or so Tommy feared he had a mutiny on his hands.

Renown was waiting at Plymouth. Although few of her ship's company had any inkling of their destination, they soon realized from the preparations being made that they were again to carry the Prime Minister. This time the attitude of the sailors was altogether different from their mood at the start of the previous voyage.

Churchill had been given a tremendous and completely spontaneous ovation as he left the ship at Greenock after the crossing from Canada, but only a few days earlier there had, unknown to the Prime Minister, been open, even bitter criticism of him by many of the ratings on board. The Russian successes, coupled with Communist propaganda which subtly encouraged the questioning of all forms of discipline, had bred a curious, unreasoning hero-worship of "Uncle Joe." And in contrast to the much advertised simplicity of the Russian leader Churchill, with his fondness for the good things of life, presented a sharply different image.

If he himself had realized this it would have saddened but not surprised him. As he knew only too well, malicious criticism and rumour in plenty had circulated about him in the London clubs ever since he succeeded to the Premiership. He paid little attention to it now; it was part of the inevitable price paid by any strong leader in a free democracy. But if people of education and influence were all too ready to spread spiteful tittle-tattle it was hardly surprising that men on the lower deck of the Navy should now accept equally petty, if less sophisticated, rumours at their face value.

H.M.S. *Renown* was a particularly happy ship, and the feeling of antagonism towards the Prime Minister was certainly not widespread among her ratings. Undeniably, however, such an attitude did exist. There was grumbling at the order to erect a canvas awning between the Admirals' cabin and the hangar space which was to be used as a cinema. "Uncle Joe wouldn't have wanted all this . . . no flannel about Uncle Joe . . ." Rumours that the cinema would have to be manned day and night in case Churchill wanted to see a film at any time spread more discontent, and since sailors are more conservative in their habits than most people some of them resented being told that work in the vicinity of the Prime Minister's quarters would have to be done with the minimum of noise.

It was not long, however, before they discovered that the rumours which had circulated about the Prime Minister's habits and routine were far wide of the mark; Mr Churchill was not the ogre they had been led to expect. The cinema was, in fact, manned for only a brief period each evening, and Churchill rarely sat through more than half the programme himself as he was invariably called away to deal with signals which had come in. Not only officers but the stewards and wardroom staff who looked after him were always invited to watch the film shows, and Mrs Churchill and Mary, who moved freely about the ship chatting to all and sundry, made it plain that the Prime Minister greatly appreciated all that was being done for him.

From resenting the crowded living conditions and the enforced change in their routine the sailors soon began to feel a sense of privilege at carrying their important visitors. And so when Churchill arrived on board H.M.S. *Renown* at Plymouth he was received as an honoured and welcome guest.

In fact the ship's company saw very little of the Prime Minister during the voyage to Malta and Alexandria. He had a heavy cold, and for a considerable time he was unable to throw off the effect of the inoculations he had received before he left London. He kept to his quarters most of the time; there was much work to do before the Conference.

In the party were Sarah Churchill (Mrs Vic Oliver), this time acting as her father's A.D.C.; Gilbert Winant, the American Ambassador; and Admiral Sir Andrew Cunningham, who had just succeeded Admiral Pound as First Sea Lord. Since the Prime Minister was looking far from well, Tommy was glad that Lord Moran, too, was travelling with them again.

"It was always a relief to have him with us on these trips. Although he insisted that he never treated himself with anything more advanced than aspirin or T.C.P., he always looked after the whole party assiduously, and he was a delightful travelling companion. He invariably brought with him an attaché-case filled with manuscript for a book he was writing. He had provisionally entitled it *The Anatomy of Fear*, but the P.M. objected to this. 'Why don't you call it *The Anatomy of Courage*,' he suggested. Under this title it was published after the war was over."[9]

When the voyage began Richard Pim and his map room staff worked out that the Prime Minister had already travelled 111,000 miles on his war-time missions. In four years he had spent no fewer than 792 hours at sea and 339 hours in the air. The early stages of this trip produced some of the wildest weather he had experienced in any of his travels, for on the first day out H.M.S. *Renown* and her escorts encountered a strong blow from the west-north-west. At 23 knots the accompanying destroyers looked like submarines, and even *Renown* and *London* were taking seas green over their bows. The quarter-deck of *Renown* was submerged for

[9] C. R. Thompson, Notes.

much of the time, and there were three inches of water in the wardroom. Off Portugal, however, the weather improved, and at dusk on November 15 they reached Gibraltar, where they picked up Harold Macmillan before heading into the Mediterranean.

On a grey depressing morning with rain falling steadily *Renown* arrived at Algiers. In recent weeks there had been considerable tension in the relations with the French Committee of Liberation, and trouble with Free French elements in Syria and the Lebanon. This may well have been in Churchill's mind when he decided not to call on de Gaulle, but apart from any other consideration he was advised that for security reasons it would be better if he remained on board. He did, however, see General Georges and Bedell Smith, Eisenhower's Chief of Staff, and de Gaulle was greatly incensed at what he considered a deliberate breach of etiquette by the Prime Minister. This was, however, a ridiculous charge. Churchill was travelling incognito, which removed any obligation for an exchange of formal calls. If the news of his presence in *Renown* had become widely known it could well have prejudiced the security of the conference in Cairo. The only reason, in fact, for calling at Algiers at all was to collect up-to-date charts of the enemy minefields, and after a few hours *Renown* sailed again for Malta.

At dawn next day the ship was making 29 knots—a remarkable speed for a battle cruiser over a quarter of a century old—and rounding Cape Bon with a favourable current she was actually doing 32 knots. A German reconnaissance aircraft sighted her near Pantelleria and action stations were sounded, but *Renown* was under almost continuous air cover and no attack resulted.

Malta was reached without incident, but as *Renown* entered the Grand Harbour Admiral Cunningham noticed that heavy weather was being made of the preparations for bringing the ship to her moorings. Chaos reigned on deck; everywhere ropes lay in tangled confusion, and Tommy thought of the day twenty years earlier when, as a young officer in charge of the quarter-deck of the battleship *Centurion*, he had wrestled with the same problems on entering Grand Harbour.

Knowing that if the Prime Minister chose this moment to go out on to the quarter-deck his arrival would only make matters worse, Admiral Cunningham endeavoured to keep him in conversation in the cabin. Eventually, when he noticed that the Prime Minister was becoming restive, the First Sea Lord remarked bluntly, "I wouldn't go out there if I was you, Prime Minister . . . it's like a snake's honeymoon!" Churchill took the hint, and *Renown*'s harassed officers were left to cope with their problems unhindered. Winant, who overheard the Admiral's picturesque description of the confusion on deck, was helpless with laughter.

Mr Churchill went ashore to stay with Lord Gort at San Anton Palace. He had been unable to shake off a feverish cold, and when Captain Pim took him his signals next morning the Prime Minister, who had had a restless night, ordered him petulantly to find some way of stopping the Governor's cows from mooing.

He spent most of the next two days in bed. The news of the fall of Leros was brought to him, and he held an anxious bedside conference to review the Ægean operations with the Chiefs of Staff; Admiral Sir John Cunningham, the new Commander-in-Chief, Mediterranean; and Air Marshal Tedder. He inveighed bitterly against the Americans for their refusal to come to British aid. Having got this off his chest, he announced that he felt very much better, and when a message arrived from Roosevelt inquiring anxiously whether after all he considered Cairo suitable for their meeting he blithely referred the President to the fourteenth chapter of St John.[10]

The President's advisers had suddenly got cold feet about Cairo. They had received reports suggesting that the enemy had discovered from U.S. Press and radio news that Egypt was to be the meeting-place of the Prime Minister and the President. Roosevelt was therefore urged to put forward the idea that the conference should be transferred to Khartoum or Malta. This found no favour with the British staff, for every conceivable precaution had been taken to ensure security at Cairo. It would have been impossible in the time available to prepare a new meeting-place at Khartoum which had anything approaching the same advantages. And Malta was even more unsuitable. Hollis, Ismay's deputy, was in fact told to report on the resources of the island for receiving several hundred visitors at short notice, but, as he soon found out, the idea was ludicrous. Food was desperately short, the rubble from the bombed buildings harboured millions of sand-flies, and it would have been impossible to find anywhere for most of the Conference party to sleep.

Conditions throughout the island were appalling at this time. At one naval transit camp a thousand men were living under canvas in a sea of mud. There were no beds and the men slept on chairs and tables. On the very afternoon that Roosevelt's signal arrived Vice-Admiral, Malta, made a tour of inspection of this particular camp, and there were angry murmurs of revolt. Officers on the camp staff reported that a mutiny was quite likely to break out if living conditions were not improved. Malta was, in fact, out of the question as a Conference venue, and in the end the Prime

[10] The passage he quoted was verses 1–4: "Let not your heart be troubled: ye believe in God, believe also in me. In my father's house are many mansions: if it were not so, I would have told you. I go to prepare a place for you. And if I go and prepare a place for you, I will come again and receive you unto myself; that where I am, there ye may be also. And whither I go ye know."

Minister persuaded Roosevelt that the safest course was to stick to the original plan.

At midnight on November 19 Churchill sailed for Alexandria. A few hours later the President himself arrived off Oran in the new battleship *Iowa*, commanded by his former naval aide, Captain J. C. McCrea. Such was the level of secrecy surrounding his arrival in the Mediterranean that when the *Iowa* appeared on the horizon H.M.S. *Sheffield*, lying in harbour there, signalled, "Who are you?" Back came the terse reply, "You know damn well who we are. Stop signalling."

On board the American battleship the atmosphere was distinctly tense. From the time she had entered the Mediterranean her officers had expected the ship to be heavily attacked at any moment, and it was plain that the responsibility of delivering the President safe and sound weighed heavily upon them.

Mr Roosevelt now came ashore, and after a meeting with General Eisenhower he completed the last lap of his long journey by air. On November 22 the Allied conference opened at Mena House, in the shadow of the Pyramids. For Churchill the five days which followed before he flew on to the rendezvous with Stalin were to provide a singularly frustrating experience.

28

The Cunning of the Bear

THE Villa Bleu, which had been set aside for the Prime Minister during his stay in Cairo, lay just off the main road to Alexandria at Mena and only half a mile from the Conference headquarters. It had been lent to the British Government by Mr Chester Beatty senior as a residence for the Minister of State in the Middle East, and the Soudanese butler and his French wife, the cook, who ran the house for the Caseys stayed on to look after Mr Churchill. The grounds had been heavily wired, and the whole Conference area was guarded by A.A. guns, troops, and fighter aircraft.

Near by the President was accommodated in the villa of Alexander Kirk, the American Ambassador, and all over the Mena area the homes of rich Cairenes had been leased to house delegates to the Conference. One wealthy woman was approached by Army Hirings to surrender her villa for three weeks at a princely rental. "Nonsense!" she said. "You can have it for nothing; I should be most honoured to lend it."

"You can't do that," said the Army. "It would place us in a most embarrassing position. We *must* pay you this money." So the owner reluctantly agreed—and she handed over the entire sum she received to King George's Fund for Sailors and the British Red Cross.

If the arrangements for the Conference involved a certain prodigality the organization of every aspect, from accommodation and transport to security and communications, was a masterpiece of efficiency. Security, indeed, was so effective that when, soon after his arrival, the Prime Minister inquired the reason for a series of deafening explosions close at hand in the desert it was discovered that an Army unit, blissfully unaware of any Conference, were carrying out a routine mine-clearance exercise.

The first plenary session was held on Tuesday, November 23. From the outset it was disturbingly plain that Roosevelt's preoccupation with the Chinese delegation headed by Chiang Kai-shek, whom he had insisted on inviting to Cairo, was going to hinder the progress of the far more urgent discussions on *Overlord* and operations in the Mediterranean. Chinese affairs were given precedence, and the whole of this first day was taken up with largely profitless consideration of Far Eastern affairs.

The staff talks broke down almost immediately, for the Chinese Chiefs of Staff and their advisers were unable to give any coherent information about their aims and resources. They were, in fact, so ill-informed at every point that Brooke and the British Chiefs of Staff became rapidly exasperated. The Chinese Vice-Admiral who was Director of Military Intelligence seemed completely out of touch with Army affairs. Strangely enough, he knew nothing about the Japanese Navy either. He explained that he had given up studying naval affairs when Chiang's forces lost their sea-ports.

Chiang Kai-shek himself revealed no impressive grasp of strategy, but he was plainly of greater mental stature than his companions. Those who watched him closely, however, found it difficult to decide whether many of the views he expressed were in fact his own or those of Madame Chiang, who interpreted for him. Of the two she appeared the dominant partner—highly intelligent, subtle, and giving an impression of ruthlessness and cunning. Never at loss for a word, she spoke fluent English, and when others were interpreting she would frequently break in to amplify or amend some statement without even a glance at her husband.

On the following day the Combined Chiefs of Staff turned their attention to Europe and the Mediterranean, and Churchill pressed strongly for a more logical attitude towards *Overlord*. He pointed out that slavish adherence to the target date for the invasion of Northern France might have a disastrous effect on the Italian theatre. If, however, some of the landing-craft due to be sent home from the Mediterranean for *Overlord* could be retained for even one more month this would enable an additional amphibious operation to be mounted.

The American reaction was guarded, for Churchill made it plain that he was still in favour of an attack on Rhodes and anxious to reopen the Eastern Mediterranean. The loss of the Ægean islands still rankled. At a lunch-party he spoke of the difficulties which had faced General Maitland Wilson in trying to hold Leros with insufficient troops. "I sent him a signal—'Improvise and dare,'" he said, adding quaintly, "So he improvose and dore."

Much of November 25—Thanksgiving Day—was spent in considering an unexpected American proposal for the appointment of a Supreme Commander for all Allied forces operating against Germany. This was strongly resisted by the Prime Minister and his advisers. They pointed out that the creation of such a post would upset the hitherto satisfactory Combined Chiefs of Staff organization; it would be virtually impossible for any one man to maintain an adequate grasp of all the military problems arising in North-west Europe and in the Mediterranean theatre as well; and the American proposal that his decisions would be subject to the approval of the Combined Chiefs of Staff, who would retain the right to overrule him whenever this was considered necessary, seemed to invite confusion. The American C.O.S. saw the strength of these objections, and for the time being the matter was not pursued further.

The Prime Minister had still not entirely recovered from his indisposition. He ate sparingly and on one of his early visits to the Map Room he advised Captain Pim and his staff to "take some of Lord Moran's special pills for warding off the Egyptian stomach." On Thanksgiving Day, however, he felt well enough to accept the President's invitation to dinner, and the traditional turkey and cranberry sauce was served, Roosevelt carving the turkey himself.

"This was a delightful family party, and afterwards there was dancing to the gramophone. Sarah being the only girl present the P.M. eventually invited General 'Pa' Watson, the President's Military Aide, to have a dance. Watson, then in his sixties, was a great character. He was taller than Mr Churchill, and very fat, and their partnership had to be seen to be believed. 'Pa' Watson had retired from the U.S. Army many years before and was unashamedly out of date in military matters. In his Southern drawl he delighted to tell of an occasion when Mr Roosevelt was cruising in the Presidential yacht. Watson sent a signal ordering a fort at the mouth of the Potomac to fire a salute. His attention had to be drawn to the fact that the fort's only gun had been removed forty years earlier!"[1]

* * * * *

At dawn on November 27 Churchill took off in the York for Teheran.

"On our arrival we found to our dismay that the road from the airfield to the centre of the city was lined by Persian troops and dense crowds had assembled. We had no alternative but to go ahead. At times the crowds slowed us to a walking pace, and when a lorry broke down in front of us we had to wait for several minutes with the car completely surrounded by people, many of whom were close enough to touch Mr Churchill. It was a very unpleasant situation. We knew there were enemy agents in the city, and it would have been the easiest thing in the world for anyone with a bomb to blow us all sky high. The P.M., who was under the impression that the crowds had gathered as a result of incompetent security precautions, was very angry. In fact the Persians were entirely unaware what was afoot.

[1] C. R. Thompson, Notes.

The streets were crowded for another reason altogether; the Shah was about to drive along the route on his own official business."[2]

Churchill was to stay at the British Legation. This was built in the form of a compound, and inside this area three hundred and fifty troops were quartered as a guard throughout the Conference. The Soviet Embassy lay just across the road, but the American Embassy was some distance away, and in view of the very real danger to the President in driving to and fro Stalin proposed that he should stay instead in a villa within the grounds of the Russian Embassy.

This greatly simplified the problem of protecting him, for whenever he moved between the Russian and British headquarters troops simply sealed off the street at either end with high barricades. These precautions were fully justified. In the next few days several reports came to Tommy that Germans had landed by parachute, and the N.K.V.D. men guarding Stalin told Mike Reilly, Roosevelt's personal bodyguard, that to their certain knowledge thirty-eight enemy paratroops had been dropped near the city.

Within a quarter of an hour of Roosevelt's arrival at the villa the Russians had placed at his disposal Stalin called on him. Only Charles Bohlen, an able young career diplomat who was many years later to become Ambassador to the U.S.S.R., and Berejkov, Stalin's interpreter, were present.

Stalin's affability at this first meeting with the President confirmed Roosevelt's impression that henceforth all would be well if the handling of the Russian leader was left to him. Long before he had remarked naïvely to William Bullitt, a former U.S. Ambassador in Moscow, "I have just a hunch that Stalin doesn't want anything but security for his country, and I think that if I give him everything I possibly can, and ask nothing from him in return, *noblesse oblige*, he won't try to annexe anything and will work for a world of democracy and peace."[3]

Furthering this hunch, Roosevelt now made it quite plain to Stalin that on a number of matters which would come under discussion he and Churchill did not see eye to eye. And when on the following morning the Prime Minister invited the President to lunch with him before the second plenary meeting he declined point-blank, on the grounds that Stalin might think he and Churchill were "hatching their own schemes."[4]

The Prime Minister was much upset by this rebuff. According to Averell Harriman, who delivered Roosevelt's reply, Churchill retorted, "I shall insist on one thing—that I be host at dinner to-morrow evening. I think I have one or two claims to precedence. To begin with I come first, both in seniority and alphabetically. In the second place I represent the

[2] *Ibid.* [3] See *Life*, August 30, 1948. [4] Sherwood, *op. cit.*, p. 779.

longest-established of the three Governments. And, in the third place, to-morrow happens to be my birthday."[5]

On the afternoon of Churchill's sixty-ninth birthday he had a private talk with Stalin. At that time he had not once seen the President alone since leaving Cairo, and he felt that Roosevelt was giving the Russians a false impression of the British attitude towards *Overlord*. The Prime Minister was in no way advocating a half-hearted policy towards the Normandy landings. What he never ceased to maintain at Teheran, however, was the illogicality of fixing an arbitrary date for the invasion of North-west Europe, and then using this as a reason for ceasing in the intervening period to exert pressure against the enemy elsewhere. It was becoming unhappily clear to him, however, that in presenting the British view at the tripartite discussions now in progress he could no longer count on the support of Roosevelt and his advisers.

He found Stalin ready to agree in principle that Turkey should be urged to enter the war, and that some good might come of providing limited aid to the Partisans in Yugoslavia, but it became increasingly obvious as the talks proceeded that the Marshal's main aim was to persuade the British and the Americans to confine their activities to the extreme west. As General Brooke noted in his diary, Stalin was by now much more satisfied with the Russian defensive position:

> The entry of Turkey was no longer so desirable . . . the opening of the Dardanelles . . . would bring in the British and Americans on his left flank in an advance westward through the Balkans. He had by then pretty definite ideas as to how he wanted the Balkans run after the war; British and American assistance was therefore no longer desirable in the Eastern Mediterranean. His new outlook on Italy was also interesting; there was now no pressure on our forces to push on up the leg of Italy. Such an advance led too directly towards Jugo-Slavia and Austria, on which no doubt he had by now cast covetous eyes. . . . We were reaching a very dangerous point where his shrewdness, assisted by American short-sightedness, might lead us anywhere.[6]

Thus it came about that the American plan for a subsidiary landing in the South of France (Operation *Anvil*) received the fullest Russian support, Stalin quickly perceiving that as the troops needed for this would have to be drawn from the Italian theatre this would put an effective brake on any advance which might threaten the Balkan area he wanted to seize himself.

The Conference was not, however, without its rewards. Russia agreed to join in the war against Japan as soon as Germany was defeated. This greatly eased American anxieties in the Far Eastern theatre, and from the

[5] *Ibid.*
[6] Bryant, *op. cit.*, Vol. pp. 90–91.

British point of view it provided welcome grounds for abandoning an over-ambitious assault on the Andaman Islands (Operation *Buccaneer*)—a project which, to Churchill's alarm, had received strong backing from the President at Cairo. The Russians also agreed to launch a major offensive to coincide with *Overlord*, and to the relief of the British Chiefs of Staff it was decided that D-Day for the Normandy landings would now take place "during May 1944."

The abandonment of May 1 as the specific date made it possible to go forward with plans for a further amphibious attack on the coast of Italy before the landing-craft began their voyage back to England. Churchill told Stalin that, as in the case of Salerno, it was planned to leapfrog ahead and put an Allied force ashore near the mouth of the Tiber.

On the last day of the Conference the three leaders reviewed many vital political problems, among them the future of Poland and Finland and the treatment of Germany after the war. In this field there could only be an exchange of views; as Churchill wrote later, "the political aspects were at once more remote and speculative" than the immediate military problems on which they had been engaged. Even at this stage, however, Stalin's attitude towards both Germany and Poland struck a vaguely disquieting note.

He called for the dismemberment of Germany, and the President supported him. Churchill, the realist and the wise student of history, counselled differently, but Roosevelt, who had without any warning produced a plan of his own for splitting Germany into seven regions—five of them self-governing and two to be controlled by the United Nations—continued to side with Stalin. To the Prime Minister it was ominously clear that such a policy would banish for a lifetime any likelihood of a united and peaceful Europe.

Stalin's intransigent attitude towards Germany had been made plain at a dinner which he gave to Churchill, Eden, and Clark Kerr, the British Ambassador to Russia, and Roosevelt, Hopkins, and Harriman, earlier in the week. When the subject of Germany was brought up Stalin said emphatically that the only way to prevent her resurgence as an aggressor nation was to round up and shoot fifty thousand officers and technicians who formed the core of the German military machine. And when Churchill protested at this suggestion—made apparently in all seriousness—Elliott Roosevelt, who had entered the room after dinner and taken a seat at the table, rose uninvited and assured Stalin that such a plan would be welcomed by the whole American Army. The Prime Minister was greatly upset.

> At this intrusion I got up and left the table, walking off into the next room, which was in semi-darkness. I had not been there a minute before

> hands were clapped upon my shoulders from behind, and there was Stalin, with Molotov at his side, both grinning broadly, and eagerly declaring that they were only playing, and that nothing of a serious character had entered their heads. . . . I was not then, and am not now, fully convinced that all was chaff and there was no serious intent lurking behind.[7]

According to Hopkins, there had been a great deal of teasing of Churchill by Stalin throughout the evening. Stalin was undoubtedly taking his cue from Roosevelt, who admitted on his return to America that he deliberately set out to win the regard of the Russian leader by making personal remarks at the Prime Minister's expense. As a result Churchill had to put up with a great deal of rather juvenile humour, and Roosevelt seemed strangely oblivious of the fact that his tactics, coming on top of his studious refusal to resume his normal friendly relationship with the Prime Minister outside the conference room or at official functions as long as the Conference lasted, was wounding to a man with whom he had for so long now enjoyed close friendship.

Even some of Roosevelt's own associates admitted frankly that they were embarrassed by his attempts to amuse the Russian leader at the Prime Minister's expense. Unhappily the President was convinced by the time he left Teheran that he had won the Marshal's complete confidence and regard. This misconception was to colour his whole attitude towards Allied policy in the days to come.

Churchill's burden at Teheran would have been easier to bear if he had been feeling fit, but throughout the Conference he was still suffering from the sore throat which had worried him ever since he left London. At times he was hardly able to speak, and only skilled medical care kept him going. On his birthday, however, he felt better, and at the dinner which he gave at the British Legation that night there was an air of genuine comradeship which had so far been woefully lacking. Both Roosevelt and Stalin paid him the warmest of tributes, Stalin toasting him as "my fighting friend."

This memorable evening, with its long succession of toasts and eloquent speeches, has often been described. Stalin was more genial than any of the British party had ever seen him, and he proposed the health of almost every one present, including Sawyers, the Prime Minister's butler. Poor Sawyers had so far had a trying trip. While shopping in Cairo he had lost his way in the Arab quarter, and when he sought help he was surrounded by a large and hostile crowd who apparently took him for a German spy. He escaped with some difficulty, and by the time he arrived back at the Villa Bleu he was late for the evening's work, and Mr Churchill was about to send out a search-party. He found himself in very hot water. Now, only

[7]Churchill Vol. V, p. 330.

a few days later, here he was in Persia, taking part in an historic occasion, and being toasted not once but twice in the same evening by the leader of the Soviet Union. His demanding job brought some strange ups and downs!

When the guests had risen from the table Stalin walked round chatting animatedly to every one in turn. Eventually he caught sight of Admiral Sir Andrew Cunningham, who said to him, "I have been waiting for the opportunity to drink a toast to the Russian Fleet, but I can find no representative of your Navy to assist me." Without hesitation Stalin replied, "I am the Commander-in-Chief of the Russian Navy. You shall drink a toast with me."

This was too much for the Prime Minister, who had come up just in time to overhear the conversation. As they raised their glasses and Cunningham said, "To the Russian Navy!" a well-known voice behind him added drily, ". . . coupled with the health of *Admiral* Stalin!"

* * * * *

When Churchill and Roosevelt returned to Cairo much ground still remained to be covered—and time was short. The President had decided to fly home on December 7. The four days which remained were fully occupied with further exhaustive discussion of *Buccaneer*, the Andaman Islands operation; talks with President Inönü about Turkey's entry into the war; the precise timing of *Overlord*; and the arrangements for *Anvil*, the South of France landings.

Still troubled by an undertaking he had rashly given to Chiang Kai-shek, Roosevelt remained stubbornly disinclined to consider cancelling *Buccaneer*, but Russia's declaration that they would turn to attack Japan as soon as the war in Europe was over had in reality removed the need for an operation which would absorb many landing-craft urgently required elsewhere. In the end the matter was resolved by a signal from Mountbatten. To guarantee success in an area where the enemy held air superiority he estimated that he would need 50,000 men, and the President, who had never contemplated an operation on this scale, realized that the project was no longer feasible.

Churchill still pressed for an attack on Rhodes but the Turkish delegates, for whom he had sent his personal aircraft, refused once again to commit themselves to any definite step. Not surprisingly, their cautious attitude strengthened American opposition to any Allied move in the Eastern Mediterranean.

Even with the abandonment of *Buccaneer* there was much anxiety over the shortage of landing-craft. Captain H. B. Ellison, the Director of Landing Craft, Mediterranean Fleet, was summoned from Algiers, and the Prime Minister cross-examined him closely to see whether the best use was being made of existing resources in the theatre. Even Churchill had to admit that the position was far from satisfactory, and in the end it was agreed that operations in the Ægean would only be considered if they could be fitted in without detriment to *Overlord* or *Anvil.* In view of the subsequent difficulty experienced in finding the bare minimum of craft for *Shingle*, the Anzio landing, it is surprising in retrospect that the capture of Rhodes kept its place for so long on the Allied agenda.

No decision had yet been announced about the Supreme Command of *Overlord*, but on his last day in Egypt Roosevelt told the Prime Minister he had made up his mind. He could not, after all, spare Marshall, and General Eisenhower was nominated in his place.

By now most of those who had taken a leading part in these long-drawn-out discussions at Cairo and Teheran were beginning to feel the strain. Ismay collapsed with exhaustion and was ordered home immediately. The Prime Minister had recovered from his sore throat, but Smuts, for one, was alarmed at his appearance and feared that he was on the verge of a complete breakdown.[8] Churchill himself knew he was ill; he complained of pains in his back and a feeling of lassitude. But he had set his mind on visiting the battle-front in Italy on his way home.

Shortly after midnight on December 11 he took off in the York for Tunis. He intended to spend one night there with Eisenhower, who had a villa on the shores of the bay near Carthage, and then go on to see Alexander and Montgomery.

"When we arrived over Tunis we were told to our surprise that the main airfield at El Aouina was closed. Instead we were directed to a desolate landing-strip some miles away. There were no buildings, no communications; apart from a small care and maintenance party from a near-by R.A.F. unit the place was completely deserted.

"The P.M., who looked ghastly, insisted on getting out of the York, and for the best part of an hour he sat chilled to the bone on one of the up-turned packing-cases which littered the field. Eventually our radio operator in the plane got in touch with Tunis, and we were told to take off again and land at El Aouina. The airfield there had been specifically closed so that the York could land without interference, and we should never have been diverted in the first place."[9]

The Prime Minister went straight to Eisenhower's villa—now known locally as The White House—and after lunch he went to bed and slept fitfully for the rest of the day. In the early hours of the following morning he woke with a raging temperature. He had pneumonia.

Lord Moran acted promptly. Wherever he went with Churchill he made a point of contacting the leading specialists and finding out everything he

[8] Bryant, *op. cit.*, Vol. II, p. 112. [9] C. R. Thompson, Notes.

could about the medical facilities in the theatre. He sent signals to Algiers and Cairo requesting that Brigadier Evan Bedford, consulting physician to the Middle East Forces, should be flown immediately to Tunis, as well as Brigadier Lionel Whitby, another distinguished specialist serving in the command, and two nursing sisters.

There was no question now of any visit to Italy by the Prime Minister. Churchill, weakened and worn out by his travels and the burden he had borne so long at the conference table, was seriously ill.

29

Christmas at Carthage

IT WAS obvious to Lord Moran that his patient could not be moved from the villa. Mrs Churchill was summoned from London, and Brigadier Hollis, who had remained behind in Cairo with a small staff to clear up War Cabinet business when Ismay returned home, was sent for to set up an emergency office. Throughout his illness the Prime Minister insisted on keeping in close touch with events. "The days passed in much discomfort. Fever flickered in and out. I lived on my theme of the war, and it was like being transported out of myself. The doctors tried to keep the work away from my bedside, but I defied them."[1]

He also defied the efforts of General Eisenhower's personal dietician, a charming and capable captain in the U.S. Women's Army Corps, to persuade him to eat the sort of meals she considered suitable for an invalid. The Prime Minister did not hold with dieticians and their abstruse theories about calories and vitamins; he demanded good, plain English fare. Luckily H.M.S. *Renown* was still at Gibraltar, and Chief Petty Officer Pinfield and the naval cook who had been drafted to the ship to look after Mr Churchill on the voyage out were dispatched post haste to Carthage. After that there were no more complaints about the food.

Although the most strenuous precautions had been taken to keep the news of Churchill's illness and his present whereabouts secret, no one was very happy about his safety. As long as he remained at Carthage there was danger of attack by long-range aircraft or submarines. The presence of the York was too conspicuous to be missed by any reconnaissance aircraft on the prowl, and so it was used as a decoy, the crew being ordered to fly back

[1] Churchill, Vol. V, p. 376.

to Cairo, where a villa, heavily and ostentatiously guarded, was taken for them on the outskirts of the city.

To protect The White House a battalion of the Coldstream Guards was brought in. The first company to arrive were rushed from Constantine and quartered in tents pitched in the ruins of Carthage. Later they were joined by two more companies, one commanded by Major Hugh Norman, an old friend of Tommy.

Although Churchill was far from a model patient he made an extraordinary recovery. He was determined to get well in the quickest possible time, and a few days before Christmas he was out of bed and walking about his room. From this moment onward he became more and more intolerant of the attempts of his medical advisers to make him take things quietly. By now he was concentrating all his attention on the vexed problem of finding enough craft to mount a two-divisional assault on Anzio, just to the south of Rome (Operation *Shingle*).

He discovered that although there were enough craft still in the Mediterranean for this purpose the bulk of them were due to sail for England not later than January 15 in order to prepare for *Overlord*. Others were said to be unavailable owing to refits. And it was pointed out that even if he was able to persuade the Americans to allow the landing-craft for *Overlord* to be held back for three weeks, and *Shingle* was launched on or about January 20, it still left too little time to train the crews for the operation.

Mr Churchill brushed all these objections aside. Bedell Smith, Eisenhower's Chief of Staff, said it was more than his life was worth to signal to Washington for a deferment of the sailing date, but the Prime Minister was fully prepared to go into action. He found, too, that he could borrow more landing-craft from the Indian Ocean now that *Buccaneer* was no longer on the Allied programme, and he began bombarding Admiral Sir John Cunningham at Algiers with demands for more realistic and up-to-date information about the craft under repair and the time needed for training.

On Christmas Eve Captain M. L. Power, Deputy Chief of Staff to C.-in-C., Mediterranean, was just about to start his lunch at the Hotel Aletti in Algiers when he was rung up and told that an aircraft was waiting at Maison Blanche to take him to a secret destination. He was to leave immediately.

Unaware that the Prime Minister had asked for a senior naval officer in close touch with current operations to be flown to Carthage he rang up the Commander-in-Chief's house, and under the impression that he was speaking to the Flag Lieutenant he said testily, "Don't you think it's about time somebody woke up and gave me some warning when they expect me to go on journeys like this? I know nothing about any trip, I've had no briefing, I've got no papers with me, and I don't even know where I'm supposed to be going!"

Admiral Cunningham, who had answered the phone, calmed him down. He explained that the Prime Minister's signal had only just come in; there was no time for any briefing. So Power left his lunch untouched and tore out to Maison Blanche, where he met Bedell Smith and two perplexed Brigadiers. They had all received a similar summons.

When they reached Carthage they were shown into the Prime Minister's bedroom. Looking like a large and apparently healthy baby, Mr Churchill was sitting up in bed, and he immediately began firing questions at Power about landing-craft—how many were there at hand, what was their state of readiness, what was the minimum time needed to train their crews for an operation, and so on. Power admitted frankly that he did not know the precise answers, and asked for time to phone Algiers.

"Where is Force S?" demanded the Prime Minister.

This was an assault force under the command of Rear-Admiral Tom Troubridge. Power remembered that two days earlier he had seen a signal from the Admiralty recalling this force to the Mediterranean. It had then been half-way across the Indian Ocean and bound for the East Indies. Not appreciating the significance of this signal at the time, he had dismissed the matter from his mind.

"I don't know their exact position, but they are coming back this way," he said.

The Prime Minister glared disapprovingly.

"Haven't you been following the progress of these great ships day by day, hour by hour?" he demanded. "You don't seem to know much. You're no use!"

By this time Power, one of the most brilliant officers in the Service, was becoming decidedly cross.

"Maybe I don't know much," he retorted, "but I can find out. Tell me what you want to do and when, and I may be able to tell you if you can do it."

"Now we're beginning to talk," said the Prime Minister. "Very well... ring up your friend at Algiers. We will meet here again at nine o'clock this evening and you shall give me your answer."

Power rang up Ellison, the Director of Landing Craft. He then dictated a brief memorandum explaining how the Anzio landing could be carried out and had it typed, with several copies. After dinner they sat round the table in Churchill's bedroom. Power chose a seat at the end, out of harm's way.

"No, no, Captain Power! Come and sit here," said the Prime Minister, pointing to a chair opposite him. He then read the memorandum. In a few concise sentences Power had shown that, making full allowance for tide training, loading, and rehearsal of the operation, the landing-craft could be ready in three weeks and their retention for a brief period could have no adverse effect on *Overlord*.

"A most remarkable paper," the Prime Minister observed. "Just what I require." Without making any addition to it, he ordered that the report should be signalled to the Chiefs of Staff and the meeting broke up.

On the following morning Power went to the airfield to meet his Commander-in-Chief. Admiral Cunningham had been up most of the night presiding over a full-scale conference at his villa to work out the answers to every conceivable question which the Prime Minister might put to him, and he was not in the best of tempers. "A merry Christmas *this* is likely to be!" he said sourly, as he emerged from his plane "—and what the devil have you been up to?" For, like most Commanders-in-Chief, John Cunningham was never easy in his mind about commitments which might have been made on his behalf in his absence, particularly where the Prime Minister was concerned. Power put him in the picture, and they set off on a devious journey to the villa, small wooden signs marked BLACK ROUTE pointing the way.

When they reached The White House, nestling low on the sloping cliff-side and ringed by A.A. guns and sentries, they found that many others had been summoned to attend this Christmas Day conference, among them Alexander, Maitland Wilson, and Tedder, and Eisenhower and two of his British Deputy Chiefs of Staff, Lieutenant-General Sir Humfrey Gale and Major-General "Jock" Whiteley. For the first time since his illness Churchill was able to leave his room, and when every one was present he emerged wearing his siren suit and a striking pair of bedroom slippers which bore his initials in gold across each foot.

He rounded up his guests, and the rest of the morning was spent hammering out the many problems of the descent on Anzio. By the end of the meeting there was general agreement that the operation was feasible provided that fifty-six of the landing-craft earmarked for *Overlord* could be retained for a period of not more than one month. Churchill envisaged *Shingle* as a gamble which would either succeed or fail in about three days. He did not at any time contemplate a long-drawn-out operation. At the same time as he signalled his conclusions to the Chiefs of Staff in London he sent a personal plea to the President to support the request for the landing-craft.

The Prime Minister had looked far from well when the meeting began, but the morning's work seemed to invigorate him. He was his old forceful self, probing relentlessly into every complex aspect of this amphibious venture from winds and tides to firepower and logistics. It was difficult for those who spent this Christmas Day at The White House, the writer among them, to believe that only a fortnight before he had been on the verge of death.

Mr Churchill had, in fact, called out for his detective at four o'clock one morning when he was critically ill. When Detective-Inspector Thompson entered the bedroom he said to him, "If this is the end it is fitting that I should die in the sight of Carthage." Now, as he presided over his large lunch-party, he seemed at the top of his form. Mrs Churchill had been to a Christmas Day service near by, conducted by a British Army chaplain. She had a strange story to tell. A white dove had flown into the tin hut where the service was being held, and had alighted on the altar just as the Blessing was being pronounced. "An ecclesiastical hoax!" declared the Prime Minister.

He twitted Admiral Cunningham about an incident earlier in the morning. "Do tell us what that little ship in the Bay is?" Sarah had asked; "is she signalling 'Happy Christmas'?" Walking over to the window, the Admiral, a stickler for discipline, was surprised to see that in blissful ignorance of war-time regulations the duty patrol vessel, apparently determined to celebrate Yuletide, had dressed overall. To make matters worse she was under way at the time when the Commander-in-Chief first set eyes on her—and even in peace-time no warship remained dressed overall when under way.

"What do all those flags mean?" Sarah asked again.

"The best translation I can give you," said the Admiral drily, "is, 'I am totally unacquainted with the customs and regulations of the Service.' "

To tea that afternoon came the Governor-General of Tunisia, General Mast, and his wife, whose son, a prisoner of war, lay under sentence of death by the Germans. In the evening Mr Churchill gave a fork supper in the large hall of the villa, and many Service guests were invited in from the surrounding district, including officers of the Guards battalion watching over the house. The Prime Minister's aircrew, headed by Wing Commander "John" Collins and Squadron Leader Bill Fraser, who was shortly to succeed him as captain of the York, had also arrived. Anxious that they should not be left out of the Christmas party Churchill had had them recalled from their hiding-place in Cairo.

He took several of his more important guests to dine with him in his bedroom. Afterwards he came out to the hall and stayed chatting for some time to the rest of his visitors. Over his siren suit he now wore his favourite black silk dressing-gown, lavishly emblazoned with silver dragons.

His appearance in the room, even in the middle of this gay Christmas-night party, produced a remarkable effect. Like preparatory schoolboys who expected at any moment to be confronted with some misdemeanour by a stern headmaster even the most senior officers instantly assumed a state of rigid and respectful alertness, stammering out halting replies to any questions which the Prime Minister put to them. Surrounded by his war leaders Mr Churchill was, however, in the happiest of moods. To one awestruck junior officer he said disarmingly, "I have asked you here to-day because I thought you might have a more enjoyable Christmas than you might otherwise have spent in your remote Algerian fastness." In the midst of war, when every one was far from their own homes and families, it was indeed a memorable and happy interlude.

Two days later Churchill flew to Marrakesh. Although much better, he was still very weak, and he found it a strain to walk more than a few paces. His doctors warned that he was in no fit state to face an immediate return to the English winter and General Eisenhower therefore arranged that the Villa Taylor should be put at his disposal while he was convalescing.

When the time came for him to leave The White House every one assembled in the hall to bid him farewell. The Prime Minister was in high spirits, for a few moments earlier Tommy had brought him a signal reporting a notable sea victory—the sinking of the *Scharnhorst* as she tried to intercept an Allied convoy bound for Russia. Spotting the young American officer Eisenhower had attached to him as a temporary A.D.C., Churchill walked over to say good-bye, and asked him where his home was. Learning that he came from Alabama, the Prime Minister immediately invited every one to join in a chorus of "When the Midnight Choo-choo leaves for Alabam," to the young Southerner's considerable embarrassment.

* * * * *

For many years His Majesty's Government had maintained a Consulate at Marrakesh, in the care of a vice-consul, but since all the arrangements for the Prime Minister's stay at Villa Taylor were in the hands of the American Army, whose guest he was to be, the British Vice-Consul, Mr Bryce Nairn, had no inkling that anything unusual was afoot until Boxing Day morning, when a Wing Commander in the R.A.F., clutching a bulging brief-case, was shown into his office. He was, he said, on an urgent and Top Secret mission, and had important papers for a Colonel Warden. Could Nairn tell him where the Colonel was staying?

Nairn, who knew the names of most people serving in the area, had never heard of Colonel Warden, but his visitor seemed so agitated that he spent most of the day telephoning to Port Lyautey and other Service bases in Morocco to ask if anyone else had met this mysterious British officer. He had no success, and the Wing Commander grew more and more depressed. Hoping to cheer him up, the Vice-Consul persuaded him with some difficulty to leave his brief-case in the Consulate safe and come back to his house for a drink. His guest was rather deaf, and Nairn had to shout to make himself understood. After an hour of desultory conversation the Vice-Consul, who was beginning to believe that the elusive Colonel Warden was a figment of the Wing Commander's imagination, felt as if he was taking part in some slightly surrealistic charade.

Next morning, however, the Wing Commander was back again at the Consulate beaming with relief. "The Colonel has arrived!" he announced, and, collecting his brief-case, he hurriedly departed. Nairn was still puzzling over this, and wondering what had brought this British Colonel to Marrakesh, when another stranger arrived—a naval Commander resplendent in gold aiguillettes—and from him he learnt at last the identity of Colonel Warden. Tommy had called on the Vice-Consul to present Mr Churchill's compliments and inquire whether the Pasha of Marrakesh, El Glaoui, should be informed of the Prime Minister's arrival.

The Nairns were asked to lunch at Villa Taylor. Bryce Nairn had not been at Marrakesh when Churchill and Roosevelt spent the night there after the Casablanca Conference. Until the previous September he had been serving at Brazzaville, but he had met Churchill on his first visit to Marrakesh in 1936. He had arrived to stay at the Mamounia Hotel with Lloyd George, who was writing his memoirs, and Nairn, who had recently joined the Foreign Service after a spell of farming in Morocco, had been asked to arrange for Mrs Churchill and Megan Lloyd George to visit the Pasha's palace. He remembered this well, for when he explained that only women could visit the harem Mr Churchill had fluffed up his hair, wrapped a scarf round his head, and asked plaintively if he could go as his own mother-in-law!

When they arrived for lunch they found the Prime Minister reading under a sunshade in the garden. He complained that he felt tired and listless, but he questioned the Vice-Consul closely about the French administration of the area. They lunched under the shade of a large olive-tree, and the Nairns gathered that the Prime Minister had had a trying flight from Tunis. His doctors had told the captain of the York that the aircraft must not be taken up to more than 6000 feet because of the strain on Churchill's heart, but at this height violent air eddies had thrown the plane about while they were over the desert. As they reached the mountains the weather had worsened and they had flown into dense cloud.

"The P.M. announced that, doctors or no doctors, he had no intention of nosing through narrow passes at a height below that of the mountains on either side. He therefore ordered the pilot to climb above the highest peak we might encounter anywhere near our route. Once over the mountains the weather improved. We never understood why we were not cleared to fly along the coast over the sea and then turn inland when west of the mountains, but Tedder flatly refused to allow this. The aircraft which followed us kept strictly to the 6000-ft. limit, and Hollis and the girl cipher officers on board had a frightening trip, one of the engines failing and a door being blown off."[2]

This lunch with the Vice-Consul and his wife was the start of an enduring friendship between the Churchill family and the Nairns. The Prime Minister soon discovered that Margaret Nairn was an accomplished artist, and they made many expeditions together into the valleys of the Atlas. Both would set up their easels, Churchill working in oils and Mrs Nairn in water-colours. Largely self-taught, although he had had some advice from Orpen and Sickert and—later in life—from French impressionist painters on the Riviera, Churchill was very diffident about his ability, but Margaret Nairn saw him to be a wonderful colourist. She noted, too, his intense concentration while he was painting. He would remain bent over the easel until sheer physical pain forced him to take a rest.

Bryce Nairn, a shrewd Scot who had spent most of his life in Morocco, was a constant help to the Prime Minister, for he knew and intimately understood both the French and the Arabs and spoke their language fluently.[3] It was he who took Tommy to pay the Prime Minister's respects to the Pasha of Marrakesh.

El Glaoui, a dignified and impressive figure, received them in the vast hall of his palace. Although he was perfectly well aware of the Prime Minister's arrival, he politely made a great show of surprise and pleasure. Arab girls brought refreshment—small cups of very thick coffee and endless plates of sweetmeats. When the time came to leave and the Pasha rose to his feet Tommy was intrigued to see that his flowing robes only partially concealed the incongruous Western garb of plus fours and golf shoes!

* * * * *

At Marrakesh the Prime Minister and his personal staff achieved the nearest approach to a normal working routine they had followed for a long time. Churchill worked in bed in the mornings; whenever possible they went off for a picnic lunch and spent the afternoons in the foothills of the Atlas Mountains.

On the day after his arrival a signal came from the President approving the retention of the landing-craft for the Anzio operation. This was welcome news indeed, but Churchill's satisfaction was short-lived. Intelligence

[2] C. R. Thompson, Notes.

[3] He was subsequently appointed Consul at Bordeaux, Madeira, and Minneapolis, and Consul-General at Laurenço Marques. In 1957 he returned as Consul-General to Tangier. An impression by Margaret Nairn of the Prime Minister painting in the garden of their villa during his holiday in France before the Potsdam Conference is reproduced on p. 336.

reports began to stress the likelihood of much sterner enemy resistance than had been estimated when *Shingle* was first considered;[4] the military planners wanted to revise their original calculations of the troops and equipment which could be carried by the landing-craft now available; and it was claimed that there were not enough craft in reserve for supply and reinforcement of the Allied divisions once they got ashore.

To iron out these problems once and for all Churchill called a conference in the first week of January, and, suspecting that many of the objections now being raised were not entirely valid, he sent for Captain Power, whose clear thinking had removed so many of the initial obstacles.

Power flew from London. He had been summoned home to discuss the planning of the South of France landings and was out of touch with recent developments in *Shingle*. When he arrived at the Villa Taylor the Prime Minister, sitting up in a bed strewn with papers, began complaining vehemently that he was meeting with considerable obstruction. "I want your views," he said.

Power pointed out that he had been at the Admiralty since the Carthage meetings and was therefore unaware of the present situation. "In any case," he added, "I am not in a position to express any definite views until I have talked this over with Admiral Cunningham first. He is the naval Commander-in-Chief of the operation."

At this the Prime Minister became annoyed and rang the bell for Hollis. "You are to cancel Captain Power's appointment to the staff of the Commander-in-Chief, Mediterranean, and attach him to the staff of the Minister of Defence," he ordered. Faced with this surprising development, Power withdrew and wrote a short report showing how the available shipping resources could be put to the best use, including the introduction of merchant ships to help the unloading of the hard-pressed landing-craft.

When he had finished this task he lunched with the Prime Minister. As they rose from the table Churchill said blandly, "Now you had better go and make your peace with your Commander-in-Chief," and Power realized that his new appointment had already lapsed after only two hours. Once again he was a member of Admiral Cunningham's planning staff.

From Italy and North Africa most of the senior officers involved in the Anzio venture were now converging on Marrakesh. At the evening meeting Power, much to his embarrassment, was called upon to read his paper. During the vigorous argument which followed several speakers maintained that the number of landing-craft which could in reality be called upon at varying stages of the assault and build-up was well below the Navy's own estimate.

[4] The Germans were, in fact, anticipating an Allied landing and had five divisions in reserve, but these were north of the Tiber.

"The soldiers are talking tripe," Power whispered to Hollis. "If we really scrape the barrel we can do a lot better than that."

Churchill, sitting alert at the head of the table, instantly called out, "What have you got to say about that, Captain Power? You'd better come and sit by me."

Power was made to repeat his analysis, and his estimate was eventually accepted. After that the meeting went well and Operation *Shingle* was finally approved.

"Now that's decided we must tell the Chiefs of Staff," said Churchill as they adjourned.

"It's really a matter for the Combined Chiefs," Hollis pointed out.

"No!" said the Prime Minister firmly. "The British Chiefs of Staff are, by agreement, responsible for the Mediterranean area."

"In that case," rejoined Hollis, "it is a matter for the War Cabinet."

"What is the quorum of the War Cabinet?" demanded Churchill.

Hollis said it was two.

"Well, then . . ." said the Prime Minister, "I have beside me Lord Beaverbrook. Are you in favour, my Lord?"

Beaverbrook said he was, and there and then the necessary approval was given.

As the meeting broke up Churchill turned to Alexander. "I do hope, General, that when you have landed this great quantity of lorries and cannon you will find room for a few foot soldiers—if only to guard the lorries," he said drily.

Admiral Cunningham and Captain Power went back to the Mamounia Hotel, where most of the Prime Minister's staff were staying. The Arab population of Marrakesh were celebrating the eve of their own New Year, and the intricate timetable for D-Day at Anzio was worked out to a ceaseless throbbing of drums which sounded all night long from the Medina.

* * * * *

The Prime Minister had many callers at Marrakesh. President Beneš came to see him on his way back from Moscow. He had long talks with Brigadier Fitzroy Maclean, whom he had summoned from Yugoslavia, about Allied aid for Tito's Partisans; and General Montgomery, about to take command of the forces for *Overlord*, spent New Year's Eve with him. Montgomery had not seen the detailed plan for *Overlord*, and he retired early to study it. Before he left next day he asked Churchill to add a further message to the leather-bound book which the Prime Minister had first inscribed on the eve of Alamein. Churchill wrote:

> The immortal march of the Eighth Army from the gates of Cairo along the African shore through Tunisia, through Sicily, has now carried its ever-victorious soldiers and their world-honoured commander far into

Italy towards the gates of Rome. The scene changes and vastly expands. A great task accomplished gives place to a greater in which the same unfailing spirit will win for all true men a full and glorious reward.

The Prime Minister had another passage of arms with de Gaulle. In the second week of his stay at Marrakesh he heard that General de Lattre de Tassigny was in Morocco, and he sent a signal inviting him to lunch. To his anger, a curt message came from de Gaulle, in Algiers, regretting that de Lattre would be unable to accept. De Gaulle was still smarting at what he chose to consider was a series of rebuffs either to him or local French commanders in various parts of North Africa. He complained that Churchill was treating North Africa as his own country; that he had not paid sufficient attention to the Governor-General of Tunisia during the time he had been seriously ill at Carthage; and that, since then, he had ignored the Governor-General of Morocco.

As it happened, the Prime Minister had already invited de Gaulle to visit him at Marrakesh. He was so incensed by the de Lattre incident that he now announced he would refuse to see de Gaulle at all. Nairn and Duff Cooper, who had just come from Algiers, tried hard to make him change his mind, and after a heated discussion lasting until 3.0 A.M. Churchill relented. By then he had discovered that de Lattre was, in fact, in Italy, and he had begun to think that he might have been a little hasty in judging de Gaulle's message.

When in due course de Gaulle presented himself at the villa the Prime Minister, gently taken to task by Mrs Churchill for being persistently unfriendly to their guest of honour, tried hard to overcome his irritation. At lunch the conversation was conducted in French, Churchill remarking cheerfully, "Now that the General speaks English so well he has no difficulty in understanding my French." Nevertheless, the atmosphere throughout the meal was somewhat strained. Afterwards they moved into the garden, and the Prime Minister brought up a number of points on which he felt de Gaulle was adopting an unreasonable attitude. Chief among these was the General's stubborn opposition to Roosevelt's policy in North Africa and the treatment of certain French politicians, among them Flandin and Peyrouton, who had recently been arrested in Algiers. "Winston was admirable, I thought, and de Gaulle very difficult and unhelpful," wrote Duff Cooper afterwards; "he talked as though he was Stalin and Roosevelt combined."[5] In spite of this, Churchill persevered, and in the end the meeting went off so well that the General invited the Prime Minister to take the salute with him next morning at a parade of the French garrison.

Nairn heard of this with some misgivings. Although the German radio

[5] Duff Cooper, *op. cit.*, p. 319.

had announced that Churchill was staying at Aswan, in Egypt, it seemed unwise for him to attend a public parade in the streets of Marrakesh. The Prime Minister had, in fact, been strongly advised to show himself as little as possible in public when he was not making one of his trips to the surrounding countryside in a properly escorted cavalcade of cars. To this he agreed in principle, but often he would be found standing at the gate at the end of the garden, talking to the children who used to gather in the hope of seeing him.

He was much moved by the tremendous welcome he received when he walked to the saluting base for the French Army parade, the cries of "Vive Churchill" rivalling the shouts for de Gaulle.

Day by day he was steadily regaining his strength in the warm Moroccan sun. Once the arguments about the Anzio landing had been resolved life at the villa became more settled. Every day there were signals to deal with and decisions to make, but to the relief of the hard-worked cipher staff the tempo slackened appreciably and the staff of the Private Office in Storey's Gate composed a long and slightly irreverent ballad which they sent upstairs to Brigadier Jacob in the Ministry of Defence. The opening verse ran:

The Warden and the Cabinet
Were working hand in hand
Between the mists of London
And a thousand miles of sand.
If we could *always* stay like this,
They said, it would be GRAND!

Nearly every day the Nairns mapped out a different expedition to the mountains. One day they went to Demnat, eighty miles to the east of Marrakesh. From the rocky ledge where they had their picnic lunch a goat track led steeply down to a pool where some native children were bathing. When lunch was over the Prime Minister, clambering down the boulder-strewn path, asked Bryce Nairn to get the boys to dive into the pool. This they did with great enthusiasm at first, but the water from the mountains was freezingly cold and eventually the shivering swimmers went on strike. Only Nairn's surreptitious bribes of fifty francs a time persuaded them to continue the entertainment.

When the time came to set off back up the mountain-side Mr Churchill found the climb more of a strain than he would admit. To gain breathing-space he carried on a series of one-sided conversations with a goat which was regarding him suspiciously from a near-by ledge. Finally he had to confess that the effort was too much for him, and with the aid of a tablecloth Diana Duff Cooper and Margaret Nairn hauled him unceremoniously up the last few yards to the plateau.

Another time the picnic party became completely lost when visiting a French military post near the snow-line.

"The road became more and more precipitous, and the sheer drop to the valley beneath looked more and more menacing as the bends became sharper. It was safe enough for the jeep leading the procession but the enormous Cadillac which the Americans had provided for the P.M. filled the entire road and it seemed certain that before long we would be faced with the nightmare task of backing on the edge of one of these ravines in order to get round a corner at all on this twisting route. The sun went down, and as the P.M. sat shivering in the open car Moran became alarmed. Fortunately the American Army drivers kept their heads and at long last we reached the plain."[6]

Marrakesh was, and is, an artist's paradise. At sunset the palm-trees in the foreground stand out against the snow-covered peaks of the High Atlas . . . now sparkling silver, now crimson-streaked with orange and changing slowly to green and mauve as the last rays vanish below the horizon.

One distinguished artist who had come to live in Marrakesh was Jean Jacques Majorelle, and the Churchills were taken to visit him. In twenty years he had created from dust, sand, and desolation one of the most remarkable gardens in the world. In one corner alone grew 360 different kinds of cacti. Vivid blue railings surrounded a pond on which a white swan sailed majestically. The pink walls of the house were mirrored in the water, and there were other striking essays in colour—a jade-green duck house . . . a tree, its trunk and branches painted blue, flaunting the natural green of its leaves with bizarre effect . . . and a blue-and-orange pavilion in the cactus garden round which every imaginable freak of nature flourished in wild profusion. Here again the rippling waters of a pool, where a pink-splashed flamingo stood sentinel, reflected weirdly distorted images of a mad, magic world.

Mr Churchill unwisely stroked one of the cacti. Immediately his hand was pierced by myriads of tiny spikes, and in sudden pain he cast away his cigar. It was retrieved by his host, who later had it mounted in silver as a memento of the visit.

The Prime Minister spent a long time admiring M. Majorelle's paintings, and when that night the artist sent a message asking if he could be allowed to present Churchill with any picture he liked to choose he said to the Vice-Consul, "I would love to *buy* a picture. Please tell him I shall be happy to accept one as a gift providing that I am allowed to purchase one myself as well." Majorelle thereupon fixed a price of £100, and with this the Prime Minister bought a delightful painting of Marrakesh. When it was brought to him as he lay on his bed in the villa he asked for it to be

[6] C. R. Thompson, Notes.

placed where he could look at it constantly. The second picture he chose he later presented to Roosevelt, but both were first returned to the artist for an exhibition M. Majorelle was holding at Casablanca. With them went a card in the Prime Minister's own handwriting, "Purchased by Winston S. Churchill." The exhibition was a triumphant success, earning a million and a half francs for the fortunate artist.

One other incident at this time deserves mention. The Prime Minister and the Pasha of Marrakesh had met before and had formed a firm friendship. In the words of one who knew them both well, "they were two great men who called to each other." El Glaoui sent Mr Churchill a warm invitation to visit him in his magnificent palace in the mountains. The Prime Minister did not feel well enough to accept, but one day he himself asked the Pasha to tea at the villa. Richard Pim and his staff had set up the Map Room in the library, and Mr Churchill was anxious to explain to El Glaoui the latest developments in the war.

When the Pasha arrived he presented the Prime Minister with an exquisitely wrought golden dagger. They had tea together, and afterwards Churchill led the way to the Map Room. With a wealth of gestures he immediately launched into a highly technical review of the war situation front by front. Nairn found great difficulty in transposing some of the military terms into Arabic, and half-way through the Prime Minister said to him accusingly, "Are you translating exactly what I am saying?"

The Vice-Consul struggled on, and after fifteen minutes Churchill took pity on him. Ending his lecture, he turned to his guest and said how greatly he was respected by the Allies for the staunch support he had given to their cause.

"I knew from the start that you would win this war," said the Pasha. "I came in on the right side."

When this was translated the Prime Minister smiled broadly.

"Tell my good friend," he said, "that he came nearer than he probably knows to backing the wrong horse."

A Guard of Honour was paraded as El Glaoui left. The Prime Minister invited him to inspect them and take the salute. Much moved, the Pasha said to him, "When I next visit London I shall take off my shoes and walk barefoot through the streets out of respect for the British people."

"No!" said the Prime Minister, "I shall call for you, and we will travel by car together."

Not long afterwards Nairn called at El Glaoui's palace to deliver a parcel from England. It contained specially bound volumes of Churchill's *Marlborough*, which the author had inscribed for him.

* * * * *

Despite his many preoccupations, the Prime Minister's stay at Marrakesh was the only real period of rest he was to have while the war lasted. On Friday, January 14, 1944, his stay in Morocco ended, and he flew to Gibraltar where the battleship *King George V* (Captain T. E. Halsey, D.S.O. R.N.) was waiting to take him home. At the last minute there was a security scare. Unwittingly some of the girl cipher staff had given away the date of departure by buying baskets of oranges to take back with them to England. This was duly reported by German agents, but the short flight to the Rock brought no untoward incident.

Admiral Sir John Cunningham and Captain Power met the Prime Minister at the Convent, the Governor's residence. The *Shingle* operation was now only a week away, and Churchill cross-examined them closely about the preparations. When Power showed him the beach maps and the coloured diagrams setting out all the gun positions and a wealth of other detail he cheered up visibly. "Now that I see all the trouble that has been taken I am quite happy," he remarked.[7]

That night there was a memorable dinner in the great hall of the Convent. In addition to General Maitland Wilson and Admiral Cunningham, Lord Beaverbrook and Mr R. G. Casey—on his way to take up a new appointment as Governor of Bengal—were present, as was Vice-Admiral Sir Harold Burrough, the Flag Officer Gibraltar. The Prime Minister seemed bent on naval reminiscence and told story after story covering the outstanding personalities of the past forty years at sea. Admiral Burrough, whose cruiser squadron had covered the early Russian convoys and had played a leading part in some of the most desperate Malta convoy actions, had some equally entertaining recollections of men and events to relate. At one stage he paused, explaining apologetically that perhaps the story he was telling might give offence. Waving an imaginary wand, the Prime Minister said reassuringly, "Pray proceed! By virtue of the powers conferred upon me in my capacity as Minister of Defence you are hereby absolved."

Although the battleship was standing by, the York was also available at Gibraltar and anxious to reach home with the least delay the Prime Minister told Tommy to make inquiries about the possibility of a return by air after all. Lord Moran was strongly against his flying except under the

[7] Power was not to see him again until the war was over. Leaving the Mediterranean shortly afterwards, he became Captain D 26 in H.M.S. *Kempenfelt* for the Normandy landings; later he took his flotilla to the East Indies, and in May 1945 they sank the Japanese cruiser *Hagano* in the Malacca Straits. For his part in this action he was awarded a bar to his D.S.O. He next met Churchill when the latter went to Portsmouth to receive the Freedom of the City long after the war. Mr Churchill recognized him instantly, and, walking over to him, he said, "We won the battle, didn't we?" Admiral Sir Manley Power became C.-in-C., Portsmouth, and Allied Commander-in-Chief, Channel, in 1959.

most ideal conditions, and had already urged the A.O.C. to present the weather report in the least rosy terms. Unfortunately the early Met forecast suggested that conditions might be passable if the York flew at 6000 feet between two layers of cloud, and all through dinner Churchill continued to toy with the idea of flying in spite of Moran's objections. Towards 11.0 P.M., however, the weather worsened, and news came that there was now doubt about landing anywhere in the United Kingdom except some airfield in the far north of Scotland. The Commander-in-Chief, Mediterranean, added his persuasion in favour of a return by sea, and the Prime Minister reluctantly gave in. "If I don't go home in this great ship," he said wryly, "I suppose I shan't ever be able to ask for a man-of-war again."

In the early hours of January 15 H.M.S. *King George V* sailed for England escorted by the cruiser *Mauritius.* On the evening before they reached Plymouth Sound the Prime Minister brought all the midshipmen into his Map Room and gave them a lecture on the war situation.

It was raining in torrents when they went ashore to join the special train. At ten o'clock next morning they arrived at Paddington, and ninety minutes later Mr Churchill was in his place in the House of Commons at question time. He had been away from England for more than two months.

30

The Alexandria Mutiny

If there was anyone in Whitehall who imagined that Mr Churchill would be content to continue his convalescence for a while, slowly gathering the reins as his strength returned, they had a rude shock. Once again the dynamo was running at full power, and from the moment of his arrival back in Downing Street the Prime Minister assumed complete control of the war machine, demanding ACTION THIS DAY on a score of points . . . driving, goading, exhorting.

He formed and took personal charge of a Committee set up to review the progress of preparations for *Overlord*. While keeping close watch on the disturbing situation at Anzio, where two Allied divisions landed unchallenged on the night of January 22—and then did nothing to exploit a dramatic opportunity—he began bombarding the Chiefs of Staff with plans for other amphibious ventures, old and new. The oft-rejected Operation *Jupiter*—his project for an Allied landing in Northern Norway—once more appeared on the agenda, and he called, too, for urgent examination of a scheme for putting another considerable force ashore on the western coast of France.

This newcomer, given the code name of *Caliph*, envisaged an attack on Bordeaux after the Normandy landings by three armoured divisions transported by sea from Morocco. Urging the adoption of this plan, Churchill dwelt on the possibilities of spreading revolt through central and southern France and thus influencing the main battle.

The Chiefs of Staff looked with little favour on either *Jupiter* or *Caliph*. In their view the resources for attempting either operation were simply not available. Churchill's wholehearted enthusiasm for some isolated operation often led him, as we have seen, to ignore vital problems of manpower and logistics and to overlook the continuing needs of a force precariously established on enemy soil. But he would not use his authority to override his professional advisers if they had a strong case. On one matter of major policy, however, he found himself in serious conflict with the Chiefs of Staff almost as soon as he returned from Marrakesh.

Looking ahead, the Chiefs of Staff considered that as soon as the war in Europe permitted the strongest possible force should be sent to Australia to take part in the fighting in the south-west Pacific. The Prime Minister disagreed. He held that the British effort against the Japanese should be based not on Australia but on India, whence an advance should be made towards the Malay Peninsula and the Dutch islands. He was therefore strongly in favour of reviving Operation *Culverin*, the attack on Sumatra, in order to secure a springboard for further assaults on Singapore and the Japanese communications with Burma. The argument raged until March, but in the end the arrival of powerful Japanese naval forces at Singapore sealed *Culverin*'s fate.

In all these discussions the disheartening example of *Shingle* was a constant reminder that the best-laid plans could easily go astray—even when the invaders had everything in their favour. Preceded by a diversionary attack on the Fifth Army front, *Shingle* achieved complete surprise. When the Allied naval Commander-in-Chief put to sea from Naples in the destroyer *Kempenfelt* to visit the invasion fleet on D-1 the landing-craft were some seventy miles to the north, proceeding slowly in two lines which stretched as far as the eye could see. A grey haze hampered enemy air reconnaissance, and the scene was so incredibly tranquil that *Shingle* seemed more like some lethargic peace-time exercise than a serious operation of war. "Reminds me of Spithead," said a sub-lieutenant on *Kempenfelt*'s bridge. . . . "Can't understand it. We haven't much surface protection, and it doesn't sound as if we've even got an air escort. What on earth is the Hun up to?"

The landings at Anzio and Nettuno that night were unopposed. In less than twenty-four hours 36,000 men and 3000 vehicles were put safely ashore, and although the Luftwaffe began to make its presence felt after three days, heavily bombing three brilliantly-lit hospital ships and sinking one of them, still no reaction came from ground forces. "The road to Rome was open. No one could have stopped a bold advance guard entering the Holy City," wrote the German General Westphal later; "the breath-taking situation continued for the first two days after the landing."[1]

General Lucas, the *Shingle* force commander, seemed paralysed by indecision. He had taken part in the Salerno landings, and with that grim

[1] *Heer in Fesseln*, p. 242.

fight for survival in mind he feared a trap. If he advanced he would surely be cut off; better by far to wait until his two infantry divisions were reinforced by the 1st U.S. Armoured Division, he argued. So while the Royal Navy continued to pour in men and vehicles and stores, and the American naval task-force commander, Rear-Admiral Lowry, sent frantic signals for help to counter the German dive-bombing of the ships lying off the beaches Lucas dug in and awaited developments.

On D+14 the Prime Minister signalled to Admiral Cunningham to inquire the number of troops and vehicles already landed. "We must have a great superiority of chauffeurs," he observed caustically when he learnt that there were now 70,000 men and no fewer than 18,000 vehicles ashore at Anzio.

From France, Hungary, Yugoslavia, and even Denmark, German divisions were rushed to seal off the bridgehead. For a time there was the agonizing possibility that the Allied force might be driven into the sea, but a major attack on February 16 was repulsed, and with General Lucian Truscott quickly showing himself an able and energetic successor to Lucas, who was relieved of his command, the danger passed. In the weeks to come the *Shingle* force was to play its part in the capture of Rome and provide useful lessons for *Overlord*, but it provided, too, a classic example of military opportunity cast away.

Only the Navy could look back on *Shingle* with pride. Their losses off the beaches were severe, but the success of their efforts to support the Army—a task which lasted far longer, and proved far more demanding than had ever been contemplated at the outset—was extraordinary. In eight weeks, with a severely limited number of landing-craft at their call, they put ashore 126,000 men and nearly 25,000 vehicles.

It was at this time that a signal from Rear-Admiral J. A. V. Morse, Flag Officer, Western Italy, to Admiral Cunningham amused the Prime Minister. After many years of smouldering inactivity Vesuvius suddenly erupted. Over the Bay of Naples a great cloud of volcanic dust hid the sun. As the dust drifted back to earth it buried scores of Allied fighter aircraft before they could be flown to safety. Down the seaward side of the mountain flowed a molten tide of lava which soon cut the coastal road to Salerno. "The Naples group of ports is now discharging at the rate of 12 million tons a year," Admiral Morse reported: "Vesuvius is estimated to be doing 30 million tons *a day*."

* * * * *

The ever-increasing weight of the Allied air offensive on Germany by day and night brought retaliation—a series of sporadic and largely ineffectual night raids on London in February and March, which did, however, cause a good deal of damage to buildings in the Whitehall area. Apart from viewing the proceedings with his usual interest from the Air Ministry roof, the Prime Minister refused to pay more than passing attention to this "Little Blitz," and indignantly objected to proposals that he should temporarily give up using the War Room in Storey's Gate.

In addition to fighting a strong rearguard action over *Culverin* he was busying himself with every aspect of the invasion, from the water-proofing of tanks to the intricacies of the naval bombardment plan. He held frequent conferences with General Eisenhower, who, anxious to avoid any late night sessions with the Prime Minister, generally angled for their business to be transacted over lunch. At the same time Churchill kept a watchful eye on political developments in Italy; in Greece, where the self-styled National Liberation Front (E.A.M.) was beginning to stir up trouble; and Yugoslavia, where the emphasis of Allied aid had now shifted from Mihailović's Cetniks to the Partisans led by Tito.

These major preoccupations did not prevent him from drawing the attention of the Minister of Supply to an unsightly rubbish dump at Chalfont St Giles, which he had noticed on his way back from Chequers. And Lord Portal, the Minister of Works, was equally surprised to receive an indignant complaint about "a very untidy sack with holes in it and sand leaking out" which the Prime Minister had seen lying "just below the Foreign Office, on the grass opposite St James's Park gate."[2]

As D-Day drew nearer Churchill set off on a series of inspection tours. Up to this time few of the American troops awaiting the invasion had set eyes on the Prime Minister, and when he visited U.S. Army units in Hampshire with Eisenhower and General Omar Bradley, the commander of the First American Army, he was given a great welcome. His friendliness, his forceful personality, and his surprisingly wide knowledge of military affairs made a strong impression on his hosts.

He went to Yorkshire to inspect the Guards Armoured Division. It was a day which brought back vivid memories, for as he watched the array of modern fighting vehicles, including the amphibious tanks and D.U.K.W.'s, being put through their paces he was told that some one wanted to speak to him. He was introduced to an old man who, nearly half a century before, had ridden at his side in the cavalry charge at Omdurman.

As the Prime Minister travelled north the Press was full of a debate which had just ended in the Commons. On March 28, in the Committee Stage of the Education Bill, the Government were defeated on an amendment calling for equal pay for men and women under the new education code. The Government had made it quite clear that, while they supported this in principle, the question of equal pay was far too large an issue to be

[2] Churchill, Vol. V. p. 610.

dealt with in a Bill of limited application, and for this reason alone they opposed its introduction at this particular stage. Nevertheless 117 voted for the amendment and 116 against.

When Mr Churchill entered the Map Room that night he was greatly upset. He saw clearly that this reverse—trivial as it seemed to British eyes when viewed against the background of a world war—would be trumpeted round the globe. By the enemy it would be hailed as striking evidence that Britain was war-weary and the Churchill Government no longer enjoyed the support of the country. No one, he pointed out, would explain that this adverse vote had been passed on one clause of a Bill dealing with pay for school teachers.

When he went to the House next day he was determined for this reason to demand a Vote of Confidence. The wisdom of this move was doubtful, however, for it played into the hands of politicians and journalists who had been loudly criticizing the Government in the past for creating a "rubber stamp Parliament" and steam-rollering all opposition by the very threat of resignation. After the Prime Minister had put his case to the House he was followed by many speakers openly critical of his tactics.

Emmanuel Shinwell said he felt it should be possible to differ from the Government on a domestic issue without conveying criticism of that Government's capacity for directing the war effort. A more violent attack was made by Aneurin Bevan, who claimed that the Prime Minister had come before the House "in a spirit of braggadocio"; the Prime Minister's attitude had killed all reconstruction legislation. "It has made a farce of it!" shouted another Member angrily.

Commenting on the debate under the heading "An Unreal Crisis," the *Daily Mail* said, "The people are 100% behind the war effort but are widely divided on domestic matters. The public can differentiate between the two but the Government are unable to do so." The paper went on to call, reasonably enough, for a free vote on Home questions and said that if the present system was continued there might well come a time when the Government might overplay their hand, goading the House into revolt. "There would then be something worse than the repetition of the present incident, which the public have found bewildering and somewhat unedifying." The *Daily Herald* spoke of the Prime Minister's "combative attitude," and remarked that "the practice of demanding synthetic votes of confidence on issues which are not vital to the Government is strongly to be deplored."

It was left to *The Times* to place the matter in fairer perspective. While conceding that it would be a grave misfortune if "the present episode induced the Government to ride the House on too tight a rein where only domestic issues are concerned," the paper pointed out that the supporters of the amendment had been ill-advised to press it to a division. In terms of educational policy Mr Butler, the Minister of Education, had had an unanswerable case for resisting them, in that teachers in publicly provided schools were not paid by the Board of Education or by Parliament, but by the local education authorities, at rates settled by the Burnham Committee. "The amendment would have laid upon him [the Minister] the duty of dictating to the Committee . . . the kind of scales upon which they should agree." Added *The Times*, "It was quite impossible for the Government to accept by way of an amendment to one clause in a departmental measure a change affecting every department of State. The vote left the Government with no alternative, but to treat it as a challenge to their authority in the House."

Churchill himself never doubted that he had taken the right course. When he spoke again next day before the House divided he received heartening support, and although he had a sharp brush with James Maxton, who said belligerently that the time to resume party politics was long overdue, the debate ended in an overwhelming Government majority. Only 23 voted for the motion—and 425 against.

* * * * *

Within a few days Churchill found himself closely involved in a political crisis of a different kind. On April 4 five warships of the Greek Navy mutinied at Alexandria, demanding the overthrow of the Greek Government and declaring their support for the Communist-dominated rebel party E.A.M. Their example was followed by the First Greek Brigade, encamped in the desert outside Cairo.

When the news reached London Churchill was deputizing as Foreign Secretary in the temporary absence of Eden. Immediately he took firm charge of the situation. He had for some months received disturbing reports of disaffection in Greece, where there were now several factions bidding for power. In addition to the tottering Tsouderos Government based in Cairo there were two military organizations—E.L.A.S., the People's Liberation Army composed of supporters of E.A.M.; and E.D.E.S., an anti-Communist force of several thousand led by a colourful, swashbuckling character named Napoleon Zervas. In both Cairo and London, too, there were supporters of King George of Greece, who were not necessarily in sympathy with either the existing Government or the rebel organizations. For some months now E.L.A.S. and E.D.E.S. had been devoting more effort to fighting each other than harassing the Germans who still occupied their country, and the mutiny at Alexandria brought matters to a head.

For three men on the spot in Egypt—Mr Reginald Leeper, the British Ambassador to the Greek Government in exile; General Sir Bernard

Paget, the British Army Commander; and Admiral Sir John Cunningham, the Allied Naval Commander-in-Chief—it was an unenviable situation. Almost immediately M. Tsouderos, the Greek Prime Minister, resigned, and Leeper had a difficult time rallying a somewhat demoralized Government. The Admiral was faced with a considerable force of rebel ships, their guns trained on the city of Alexandria, which they threatened with point-blank bombardment if any attempt was made by the Royal Navy to attack them. And General Paget had under his command a large military force which no longer obeyed his orders.

Upon the harassed Ambassador Churchill directed a characteristic stream of exhortation and salutary advice. "This is an occasion for you to show those qualities of imperturbability and command which are associated with the British Diplomatic Service," he signalled. And when Rex Leeper drew attention to his difficulties with the vacillating Greek politicians the Prime Minister replied tersely, "You should stick to the line I have marked out and not be worried about the consequences. You speak of living on the lid of a volcano. Wherever else do you expect to live in times like these?"[3]

He made it plain to the Admiral and General Paget that, while every effort must be made to persuade the mutineers to surrender without the use of force, he was firmly behind the British commanders in any action they felt necessary to bring the rebellion to an end. At Alexandria the situation was grave, for apart from the cruiser *Phœbe*, in dock, there were no British warships in the harbour. Two hundred Greek sailors who barricaded themselves in a house in the city were prised out without much difficulty, but the destroyers showed no signs of capitulating. As they were provisioned for three months and could distil their own drinking water they were well able to stand a siege. A signal was therefore made recalling H.M.S. *Ajax* from Anzio; a number of destroyers were detached from vital escort duties and ordered to proceed at full speed for Alexandria.

While the Royal Navy awaited reinforcement appeals were broadcast to the rebels by loud hailer, and as a novel experiment in psychological warfare a Greek Bishop was dispatched in a rowing-boat to excommunicate the ringleaders. This latter move proved singularly unsuccessful, for as soon as the Bishop got within earshot the mutineers shouted such uncomplimentary remarks at him that he became speechless with rage and forgot to excommunicate anybody.

Eventually Admiral Cunningham sent for the Greek naval C.-in-C., Admiral Alexandris. He told him bluntly that if he was not prepared to take any positive action to end the mutiny in his own navy the task would be given to the Sacred Heart, a Greek Army Brigade who had remained loyal to their Government. As Alexandris continued to shilly-shally he was

[3] *Ibid.*, pp. 479–480.

relieved of his command, and under a more resolute Commander-in-Chief, Admiral Voulgaris, plans were made for an attack on three of the ships by a band of Greek naval volunteers in the early hours of April 23. Their leader was shot dead, but within an hour his companions had gained control of all three destroyers. A smoke screen was then laid over the remaining two rebel ships, lying farther out in the harbour, and the rest of the mutineers lost their nerve. A few hours later they surrendered unconditionally.

At Amiriya, in the desert, General Paget prepared for an assault on the Greek Brigade with tanks and artillery, but the besieged troops, who had already been cut off from the food and water supplied to them by Arabs in the early stages of their revolt, offered only slight resistance. The rebellion was over, and three days later M. Papandreou, leader of the Social Democrats, formed a new all-party Government.

Churchill's shrewd political sense, his insistence on firm diplomacy, and his clear directives to the men on the spot had undoubtedly removed the immediate threat of a Communist take-over in Greece. To act as he had done required considerable courage, for inevitably it invited a charge of meddling in the internal affairs of another country. More clearly than his critics he saw, however, the significance of E.A.M.'s challenge, and the effect it might have throughout the Balkans.

Coming as it did almost on the eve of the Normandy invasion the Greek mutiny in Egypt attracted little widespread attention. Perhaps for this reason Churchill's skilful handling of a complex and delicate situation has received all too little credit in subsequent assessments of his war-time leadership, but Roosevelt, for one, realized the significance of this uprising and the Prime Minister's achievement in bringing about a peaceful settlement. For his part Churchill was quick to recognize that the firmness, patience, and sound judgment of Admiral Cunningham and General Paget had unquestionably averted much bloodshed. Both received signals of warm congratulation from Downing Street.

31

Colonel Warden Returns to France

On Monday, May 15, Montgomery staged a final presentation of his plans for *Overlord* at his headquarters at St Paul's School, in London. It was a bitterly cold day, but the Prime Minister, huddled in his greatcoat, sat through the whole proceedings from mid-morning to 5.0 P.M., and made a vigorous fighting speech at the end of it. He had been driving himself hard throughout the preceding month, and several times he had admitted to those close to him that he was feeling the strain, but he had continued to carry out his programme of visits to the invasion troops.

He had been to Lydd and Hastings; to Portsmouth, where he went out in an M.T.B. to have a closer look at the floating piers and all the Wellsian paraphernalia of Mulberry Harbour now massed in the Solent; and after his day at St Paul's he went back to Sussex for a further tour of armoured and infantry units, taking with him Smuts, Mackenzie King, and Godfrey Huggins, the Prime Minister of Southern Rhodesia.

Two aspects of the preparations for the assault on France were much on Churchill's mind. To seal off the battlefield a methodical bombing programme had been launched against the Axis rail and road network. It threatened to inflict grievous casualties on French civilians, and, appalled by this prospect, the Prime Minister raised with the President the advisability of continuing this offensive. "It is not alone a question of humanitarianism. It is also a question of high State policy," he said. "Post-war France must be our friend."[1] With great reluctance, however, it was decided that the bombing must continue.

The Prime Minister was also disturbed by a factor which had been

[1] In a letter to General Eisenhower. (See *Crusade in Europe*, p. 255.)

ominously apparent in the *Torch* and *Shingle* landings—the proportion of vehicles to men put ashore, and the number of administrative personnel compared with fighting troops. By D+20 it was planned to have one vehicle ashore for every 4·77 soldiers in the bridgehead. By D+60 there would be no fewer than 365,000 Allied vehicles in France. He raised this question with Montgomery when he visited him on May 19. By then, however, it was too late to alter the loading plans.

The immensity of the preparations staggered even Churchill, who had followed every stage of their development. The assault force consisted of 176,000 men and 20,000 vehicles, protected during the assembly period by 7000 guns and rockets. The marshalling of the ships involved—80 per cent. of the naval forces were to be British—set intricate timing problems, for the berthing overflow extended to Milford Haven, Harwich, the Humber, Belfast, and the Clyde. The minesweeping task presented special difficulties, and so did the deception plan, which aimed at convincing the enemy that the landings were to take place in the Pas de Calais.

From May 28 the coastal area was sealed, all troops being confined to their camps. By now foreign embassies could no longer communicate with the outside world, and passenger traffic with Eire had ceased. The fear of a major security breach which had haunted Eisenhower's staff before the *Torch* landings was a far more terrifying prospect now, and there were repeated alarms.

An envelope with detailed information about *Overlord* found its way to a private house in Chicago through a mistake in writing the address, and it was discovered that at least a dozen people had inspected the contents. A Major-General and a senior naval officer were swiftly removed from England after they had been overheard recklessly discussing the invasion timetable at cocktail parties. And three days before the invasion fleet sailed a news agency actually put out a flash that Eisenhower's forces were landing in France—an item monitored and repeated in Moscow and Berlin.

Miraculously the Germans remained in complete ignorance of Allied intentions, and their air reconnaissance was so firmly restricted that for day after day at the vital period when the armada was massing along the South Coast not a single report of any value reached Rundstedt's H.Q.

The total inability of the Luftwaffe to interfere with the vast force gathering only a few miles from the German-held coast made it possible to take risks which no one would have contemplated a year earlier. When Churchill learnt that American transport was being dangerously slowed up at night by the need for driving with masked headlamps he promptly gave orders that all Service vehicles should be allowed to proceed with lights undimmed.

A week before D-Day maps of the landing areas were put up in the

Prime Minister's Map Room. The door to the outer office was then locked, and a duty officer remained on guard day and night. The Americans provided a wonderfully constructed model of the beaches in *papier mâché*. Since it showed the whole coast-line from Bremen to the Spanish border, Lieutenant-Commander Sayers, one of Richard Pim's deputies, had no qualms about drawing Mr Churchill's attention to it, but the Prime Minister took one quick look and said gruffly, "Cover it up!" The vital beaches stood out like beacons to him.

To the alarm of Admiral Ramsay, the Naval Expeditionary Force Commander, the Prime Minister had made up his mind that he would sail himself with the bombarding force on D-Day. When Eisenhower heard of this he said firmly that he could not allow it, but Mr Churchill then pointed out that the General's authority did not extend to the administrative control of the British organization, adding blandly, "Since this is true, it is not part of your responsibilities, my dear General, to determine the exact composition of any ship's company in His Majesty's Fleet. . . . By shipping myself as a bona fide member of a ship's company it would be beyond your authority to prevent my going."[2]

Admiral Sir Andrew Cunningham, whom he summoned to the Map Room on June 2 to discuss the arrangements for his accommodation in H.M.S. *Belfast*, told him bluntly that he could not agree to the idea, but fortunately decisive intervention came from an unexpected quarter, the King pointing out that if it was right for the Prime Minister to take part in the invasion then he himself had an even stronger claim as the head of all three fighting Services.

Mr Churchill gave in. He was bitterly disappointed and not a little resentful. He had formed his own very decided philosophy on the right of a leader to share in the hazards of any venture for which he might have some measure of responsibility.

> His field of personal interest, and consequently his forces of action, are stimulated by direct contact with the event. . . . I had seen many grievous errors made through the silly theory that valuable lives should not be endangered. No one was more careful of his personal safety than I was, but I thought my view and theme of the war were sufficiently important and authoritative to entitle me to full freedom of judgment as to how I discharged my task in such a personal matter.[3]

Churchill undoubtedly felt a sense of affront at this rejection of his plan. He claimed that he never took an 'unnecessary' risk, but those who accompanied him often felt that his interpretation of what was necessary was disturbingly elastic. And before long even that intrepid sailor, Admiral Sir Philip Vian, was to remark on the Prime Minister's disregard of

[2] *Ibid.*, p. 276.

[3] Churchill, Vol. V, p. 551.

danger. On this eve of D-Day, however, he could not ignore the King's earnest appeal.

The letter from Buckingham Palace reached him while he was making his final visit to Hampshire. His special train had been shunted into a siding at Droxford, close to Eisenhower's H.Q. at Southwick Park, a Georgian country house hidden in the woods outside Portsmouth. Smuts and Ernest Bevin accompanied Churchill. Later they were joined by de Gaulle, for whom the Prime Minister had sent his own aircraft to Algiers.

For security reasons de Gaulle had been kept out of the picture until this moment, and he was bitterly resentful. His ruffled feelings were partially soothed by Smuts, whose sincerity and practical common sense, combined with his rather terse way of speaking, seemed to disconcert the General. De Gaulle refused to be won round, however, and after a few hours he departed for London in a huff, haughtily declining an invitation to dine on board the train.

On June 3 Churchill drove to Southampton to watch the 'Geordies' of the Tyneside Division embarking. It was during dinner in the train that night that news came of worsening weather, and after a 4.0 A.M. conference at Eisenhower's headquarters on June 4 the decision was taken to postpone the invasion for at least twenty-four hours.

The agonizing dilemma which faced General Eisenhower as the bad weather continued is now part of history. He knew that if the invasion could not be launched in the next forty-eight hours it would be a full fortnight before moon and tide offered another favourable opportunity. Until the die was cast the Prime Minister was reluctant to leave the area, but he kept away from Eisenhower's H.Q.

A gale was raging round Southwick Park as the vital 'Met' conference took place in the early hours of June 5, but to every one's surprise a brief spell of finer weather was predicted and Eisenhower decided to go ahead. The landing in Normandy would take place on June 6. After visiting the Supreme Commander and Montgomery to wish them luck Churchill returned to London.

He spent most of the succeeding hours in the Map Room. He was much on edge. Once again he could hear the tramping of Housman's ghostly legions:

Far and near and low and louder
  On the roads of earth go by,
Dear to friends and food for powder,
  Soldiers marching, all to die.

When Mrs Churchill joined him for a few moments before retiring he said to her, "Do you realize that by the time you wake up in the morning twenty thousand men may have been killed?"

* * * * *

Within a week of the descent on Normandy Churchill himself set foot once again on the French shore. It was four years to the day since he had left Briare on his hazardous flight home in the Flamingo after the last fateful meeting with Pétain, Weygand, and Darlan.

Smuts, Brooke, and Tommy crossed the Channel with him in the destroyer *Kelvin*, and they drove in brilliant sunshine through a smiling, unscarred countryside to a château at Creully, five miles inland from the invasion beaches, where Montgomery had established his tactical headquarters. The front line was only three miles away, but apart from an occasional dog-fight overhead all seemed strangely peaceful.

Montgomery led the way to his mobile map room, set up in one of three caravans hidden among the trees in the garden. In his usual clear way he described the course of the battle, and then they adjourned for lunch.

As they emerged from the caravan Smuts paused and sniffed the air. Then, turning to Major Noel Chavasse, Montgomery's A.D.C., he said quietly:

"There are some Germans still here—quite close to us."

Chavasse looked at him in astonishment.

"There can't be, sir. We've been through these grounds with a fine-tooth comb."

"I can't help that," replied Smuts. "There are Germans near us now . . . I can always tell."

Standing bare-headed in the sunshine, Smuts continued to frown in a puzzled way, staring suspiciously at the clumps of laurels and rhododendrons which almost surrounded the caravans, but he said no more, and they followed Montgomery into his Mess tent.

Two days later, from the centre of a huge rhododendron-bush growing within a few yards of the spot where Smuts had halted, emerged two young German paratroopers. Both were armed, and they could have shot the Prime Minister and his party at point-blank range. But their morale was at zero. Long ago they had finished the last of their rations. Now, soaked to the skin and weak from hunger, they were weeping with fright for they expected to be shot out of hand.

When they had found themselves cut off from their unit they had dug a hole to shelter them in the roots of the rhododendron-bush, and once there they had not dared to emerge from their hiding-place. Time and again Montgomery had stood talking a few feet away from them. But of all the visitors to the caravans only Smuts, with that uncanny sixth sense of his developed in a lifetime of campaigning, had sensed they were there.

Before returning to H.M.S. *Kelvin* the Prime Minister visited Mulberry Harbour and a small port just west of Arromanches which was being prepared as the terminal point for *Pluto*, the submarine pipeline which was to feed the Allied armies with fuel. When Churchill reached the easternmost beach he insisted to every one's alarm on climbing to the top platform of a lighthouse. In such an exposed position there was serious danger from shellfire—one shell landing on the base of the building would have brought it toppling down—and Admiral Vian pointed this out.

Churchill took not the slightest notice. He had had several miraculous escapes from shellfire in the First World War, and he had a strong presentiment that he was protected by a larger measure of good fortune than other men. This did little to reassure his companions.

When they arrived back on board H.M.S. *Kelvin* they sailed along the coast while Admiral Vian explained the activities of the various warships they passed. An R Class battleship was bombarding German positions twenty miles inland towards Caen, and on reaching the end of the British line the Prime Minister suggested that *Kelvin* should do some bombarding on her own account. Six rounds were therefore fired into the area beyond Trouville. Churchill was delighted. "Who knows? We may have just killed a German general capable of winning the war for them," he remarked with obvious satisfaction.

That same night, only a few hours after the Prime Minister arrived back in Whitehall, the first flying bomb landed on London. Only one of the opening salvo, launched in the early hours of June 13, did much damage. Falling on a viaduct outside Liverpool Street Station, it blocked all lines into the terminus. For three days after that there was an ominous lull, and then a torrent of high-explosive rained down on the capital.

Churchill was at Chequers when the first heavy raid took place, but Mrs Churchill had chosen that morning to inspect her youngest daughter's A.A. battery in Hyde Park. She found the unit in action and saw one of the 'doodle-bugs,' as they were soon christened, dive on Whitehall. It struck the Guards Chapel in the middle of the morning service, killing scores of the congregation, which included many of the Churchills' friends. That evening, when the Prime Minister returned early to London, rescue work was still in progress.

To the War Cabinet the onslaught came as no surprise. For the past year fragments of information about Germany's secret weapon had been under constant review, and Lord Cherwell had worked out in advance the likely size of the war-head. From the start the Prime Minister had kept in close personal touch with every development reported by intelligence agents abroad.

With the same extraordinary insight which had led him to see the possibilities of prefabricated harbours during the First World War he had written, as far back as 1925: "Could not explosives, even of the existing type, be guided automatically in flying machines, by wireless or other rays, without a human pilot, in ceaseless procession upon a hostile city, arsenal, camp, or dockyard?"

Now this very thing had come to pass, and but for the energetic measures already taken against the launching sites of the bombs London's ordeal, which lasted ten weeks, would have been infinitely worse.[4] Ordeal it was, nevertheless, for three thousand of these missiles came over in the first five weeks. Although the men and women of London behaved with their usual stoicism, it was impossible to treat the 'doodle-bugs' with the same resigned indifference accorded to the bombing in the Blitz of 1940–1941. There was a dreadful inevitability about a flying machine controlled by mechanism alone. To a casual observer, however, Londoners went about their business with the same apparent unconcern, and when, one lovely summer's day, Mr Churchill walked to the window of the Map Room and stood gazing out across St James's Park crowds were sitting on the grass in the hot sunshine eating their sandwich lunches. "If only Goebbels could see this!" he said thoughtfully. Then, apparently recalling the menacing TOP SECRET messages which kept reminding those in the Inner Circle of the imminence of the V 2 rocket bombs, he added, "Of course, they don't know what may be coming soon."

At first the flying bombs proved extraordinarily difficult to destroy, for they came in at between 2000 and 3000 feet—a height which greatly complicated the task of the anti-aircraft gunners and prevented the radar screen from giving any adequate warning. A vast redeployment of guns, radar equipment, and barrage balloons was necessary, and on July 14 the heavy guns, which had already been moved from London to the North Downs, were uprooted again and sent to the coast, where they were re-sited in a dense belt stretching from Dover to Beachy Head.

The V 1 defence system now consisted of four distinct elements—the fighter aircraft who first tried to intercept the flying bombs over the Channel; the coastal guns which opened up at them over the last 10,000 yards to the English shore; another fighter zone inland; and then the balloon barrage. By the end of August few of the flying bombs were penetrating this elaborate network, and soon afterwards the Allied armies, thrusting deep into Belgium, overran most of the launching sites.

London's affliction was not entirely at an end, for in the closing months of the war five hundred V 2's—rocket bombs travelling beyond the speed of sound and therefore impossible to intercept by any means then available—reached the capital from launching points in Holland. But the development of the V 2 had come too late to allow it to play the part which Hitler had boastfully predicted for it.

[4] Over 6000 civilians were killed and 18,000 seriously injured by the flying bomb (V 1). The rocket bomb (V 2) killed 2724 and seriously injured 6476.

32

Dragoon at a Distance

WITH the Allied bridgehead firmly established in Normandy the illogicality of proceeding with the major amphibious assault on the South of France became more and more apparent to British eyes. Operation *Anvil*—now, for security reasons, rechristened *Dragoon*—had been originally conceived as a diversionary attack. Its sole purpose was to draw off German troops from Eisenhower's armies as they fought for a toehold on the Channel beaches. It had been realized that the bulk of the Allied force for this operation would have to come from Italy. At the outset, however, it had not been foreseen that *Anvil* would seriously affect the situation there, for it was confidently expected that Rome and its important airfields would be in Allied hands by the early spring.

This proved an over-optimistic forecast. Hitler's determination to stand at Cassino and the fierce German reaction to the Anzio landings wrecked the Allied timetable. But, as it turned out, the enemy decision to fight for Rome right up to D-Day for *Overlord* played right into Allied hands. Ten Axis divisions which could have been used to reinforce Rundstedt in the west had instead to be diverted to the Italian front, and the heavy fighting there removed any need for a ponderous diversionary operation in the South of France.

In the Prime Minister's opinion the mounting of *Dragoon* long after *Overlord* could only be justified if a different target altogether was chosen for the invading force. He therefore put forward the suggestion that the divisions earmarked for assaulting the Riviera coast should instead be dispatched to Brittany. By landing at Saint-Nazaire they could link up swiftly with Eisenhower's armies and create the precise effect he had had in mind when pressing the claims of Operation *Caliph*.

He only suggested this compromise, however, when he found American opinion ranged solidly against a cancellation of the move against Southern France. In his heart he felt that the withdrawal of Allied troops from Italy for any new enterprise was a grave strategic blunder because far greater rewards awaited Alexander's armies beyond the Po Valley.

To Churchill their obvious goal was Austria, to be reached by way of Trieste and the Ljubljana Gap. But no one would listen to him. Roosevelt who had still failed to fathom the real reason for Stalin's support of a South of France landing, was adamant that *Dragoon* should be carried out in its original form. Hopkins, whose influence with the President had declined, thought it unlikely that Roosevelt could ever be persuaded to consider a switch to Brittany. And Eisenhower, wary of becoming involved in a change of plan dictated by what he felt were purely political considerations, would have nothing to do with any "Balkan diversion." When, on August 5, Churchill made a final attempt to persuade him to cancel the South of France invasion the General "said No, continued saying No all afternoon, and ended by saying No in every form of the English language at his command."[1]

In Rome another American general, Mark Clark—commander of the Fifth Army—took a very different view. When General Marshall visited Italy in June Clark pleaded with him for a reconsideration of the Allied plan. At the very moment when, to quote his own words, the Germans in Italy were "defeated, disorganized, and demoralized" seven divisions were to be taken from him. Clark wrote afterwards:

> The weakening of the campaign in Italy in order to invade Southern France instead of pushing on into the Balkans was one of the outstanding political mistakes of the war. . . . Had we been there before the Red Army, not only would the collapse of Germany have come sooner but the influence of Soviet Russia would have been drastically reduced.[2]

The *Dragoon* controversy provoked one of the very few serious disagreements between Churchill and Eisenhower, but although the Prime Minister brought the utmost pressure to bear their arguments were conducted without the slightest acrimony. By now there was a firm bond between the two men. Apart from current military topics they had an unexpected meeting ground in their encyclopædic knowledge of English history. When Churchill discovered that Eisenhower could not only review most significant events over a period of a thousand years but explain their political implications as well he was greatly impressed.

Churchill himself was never happier than when discussing the great campaigns of history and the lessons they taught. Lunching at Chequers

[1] Butcher, *op. cit.*, p. 545. [2] Clark, *op. cit.*, pp. 348–351.

one day, he remarked to Eisenhower that he had studied every campaign since the Punic Wars. "And he's taken part in most of them!" was Tommy's comment, *sotto voce*, to his neighbour. The Prime Minister overheard. "I'm not as old as all that," he said gruffly.

Once the decision to proceed with *Dragoon* had been confirmed—even Churchill's eloquence and the force of his case failed to shift American opinion one iota—the Prime Minister decided to visit the Italian front. Despite the weakening of his armies Alexander was preparing for another major offensive—a two-pronged attack on the Gothic Line by the Eighth Army under General Leese on the Adriatic side and Clark's Fifth Army striking through the mountains towards Bologna. There were important political problems to discuss with the new Greek Prime Minister, with Marshal Tito, and with the Italians. And Mr Churchill had a sneaking desire to see something of the much maligned *Dragoon* at close quarters. The rejection of his plan for taking part in the launching of *Overlord* still rankled!

Before he set off for Italy, however, he paid two more visits to France. Montgomery was about to begin a fresh offensive towards Caen, and the Prime Minister signalled his intention of flying to Normandy once this was under way.

With his passion for talking to the men on the spot and examining problems at first hand, it never occurred to Mr Churchill that his visits to the battlefields were often highly unpopular. When Minister of Munitions in the First World War he had frequently flown to France from Hendon after a morning's work in Whitehall, talked to the Army commanders, and flown back to England the same evening. Like Clemenceau, who had remarked, "C'est mon grand plaisir!" when reproached for spending so much time under fire, danger was exhilarating to him, and he hotly resented any attempt to confine his visits to the rear areas.

On this particular occasion there was a considerable rumpus, for Eisenhower laid down that while he had no objection to the Prime Minister exploring Cherbourg and the American harbour installations he did not want him to go forward. Unfortunately the signal reached him in garbled form, and Churchill got the impression that it came from Montgomery. Declaring that he was not going to be dictated to by one of his own generals he had a heated conversation with Eisenhower on the phone. Eventually all was smoothed over, and on July 20 Churchill landed on the Cherbourg Peninsula.

After watching American activities at Utah Beach and inspecting a rocket launching site, massively built into the hillside behind the port and apparently designed for bombarding Plymouth, he set off in an M.T.B. for the British harbour at Arromanches.

"The journey took us far longer than we had expected, for a heavy sea was running. The P.M. soon became both sick and bored, but as soon as we arrived at Mulberry Harbour he was in his element, for the port was seething with activity. From the store ships to the beach plied a constant stream of D.U.K.W.'s. We watched them waddle out of the water and set off up the beach to dump their loads.

"Mr Churchill spent most of the following morning inspecting the working of the port. We visited Army units and field hospitals, and after he had had his talk with Montgomery on the third day he took off with Air Marshal Broadhurst in a captured Fiesler Storch on a hedge-hopping tour of near-by airfields, where he talked to the squadrons.

"Ismay and I decided to make a tour of our own. We visited several observation posts commanding the front line and then drove into Caen. The town was in a state of indescribable ruin. Many of the streets had disappeared completely, and we made our way along lanes bulldozed through the rubble. Miraculously the Cathedral had escaped. Hardly a pane of glass in the building was broken, and although thousands of people had taken refuge there when the bombardment began only one man had been slightly injured by falling masonry.

"When we rejoined the P.M. we were taken to task because we had managed to get nearer to the front line than he had. Although we had been expecting to stay a final night on board the cruiser, Mr Churchill announced that he had decided to return to London immediately. In the rush to pack and get to the plane Ismay, to his great mortification, left behind several excellent Camembert cheeses—a delicacy with which, surprisingly enough, Caen's surviving shops seemed to be lavishly stocked."[3]

A fortnight later the Prime Minister was once again on his way to Cherbourg. He had been disturbed by American criticism that Montgomery was leaving Bradley's United States troops to do most of the fighting in a fresh offensive designed as the final break-out from the bridgehead. In fact, Montgomery's plan, which Eisenhower himself had approved, sensibly aimed at tying down the considerable enemy armoured forces on the eastern flank while Bradley pushed forward to seal off the Cotentin peninsula and then swung round eastwards for the major break-out from Saint-Lô. The American Press had, however, made much of the failure of the Canadian Corps to gain ground in the early stages, contrasting their rate of progress with Bradley's energetic advance on the opposite flank (where the opposition was much less formidable).

When Churchill's plane was half-way across the Channel the pilot reported that he would be unable to land in France. The weather was deteriorating fast, and the airfield at Cherbourg was already hidden in fog.

[3] C. R. Thompson, Notes.

The Prime Minister was extremely reluctant to turn back. His attitude to flying was often coloured by the needs of the moment, and at times he plainly regarded the limitations of the flying machine as a factor to be overcome by sheer determination; the pilot had only to impose his will on the plane, and all would be well. Certainly he himself had adopted this principle many years before, when he took flying lessons at Croydon. On that occasion, admittedly, the results had not been encouraging, for early on he had attempted to climb with insufficient flying speed, and when, inevitably, the plane stalled into the ground Mr Churchill abandoned the course of lessons in disgust.

But that had been many years earlier. A modern aircraft should, he felt, be capable of delivering him to his destination even if the weather *was* a little threatening. And on this particular morning it was not until the pilot told him that the Dakota ahead of them had just crashed, killing all its passengers, that the Prime Minister consented to return to Thorney Island, which they reached with some difficulty. He lunched with Eisenhower and had his final abortive discussion on *Dragoon*. On August 7 he set off again with Tommy and General Hollis for Normandy.

By now the Allied armies were on the eve of overwhelming victory. Caught in a vast pocket stretching west from Falaise, eight German divisions were about to be cut to ribbons. After talking to Montgomery the Prime Minister went on to see Bradley at Saint-Sauveur-Lendelin.

"We passed through the most terrible devastation I ever saw during the war I remembered Saint-Lô as a delightful place built on both sides of the river which flowed through the town. Now there was not a building left standing on either bank. Even the river had vanished. We could see it further up the valley. Then it disappeared altogether under the rubble and only emerged again half a mile further on."[4]

When the Prime Minister arrived at Bradley's Command Post he found an extremely tense atmosphere. The great battle was at its height, and, realizing that the General and his staff had their hands full, Churchill did not stay long. Plainly all was going well, and he returned to London much heartened. Three days later he flew to Italy.

* * * * *

When the visit to Italy was first discussed the Prime Minister had announced that he intended to have a few days' rest in the sunshine. Wearing a light tropical suit and an enormous sun-helmet he emerged from his plane at Pomigliano, the great airfield behind Vesuvius, to find rain falling in torrents—so heavily, indeed, that none of the motor-cyclists escorting his car got as far as Naples. Blinded by the downpour two fell off at a level-crossing, and the rest retired with engine-trouble.

[4] *Ibid.*

Churchill went to the Villa Rivalta, a large, rambling house at Posillipo —on the shores of the Bay—which had been requisitioned for General Wilson. Immediately he began planning a series of conferences and interviews. His first visitor was Marshal Tito, resplendent in a blue uniform heavily decked with gold braid. The Marshal was accompanied by two powerfully built bodyguards and an attractive girl in battledress, Madame Olga Homo, who acted as interpreter. Her initial task was to persuade Tito to dispense with his heavily armed henchmen while he conferred with the Prime Minister. He agreed to this with obvious reluctance, and the guards retired to the basement, where they were so hospitably entertained that both fell fast asleep. They were still recovering from British hospitality some hours later when Tito took his departure, and he drove off without them.

The talks with the Yugo-slavs were spread over two days. They covered forthcoming military operations, the stepping up of Allied supplies to the Partisans, and the Marshal's plans for the future political control of his country. Tito's attitude towards the Royalist faction in London was still extremely guarded, but Churchill brought him together with Dr Subasic, Premier of King Peter's Government in exile, and then left them alone to work out their problems.

Before Churchill's final meeting with Tito he took one of his rare days off, and with Rear-Admiral Anthony Morse as his guide he went to Ischia, where he swam for a while, and then lay contentedly in the sun, letting the grey volcanic sand trickle through his fingers while the hot water from the island's subterranean springs bubbled around him. As they returned to Naples landing-craft were steaming slowly up the bay packed with American troops about to take part in *Dragoon*. They were bound for the assembly area off Ajaccio, in Corsica. When the soldiers caught sight of the unmistakable figure in the Admiral's barge they cheered wildly. Mr Churchill saluted them with a wave of his ten-gallon hat.

On the eve of the invasion the Prime Minister himself went to Ajaccio, where General Wilson, Admiral Cunningham, and their staffs were already on board the headquarters ships *Royal Scotsman* and *Largs*. After dinner, wearing his Trinity House uniform he sat on the *Royal Scotsman*'s sun-deck and listened to the weather experts. "We'll go in even if the cloud's at nought feet," said Lieutenant-General Ira Eaker, the American who was commanding the Allied air forces. Churchill looked at him approvingly.

He had already told Admiral Cunningham that he wished to visit the invasion area on the following day, and the Commander-in-Chief had placed H.M.S. *Kimberley* at his disposal. What the Admiral did *not* tell the Prime Minister was that he had already given strict orders to the captain of the destroyer to approach no closer to the enemy coast than the hundred-fathom line. And, to make sure that the Prime Minister—intent on seeing as much action as possible—did not run into any unnecessary danger, he had arranged for an experienced senior officer, Commodore G. R. G. Allen, to accompany him.

Dragoon opened with a tremendous combined bombardment of the French coast by aircraft and warships, and the dropping of 14,000 parachutists. In the early hours of August 15 the landings were made along a fifty-mile stretch of the Riviera running from Cannes towards Toulon. By 10.30 that morning came news that the whole of the central sector had been taken with few casualties.

The Prime Minister returned to Ajaccio in a distinctly disgruntled frame of mind. He complained that he had not been allowed within six miles of the coast, he had seen no opposition of any kind—and to make matters worse he had run out of cigars. He had become so bored that he had borrowed a novel from *Kimberley*'s captain and retired to his bunk.

Tommy confirmed that it had indeed been an uneventful day and Mr Churchill had not exaggerated when he wrote on the fly-leaf of the borrowed book, "This is a lot more exciting than the invasion of Southern France." When they arrived off the beaches they found the battleship *Ramillies* carrying out a desultory bombardment of an untenanted right flank. Fires were blazing in the pinewoods running down to the sea, but already the Allied troops had pushed far inland, and the unloading of stores was proceeding completely unhindered. With virtually no aircraft to support them the depleted German forces were unable to offer more than a token resistance. In less than a month the Allied armies from north and south were to join hands.

From these placid naval proceedings Mr Churchill turned his attention to the battle scene in Italy, and two days later he was driving through Capua to the Cassino front. Alexander was waiting there to take him in his Dakota to Siena. The days which followed were spent in conferences at Alexander's H.Q., visits to General Mark Clark's troops, and a tour of Leghorn, where Admiral Morse had quickly restored the shattered port to full working order.

By now there were soldiers of many nations fighting on the Allied side in Italy, ranging from a Japanese-American combat unit to Goums and Basutos, Senegalese and Mauritians. Among the newcomers inspected by the Prime Minister was a Brazilian Brigade.

The villa at Siena where Churchill put in long hours each evening working on the papers which reached him from England had been specially prepared for its distinguished visitor, but the information that the whole building had been deloused with blow-lamps and copious quantities of

D.D.T. "as well as possible in the time available" was not entirely reassuring to its occupants. Soon it became evident that both animals and insects had survived the holocaust, for with unfailing regularity a mouse took up its position every night on a curtain rod in the drawing-room and sat for hours surveying the Prime Minister with close interest. And when General Alexander and some of his staff came to dinner the meal was rudely interrupted by an invasion of hornets.

Rome was the next port of call. In the sweltering heat, more meetings, day and night—with M. Papandreou, to discuss the activities of E.A.M. in Greece; with the elderly Italian Premier, Bonomi; the Communist leader, Togliatti; and Marshal Badoglio. And with Prince Umberto, who impressed Churchill with his personality and his shrewd understanding of Italy's problems. Taking Moran, Rowan, and Tommy with him, the Prime Minister had an audience at the Vatican. Afterwards Kinna and Sawyers, both Roman Catholics, were received by the Pope.

So far the Italian 'holiday' had been even more arduous than Churchill's daily round in England, and Tommy began to wonder how long the tempo could be sustained. They flew back to Siena, visited Freyberg's New Zealand Division, and then crossed to the Eighth Army front to see General Leese and the Polish C.-in-C., Anders. In an olive-grove on the eastern flank of the front and only a few hundred yards from German machine-gun posts the Prime Minister found himself, to his delight, closer to the enemy than at any time in the war. But these stirring days in the field were at last drawing to an end. On August 27 Mr Churchill left Eighth Army Tactical H.Q. and flew back to Naples.

With the front line now far to the north, the city was besieged by visitors anxious to savour the atmosphere of a conquered country. Mr Attlee and Mr George Hall, Under-Secretary of State for Foreign Affairs, had just arrived there. So had Sir James Grigg, the Secretary of State for War.

At Villa Emma, where nearly one hundred and fifty years before another Commander-in-Chief, Mediterranean, had been the frequent guest of the British Ambassador, Sir William Hamilton, Admiral Cunningham received a stream of callers from England, among them the King, travelling as 'General Collingwood'; Mr A. V. Alexander, the First Lord of the Admiralty; Mr Emlyn Williams, and several Bishops. On the King's last night in Naples he had sat on the terrace at Villa Emma and seen one of Churchill's favourite films, *Lady Hamilton*. Told of this later, Alexander Korda remarked, "Little did I imagine that my paste-board Vesuvius would have to stand such close comparison with the original," for as the volcano appeared on the screen the red glow from the peak of the real Vesuvius loomed in the background at the foot of the darkened bay.

As soon as the Prime Minister reached Naples he had a set-to with Admiral Cunningham, accusing the Royal Navy of failing to give adequate gun-fire support on the Eighth Army flank. He had got his facts wrong, and for once he had the worst of the argument. When, on the defensive, Churchill quoted Alexander as his authority for certain statements Cunningham taxed the General with these charges by signal and received, not surprisingly, a handsome exoneration, for the Navy had been co-operating very closely with the Allied advance. The Prime Minister climbed down, ruefully remarking that the naval Commander-in-Chief had been "a little hard" on him.

The truth was that Mr Churchill was beginning to feel the strain of incessant travel in the heat and the dust, and the combination of arduous days in the field with equally exhausting political discussions which called for intensive preparatory briefing. He was a very tired man, and he was in no fit state to face the rough flight he encountered when the York took off for home. They ran head-on into a stiff Levanter, and by the time the plane neared Rabat Churchill was feeling so ill that Moran advised a stop there for the night. The rest refreshed him, and next day they flew on to Northolt.

He had meant to call at Gibraltar, but a treacherous shift of the wind made landing there impossible. Affairs at the Rock were on his mind as he flew home, however, and soon after he reached London he asked the Colonial Office to inquire whether the orders given on his last visit there had been carried out.

On the way back from Marrakesh he had made a disturbing discovery. The population of Barbary apes which from time immemorial had roamed the Upper Rock was dwindling alarmingly. No one knew for certain where the apes had come from originally. Legend told of a tunnel under the Straits running from St Michael's Cave, a thousand feet above sea-level at Gibraltar, to Mount Abyla, the second pillar of Hercules, on the African shore. A later legend prophesied that if the apes ever left Gibraltar British rule there would end, and, aware of this, Churchill decreed that the monkey colony must be brought up to strength without delay.

Occupied with more pressing problems the Governor had felt that this particular task could be safely shelved for the time being. He had, in fact, forgotten all about it when out of the blue came this signal, three days after the Prime Minister's return from Italy:

> The establishment of the apes on Gibraltar should be 24 and every effort should be made to reach this number as soon as possible and maintain it thereafter.[5]

The Governor rang up Edward Cottrell, the Consul-General, who in

[5] Churchill, Vol. VI, p. 607.

turn passed the problem to his friend, Cecil Hope-Gill, the Consul-General at Tetuan, in Spanish Morocco.

"If you can get hold of twenty apes and bring them by sea to Algeciras I'll meet you at the Customs, and the Admiral has promised to send a boat to take you on to the Dockyard," Cottrell told him.

When Hope-Gill set out from Tetuan with his captives it was a very hot day and by the time he reached Algeciras he was tired and fed up with the apes, and much in need of refreshment. Cottrell suggested that he should send the apes on in the boat and stay to lunch with him at the Reina Cristina, but Hope-Gill reluctantly declined.

"I suppose I'd better see the thing through now; something might easily go wrong," he said. Sure enough, his misgivings were justified, for as Edward Cottrell lunched alone on the terrace of the Reina Cristina, on the opposite side of the bay to Gibraltar, he received a telephone call. It was the Admiral, inquiring anxiously where the apes had got to; they were now long overdue at the Dockyard, and he feared they might have been kidnapped by Spaniards who knew of the legend.

The Consul-General returned to the terrace. With the aid of the hotel telescope he soon spied the boat with Hope-Gill and the apes on board. It lay becalmed, half-way across the bay. The engine had apparently broken down.

Admiral Burrough dispatched a rescue boat with all haste and twenty rather sea-sick monkeys reached the Rock without further misadventure. Mr Churchill's orders had been faithfully carried out. With the Barbary apes once more at full strength Gibraltar's future was no longer in jeopardy, and the Governor and the Colonial Office could breathe again!

33

The Last Atlantic Crossing— and Back to Moscow

WITHIN a week of arriving back in Downing Street Tommy found himself preparing for his sixth—and final—transatlantic mission with the Prime Minister. Churchill and Roosevelt had not met for more than nine months and a further Allied conference was imperative, for since D-Day the face of Europe had already changed with dramatic speed.

Churchill was anxious to establish a clear-cut agreement with the Russians as to precisely what areas they intended to bring under their control. The Soviet armies were rolling forward towards the west, but as yet Stalin had given no undertakings about his plans for Poland, Hungary, Roumania, or Bulgaria. When, however, the Prime Minister urged the need for concerted Anglo-American pressure on Soviet Russia to clarify her intentions Roosevelt seemed at first reluctant to come to grips with this situation and talked vaguely of the possibility of setting up 'consultative machinery.' Churchill replied:

> I am much concerned to receive your message. Action is paralysed if everybody is to consult everybody else about everything before it is taken. Events will always outstrip the changing situations in these Balkan regions. Somebody must have the power to plan and act. . . .[1]

Once again he drew attention to the position in Greece, where the Russians were still giving furtive support to E.A.M. He reminded the President that firm action at the time of the revolt at Alexandria had done much more to thwart Communist plans than any elaborate consultations could have achieved:

[1] Message to Roosevelt dated June 11, 1944. (See Churchill, Vol. VI. p. 66.)

> Your telegrams to me . . . worked wonders. We were entirely agreed and the result is entirely satisfactory. Why is all this effective direction to be broken up into a committee of mediocre officials such as we are littering about the world? Why can you and I not keep this in our own hands, considering how much we see eye to eye about so much of it?

If Roosevelt's reluctance to intervene at this stage in the shaping of post-war Europe was due to an exaggerated belief in Stalin's good intentions the sequence of events in Warsaw early in August must have made it belatedly but all too ominously clear to him that Soviet policy was ruled by cold-blooded self-interest. Encouraged by the swift Russian advance on the city, the Polish population rose against the Germans, confidently expecting the momentum of the Soviet attack to be redoubled, and expecting, too, that their appeals for weapons and food to be dropped to them would be quickly answered.

Instead, at the first news of the rising, the Soviet advance came to an immediate halt. With an eye to the future domination of Poland Stalin flatly refused to aid Polish patriots; none of these people, he argued, was likely to side with his Russian-sponsored Lublin Committee, set up in Moscow as a puppet Government to ensure that post-war Poland would remain a vassal state. So the Germans were left to put down the rising unmolested, and the men and women of Warsaw were butchered in their thousands.

Apart from these grave developments in Poland Churchill was anxious to discuss a number of other matters which called urgently for decision. Chief among these was the contribution which British and Commonwealth forces could make to the operations against Japan in the Pacific as well as the Indian Ocean. He was now occupied with a plan for a new amphibious assault (*Dracula*) aimed at seizing Rangoon before the next monsoon season, but he was determined, too, that British sea and air forces should play their part in the Pacific fighting. The forthcoming conference, for which Quebec was once again chosen as the venue, would also have to decide the future of the Italian campaign. Churchill was still firmly in favour of an advance into Austria to forestall complete Russian domination in that sphere, but no progress in that direction could be contemplated if more and more troops were to be withdrawn from Alexander's command for other ventures.

The Prime Minister's doctors learnt of the Quebec trip with some concern. Mr Churchill had arrived back from the Mediterranean feeling wretchedly ill. Intermittent bouts of fever forced him to spend much of the following week in bed in the Annexe, and the King went to his bedside to sign the submission for Montgomery's promotion to Field-Marshal. On September 4, the eve of his departure for Canada, the Prime Minister still had a high temperature, but he insisted on getting up to attend a Cabinet meeting on the Warsaw crisis. On the following evening he travelled north to the Clyde to board the *Queen Mary*.

Mrs Churchill was with him, and Lord Moran arranged for a nursing sister from St Mary's Hospital to accompany them. He also brought along Brigadier Lionel Whitby, who had helped to look after the Prime Minister at Carthage.

The *Queen Mary*, commanded by Captain James Bissett, who was about to become Commodore of the Cunard Line, was escorted by the cruisers *Kent* and *Berwick*. She took a southerly course, and for two days the Gulf Stream made conditions trying for the harassed staff officers grappling till all hours with Pacific war plans. Mr Churchill was in an exacting mood, and even Tommy, who was not involved in the acrimonious planning sessions, soon found himself in the Prime Minister's bad books. On the first day at sea he asked to see some news reels. Before leaving London Tommy had given instructions that several recent news films should be sent to the ship, but now they were nowhere to be found, and deprived of his favourite relaxation Churchill waxed more and more indignant about this as the voyage continued.

Knowing these moods, which invariably resulted from physical and mental exhaustion, and realizing that part of his job was to act as a safety valve whenever the Prime Minister felt put out about something, Tommy took his daily upbraiding over the films in his usual philosophical way. He was soon in trouble again, for, looking through the programme beginning with their arrival at Halifax on September 10 Churchill came to the conclusion that if he went by train to Quebec as arranged he would not get there before Roosevelt. "I must fly to Quebec and beat the President to it," he announced. Tommy pointed out that this was impossible to organize as the *Queen Mary* had to keep wireless silence throughout the voyage and the Prime Minister decided that he was being deliberately obstructive. The storm only blew over when, checking the timings once again, they discovered that Mr Churchill was basing his calculations on an error of one day in the President's plans.

As it turned out, Mr Roosevelt was the first to arrive at Quebec after all. Unknown to the British party, he changed his programme, and his train drew into Wolfe's Cove station nearly an hour ahead of the Prime Minister, but with the Governor-General, the Earl of Athlone, and Princess Alice he waited till the Churchills arrived and they drove to the Citadel together.

The *Octagon* conference, which lasted only five days, produced several important decisions. The Prime Minister offered to send the main British Fleet to the Pacific, and the President readily accepted, but this was not at all to the liking of Admiral King. At a meeting of the Combined Chiefs of Staff on the following day he tried to repudiate the agreement, implying that the President's answer had been misunderstood. The wind was taken out of his sails, however, when Hollis produced a written note of the conversation. Even then King still seemed disposed to dispute the decision, but in the argument which followed he was roughly handled by Portal, and when the American chairman, Admiral Leahy, also ruled against him he grudgingly gave way.

In addition to the British Fleet the Prime Minister also offered a substantial bomber force for operations against Japan. He explained the British proposal for *Dracula*—the capture of Rangoon—and spoke at some length about the Italian front, urging that no more troops should be withdrawn from that theatre unless the Germans staged a full retreat, for the capture of Vienna, he argued, might well be hastened if Alexander's forces were left with sufficient means to launch an amphibious assault on the Istrian peninsula.

The Combined Chiefs of Staff eventually recommended that no major Allied units should be removed from Italy until the outcome of the current offensive there was known. They also ruled that if General Wilson wished to retain landing-craft for the Istrian venture this project would be considered, providing that he submitted a plan within the next month.

They approved Eisenhower's intention to press on with his attacks towards the Ruhr and the Saar. At the same time they stressed the desirability of seizing the ports of Antwerp and Rotterdam as soon as possible. For planning purposes the date for the end of the war with Japan was set at eighteen months after the defeat of Germany.

On the final day at Quebec the Senate of McGill University, who had made a special journey from Montreal, conferred Honorary Degrees on the Prime Minister and the President at an impressive ceremony on the terrace of the Citadel.

Churchill sadly missed Harry Hopkins, who had taken no part in the Conference. It was only when the Prime Minister arrived to stay with the Roosevelts on the way home that he heard—from Hopkins himself—that he was no longer a member of the President's inner circle. Roosevelt, indeed, made this plain, studiously ignoring his old friend when he arrived for lunch at Hyde Park.

Three factors had apparently led to their estrangement. Hopkins, always a sick man, had been much more ill in recent months. In his absence political rivals and persistent Press criticism had persuaded the President that he was a liability in the higher councils of the State—an adviser too easily influenced by the statesmen of other nations. Roosevelt himself did not altogether believe this charge, but he had grown tired of defending

Hopkins from these incessant attacks. Tommy gathered that the recent marriage to Louise Macey had widened the breach. At first Hopkins had continued to occupy his old quarters in the White House with his wife and small stepdaughter, but the arrangement did not prove a very happy one, and latterly he had moved into a house of his own in Georgetown.

To Churchill, whose admiration and affection for Harry Hopkins had grown with the years, it was distressing to find his host so obviously ill at ease with the man who had once been an inseparable companion.

"That evening at Hyde Park there was the usual family dinner-party, but to us it seemed to misfire. The President and Hopkins were worlds apart, and the forced cheerfulness was just a façade. It was all most depressing and in such sharp contrast to our happy times together in the past.

"Next day Mrs Roosevelt took us up to her cottage high in the hills for a barbecue lunch, which she cooked herself on a charcoal brazier in the garden. After dinner we left by train for Staten Island to avoid the publicity of a drive through New York City. On our arrival at the dockside we heard that Lord Moran, who had lost his pass, had been turned away by the guards when he tried to board the *Queen Mary*. He had been found by a member of the Mission sitting disconsolately on his suitcase at the foot of the gangway."[2]

The Prime Minister was determined to be back in London in time for the opening of Parliament on September 26. Early in the voyage home the *Queen Mary* was forced to alter course to the south to avoid a U-boat and although all next day she steamed at thirty knots it seemed doubtful if she could reach the Clyde in time. Churchill then had a brainwave. If the ship headed for the south of Ireland he could be landed by tender at Fishguard and thereby save the overnight train journey from Scotland. Tommy viewed this plan without much enthusiasm for the stopping of the ship in anything but a flat calm would have made a landing by tender extremely hazardous.

In the end the weather worsened and the *Queen Mary* carried on. They landed at Greenock at 5.30 P.M. on Monday, September 25, and by breakfast-time next morning the Prime Minister was back in Downing Street. Although this had been the shortest of all the Allied conferences, they had covered nearly 9000 miles in the three weeks they had been away from England.

* * * * *

Tommy had hardly unpacked when Mr Churchill called for a progress report on the new aircraft—a Skymaster with a much greater range than the York—which was being specially equipped at Coventry for his use. Tommy found that the Skymaster was not likely to be ready for some weeks,

[2] C. R. Thompson, Notes.

and even then Bill Fraser, who had now succeeded Wing Commander Collins as the Prime Minister's personal pilot, had still to go through a conversion course in America.

Churchill then asked for details of their last flight in the York to Teheran, and Tommy guessed that another Moscow visit was in the offing. They had been back in England only five days when an unusually cordial message from Stalin decided the Prime Minister's plans.

At the end of August Smuts had sent one of his periodic surveys of the world scene. In the course of this he had urged Churchill not to let strategy absorb all his attention:

> From now on it would be wise to keep a very close eye on all matters bearing on the future settlement of Europe. This is a crucial issue on which the future of the world for generations will depend. In its solution your vision, experience, and great influence may prove a main factor.[3]

Churchill had not seen Stalin since their meeting at Teheran in the previous November, and although the tone of messages from Moscow at the time of the Warsaw rising had struck a chill note it seemed to the Prime Minister that frank discussion with the Russians on the situation in Poland and Greece, and, indeed, on the whole problem of world organization following the defeat of the Axis Powers, could not be long delayed. Accordingly he informed the President that he was considering a visit to Moscow with the Foreign Secretary. He hoped, he said, to clinch Russian intervention against Japan, obtain a settlement of the Polish problem, and reach an understanding with Stalin over Greece and Yugoslavia. Roosevelt warmly approved of the plan, and when word came from Stalin on September 30 welcoming Churchill's proposal it was decided to start for Russia as soon as possible.

In the early hours of October 8 the Moscow party left Northolt in two aircraft. Mr Churchill's York carried Moran, John Martin, Tommy, and Detective-Inspector Hughes. In the second plane were Eden, the C.I.G.S., Ismay, Jacob, and several staff officers and typists. Inspector Hughes, who had recently replaced Inspector Thompson as the Prime Minister's senior personal detective, was a quiet, self-effacing Scot from Fifeshire who had once been an officer in the Merchant Navy. He was no stranger to the Downing Street routine, for off and on he had been a member of Churchill's bodyguard since 1940.

There had been the change, too, in the Prime Minister's aircrew. Although Bill Fraser had already made a number of trips in the York as first pilot—he had brought de Gaulle from North Africa for the meeting in the train on the eve of D-Day—this was his first flight in command with

[3] Churchill, Vol. VI, p. 90.

Churchill on board. After careful vetting of his flying record and personal background—a mysterious Scotsman who professed to be an old friend of his father's had called on his wife one day and questioned her closely about his activities and interests—he had been posted to the Prime Minister's aircrew some eighteen months earlier.

From the start he had found the new job intensely interesting. When a long flight was imminent the captain of the aircraft would be summoned to Downing Street. There Tommy would give him a general briefing, and operating heights and refuelling stops would be discussed. With the Prime Minister on board the aircraft was normally taken no higher than 8000 feet, but each passenger had oxygen equipment if he wanted to use it. During the flights Churchill would often work in bed during the daytime. At least once on every trip he would go forward, take over the second pilot's seat, and chat to the crew. He was keenly interested in navigational problems, and in spite of his brief and elementary training at Croydon he seemed to Fraser very much *au fait* with everything going on in the York's crowded cockpit.

On this occasion the first leg of the flight, to Naples, was uneventful, and at 7.30 A.M. Fraser put the plane down on the long runway at Pomigliano, where Alexander and "Jumbo" Wilson had been waiting for an hour in the cold dawn to greet them. Churchill, this time officially disguised as "Colonel Kent," drove to the Villa Rivalta. There he had a brief talk with M. Papandreou, the Greek Premier, and a longer and not altogether harmonious discussion with Alexander and Wilson about the progress on the Italian front. Alexander felt that the Allied armies in Italy had not been sufficiently supported at the conference table. As a result of the severe drain on his resources, and the fierce resistance now being offered by Kesselring, he had been able to make little headway recently.

Talking to him, it was soon obvious to the Prime Minister that the staging of *Dracula*—the amphibious assault on Rangoon—would have to be deferred. Eisenhower had already declared that he would be unable to spare British troops from France and the Netherlands for this venture. Neither could Alexander, it seemed, supply troops from Italy. He badly needed reinforcements himself, and Churchill drafted a message to the President urging that two or three fresh American divisions earmarked for North-west Europe should instead be diverted to strengthen the Fifth Army in Italy.[4]

Before noon the journey was resumed, the York heading first for the Straits of Messina and then Benghazi, where Fraser altered course to start

[4] The plea failed, Roosevelt eventually replying that in the American view it was more important to give all available support to the attempts to break into Germany from the west.

the final thousand miles across the desert to Cairo. As they landed in the darkness on the military airfield near the Pyramids one of the oleo legs of the York's undercarriage was slightly damaged.

"We only learnt of this when we returned to the airfield later that night, after dining at the British Embassy. As this was obviously going to delay us considerably we transferred to Brooke's aircraft. We took off for Russia about 1.0 A.M. Mr Churchill was dead tired and slept for most of the onward flight. When we arrived over Moscow there was some delay, for it was now the turn of the C.I.G.'s aircraft to develop undercarriage trouble and for a time the wheels refused to go down. In the end we landed safely just before noon.

"We were driven out of the city to a different *dacha* to the one we had stayed in on our previous visit. A feature of our new house which, we gathered, was normally occupied by Molotov, was an elaborate nursery suite, decorated with gay chintzes and equipped with masses of charming and ingenious toys.

"We sensed a marked difference in the attitude of our hosts. This time every one seemed extraordinarily friendly and anxious to talk to us. The domestic staff was headed by a very pleasant middle-aged woman dressed in the black alpaca garb of a Victorian English housekeeper; round her waist was a chain bearing an enormous bunch of keys. On our last stay in Moscow the Secret Servicemen had swarmed all over the house, never letting the Russian staff out of their sight for a moment. Now the N.K.V.D. guards no longer entered the building; the sole custodian was an elderly doorkeeper who spent all day long sitting placidly in a hooded wicker chair just inside the main entrance."[5]

For the British Mission the pattern for the next few days was very much the same as before—meetings which dragged on long into the night (for no one seemed to come to life in the Kremlin until the afternoon of each day), and gargantuan meals. On their first evening in Moscow the Prime Minister and the Foreign Secretary discussed the Polish question with Stalin and Molotov until 3.0 A.M. Next day Stalin gave an official lunch which lasted from 2.30 to 6.15, course after course of rich food—caviar, scallops, sucking-pig, partridge—being dispatched to the accompaniment of interminable speeches and toasts.

There was an official reception at the Government Hospitality Centre, at which, for the first time, Churchill met many of the lesser Russian officials and their wives, and the whole British Mission was invited to a gala performance of the Ballet at the Bolshoi Theatre.

"When we arrived at the theatre we had a strange glimpse of the working of Russian democracy. Some of the British N.C.O.'s who were doing

[5] *Ibid.*

clerical work at the conference had been given tickets for the stalls, but they were refused admission on the grounds that only officers could sit in such exalted seats. So Ismay and one or two others who had been allocated boxes changed places with them. When they went in search of refreshments during the intervals all the unfortunate N.C.O.'s could find was apples and bottles of fizzy lemonade, both on sale at prices far beyond the reach of a British Army sergeant."[6]

As the Conference dragged on depressingly little progress was made towards reaching any agreement on the future of Poland. The Lublin Poles, headed by M. Bierut, spoke their parts like well-drilled parrots. They refused to acknowledge that Mikolajczyk, Premier of the exiled Polish Government in London, and Romer, his Foreign Minister, who had been persuaded by Churchill to take part in the talks, had any standing whatever. And when the redrawing of the Polish frontier was raised Bierut's servile anxiety to favour Russia at the expense of his own country made negotiation a mockery. Although feeling far from well—at one stage he had to retire to bed with a fever—Churchill worked with great patience to bring the two sides together. But the task was clearly beyond him.

On this one question of Poland Stalin himself remained carefully noncommital, pretending a measure of sympathy with the British and Mikolajczyk and at the same time adroitly manipulating the Lublin Committee to ensure that no significant concessions were made. On a number of other points at issue, however, the Russian leader was more friendly and accommodating than he had ever been before.

He made it plain that Russia would enter the war against Japan as soon as she could move sufficient men and equipment to the Far East. And he took an unexpectedly reasonable line over joint spheres of influence in the Balkans, conceding to Britain equality of rights in the case of Yugoslavia and Hungary and admitting her predominant interest in Greece. Although it had been decided, after all, not to deal with broader questions of world organization at this conference but to wait for a Three-Power Meeting in the near future, Churchill found himself in agreement with several suggestions which Stalin put forward informally for the post-war control of Germany.

Throughout the ten days the British Mission was in Moscow Stalin went out of his way, in fact, to treat his guests with a friendliness and courtesy quite out of keeping with his brusque and domineering attitude at the previous meetings. As a special mark of goodwill he visited a foreign embassy for the first time to dine as Churchill's guest, and on the night the British party went to the Bolshoi he insisted—again for the first time—on going to the theatre so that he could appear at Churchill's side. When the Prime

[6] *Ibid.*

Minister left Moscow on the morning of October 19, a cold, cheerless day with rain falling in torrents, Stalin was waiting at the airfield to bid him farewell—yet another unprecedented gesture.

"In order to arrive in Egypt by daylight on the following morning we had to break our journey. So we landed at Sarabuz, in the Crimea, and leaders of the local Soviet took us to Simferopol, where a rest house had been prepared for Mr Churchill. The road we drove along was lined with troops, and we passed several strings of the most miserable specimens of humanity I had ever seen in my life. Dressed in rags, filthy, and obviously near starvation, they were chained together and working in labour gangs. I asked if they were Germans. My interpreter seemed embarrassed, and after a pause he said they were Russian criminals. To this day I believe they were German prisoners of war.

"We sat down to a dinner of Moscow lavishness. At midnight we took off again, to the great disappointment of our host, General Yermetchenko. He had obviously taken a fancy to one of the P.M.'s attractive girl secretaries, whom he lured into a private room on the pretext of drinking a few special toasts!"[7]

On reaching Cairo Churchill had a meeting with Admiral Mountbatten. Early on the following morning he flew on to Naples and thence to England. The arrival back at Northolt had an entertaining sequel, for when the baggage was unloaded several strange crates appeared. As Tommy had been told before leaving Moscow that the Soviet Government intended to make a present of caviar and vodka to the British Mission he assumed that the crates contained the promised gifts. One was addressed to Mr Churchill and one to the Foreign Secretary. Admittedly the remainder bore no name, but every one concluded that the contents were meant to be shared out among the rest of the Mission. Sure enough, when opened in the Cabinet Office, they were found to contain enough vodka, caviar, and Georgian champagne for every one who had made the trip.

A few days later, when most of the food and drink had been avidly consumed, the Russians asked the Foreign Office what had happened to a special consignment of caviar and vodka sent from Moscow in the Prime Minister's aircraft. It was, they said plaintively, intended for the Russian Embassy's celebration of Red Army Day.

When Mr Eden replied apologetically that the contents of these crates had been distributed among the British party, and pointed out that he had already thanked the Ambassador for the welcome present, his explanation was coldly received. Declaring that the cases had been specially sealed—a fact which no one seemed to have noticed—the Embassy complained indignantly of a breach of diplomatic privilege.

[7] *Ibid.*

Much taken aback, the Foreign Secretary offered to try to round up what was left of the caviar, the vodka, and the 'champagne.' By then, however, M. Gousev, the Russian Ambassador, had had second thoughts. Reflecting that his staff would fare rather badly on the remnants, he announced philosophically that he would cable to Moscow for a fresh consignment.

34

"To Athens To-night"

AT THE end of October the three major Allied Powers granted formal recognition to de Gaulle's Provisional French Government. Two months earlier Paris had been liberated by General Leclerc's 2nd French Armoured Division, and de Gaulle now sent an invitation to Mr Churchill to visit the capital for the Armistice Day Parade on November 11.

To the Prime Minister's advisers the suggested programme appeared to involve a considerable security risk, and before the invitation was accepted Ronald Howe, Assistant Commissioner of Police, and a Chief Inspector from Scotland Yard attended a meeting in the Annexe. At this time no one knew how many Germans were still in hiding in Paris and the chief danger to the Prime Minister seemed to lie in his proposed visit to the Tomb of the Unknown Warrior at the Arc de Triomphe, and his subsequent journey on foot down the Champs-Élysées to the saluting base. Apart from vast crowds in the street thousands of people would be overlooking the route from the windows and roofs of houses on either side.

Duff Cooper, who had now arrived in Paris from Algiers, considered that the risk of an assassination attempt was remote. He argued that any Germans who had so far escaped capture would hardly want to draw attention to themselves, and although the Scotland Yard team felt the arrangements were far from ideal they eventually agreed with the Ambassador that the hazards should be accepted. On November 10, accompanied by the Foreign Secretary, Mary Churchill, and Tommy, the Prime Minister flew to Orly.

His return to the city he had last seen in the tragic spring of 1940 was greeted with almost hysterical emotion. The entire population seemed to have massed along the route, and the ceaseless roar of cheering as he drove into Paris in an open car with de Gaulle echoed a nation's thankfulness for deliverance from the long years of servitude. It was a breath-taking welcome, which moved Churchill to tears.

At the Quai d'Orsay a whole floor had been reserved for him and his party. During the visit to Italy he had twitted John Cunningham about the black marble bathroom which the Admiral used at Villa Emma, but the suite set aside for the Prime Minister during his stay in Paris had a far more spectacular attraction—a gold bath which had been specially installed for Goering.

The scene in the Champs-Élysées next morning made Churchill's reception of the day before seem almost commonplace. The tree-lined avenue leading up to the Étoile, and the balconies, windows, and rooftops of every building within sight of it were crammed with wildly excited men, women, and children. The Prime Minister and de Gaulle laid their wreaths, and then began what to Tommy still seemed a hazardous walk of half a mile to the Tribune, where there was to be a march-past of French troops. The only untoward incident, however, occurred when some American Servicemen, intent on taking photographs, broke through the cordon and surged towards the Prime Minister and the General. When police tried to drive them back they became truculent and abusive.

After the parade Churchill went to Les Invalides to place wreaths on the tombs of Clemenceau and Foch. An official luncheon in the Rue Saint-Dominique was followed by a two-hour discussion of current problems facing de Gaulle's administration, "Winston talking most of the time in his uninhibited and fairly intelligible French. . . . Both he and de Gaulle were in the happiest of humours. It was all very different from the interview at Marrakesh," wrote Duff Cooper afterwards.[1]

Next day Churchill visited the Allied Expeditionary Forces Club which Mrs Eden had organized, and then lunched at the Hôtel de Ville with the Mayor and civic authorities.

> Here the Prime Minister surpassed himself. Unwarned and unprepared he plunged into a speech in French which entirely delighted his audience. He used to say sometimes when defending Spears that the only reason why the French disliked him was because Spears spoke French better than they did. His own method of dealing with the language is certainly more endearing.[2]

In his reply the Mayor made it evident that de Gaulle was not going to have matters all his own way in controlling the immediate destiny of France. He implied that the Resistance movement who had borne the

[1] *Old Men Forget*, p. 341. [2] *Ibid.*

heat and burden of the day under the German occupation would demand a much greater say in the running of the country than they had so far been offered. But on such an occasion few of those present paid more than passing heed to this sudden injection of political realism. It was a day for rejoicing. The problems of France reborn could wait till the morrow.

"After dinner with the Duff Coopers at the Embassy we joined de Gaulle's train and set off for Besançon to visit General de Lattre de Tassigny, whose troops were about to launch a major attack on the mountainous Vosges frontier. Just as we were boarding the train Cecil Beaton arrived brandishing a pass from the British Embassy which, he claimed, entitled him to travel with the Prime Minister as an official photographer, and asked where his accommodation was. I had to point out to him that the Press were all travelling together in a separate part of the train and he retired, distinctly crestfallen. As the P.M. invariably worked during his journeys by train, or wanted to discuss confidential matters, he could not have reporters and photographers travelling with him, but he always took a close interest in the Press representatives who covered his engagements. On this trip he had a long talk with Ward Price, of the *Daily Mail*, whom he had last seen at Casablanca.

"The reporters who came with us on this occasion had a difficult time. There had been a heavy fall of snow and it was bitterly cold when we reached Besançon. The car waiting for us seemed in reasonably good order, but judging from the dilapidated appearance of several others provided for the Press their chances of keeping up with us seemed remote. Sure enough, several only covered a mile or two before burst tyres or mechanical breakdowns ended their attempts to follow us to de Lattre's H.Q. at Maiche.

"On icy roads we went off at a great pace towards the Swiss frontier, but half-way we ourselves were held up by a jeep which was pulling a small car out of a ditch. As soon as it was safely back on the road our Police escort began shouting at the driver: 'Dégagez la piste!' This so unnerved him that he revved up his engine, let in the clutch with a bang, and shot straight across the road into the ditch on the opposite side, where we left him more firmly wedged than ever!"[3]

The weather grew worse and worse, and by the time Churchill arrived at Maiche a further heavy snowstorm had blocked the mountain road ahead. There was now no hope of reaching the front. De Lattre therefore suggested that the Prime Minister should return to Besançon by way of Valdahon, where a large body of French troops were encamped.

"As we drove off I saw poor Cecil Beaton standing miserably at the gates of the headquarters in the middle of a group of frozen Press photo-

[3] C. R. Thompson, Notes.

graphers. The snow clouds were still massing, and although the P.M. had luckily brought a fur-coat the prospect of him spending the rest of the afternoon in the open in the icy cold worried us all.

"At Valdahon we were given cups of coffee laced with brandy, and then, standing on a hastily improvised daïs, Mr Churchill took the salute as several hundred troops marched by in the gathering dusk. It was almost dark when the last unit passed, and I thought the parade was over, but then we heard the sound of approaching tanks, which thundered by with headlights glaring. Now at last there seemed an opportunity to hustle the P.M. back indoors, but as we turned to leave the platform a man, barely visible in the gloom, jumped on to a farm cart among a crowd of soldiers and cried out: "Attention! On va chanter!" For twenty minutes longer we stood in the freezing night air while the French troops sang martial songs for Mr Churchill's benefit."[4]

In all the Prime Minister had been in the open for ten hours that day, standing for most of the time in melting snow and a bitter wind. Miraculously he seemed completely unaffected by the ordeal. He dined with de Gaulle, and when the General left the train next morning Mr Churchill went on to Rheims for a meeting with Eisenhower before he flew back to Northolt.

* * * * *

As the month ended the Prime Minister celebrated his seventieth birthday. One present he received—from the officers of his Map Room—particularly delighted him. It was a silver menu-holder which bore a picture, coloured on enamel, of the prefabricated harbour at Arromanches. On the reverse side was inscribed his own farsighted directive:

PIERS FOR THE BEACHES. THEY MUST RISE AND FALL WITH THE TIDE.

With this was engraved the date, 1942, when the directive was written—two years before Mulberry Harbour played its vital part in the invasion of Normandy.

America had just been to the polls, re-electing Franklin Roosevelt for a fourth term. Churchill, whose attention in recent months had been mainly centred on world affairs, now began to reflect, a little despondently, that although so much still remained to be done in the field of international organization the life of the British Coalition which had so far subordinated party politics to wider interests was drawing inexorably to a close. To Smuts, who had sent him a message on his birthday, he wrote:

> there approaches the shadow of the General Election which before many months have passed will certainly break up the most capable

[4] Ibid.

> Government England has had, or is likely to have. Generally we have a jolly year before us. Our financial future fills in any spaces in the horizon not already overcast with clouds. However, I am sure we shall master all these troubles as they come upon us, singly or in company, even though the tonic element of mortal danger is lacking.[5]

The troubles which he foretold were not long delayed. Throughout November the advance towards the Rhine had continued, but attacking along a wide front progress was slow. "I am trying to have Holland cleared up behind us. But it is not so easy as it used to be for me to get things done," Churchill noted sadly as December came.

In Italy and far-off Burma as well as in Germany the momentum of the Allied effort had slackened perceptibly. He warned Roosevelt of the dangers facing them if they allowed the initiative to pass to the enemy and urged that the U.S. Chiefs of Staff should visit Eisenhower as soon as possible to study the situation on the spot and formulate fresh plans, but he received a disturbingly complacent reply. Within a week the Germans, who had assembled a striking force of more than 375,000 men, launched a violent counter-attack in the Ardennes with ten Panzer and fourteen infantry divisions. Their aim was to break through the Allied centre and swing north to capture Antwerp, thereby cutting off Eisenhower's northern armies from their main supply base.

At the moment when this alarming development occurred Churchill found himself with a political crisis on his hands. Civil war had broken out in Greece, and when the Prime Minister took immediate and decisive steps to bring the situation in Athens under control he was instantly assailed on all sides for intervening in what appeared to ill-informed critics to be a purely domestic matter concerning Greeks alone.

As far back as the summer of 1943 Smuts had written with characteristic foresight, "I very much fear that in the inflamed conditions of public feeling, not only in Greece but also in other Balkan countries, chaos may ensue . . . unless a strong hand is kept on the local situation; the Bolshevization of a broken and ruined Europe remains a definite possibility."[6] The revolt in Egypt in the following April had shown that Communist influence was already spreading fast, and although for a while the rebel movement, E.A.M. made a pretence of co-operating with the new Prime Minister, Papandreou, they were only biding their opportunity.

In the middle of October, as the Germans retreated, British troops occupied Athens and the Greek Government began the herculean task of administering a shattered country. The invader had departed; behind him he had left the seeds of chaos and anarchy. Money had lost all its pur-

[5] Churchill, Vol. VI, p. 234.
[6] Churchill, Vol. V, p. 475.

chasing power, and million-drachma notes blew about the streets. There was a desperate shortage of food and clothing. Strong leadership, backed by military power, could alone restore law and order, but Papandreou had too few Greek troops to aid him in asserting the authority of the new Government. And the rebel factions saw their opportunity. On December 3 they rose against the Government, seizing a number of police stations at key-points in the city and murdering the occupants.

Aware that any hesitancy or half-hearted measures in dealing with this Communist challenge would be fatal, Churchill ordered General Scobie, commanding the British troops in Greece, to meet force with force. In a forthright signal he promised Scobie the fullest support in whatever action he took to put down the rebellion. "It would be a great thing for you to succeed in this without bloodshed if possible, but also with bloodshed if necessary," he concluded.[7] He had chosen his words deliberately. They formed part of a carefully considered message which emphasized the vital need to restore order before the outbreak assumed grave proportions. Unhappily this signal, intended for Scobie and Maitland Wilson alone, was to achieve considerable notoriety.

Even before this happened, however, news of the intervention provoked an immediate and hostile reaction in the British Press. At the same time as the storm broke Mr Stettinius, the American Secretary of State, issued an implied rebuke to the Prime Minister for allegedly bringing undue influence to bear in Italian politics—a reference to Churchill's critical attitude towards Count Sforza, who was at this time trying to re-establish himself in his native land after many years' exile in America. This prompted the *Manchester Guardian*, which quaintly described the supporters of E.A.M. as the "most energetic and progressive" section of the Greek population, to declare scathingly that British diplomatic prestige had reached its lowest ebb since Munich: "We are alienating all the renascent democracies. The mischief does not stop in Europe. The U.S. Secretary of State has chosen this moment to rebuke us, and thus Britain and the U.S.A. have made nonsense of the principles of co-operation."

American public opinion had, of course, long cherished a curiously distorted image of Britain's rapacious foreign policy. The hostility of a large section of the British Press towards intervention in Greece was due to a total misunderstanding of the motives and mentality of the rebel leaders they sought to champion. While the *Times* correspondent on the spot in Athens was eloquently confirming that E.L.A.S. troops had embarked on a coldblooded campaign of "terrorism, extortion, and killings" the *News Chronicle* seemed unmoved by this aspect—or perhaps unaware of its existence: "We must never run the risk of using our bayonets to force an

[7] Churchill, Vol. VI, p. 252.

unacceptable Government upon a liberated people. On the contrary we must keep the field clear until genuine popular opinion can express itself." This view completely ignored the fact that at that very moment the bayonets of E.L.A.S. were endeavouring to ensure that genuine popular opinion in Greece was stifled for ever by Communist control.

In a long and convincing speech in the Commons on December 8 the Prime Minister hotly defended the Government's policy. They had been charged, he said, with using His Majesty's forces to disarm the friends of democracy in Greece and other parts of Europe.

"Democracy is not based on violence and terrorism, but on reason, on fair play, on freedom, on respecting the rights of other people. Democracy is no harlot, to be picked up in the street by a man with a tommy gun. I trust the people, the mass of the people, in almost any country, but I like to make sure it is the people and not a gang of bandits who think that by violence they can overturn constituted authority."

Speaking with considerable emotion he went on: "We are told that because we do not allow gangs of heavily armed guerrillas to descend from the mountains and install themselves, with all the bloody terror and vigour of which they are capable, in power in great capitals, we are traitors to democracy. . . . I shall call upon the House as a matter of confidence in His Majesty's Government, and of confidence in the spirit with which we have marched from one peril to another till victory is in sight, to reject such pretensions with the scorn that they deserve."[8]

In spite of the overwhelming support he won from Parliament certain national newspapers continued to press for the withdrawal of British troops from Greece, one well-known writer on foreign affairs declaring that the country would not tolerate a war between "British soldiers and the Greek people"—an over-simplification which caused much resentment among the British soldiers concerned, who by now had seen enough of the rebel atrocities to form their own bitter opinions of the agitation in England. The Labour Party Conference joined in the clamour, calling for an armistice without delay, and a mass meeting in Trafalgar Square added its further hysterical protest.

Fortified by his long experience, and comforted in no small measure by the emphatic endorsement which Parliament had given to him, the Prime Minister was prepared to ignore these domestic pinpricks. But in America the chorus of criticism suddenly swelled anew as the result of an astonishing security leak. To the embarrassment of the British Government, the text of Churchill's outspoken TOP SECRET message to General Scobie was suddenly reproduced almost verbatim by an American gossip columnist.

[8] *Ibid.*, pp. 256–258.

To many cynical British observers the American attitude towards security often seemed to be exemplified by a story widely current in Allied Force Headquarters at Algiers after the North African landings. Having decoded a vital message from Washington to the Supreme Commander, an American cipher officer had handed it to a messenger. As the latter passed through the next room he called out, "Here's an EYES ONLY for Ike. . . . Anyone want to see it before it goes up?"

In the case of the Scobie signal investigation failed to establish whether the leak had occurred in the American Embassy in Rome or in the State Department in Washington. At first sight it seemed inexplicable that a highly confidential message addressed to General Scobie and repeated to General Wilson alone should have found its way into American hands at all. It had not, however, been realized in Whitehall that all messages of a certain grading which reached Wilson, the Supreme Allied Commander in Italy, were shown as a matter of course to the American Ambassador in Rome, who was fully entitled to pass to Washington any information he gleaned from them. Even with this wider distribution which the signal received it was still difficult to comprehend how its contents had got into the hands of an American journalist, but somewhere along the chain of cipher officers, messengers, and junior and senior officers or officials who handled it this flagrant leak occurred, and publication of Churchill's order to meet force with force caused a sensation throughout America.

It stirred up afresh all the deep-seated mistrust of British 'imperialist' aims which had been firmly rooted in the American mind for more than a hundred and fifty years. And the wave of emotionalism over Churchill's realistic attitude to the Athens rebels made all subsequent efforts to reach a settlement in Greece infinitely more complicated. Relations between Britain and her principal ally had already been strained by the action of Admiral King, who without any reference to the Joint Chiefs of Staff had ordered that no American landing-craft in the Mediterranean should be used to carry urgently needed supplies to Greece. Now they seemed almost at breaking-point.

As Christmas approached the fierce fighting in Athens continued. Without considerable reinforcement General Scobie had no hope of inflicting a decisive military defeat on the E.L.A.S. guerrillas and Alexander made it plain that for the time being at least no more troops could be spared from the Italian front. By now Churchill was well aware that no satisfactory truce would be negotiated while the existing administration remained in office. Nominally it continued to function after a fashion, but its members had lost all confidence in themselves; they had been overwhelmed by events. A new leader was wanted, but where could he be found? In different circumstances the Monarchy might have provided a rallying-point, but the return of the King under the protection of British arms could not be considered in the present *impasse*.

The only promising alternative seemed to lie in the creation of a Regency, headed by some one who exerted influence over a wider sphere than the disintegrating Papandreou Government. In this connexion the name of Archbishop Damaskinos had been submitted to the King of Greece, but so far the latter had refused to regard the setting up of a Regency as a desirable step.

Reluctant as he was to become involved in a constitutional crisis, Churchill saw that the deadlock could not be allowed to continue. No doubt the King of Greece could be persuaded to change his mind and accept the Archbishop as Regent if sufficient weight of evidence suggested that Damaskinos was the right man to hold such an office. But the Prime Minister had no personal knowledge of him. The more Churchill turned the matter over in his mind the more convinced he became that one course alone lay open to him.

On Christmas Eve he left London for Chequers. Tommy stayed behind for an hour or two at Downing Street. Then he packed a suitcase, intending to drive down to Henley and spend Christmas with friends. First of all, however, he headed for Chequers to see if there were any last-minute orders.

He ran into the Prime Minister in the hall. "I'm afraid you'll have to cancel your plans," said Mr Churchill. "We're going to Athens to-night."

35

Conference by Candlelight

FOR some days Tommy had been aware that a journey to Greece was in Mr Churchill's mind, and he had warned the aircrew to remain on duty. When Christmas Eve came and there was no further news he assumed that the idea had been dropped. As a precaution, however, he had rung up Fraser before he left Downing Street, and checked that the crew were still standing by the new Skymaster. Now he began feverishly contacting the others chosen to accompany the Prime Minister.

The Foreign Secretary had already been warned to prepare for the journey. In addition to Moran, Jock Colville, and Pierson Dixon, Eden's Private Secretary, Churchill took with him Detective-Sergeant Davies and two girl secretaries, Elizabeth Layton and Marianne Holmes.

Cyril Davies, who had joined the Prime Minister as second detective in the previous year, was probably the least surprised of all when the phone rang at his home in Croydon. Although he had just been told he would not be wanted throughout the Christmas period he was quite resigned by now to these sudden changes of plan. As a rule both detectives were on duty for at least twelve hours daily and saw little of their homes even when they were in England. Davies himself had already accompanied the Prime Minister to Cairo, Teheran, Tunis, Marrakesh, and Quebec. Now he was warned to pack immediately for another trip abroad lasting several days. A car arrived, and he went straight to Chequers. Towards midnight the cavalcade set out for Northolt.

The Skymaster, now starting its maiden flight with Churchill on board, had been made available on Roosevelt's instructions as soon as he learnt of the relatively restricted range of the York which the Prime Minister had been using. The new plane had an endurance of twenty-five hours and could cover 4500 miles without refuelling. Its fitting-out had given M.A.P.'s designers a welcome opportunity to experiment with a number of new features and appliances which could be adapted to British civilian aircraft when peace came, and starting with a bare, unsoundproofed fuselage they had made a wonderful job of it.

In the tail was the Prime Minister's private cabin. Next came a saloon which could be used for meals or conferences. In the forepart were seats for twelve passengers which could be converted into bunks at night; there were two cloakrooms, a pantry, and a kitchen. Extra fuel-tanks, housed internally, made it possible to fly as far afield as Singapore and Australia. Bill Fraser, who had just returned from a successful trial flight to Montreal, was delighted with his new charge.

Churchill slept fitfully during the flight to Naples. He awoke tired and dispirited. The telegrams which had come in to Downing Street on Christmas Eve suggested that the situation in Athens was growing hourly more grave and to Admiral Cunningham and Air Marshal Slessor, who were waiting on the airfield at Pomigliano, it was plain that the criticism of the Prime Minister's policy towards the Greek rebels had surprised and wounded him by its venom.

He was angry, too, with the Greeks for their unrelenting repudiation of the Caserta Agreement—a pact which had bound them to co-operate with the Papandreou Government. "If only I had known they were going to do this," he kept repeating. Then, smashing his fist in the palm of his hand, he demanded bitterly, "Why didn't they fight the Germans like they are fighting us now?" Apart from sizing up the Archbishop he did not seem to have any cut-and-dried plan of action, but he mentioned that he hoped to persuade the rebel leaders to attend a meeting with representatives of the Greek Government on the morrow.

In little more than an hour the Skymaster resumed its journey towards the Peloponnese. They flew low over the Corinth Canal, still blocked by the debris of German demolition. As he approached Hassani airfield Fraser could see bright flashes of gunfire all round the aerodrome. In the plane there was a hurried conference and then it was decided to take the Skymaster down and risk the consequences.

Alexander and Scobie, Harold Macmillan and the Ambassador, Mr Leeper, were awaiting them. While a strong R.A.F. detachment guarded the perimeter of the field they held a meeting in the plane. Once the engines were switched off it soon grew bitterly cold, and when Elizabeth Layton was summoned in to take down a statement for the Press her fingers were so frozen that she could scarcely use her typewriter. An icy wind bearing occasional flurries of snow howled mournfully round the aircraft. Not far away they could hear bursts of machine-gun fire.

At four o'clock they emerged from the Skymaster and set off to drive through the E.L.A.S. lines to the Piraeus, the port of Athens, where H.M.S. *Ajax* was waiting to accommodate the party. Tommy was in the leading car, a station-wagon. Immediately behind followed an armoured car carrying the Prime Minister, who sat with his heavy Colt revolver across his knees.

* * * * *

The first intimation that she was to receive visitors on Christmas Day had reached H.M.S. *Ajax* at three o'clock that morning, when a TOP SECRET signal bearing the injunction, ONLY TO BE DECIPHERED BY ADMIRAL'S SECRETARY, was brought to Paymaster-Commander Morrice MacMullen's cabin. *Ajax*, dispatched to Greek waters to support General Scobie's small British Army contingent, was flying the flag of Rear-Admiral J. M. Mansfield, a submarine specialist who now commanded the 15th Cruiser Squadron in the Mediterranean, and when MacMullen had decoded the signal he took it along to him. Admiral Mansfield was puzzled, for the message gave no clue to the identity of the party for whom he was asked to find room on board. It merely stated that two V.V.I.P.'s and a staff of fourteen, including one female, were to be given accommodation. An hour later came the single, unrevealing amendment, —"For one female read two."

His Majesty's Ambassador had also received a puzzling message from Whitehall. Admittedly this came from the Prime Minister in person, but it said that he was "sending trusted emissary." The first visitor to arrive in Athens that day was not, however, an envoy from Churchill; a frigate entered the Piraeus bringing Alexander, recently promoted to Field-Marshal. He seemed as puzzled as every one else. A brief signal from the Prime Minister had just reached him warning that "an old friend" was on his way to the Greek capital.

After some discussion he and the Ambassador came to the conclusion that Anthony Eden was probably the senior of the Very Very Important Persons mentioned in the Admiral's signal. No one in Athens on this Christmas morning was prepared for the descent from the skies of both the Foreign Secretary *and* the Prime Minister.

When Mr Churchill came off in the Admiral's barge the commanding officer of *Ajax*, Captain J. W. Cuthbert, said to him, "I hope, sir, that while you are with us we shan't have to open fire, but as you know our purpose here is to assist the Army. If we are asked to give supporting fire I must do so."

The Prime Minister seemed delighted at this prospect. "Pray remember, Captain, that I come here as a cooing dove of peace, bearing a sprig of mistletoe in my beak—but far be it from me to stand in the way of military necessity," he remarked blandly.

At the conference in the aircraft it had been decided to summon the Greek Prime Minister, M. Papandreou, on board the cruiser, followed by Archbishop Damaskinos. Churchill emphasized that he wanted to see them separately; if by any mischance they arrived together the Archbishop must be suitably entertained until he was ready to receive him.

Sure enough, they did arrive together—Papandreou a greying, worried-looking man in a dark suit; Damaskinos a magnificent, commanding figure with a long black beard and dressed in flowing robes. He wore a stove-pipe hat; in his left hand he carried a crook. Well over six feet tall, he towered above Tommy and Commander Roy Foster-Brown, who had been deputed to shepherd him to the Captain's cabin.

As they passed through the screen door there was a dramatic and entirely unforeseen development. To the Commander's horror he saw advancing towards them the ship's "Funny Party." In the Royal Navy the Funny Party is a traditional form of amusement at Christmas-time; a group of sailors, garbed in extravagant fancy dress, go their rounds of the ship clowning and generally making fun at everyone's expense. Bearing this in mind Foster-Brown had stationed sentries to head off this team from the conference area. But somehow or other they had succeeded in getting into the Captain's Lobby, and there they stood—a hula-hula 'girl' with a grass skirt and a brassière with winking red and green lights on either side; the clown Coco; Charlie Chaplin; and three other equally bizarre characters with grotesquely blackened faces.

Like all Funny Parties, they thought they were excruciatingly amusing, but when they caught sight of Archbishop Damaskinos they concluded with grudging admiration that the Commander had turned the tables on them. He had produced someone far funnier than they were—a rival one-man Funny Party, in fact!

They gaped unbelievingly at the Archbishop with his immense black beard, his tall hat, and his long robes. Then they howled with laughter. From behind the Archbishop's back Tommy made frantic signs to them to clear off. The Commander, realizing that anything *he* said to the sailors at that juncture would probably only make matters worse, could only mutter apologetically, "You know, sir . . . Christmas Day, sir . . . very funny, sir!" as he steered the amazed Damaskinos rapidly past.

As soon as they reached the Captain's cabin he sent for the interpreter and asked him to explain to their guest that it was an old British custom in the Royal Navy to have Funny Parties on Christmas Day. From the look of utter incredulity on his face it was quite clear that the Archbishop thought he was imprisoned in a gathering of lunatics. His meeting with Churchill went well, however, Damaskinos making a very favourable impression, and it was agreed to hold a conference ashore on the following afternoon at which representatives of all Greek political parties would be present.

Dinner that night was a cheerful affair, and Churchill seemed much more relaxed than he had been for some days. Chatting across the table to Alexander he suddenly noticed that the Field Marshal was wearing an unusual medal, and he leant forward to inspect it more closely.

"It's a personal medal I have had made for my staff who have been with me since Alamein," said Alexander, detaching it and passing it across for Churchill to look at.

"Very nice, too," said the Prime Minister, pinning it in place on his own breast. And there it remained!

When conversation turned to the difficulty in reaching agreement with the rebels the Prime Minister said gravely: "We must make our decision uninfluenced by our closeness to the battle. We must adopt a course of action which in England will be regarded as right in fifty to a hundred years." Dinner at an end he retired to the Admiral's cabin. There he drafted two signals pleading for understanding of what he was trying to do to overcome the crisis. They went to Roosevelt and Stalin.

At six o'clock on the evening of Boxing Day the conference with the E.L.A.S. leaders was held in the Greek Foreign Office. When Churchill left the cruiser earlier in the afternoon to drive in his armoured car to the Embassy the sound of gunfire was still reverberating across the water. Every now and then shells were landing in the harbour, though it seemed fairly plain that H.M.S. *Ajax* was not intended as the target. During the previous night, however, an E.L.A.S. raiding party had attempted to break through the cordon of British troops guarding the airfield, and bullets had struck the undercarriage of the Skymaster.

On reaching the Embassy Churchill learnt that a plot had been discovered to blow up the Grande Bretagne Hotel, in the centre of the city, where General Scobie had his headquarters. The Prime Minister's decision to visit Athens had been a well-kept secret and it seemed highly improbable that the plot was aimed at him. Shortly before his arrival, however, the Chief Engineer of 3rd Corps, Brigadier Frank Hards, had had a strong premonition that E.L.A.S. might attempt a major coup by dynamiting some part of the city in British hands.

Sending for plans of the sewerage system, he had discovered that one tunnel ran right under the front of the Grande Bretagne. He therefore decided to search the tunnel himself. Six feet seven inches in height, with the build of a Rugby forward—he had played in the Army pack before the war—Hards at first had some difficulty in squeezing through the manhole outside the hotel. Almost as soon as he landed on the slimy floor he heard men moving in the darkness, and he stumbled on several boxes of dynamite which a gang had been placing in position immediately under General Scobie's office. The cache was almost complete, and some of the fuses had already been connected. There was nearly a ton of high explosive and Hards and his Sappers had a hazardous time before they were able to report that the danger was over.

The drama of the conference in the Greek Foreign Office was heightened by the eerie setting.

"The windows were heavily shuttered. The only illumination in the room came from hurricane lamps which cast small pools of light on the table, and pitch-black shadows partially hid the faces of the delegates. Mr Churchill sat in the centre at one side of the oblong table, with Eden on his right and the Archbishop on his left. Alexander was on the other side of Damaskinos, and then came Macmillan and Scobie. The American Ambassador, the French Minister, and a Russian military representative were also present. Damaskinos wore a large gold eagle suspended round his neck. In his dark robes and his tall hat he looked like some ancient magician, and I thought of a remark the P.M. had made on his arrival. He had asked what the Archbishop was like, and some one had said, 'He's a crafty mediaeval priest.' To which Mr Churchill had retorted, 'Splendid . . . just the man we are looking for.'

"We waited for some time as the E.L.A.S. leaders had not arrived. Most people were shivering, and I went out in search of an oil-stove. Eventually the P.M., who was feeling the cold acutely in spite of his overcoat and the thick rug he had wrapped round him, made his opening speech. He said how glad he was to have brought all the Greek representatives together, and how greatly he welcomed the Archbishop's decision—given to him that morning—to act as Regent until the King's return. Now it was up to the Greek people to settle their differences among themselves; he would take no part in their discussions. Having brought them together, his work was done, and he got up to leave the room.

"Just then news came that the E.L.A.S. leaders had arrived. They were received in grim silence by their fellow-countrymen and Mr Churchill, feeling that this was no way to get them together, moved round the table, shook hands with the latecomers, and asked them to be seated. I noticed that the rest of the Greeks looked none too pleased, but after the P.M. had repeated his few words we left the room and returned to the Embassy."[1]

All next day the Greeks argued over the truce which Churchill had urged them to accept. The titular leader of E.L.A.S., General Sarafis, was a Regular Army officer of limited capacity and no great strength of purpose. But behind him stood a man of very different calibre named Siantos.

[1] C. R. Thompson, Notes.

A tobacco worker from Volos, he was Secretary of the Party and a fanatical Communist, Moscow-trained and completely unscrupulous. At the Candlelight Conference with the rebel leaders Churchill, who had an extraordinary gift for summing up the people he was dealing with, quickly recognized him as the chief stumbling-block and noticed that the other delegates seemed to fear him. As he left the room he had deliberately stopped in front of Siantos, and, with a searching look, he said to him, "Greece for ever!"

Having made it plain to Greeks of all parties, however, that he was not going to intervene directly in their negotiations after that initial meeting Churchill's own efforts were now perforce confined to advising and encouraging the Archbishop, whom he saw again on the evening of December 27. When the Communists sought an interview with him he refused to meet them.

For the Prime Minister's party and the staff of the British Embassy it was a strange and incongruous existence. While the meetings continued British troops and a growing number of loyal Greeks recruited at night in a basement of the old Palace to form battalions of a National Guard were still under fierce attack, and at the Embassy work was carried on under extreme difficulties. The Ambassador and his staff and guests, among them Alexander and Harold Macmillan, lived on Army rations which had to be collected from dumps under constant fire. For safety every one attached to the Embassy moved in to live in the main building. As bullets frequently struck the outer walls and windows many of the rooms could not be used, and at night most people, including the Ambassador and his wife, slept on camp-beds in the corridors.

By day Rex Leeper insisted on working as usual in his study, but his desk had to be moved into a corner as half the room was under observation from a rebel machine-gun post. Although the Prime Minister was warned of this Leeper entered the room on the first day to find him sitting unconcernedly in full view of the window reading dispatches from London, and Mr Eden had to be summoned to persuade him that the danger was not exaggerated. It was not long, however, before he discovered this for himself. Alexander offered to take him to Observatory Hill—a coign of vantage commanding a panoramic view of the E.L.A.S. positions—and as they emerged into the courtyard of the Embassy there was a volley of rifle-fire from the direction of the Stadium. Several people crossing the road fell dead or wounded, and the Prime Minister was showered with plaster as bullets struck the Embassy wall.

Wherever they went, in fact, the visitors found they were liable to come under fire from one side or the other, the National Guard showing an alarming readiness to blaze away at friend and foe alike. They lost no time in arresting Jock Colville when he ventured ashore from the *Ajax* for a quiet walk through the orange-groves near the port.

By the time Mr Churchill and his party reached Athens the British Embassy staff, which included a number of girl cipher officers, had become almost inured to their life under siege. In spite of the hazards of war, the intense cold, and the meagre rations, morale was high. One man who did much to foster this was Harold Caccia, Leeper's second-in-command. Although still in his thirties Caccia already held the rank of Minister. A former Rugby blue and all-round athlete of note he was completely unperturbed by any alarm, and did invaluable work as chief liaison officer between the Embassy and General Scobie's H.Q.[2] Another who soon became acclimatized to the perilous and uncomfortable life of a diplomat in the besieged capital was Osbert Lancaster, the cartoonist, who had volunteered to join Leeper's staff as Press Attaché.

At their final talk Archbishop Damaskinos assured Churchill once again that he would do his best to form a new administration. The Prime Minister told him that British troops would fight on until E.L.A.S. agreed to a truce and would, he hoped, remain until a Greek National Army could be re-formed. Churchill was well aware, however, that if no truce came and the British Army continued to intervene for any length of time the effect on world opinion might well be disastrous. This was much on his mind and he complained to those around him that the British efforts to clear the E.L.A.S. forces from the capital were not being pressed with sufficient vigour. He was speaking in this strain during dinner on board *Ajax* when Alexander, who had been listening patiently, asked if he might be allowed to clarify the situation.

"Pray proceed!" said the Prime Minister.

"Well, sir, I now have my military boots on," said Alexander firmly, "and if you will listen to me I will explain to you exactly what, in fact, the position is." He then gave a brilliant dissertation, lasting some ten minutes, in which he pointed out with considerable emphasis that he could achieve nothing more in Greece unless the Joint Chiefs of Staff provided him with reinforcements from another theatre. Any weakening of the Fifteenth Army Group in Italy at this juncture might gravely endanger the military situation in the Western Appenines.

The Prime Minister saw the force of his argument. A few hours later a signal went to the British Chiefs of Staff asking them to examine the possibility of moving a Brigade from Palestine to Italy to compensate for any units which might be called upon to aid General Scobie.

* * * * *

[2] Now Sir Harold Caccia, G.C.M.G., K.C.V.O., British Ambassador at Washington, 1956–61; Permanent Under-Secretary of State, Foreign Office, from 1961.

On board H.M.S. *Ajax* the comings and goings of Mr Churchill, Mr Eden, and the various diplomats and senior officers had been watched with fascinated interest by the ship's company.

As the Commander was pacing the quarter-deck one morning he caught sight of Leading-Steward Torrance, the Admiral's valet, who had been assigned to look after the Prime Minister. In his time Torrance had acted as valet to several Commanders-in-Chief in the Mediterranean before retiring from the Service. On the outbreak of war he had been recalled to duty. He was the embodiment of Wodehouse's perfect manservant—grave and dignified, impeccably correct, and speaking with the somewhat pontifical manner of a British diplomat of the old school.

Seeking to discover what impression his temporary service with the Prime Minister had made on this austere and normally uncommunicative pillar of the Admiral's retinue, the Commander said to him, "Torrance, you are a very lucky man."

"Indeed, sir . . . and why?"

"Because, Torrance, you happen to be the valet at the moment to the greatest man alive."

"Really, sir?" Leading-Steward Torrance paused reflectively. "Mr Churchill, I regret to say, sir, is no good to me."

The Commander looked at him in astonishment. "That is a most extraordinary statement," he said.

"What on earth do you mean?"

Torrance stood his ground. "I must repeat, sir. . . . Mr Winston Churchill is not the sort of gentleman I altogether approve of," he insisted doggedly. . . . "A man who breakfasts at nine-thirty in the morning off a wing of chicken and a bottle of white wine is no good to me, sir!"

Mr Eden too came in for criticism on unexpected grounds. As he was preparing to leave the ship one afternoon an elderly Able Seaman was elbowed to one side by a Petty Officer clearing the way for him. "Gangway, there!" shouted the Petty Officer. "Gangway for the Foreign Secretary!"

The Able Seaman gave Mr Eden a penetrating stare as he walked past. "Foreign Secretary my Aunt Fanny!" he was heard to observe in a tone of indignant disbelief. . . . "Bloke's a ruddy Englishman!"

* * * * *

On the morning of December 28 the Prime Minister left Athens for Naples in the Skymaster. He had been greatly cheered by his talks with Damaskinos and was full of hope that the Archbishop would succeed in forming a Government which would bring peace and a measure of stable control to the country. All that now remained was to persuade the King of Greece to agree to the Regency.

While Fraser was running up the Skymaster's engines Lord Moran, who had been rummaging in a suitcase at the rear of the plane, went up to Admiral Mansfield, who was bidding farewell to Mr Eden and thrust a faded woollen jacket into his hand. "This isn't mine," he said; "the steward must have packed it by mistake. Could you take it back to the ship with you or dispose of it somehow? I think the moths have been at it."

As the Prime Minister's party settled down in their seats and the Skymaster gathered speed down the runway sudden misgivings assailed Mr Churchill's physician. He dived for the suitcase again and his fears were confirmed. The case he had been searching was not his at all. He had just given away Harold Macmillan's favourite cardigan!

* * * * *

When Churchill arrived back in London he found a very different atmosphere. His courageous journey on Christmas Eve, and the success of his efforts—already becoming apparent from the dispatches of correspondents in Athens—had dramatically changed the climate of opinion. Even the *Manchester Guardian*, whose bitter criticism had so distressed him, now praised him for seizing the initiative and hailed his decision to fly to Greece as "one of those flashes of courage and imagination which will always cause his countrymen to forgive his occasional errors of judgment."

The Prime Minister and the Foreign Secretary sat up most of the night of their return discussing with King George of Greece the developments of the past few days. Eventually the King assented to recognition of a Regency for a limited period. Within three days General Plastiras, a Republican, became the new Premier at the head of a non-Communist Government. A week later the civil war in Greece was over.

To a meeting of the Cabinet on New Year's Eve Churchill was able to report not only further evidence that Damaskinos was making headway, but better news from the Western Front. The German thrust in the Ardennes had spent its force, and the enemy had sustained losses from which they were never to recover.

When the business of the meeting ended the Prime Minister invited his colleagues to dine with him. The German rocket attacks were still proceeding, and Herbert Morrison asked if it was wise to risk gathering so many of the nation's leaders together in one place for the whole evening. Mr Churchill brushed the suggestion aside. "I have consulted Lord Cherwell," he said reassuringly. "He tells me that the odds against our meeting our Maker are not more than one in 600,000." And with that they adjourned to Downing Street.

36

The Tragedy of Yalta:— Churchill Plays a Lone Hand

ON New Year's Day 1945 the Luftwaffe carried out its last major operation of the war on the Western Front, hurling every available aircraft into a series of low-level raids on the Allied forward airfields. It was a costly gamble which sealed the fate of the German offensive, for from this moment the vastly stronger British and American air arm ranged virtually unopposed, and fighting with great gallantry the American ground forces, who throughout bore the brunt of the Ardennes offensive, gradually drove the enemy back towards the east.

Although the crisis was over when Churchill flew to France on January 3, he found a worried Eisenhower awaiting him. For some days there had been disagreement with Montgomery, who had been pressing for operational control of General Omar Bradley's Army Group. Now the Supreme Commander was involved in impassioned argument with de Gaulle, who violently opposed Eisenhower's plan to pull back Allied troops from Strasbourg, at this moment forming an awkward salient in their line.

Since such a move would have left the population of the city at the mercy of a vengeful German army Eisenhower's initial decision, militarily correct though it was, alarmed the Prime Minister. Realizing the effect on public opinion throughout the world if a defenceless Strasbourg was abandoned to the enemy he added his own strong appeal for the plan to be modified. Eventually Eisenhower agreed that two French divisions should be left to hold the city, and the German attacks on that sector were successfully repulsed.

From Paris Churchill travelled in Eisenhower's train to Hasselt, headquarters of 21 Army Group, had a talk to Montgomery after breakfast on the following morning, and at midday he flew back to London from Brussels.

By now arrangements were well advanced for the forthcoming meeting with Roosevelt and Stalin. A personal message from Stalin which he found on his return to Downing Street was an ominous reminder of the problems awaiting solution. Without any further consultation with the United States or Britain the Russians had formally recognized Bierut and his Lublin Committee as the Provisional Government of Poland—a calculated gesture of independence which made a mockery of the Alliance.

The President condemned the Russian action in no uncertain terms. "I am disturbed and deeply disappointed over your message," wrote Roosevelt to Stalin on December 30:

> I felt you would realize how extremely unfortunate and even serious it would be at this period in the war in its effect on world opinion and enemy morale if your Government should formally recognize one Government of Poland while the majority of the other United Nations, including the United States and Great Britain, continue to recognize and to maintain diplomatic relations with the Polish Government in London. I must tell you with a frankness equal to your own that I see no prospect of this Government's following suit. . . . This is in no sense due to any special ties or feelings for the London [Polish] Government. The fact is that neither the Government nor the people of the United States have as yet seen any evidence either arising from the manner of its creation or from subsequent developments to justify the conclusion that the Lublin Committee as at present constituted represents the people of Poland. . . .[1]

Unabashed, Stalin notified Churchill of the Russian action on January 4, ending his message—as he had done to the President—with warm New Year greetings. "Naturally I and my War Cabinet colleagues are much distressed at the course events are taking," replied the Prime Minister; "the best thing is for us three to meet together and talk all these matters over. . . ."[2]

By now the Polish question was only one of many grave problems awaiting a decision. Churchill had touched on some of them during his visit to Moscow three months earlier, but in the absence of the President the talks then had been mainly exploratory. As yet no policy had been hammered out for the control of a defeated Germany; other European nations had already been overrun by the Soviet armies and their future independence seemed in jeopardy; and although Stalin had given an assurance that Russia would enter the lists against Japan neither Churchill nor Roosevelt had any precise information of the timing or likely extent of Soviet aid in the Far East.

[1] Churchill, Vol. VI, pp. 290–294. [2] *Ibid.*

The venue of the Conference, given the code name of *Argonaut*, had now been decided. Reluctant as ever to leave Russian soil, Stalin had agreed to act as host to the American and British missions at Yalta, on the southern shore of the Crimea. Roosevelt signalled that he would leave America as soon as possible after his inauguration as President for his fourth term, and proceed to the Mediterranean by sea. He suggested that the business of the Conference could be discharged in five or six days, and when the Prime Minister pressed for a preliminary meeting of the British and American staffs at Malta, on the lines of the talks in Cairo before the Teheran Conference, with Eden and the U.S. Foreign Minister, Stettinius, taking part, this at first met with little support.

Roosevelt plainly felt that discussions at Malta might put back the timetable for *Argonaut*, and might offend Stalin. The more he studied the agenda, however, the more Churchill was convinced that some initial problems at least must be disposed of before the main talks began. "I do not see any other way of realizing our hopes about World Organization in five or six days. Even the Almighty took seven," he telegraphed.[3] "The Old Man's overlooked one point," said a member of his secretariat as the message was being typed. ". . . The Lord didn't have the Joint Planners to help him!"

The President replied that he was unable to spare Stettinius for preliminary discussions with Eden before January 31, but he announced to Churchill's surprise and pleasure that Harry Hopkins would fly to England. After that the Joint Chiefs of Staff could hold a series of meetings at Malta, and the whole party would proceed to the Crimea on the night of February 2.

For three days in London Churchill and Hopkins explored the ground for the Conference. And recent rifts in Anglo-American opinion were frankly discussed. To the President—now crossing the Atlantic in the U.S.S. *Quincy*—Hopkins radioed that the talks had proved "very satisfactory." He added that discouraging reports had reached London from the advance party at Yalta, and passed on Churchill's comment—"We could not have found a worse place for a meeting if we had spent ten years on research."[4]

The President had intimated that he intended to bring only a small staff but it soon became evident that the limited accommodation ashore at Yalta would be taxed to the full. The size of the respective missions grew and grew, and although arrangements were made to send some of the junior officers and secretarial staff by sea from England it was obvious that a large air-lift would be necessary. The R.A.F. sent a party ahead to prepare a landing base at Saki, some ninety miles away across the moun-

[3] *Ibid.*, p. 298.

[4] Sherwood, *op. cit.*, p. 839.

tains from Yalta. The Cunard liner *Franconia* was also sailed to Sevastopol, much closer at hand, to provide additional accommodation and act as a communications centre.

Mr Churchill decided to take off from Northolt in the Skymaster at midnight on January 29, in order to arrive at Malta after daybreak. He was attending a Cabinet meeting when Tommy got a call from the Air Ministry warning that snow was on the way and unless they were in the air by 9.30 P.M. they would not be able to get away that night. Luckily Lord Moran, the only member of the Skymaster party then out of London, was at his cottage at Uxbridge, close to Northolt, and, ringing up his wife, who always drove him to the airfield, Tommy gave her a cryptic message which she fortunately interpreted right.

"Before leaving I wrote out a signal for Ismay in Malta giving him our new E.T.A of 4.30 A.M. (Malta time) and telling him that the P.M. would remain in bed in the aircraft on arrival; he did not wish anyone to stay up to meet him.

"As the Skymaster approached the island I got up and put on a monkey-jacket over my pyjamas as I wanted to leave the aircraft on arrival and explain to Air Commodore Whitney Straight, who was in charge of the R.A.F. arrangements there, that Mr Churchill would need transport to the dockyard at eight o'clock. When we stopped on the tarmac and I left the plane I was blinded by floodlighting. As my eyes became accustomed to the glare I saw to my horror that every high-ranking officer and civilian from the Governor downwards was standing to attention in front of me. Our message from Downing Street had not been received. To make matters worse at least three other signals had come in during the night, all giving different times of arrival; the final one had announced that the P.M. would land at 3.30 A.M., but this was Greenwich Mean Time. As a result General Sir Edmond Schreiber, the Governor; John Cunningham, the Commander-in-Chief, Mediterranean; Pug Ismay, and many others had all been waiting on the airfield for over an hour, cursing our lack of consideration. Surrounded by this bunch of nearly explosive V.I.P.'s, I felt I was lucky to regain the Skymaster without being torn limb from limb!"[5]

When Churchill woke he had a high temperature, and Moran made him stay in bed in the aircraft until a specialist had examined him. He was then driven to the harbour and went on board H.M.S. *Orion*. For the rest of the day he remained in his cabin but characteristically he was soon complaining that his medical advisers were making a lot of fuss about nothing, and to show he was feeling perfectly well again he invited Averell Harriman and General Schreiber to dinner.

In spite of stringent security precautions the Maltese soon discovered

[5] C. R. Thompson, Notes.

that the Prime Minister had arrived in the island, and all day dense crowds waited in the streets in the hope of seeing him. They gave a tumultuous welcome to the First Sea Lord, Admiral Sir Andrew Cunningham, who had played such a prominent part in Malta's survival, when he appeared outside the Union Club.

By the following day, when the pre-Yalta talks began, all the Chiefs of Staff had arrived, and Churchill had a long discussion with General Marshall. That evening the Joint Chiefs of Staff dined with Sir John Cunningham at Admiralty House, Valletta. It was a historic and unforgettable occasion, and the setting was worthy of it. As far back as the sixteenth century the old house had been occupied by the Captains of the Galleys when the Knights of St John ruled Malta. And as the guests, who included three Field-Marshals, two Admirals of the Fleet, five Admirals, four Generals, and an Air Marshal, mounted the wide staircase on their way to dinner they saw above them the great marble scrolls bearing the names of every British C.-in-C. in the Mediterranean for one hundred and fifty years, Hood and St Vincent, Nelson and Collingwood among them.

The "Commander-in-Chief's String Orchestra"—a delightful anachronism miraculously preserved from more spacious and peaceful times—went through its traditional repertoire, and even Field-Marshal Brooke, who had arrived "feeling very old and tired" after an exhausting day at the conference table, soon fell under the spell of naval hospitality in the great room where Nelson had dined with his captains. "I felt swept off into the old ages, imagining him here with his romance and his wars," he wrote in his diary that night.[6]

Next day, as more and more Americans arrived in the island, including Stettinius, they were met with the disconcerting news that the advance party at Yalta were at their wits' end to find suitable accommodation for every one. "REGRET NECESSITY FOR 19 FULL COLONELS SLEEPING ONE ROOM," signalled a distracted member of Ismay's staff. By now the air-lift from Malta alone involved some seven hundred people.

In the forenoon of February 2 the *Quincy* entered Grand Harbour. She passed close by *Orion* on the way to her berth in French Creek, and Churchill waved a greeting to the President. As soon as the ship made fast he went on board. Roosevelt had aged greatly. He looked fragile and ill, but he plunged straightway into discussion of the staff talks, which by now had covered much ground. Eisenhower's plans for the Rhine crossing, new measures for the U-boat war, the situation in Italy and Greece, and operations in South-east Asia and the Pacific had all been reviewed.

The Prime Minister stayed to dinner. Then he drove out to Luqa to

[6] Bryant, *op. cit.*, Vol. II, p. 396.

board his plane for the 1400 mile flight to Saki. It was a cold, starlit night. All over the airfield huge throbbing silver shapes of Skymasters and Yorks gleamed in the pale light of the rising moon.

The air-lift began in the shadow of tragedy. On the previous evening York EW 617 had left London carrying a party from the Foreign Office, a number of Army and R.A.F. staff officers, including Captain "Barney" Charlesworth, who had been Brooke's A.D.C. ever since Dunkirk, and additional members of the Conference secretariat. Although scheduled to land at Naples to refuel it did not do so, and when first heard of it was circling the tiny rocky island of Lampedusa, 90 miles to the south-west of Malta.

Apparently under the impression that he had reached his destination, the pilot asked Luqa to switch on landing sights. "They are on already," came the reply. By the time the mistake was realized the York was almost out of fuel, and its captain decided to put the plane down on the sea as close to the shore as possible. He did this with some skill, but an underwater obstruction ripped the bottom out of the fuselage and the aircraft sank almost immediately.

Destroyers escorting the President's ship, which was close at hand, found only six survivors. Captain Charlesworth was one of those who lost their lives.

* * * * *

Molotov, several Russian Generals, and a guard and band were waiting on the snow-covered field at Saki. Half an hour after Churchill's Skymaster landed the President flew in in his new plane, *The Sacred Cow*. This was fitted with an ingenious device—a lift, just large enough to take Roosevelt's wheeled chair, which obviated the need for the usual ramp. With Churchill walking at his side the President drove slowly along the line of troops in a jeep, and then in two separate convoys the American and British parties set out on their long journey across the mountains to the Black Sea.

"Our route, mainly over barren and desolate country, was lined by soldiers, some of them women. Although in the more remote districts they were stationed several hundred yards apart they were always in sight of their neighbours; in the villages the concentration was much thicker. After three hours we stopped at Alushta, a small coastal town some twenty-five miles from Yalta, where Molotov entertained us to a lavish lunch. We then went on to the house which had been set aside for the P.M.

"The Vorontzov Villa, perched on a promontory overlooking the sea, was a luxurious and lavishly furnished house of extraordinary design. From the angle we first approached it it resembled an austere Scottish castle. On the seaward side, however, the architecture was Oriental—a gay conception adorned with cupolas like some Turkish palace. Unlike the Yousupov Palace, where Stalin was staying, and the Livadia Palace, which had been made ready for Roosevelt, it had survived the German occupation relatively undamaged, for Field-Marshal von Mannstein had made his headquarters there. It contained many fine pictures, and Mr Churchill was greatly intrigued by a portrait which hung over the fireplace in the dining-room. 'I know I have seen that before,' he said to me as soon as he caught sight of it. This seemed unlikely, but he soon identified it. The picture was a copy of one still in the possession of the Herbert family at Wilton and we found later that one of the Vorontzovs had married a Herbert in the previous century."[7]

Yalta itself is a somewhat dismal seaside resort sprawling across a beautiful amphitheatre with snow-capped mountains towering behind it. From the British point of view it was far from ideal as a conference centre, for as the port was still heavily mined and littered with sunken ships much time was wasted travelling to and from Sevastopol, the nearest safe anchorage, where the *Franconia* lay handling all the signal traffic.

For anyone below the rank of General living quarters ashore were cramped and primitive, but considering the difficulties which had faced the Russians in making any workable arrangements at all they had achieved miracles. A labour force of 3500 men had transformed many of the buildings wrecked by the Germans; in some cases every stick of furniture had been brought from Moscow. In the winter garden of the Vorontzov Villa stood a lemon-tree in a gaily painted tub. Several of these had been flown from Batum, in the Caucasus, to decorate the residences of the principal delegates, and when the Prime Minister jokingly remarked to Stalin that the President's tree bore more fruit than his a bigger and better tree was produced in a matter of hours. On the day after Churchill's arrival Stalin and Molotov called on him at the Villa, and they had a long discussion on Germany. Afterwards the Prime Minister took his guests into the Map Room. Stalin immediately pointed out that the position of the Russian front line was inaccurately marked. Next morning a Russian Colonel, drenched in scent, reported to Captain Pim. He had been ordered by Stalin to bring the map up to date.

The Conference, which opened on the afternoon of February 5, lasted for a week. To save the President from making a daily journey by road all the plenary meetings were held at the Livadia Palace. Much of the first day was occupied by discussions of plans for Allied control of Germany after her defeat, and it was eventually agreed that one of the zones of occupation should be administered by France. Maisky brought up the question of German reparations and submitted a scheme for dismantling her indus-

[7] C. R. Thompson, Notes.

trial plants. Both matters were referred to a special committee, to be set up in Moscow, for detailed examination.

On the subject of reparations Churchill and Eden immediately recognized the fallacy of imposing a crippling financial burden on a defeated country and at the same time reducing her industrial capacity to such an extent that she would be no longer able to maintain herself economically. They therefore stood out firmly against the Russian contention that a set figure—the Soviet demand was for twenty billion dollars—should be embodied in the final Conference record. In the British view it was entirely unrealistic to decide on the exact amount of reparations due from Germany before discovering precisely what her capacity was for meeting such a commitment.

In the end, however, Stalin, who throughout the Conference played with the greatest skill on Roosevelt's obvious determination to conciliate the Russians whenever a deadlock threatened, gained his point. And the sum of twenty billion dollars was written into the records "as a basis for discussion"—a phrase soon to be recognized as synonymous in the Soviet vocabulary for acceptance in principle.

At meeting after meeting Russian diplomacy followed a set pattern. Extravagant demands would be presented. Concessions would then be offered—all too frequently at points where a partial retreat involved no real loss of ground—and the bargaining would then begin anew with the American delegation convinced that each Russian surrender betokened a change of heart. When discussions switched to ways and means of safeguarding world peace Molotov eventually accepted the American plan for a United Nations organization in which the Big Four would have the right of veto, and although he had begun by demanding voting rights for all sixteen States of the Soviet Union this was ultimately reduced to a request that two only should be admitted as founder members of the organization.

Since it had been already agreed that Britain and her four Dominions should have individual votes Churchill was in no position to object. And Roosevelt, who had declared not long before that if the Russians demanded any additional votes he would insist on forty-eight votes for the United States, appears to have decided early on in the Conference that the need to humour Stalin now outweighed the importance of challenging him on this particular ground.

From the British point of view the crux of the Conference came with the consideration of Poland and her future. The Yalta Agreement has since been branded as a betrayal of the Polish nation, but the majority of critics have conveniently ignored the peculiarly difficult situation facing the British delegation.

Determined to obtain a revision of the Polish boundary favourable to

Russia, and determined, too, to retain the servile Lublin Committee as his instrument of government, Stalin had no scruples about giving undertakings which he had no intention of honouring. Roosevelt, a sick man, was only too anxious to take Stalin's assurances at their face value, and he plainly felt that Churchill's intransigence on certain points was unnecessarily provocative. The President was far more concerned in reaching a satisfactory agreement with Stalin over Soviet intervention against Japan; he was not prepared to ruffle the feelings of the Russian leader by opposing him to the limit on any matter connected with Poland.

Churchill was therefore left to play a lone hand. He played it with considerable resolution, but at this stage in the war, with Great Britain's resources in manpower and money drained almost to vanishing-point, he was in no position to jeopardize the American alliance by a flat refusal to remain at the Conference table—which was the only course left to him if all his eloquent attempts at persuasion failed.

Roosevelt did, in fact, speak out strongly against the Lublin Committee, and between sessions he wrote a note to Stalin urging him to summon two representatives of that Committee and two from the London Government of Mikolajczyk or from independent circles inside Poland to attend the Conference and reach a definite agreement there and then on the constitution of a provisional Polish Government. But Stalin said hastily that it would be impossible to arrange this in the time available, and countered with a vague undertaking to hold free elections as soon as possible. He proposed that Molotov, Harriman, and Clark Kerr should discuss the constitution of an enlarged Polish Government and report back.

Soon Molotov was harping once again on the immense popularity of Bierut and his associates among the Polish people. He now promised free elections in Poland within a month, but when Churchill pressed for an assurance that Mikolajczky would be allowed to return to his country and organize his party in preparation for these elections Stalin was ominously evasive. On every major point raised for discussion he played on Roosevelt's sympathies. The subject of reparations produced an emotional harangue about Russian sufferings; the boundary question—reviewed, astonishingly enough, without recourse to maps at a vital stage—was left in a dangerously vague state after an impassioned plea by Stalin that he should not be sent back to tell his people that he had secured for them less than Curzon and Clemenceau had conceded in 1918; and he laid such a catalogue of evildoing at the door of the Polish Government in London that Roosevelt cut short Churchill's attempt to present the other side of the picture. "Poland has been a source of trouble for over five hundred years," observed the President judicially.

When the Conference ended, after Roosevelt and Stalin had held a private discussion about Russian intervention in the Far East and Stalin had driven a series of shrewd bargains as the price for his support, all three Heads of State approved a joint declaration the preamble of which stressed their desire to see the establishment of a "strong, free, independent, and democratic Poland."

The agreement called for the reorganization of "the present Provisional Government"—in retrospect a regrettable and surprising concession by Britain and America, who had not hitherto acknowledged any such formal status for the Lublin Committee. It next pledged the reorganized Government to hold "free and unfettered elections as soon as possible," at the conclusion of which Britain and the United States would open diplomatic relations with the newly elected Government.

On the boundary question the three signatories declared that the eastern frontier of Poland should follow the Curzon Line, "with digressions from it in some regions of five to eight kilometres in favour of Poland." They recognized that Poland must receive substantial accessions of territory in the north and west . . . and agreed that the final delimitation of the western frontier should thereafter await the Peace Conference.

This partition of Poland was to bring bitter criticism on Churchill's head. At the time it came under review, however, the majority of delegates undoubtedly considered that in all the circumstances the settlement secured for the Polish people was the best that they could hope for if future Russo-Polish relations were not to be exacerbated from the outset. They were convinced, too, that Russian agreement to the proposal for a meeting at San Francisco in the near future to establish an organization of United Nations which would safeguard the peace of the world was firm evidence of the Soviet desire to co-operate with the West.

Robert Sherwood has described the mood of the United States delegates at the conclusion of the Conference as one of "supreme exultation." Harry Hopkins said to him, "We really believed in our hearts that this was the dawn of the new day we had all been praying for and talking about for so many years. We were absolutely certain that we had won the first great victory of the peace—and by 'we' I mean all of us, the whole civilized human race. The Russians had proved that they could be reasonable and far-seeing, and there wasn't any doubt in the minds of the President or any of us that we could live with them and get along with them peacefully for as far into the future as any of us could imagine."[8]

To Congress Roosevelt declared, "I am sure that under the agreement reached at Yalta there will be a more stable political Europe than ever before."

Precisely sixteen days later Stalin, who at Yalta had signed a Declara-

[8] Sherwood, *op. cit.*, pp. 858–859.

tion on Liberated Europe calling for free elections and the establishment of democratic Governments in all countries occupied by Allied armies, staged a *coup d'état* in Roumania, and a Communist Government took office.

In less than a month it was tragically apparent to the world that the Russians intended to violate the spirit and the word of every undertaking they had given about Poland.

37

Roosevelt: The Last Farewell

THROUGHOUT the Conference Roosevelt had looked increasingly tired and ill. Churchill was therefore astonished when the President told him that instead of returning straight home at the end of the talks he intended to carry out an elaborate programme of discussions with Middle East rulers; he had invited Ibn Saud, Haile Selassie, and Farouk to meet him at a rendezvous in Egypt.

Churchill himself had made no firm plans, but for some days he had been contemplating a brief visit to Athens. Archbishop Damaskinos had sent him a warm invitation to return to the Greek capital and see the progress which had been made since the Civil War ended. He now decided that after leaving Greece he would fly to Alexandria, say farewell to Roosevelt there, and then himself meet Ibn Saud, for long a staunch ally of Britain.

Tommy was glad to be on the move again. While the Conference was in session there had been little for him to do, and the possibilities of sight-seeing in Yalta and the surrounding district were soon exhausted. With Sarah Churchill he had made one interesting expedition—to Chekhov's former home, which was now a "State-maintained Cultural Institution." The resident curator was a sister of the great Russian writer. She seemed flustered and nervous in the presence of the interpreter, so they talked to her in French, which he could not understand. Even so she would only speak freely when she was certain that the watchdog was out of earshot.

On their way to the house—a sad little brick-built châlet set in a wild, overgrown garden filled with cypress-trees—they passed many villas in ruins. The interpreter announced with a great show of indignation that they had been wantonly destroyed by the Germans, but Tommy could not resist pointing out that fully grown trees were flourishing in the rubble. Even allowing for the fertility of his sub-tropical region these could hardly have reached their ripe old age in a few weeks. Most of the damage had, in fact, been caused during the Russian Revolution.

Another expedition, this time initiated by Mr Churchill, had an embarrassing start.

"Soon after we were installed in the *Franconia* Molotov came on board to say good-bye. When he left the P.M. said he would like to see the battlefield of Balaclava nearby. I explained this to the interpreter, and off we went to the little fishing village after which the battle is named. We were shown where German submarines had been moored, but no reference was made to the battle of 90 years before, and it turned out that none of the Russians present had ever heard of it. The situation was saved by Brigadier Peake, of the War Office Intelligence Staff, who had been brought along by Brooke. As he had made a study of the Crimean War and knew the lie of the land by heart we soon found the actual scene, but when he started to explain the events leading up to Cardigan's famous Charge with the Light Brigade the Russian Flag Officer commanding the Black Sea Fleet, who had come with us, kept butting in with entirely irrelevant remarks under the impression that we were discussing recent German troop movements."[1]

Next day they drove to Saki and took off for Greece. It was a lovely sunny afternoon, and soon after leaving the Turkish coast the Prime Minister's plane passed low over Skyros. The grave of Rupert Brooke in a little hill-top clearing in the centre of the island could be plainly seen from the air.

When they landed in Athens the Ambassador was waiting for them. "What have you let me in for . . . a speech?" asked Churchill. "And what have you and Harold been up to at Varkiza? I trust you did not do anything merely to ease my position in the House."[2]

The welcome which the Prime Minister received from the people of Athens was breathtaking to those who had accompanied him on his previous visit. Only six weeks earlier the Civil War had been raging. Now an almost incredible change had come over the city. Long before the moment when Churchill drove with Damaskinos into Constitution Square, with picturesquely garbed Evzone soldiers standing on the running-boards of the open car, every road leading to it was packed with happy, cheering

[1] C. R. Thompson, Notes.

[2] A few days before a hitch had occurred in the negotiations between the new Greek Government and E.L.A.S. to reach a settlement following the Armistice. At the invitation of both sides the British Ambassador and Mr Macmillan had gone to Varkiza, just outside Athens, to act as mediators. After discussions lasting all night they had worked out a solution which satisfied both parties.

crowds. While they waited for him to appear on the balcony of the old Palace some one in the Square called out for General Scobie, and the whole crowd, applauding, broke into a chant of "Scobie! Scobie! Scobie!"—an extraordinary tribute to a man who had so recently been leading British troops against Greeks.

After the Regent had introduced him Churchill spoke, for ten minutes only. It was a brilliant oration, phrased so simply and poetically that although each passage was translated over the microphone many of his listeners who did not know a word of English understood the sense of his remarks before the interpretation came, and clapped and cheered him. He ended:

"Let no one fail to rise to the occasion of this great moment and of these splendid days. Let the Greek nation stand first in every heart. Let it stand first in every man and woman. Let the future of Greece shine brightly in their eyes. From the bottom of my heart I wish you prosperity. From the bottom of my heart I hope that Greece will take her proper place in the circle of victorious nations—of nations who have suffered terribly in the war. Let right prevail. Let party hatreds die. Let there be unity. Let there be resolute comradeship. Greece for ever! Greece for all!"[3]

The ovation which greeted this seemed as if it would never cease, and the Prime Minister, who said afterwards that it was the greatest and most enthusiastic audience he had ever addressed, was in tears as he left the balcony. When they got back to the British Embassy Damaskinos presented the members of the new Government. Afterwards Churchill dined with the Leepers and drove back to the aircraft to sleep before an early take-off for Egypt.

They reached Aboukir soon after breakfast, and Churchill went on board the cruiser *Aurora*, where he intended to stay that night. Roosevelt arrived from Ismailia in the *Quincy* much sooner than anyone expected, and the Prime Minister went on board with Randolph and Sarah to lunch. He wrote afterwards, "The President seemed placid and frail. I felt that he had a slender contact with life. I was not to see him again. We paid affectionate farewells."[4]

Soon after lunch the *Quincy* sailed, and as there was now little point in remaining at Alexandria Churchill decided to fly to Cairo, where he would be more closely in touch with London through the British Embassy. Before he left H.M.S. *Aurora* he spoke to the ship's company about the war and the tasks which still lay ahead.

In the light of subsequent events their reaction was prophetically significant. To their officers who knew them well it was obvious that the sailors

[3] Churchill, Vol. VI, pp. 347–348.
[4] *Ibid.*

were bored. They showed little or no enthusiasm. Their attitude seemed to be—"Well, he did his stuff all right, but the war's virtually over now, and it's no use him ramming speeches like this down our throats . . . we're just not interested."

In Cairo the Prime Minister had talks with the Emperor of Ethiopia, Haile Selassie; with King Farouk; with President Shukri of Syria, whose relations with the French were becoming tense; and with Moyne and Killearn. The British Ambassador had long been anxious that Churchill should meet a certain leading Egyptian politician, and the latter was asked to lunch. Nervous and plainly anxious to make an impression, he embarked at tedious length on an exposition of his life's principles which involved frequent reference to "ma conscience." Eventually Mr Churchill, by now extremely bored, felt that some comment was expected of him, and, turning to the guest of honour, he remarked quizzically, "Et moi, Excellence . . . quand à moi, j'ai toujours préféré traiter ma conscience en bonne camarade."

The meeting with Ibn Saud took place at the Hôtel du Lac, in the Fayoum Oasis. A cruiser had been sent for him, which greatly impressed him as the Americans had only provided a destroyer, and he was even further impressed when a gyro compass repeater was rigged up in his tent on the quarter-deck in order that, whichever way the ship was heading, he would always know the direction of Mecca.

Transporting the Royal party in fitting style presented some intriguing problems for the ship's officers. His Majesty Abdul Aziz Ibn Rahman Al Faisal Al Saud, ruler of Saudi Arabia, was accompanied by three Royal Princes—a brother and two sons—and forty-four of his subjects. His entourage was headed by the Minister of Finance, the Deputy Minister for Foreign Affairs, and the Saudi-Arabian Minister to Great Britain. Then came the King's Physician, the Royal Astrologer, the Imam who led the Palace prayers, the Commander of the King's Guard, Ibn Saud's personal Radio Officer, and the Royal Monitor of English Broadcasts. There were leaders of various tribes, the Royal Food Taster, the Royal Purse Bearer, the Chief Server of the Ceremonial Coffee, and a Second Server of the Coffee. Completing the party were ten guards, armed with sabres and daggers and chosen from the principal tribes, three valets, and "nine miscellaneous slaves, cooks, porters, and scullions."

They brought with them a flock of sheep, and to the mortification of the Commander these were killed at regular intervals on his normally spotless deck. The survivors from the flock caused even more consternation when they were driven to the hotel at Fayoum. Soon after Ibn Saud was installed in his suite there clouds of smoke began pouring from a near-by bedroom. Rushing upstairs a liaison officer discovered that some of the

King's Bodyguard had built a fire on the bedroom floor and were busy roasting a sheep they had just killed.

"One thing which worried us was the question of presents for our guests. We already knew that the King was bringing rich and elaborate gifts for every one in the Prime Minister's party, so Mr Churchill asked me to go to the Mousky in Cairo and buy whatever seemed suitable. It could be nothing more than a token—the real present for Ibn Saud from the British Government was to be a bullet-proof Rolls Royce which the P.M. had boldly decided upon, hoping that the Treasury would foot the bill. Perfume seemed the only acceptable token gift we could manage with our depleted funds, and I spent £100 on a handsome cabinet containing a collection of the most powerful essences I could lay hands on.

"The lunch was a great success once the P.M. had broached the awkward difference between British and Arabian social custom. Since his religion forbade Ibn Saud to drink and smoke, and the Prime Minister's invariable habit was to do both, Mr Churchill was a little apprehensive, but the King readily agreed that every one should follow his own conscience. There was a tense moment when the P.M. was given some holy water from Mecca to drink, but he managed to give the impression that he really enjoyed it!"[5]

The gifts brought by Ibn Saud for the majority of the British party were of two kinds. Some people received gold wrist-watches. Others, Tommy among them, were presented with golden daggers. Sarah Churchill was given an enormous trunk filled with silks, Arab robes, jars of rare perfumes, and diamonds and pearls. Sad to relate, all these priceless presents had to be surrendered to the British Treasury to pay for Ibn Saud's Rolls Royce.

A few hours later this Arabian Nights interlude was over and Churchill was flying across the Mediterranean on his way home. England lay shrouded in fog, and Mrs Churchill had an anxious wait in the Station Hotel at Reading before word reached her that the Skymaster had landed safely at Lyneham.

[5] C. R. Thompson, Notes.

38

A Challenge Defeated

WHEN the Debate on the Yalta Agreement opened in the Commons it was soon evident that opinion differed sharply on the subject of Poland. Reminding the House that Stalin had given "most solemn" undertakings to safeguard Polish independence, Mr Churchill emphasized that no satisfactory international negotiations could be pursued if Russian motives were to be mistrusted from the outset. He called on Parliament to approve the Allied declaration of policy, but an Amendment was moved by Mr Maurice Petherick, Conservative Member for the Penryn and Falmouth Division of Cornwall.

"Remembering that Great Britain took up arms in a war of which the immediate cause was the defence of Poland against German aggression, and in which the overriding motive was the prevention of the domination by a stronger nation of its weaker neighbours," he regretted the decision to transfer "to another Power the territory of an ally contrary to treaty and to Article 2 of the Atlantic Charter." His Amendment also deplored "the failure to ensure to those nations which have been liberated from German oppression the full right to choose their own government free from the influence of any other Power."

In his reluctant decision to challenge the Government Petherick had the support of a number of influential back-benchers, and a series of meetings had been held in his London flat to concert the attack. All the members of this group were deeply distressed at what they considered an unjustifiable betrayal of specific British undertakings given to Poland. They were, too, hotly opposed to any form of negotiation with the Lublin Committee.

Before the Amendment was moved there were outstandingly able speeches on the first day of the Debate from Lord Dunglass and Captain J. H. F. McEwen, who, significantly, was Chairman of the Conservative Members Committee in the House. Both were strongly critical of the Yalta concessions.[1]

When his turn came to speak on the second day Petherick claimed that the partition of Poland had been approved in defiance of British treaty obligations and was, in addition, directly in conflict with the ideals expressed in the Atlantic Charter. He pointed out that Poland would lose nearly half her territory, a third of her population, and a very great part of her natural wealth. This could not possibly be made good by issuing a post-dated cheque for slices of Germany. And he could not agree that British assent to such a proposal had been in any way necessary. In his view delegates to international conferences must be prepared to say No—in recent times both Philip Snowden and Lord Swinton had rightly refused to accept damaging compromises—and it was vitally important to respect the sanctity of treaties. If we were not prepared to return to this principle there would be no peace in Europe for a hundred years.

Commander Sir Archibald Southby (Epsom), who seconded the motion, said that our treatment of Poland was the touchstone by which our post-war relationships would be measured. He claimed that in addition to Poland there was widespread anxiety about our possible attitude towards Syria and the Lebanon, and he quoted the disillusioned comment of a young officer of his acquaintance—"Of course it is perfectly obvious that we have fought the war in vain; every principle for which we started the war has been sacrificed."

Several speakers who followed, including Major E. G. R. Lloyd (Renfrew East), Lord Willoughby de Eresby (Rutland and Stamford), and Mr H. V. A. Raikes (Essex, South-east) made telling points in support, but a sense of realism seemed lacking in much of the criticism directed at the Government. Two of the most effective speakers against the Amendment, Captain Peter Thorneycroft (Stafford) and Mr W. J. Brown, the Independent Member for Rugby, shrewdly exposed this weakness. "In statesmanship and politics what counts is not the art of getting what is best, but the art of getting what is possible," Thorneycroft reminded the critics. And Brown, who pointed out that the whole House would have been ringing with complaints if an agreement had not been reached at Yalta, claimed that the Prime Minister had secured more than anyone could reasonably have expected, "*having regard to the historical, political, and military realities of the situation.*" Mr Harold Nicolson (Leicester, West) was

[1] Dunglass, Conservative M.P. for Lanark, had been Parliamentary Private Secretary to Chamberlain when Prime Minister. As Lord Home he was destined later to become Foreign Secretary. Captain (now Sir John) McEwen was Conservative M.P. for Berwick and Haddington.

equally emphatic. He considered it out of the question to restore the exact geographical and political position occupied by Poland in 1938, and strongly defended the adoption of the Curzon Line. It was amazing that so much had been achieved at Yalta; "I do not see what else could have been done," he said.

The Foreign Secretary, who denied that Great Britain had guaranteed the pre-war frontier of Poland in any treaty, declared that to have left the situation unresolved, as some of the Opposition speakers had advocated, would have been to adopt a policy of despair. "There is no such thing as a perfect solution of this problem, but surely it is a step forward that the three Great Powers have agreed on a method of handling it," he said.

When the House divided the Government had a majority of 371. Twenty-five Members voted for the Amendment and eleven members of the Government abstained. At the conclusion of the Debate on the following day the original motion was put to the House, and this time the Government vote was 413 to nil. Once again Mr Churchill's authority and leadership had received emphatic endorsement.[2]

The Prime Minister himself was firmly convinced that the British delegation had done all that was possible for Poland in the climate of opinion prevailing at Yalta. At the same time he realized only too well that everything depended on the spirit in which Russia interpreted the resolutions put forward at the Conference.

The Debate had not even ended when Stalin showed his hand. In defiance of his pledge to restore the sovereign independence of the countries freed from German occupation he struck at Roumania. Following the hideously familiar technique of Hitler's pre-war diplomacy Vishinsky demanded an interview with King Michael and ordered him to dismiss his Government. Then, with the backing of Soviet tanks, a puppet administration headed by the Communist leader, Groza, was promptly installed in its place.

* * * * *

The Allied armies had now reached the Rhine on a broad front and were preparing to cross the river. On the day following the Yalta Debate Churchill visited Eisenhower's headquarters. During lunch there the conversation turned to the swiftly changing pattern of warfare. The Prime Minister predicted that rocket weapons would supplant piloted aircraft and that Britain would then become "one vast bazooka aimed at the aggressors who threaten Europe." "There may come a day," he continued prophetically, "when we shall walk into a Cabinet room, break a glass over a

[2] The first day of the Debate and the speeches on the Amendment are covered by Hansard 1944–45, Vol. 408, columns 1267–1346 and 1416–1519.

switch, dial to the nation to be bombed, and press a button to declare war."[3]

When he arrived at Montgomery's headquarters in Holland, just west of the Meuse, Churchill raised a matter which had been much in his mind in recent weeks. He had been anxious to bring in Alexander as Deputy Supreme Commander in place of Tedder, feeling that Alexander's experience would enable him to take some of the burden from Eisenhower's shoulders in directing the fighting which lay ahead east of the Rhine. Montgomery, however, had already made his views known to Eisenhower. He did not want Alexander placed over him, and had said so in no uncertain terms. When he learnt this Churchill was far from pleased, but since Eisenhower himself seemed opposed to a change the suggestion was dropped.

Even the Prime Minister, who was invariably dissatisfied with people who would not stand up to him in argument, found General Montgomery's uncompromising independence a little disconcerting at times. He was oddly inflexible on quite trivial matters, and during this visit he flatly refused to have Jock Colville accommodated in his camp, although Colville, a Flight Lieutenant in uniform, was the Prime Minister's Private Secretary and was accompanying him in that capacity. Colville was therefore banished to the H.Q. Mess camp at least a mile away. This arrangement was thoroughly inconvenient from Churchill's point of view, but by now he had become resigned to the General's autocratic behaviour and he accepted the position with surprisingly good grace.

By the middle of March units of Patton's Third Army dislodged the Germans from their last toehold west of the Rhine, and the scene was now set for the crossing of the great river. The Prime Minister was determined to be present on this historic occasion, and although de Guingand, Montgomery's Chief of Staff, ventured with some temerity to suggest a number of reasons why Mr Churchill should not descend on the British headquarters at such a critical time this seemed to make him all the more determined. When Montgomery realized he was in earnest he sent him a cordial invitation, and, accompanied by Brooke, Colville, and Tommy, the Prime Minister drove out to Northolt on the afternoon of March 25.

The Skymaster could not put down on the landing strip near Montgomery's H.Q. at Venlo, and the flight was made in a Dakota piloted by Squadron Leader S. R. Hinks, with Flight Lieutenant H. S. Hobday, who had gained a D.F.C. in the Dam Busting raid, as navigator.[4] When Hobday explained the flight plan, pointing out that they would have to keep to a safety corridor through France as the Allied anti-aircraft gunners were

[3] Omar Bradley, *A Soldier's Story*, p. 508.

[4] Squadron Leader Hinks became a civilian pilot for El Al, the Israeli airline, after the war. He was captain of the Constellation Aircraft shot down by Bulgarian fighters with the loss of all on board on July 27, 1955.

apt to be 'trigger happy,' Churchill pointed to a spot just off their estimated course. "You'd better avoid that," he said. "My daughter Mary is stationed there. It would be unfortunate if she shot us up."

Montgomery's caravans were parked in a small forest clearing. After an early dinner the Prime Minister went to the map-room, and the plan for the assault was explained to him. Eighty thousand men were to be hurled across the river at ten points between Reinsberg and Rees; in the early hours of the following day, just as it began to grow light, two airborne divisions were to be dropped in the area around Wesel.

That night two American and two British divisions made the initial crossing in the face of surprisingly light opposition. Among the units taking part were three troops of C.D.L. tanks, in action at last after their weary years of training on the Cumberland fells, where Churchill had seen them in the winter of 1942.[5] Their powerful flood-lamps were used to light the passage of the 15th Scottish Division across the river.

The inventor's claim that his oscillating device made the tanks a difficult target was certainly borne out, for during a stay of three hours on the river-bank not one was hit; the crews could hear the swish of machine-gun fire sailing harmlessly overhead. When the enemy began floating saboteurs and explosive motor-boats controlled by radar against the crossing areas the C.D.L. tanks were sent upstream to illuminate the river from dusk to dawn near Wesel.

At first light Mr Churchill, watching from an observation post on high ground overlooking the Rhine at Ginsbeck, heard the roar of aircraft approaching from the west. Overhead passed a veritable air armada—2898 aircraft and gliders, escorted by nearly 900 fighters. Forming a defensive screen to the eastward, and giving cover over the dropping area, were a further two thousand fighter aircraft. There was so much haze and smoke from the German barrage that little could be seen of the actual drop, but soon the planes began to return, some of them in flames. The operation had, however, been a spectacular success and casualties were relatively light.

From Ginsbeck the Prime Minister was taken to another observation post at Marienbaum. "Get rid of the whole party until well after tea—and make certain no one is killed," was Montgomery's parting injunction to Noel Chavasse, one of his A.D.C.'s Chavasse found this was easier said than done, for as soon as lunch was over Mr Churchill announced that he himself wished to cross the Rhine. Chavasse hurriedly consulted Tommy, who advised him to have a word with the C.I.G.S. This did the trick, and the Prime Minister was persuaded instead to visit Schloss Moylan, the headquarters of General Whistler's 3rd Division.

[5] See pp 218–221.

He returned to Montgomery's camp in great good humour, and during dinner that night he gave a series of dramatic recitations from Maeterlinck's *Life of the Bee*. Afterwards he sat in the map-room listening fascinated as Montgomery's personal observers—young officers sent to every sector of the front to gather information and impressions for the Commander-in-Chief—rendered their graphic reports of the battle.

After attending a church service in the headquarters camp on the following morning the Prime Minister met General Eisenhower and went with him to a boathouse on the bank of the Rhine at Buderich. Eisenhower had no intention of allowing him to cross the river, but as soon as the Supreme Commander left Churchill pointed to a near-by landing-craft and suggested that there would be no harm in paying a brief visit to the far side. Surprisingly enough, Montgomery agreed.

Once the symbolic gesture had been made and they had set foot in a featureless meadow running down to the eastern bank no one could think what to do next. There was nothing to see, and no one in authority to talk to, for the main tide of fighting men and all the impedimenta of war had already swept far ahead of the river border. But for the sound of the guns this might have been any peaceful field in the heart of England. After a quarter of an hour they embarked again and went back across the Rhine to inspect a damaged bridge at Wesel. There, to Churchill's apparent gratification, they came under desultory shell-fire.

"When the American General Simpson, whose sector we were in, insisted that he must leave immediately the P.M. looked so bitterly disappointed that I couldn't help laughing. It seemed so incongruous to see him clutching hold of the bridge and almost defying Simpson to spoil his afternoon by taking him away to some dull place out of range of the German guns.

"Before we returned to England we made a second crossing of the Rhine, General Dempsey taking us in his jeep over a pontoon bridge which had just been completed at Xanten. On the far side we saw a large number of very woebegone and dishevelled German prisoners who had been herded into a barbed-wire enclosure. Some of them recognized the P.M., and they gaped at him in absolute astonishment. Mr Churchill spoke to many men of the Highland Division. They were all downcast at losing their very popular commander, Major-General Rennie, during the crossing, but the P.M.'s unexpected arrival seemed to cheer them up.

"Eventually we went back across the Rhine in one of General Hobart's tracked amphibious craft, and then began one of the most hair-raising drives I can remember. Keen to get rid of us by this time Monty was determined we should reach the airfield at Venlo before dark. In the leading car he set a furious pace, and as the sun went down we went faster and faster, the convoy often reaching 80 m.p.h. Even so it was almost dark when the Dakota took off."[6]

* * * * *

It was Mr Churchill's last visit to the battlefield—the last journey he and Tommy were to make together before the war with Germany was over. In Downing Street the hectic weeks which followed presented a strangely conflicting pattern. Every day now brought news of some fresh Allied success, some significant sign that the Third Reich was in its death throes.

Mannheim and Frankfurt fell, the Russians captured Danzig, the French entered Karlsruhe. On the day following the Prime Minister's return from the Rhine the last German rocket fired against England fell at Orpington. Within a few hours London's air-raid sirens wailed for the final time. The scent of victory was in the air—victory over Nazi Germany, her once-arrogant armies, her bomber fleets which had crushed peaceful cities to rubble, her U-boat packs which had all but cut the Atlantic lifeline.

For most people it was a time to rejoice. But the Prime Minister and the War Cabinet saw a different picture. For them each day brought grave news as well as good news . . . news of Allied dissension, news of Russian treachery which threatened the very fabric of future civilization.

Discord over a decision by Eisenhower to ignore Berlin and throw the main weight of the Allied offensive into a thrust by Bradley's troops through Central Germany was aggravated when the Supreme Commander revealed his intention to Stalin before his plan had been considered by the Combined Chiefs of Staff. Churchill was quick to point out that if the Soviet armies were to secure Berlin as well as Vienna it would appear to the world that the decisive victory had been gained by Russia.

This sharp controversy followed hard on the heels of a series of insulting messages from Moscow accusing Britain and America of attempting to negotiate a separate peace with the German armies in Italy. The mood of the Russians was now openly hostile, and one by one Stalin's glib promises at Yalta were repudiated with a cynicism which showed that plans for the subjection of occupied territory had long been cut and dried.

Already Poland was firmly in the Soviet grip. Molotov refused point-blank to allow Allied observers to enter Polish territory; not a single independent newcomer was brought into Bierut's puppet Government; and as the Russians declined to co-operate in any of the matters which the Allied subcommittee had been appointed to consider the Moscow talks achieved nothing. Rubbing salt into the wound, the Soviet Government formally applied for Poland to be represented at the inaugural United Nations Conference at San Francisco by the very Lublin Committee whose authority

[6] C. R. Thompson, Notes.

had been rejected by the United States and Britain at Yalta. And when this was refused word came that Molotov would not attend the Conference.

To the President Churchill wrote—"We are in the presence of a great failure and an utter breakdown of what was settled at Yalta, but . . . we British have not the necessary strength to carry the matter further . . . the limits of our capacity to act have been reached."[7] Britain and the United States sent strongly worded messages to Stalin protesting at the violation of the spirit of the Crimean agreement. They received an evasive reply.

At this critical time Roosevelt's strength was failing fast. He was, in fact, no longer well enough to direct the business of government. One of the last messages which Churchill received from him concerned the arrival in England at the end of March of Bernard Baruch, who crossed the Atlantic at the President's invitation to discuss the Polish question and other matters with the Prime Minister.

Baruch was an old and valued friend. It had been at his instigation that Churchill received the Distinguished Service Medal from the American Government at the end of the First World War, for Baruch had been Chairman of the American War Industries Board at the time when Churchill was Minister of Munitions. He was a welcome visitor to Chequers, where Smuts and Fraser, the New Zealand Premier, were also spending the week-end, and they were joined by another close friend of the President, Judge Rosenman. An economist and an astute financier, Bernard Baruch had made and lost more than one fortune. At Chequers he told Tommy of a fortune he *almost* lost.

"He had received information that an unknown company in the South was about to strike oil. He therefore bought up all the shares he could on margins. But the shares went down and down until he had only a cover of a few thousand dollars left. Baruch became desperate. Finally he decided to sell next morning; he would cut his losses and start afresh. Hardly had he made up his mind when he got a message from his mother. Pointing out that it was the eve of Yom Kippur she said she hoped he would be loyal to his faith.

"This presented him with a nice problem, for the Jewish faith forbade the transaction of any business before sundown at such a time. After wrestling with his conscience he decided to respect his mother's wishes and he spent a miserable day in Central Park convinced that he was now ruined.

"At sunset he hurried from the Park and bought an evening paper. To his astonishment and relief he read that the oil 'strike' by the company had been confirmed. The price of the shares had soared, and instead of facing ruin he found himself a fabulously rich man.

"He was certainly a generous man. During the time he spent at

[7] Churchill, Vol. V, p. 374.

Chequers he loved roaming about the estate and talking to the men of the Coldstream Guards and the Metropolitan Police who shared the security duties. Just before he left he told me he would like to give me a sum of money to pay for a good party for the Guard. Asking if I thought it would be enough, he then handed me £125 in five-pound notes!"[8]

By the time Baruch arrived back in America the President had left for Georgia, where he intended to rest for a few days before travelling to San Francisco to open the United Nations Conference. It was there, at Warm Springs, on the afternoon of Thursday, April 12, 1945, that he died of a cerebral hæmorrhage. The news reached the Prime Minister's Map Room at midnight, and Churchill, who was dining out that evening, was told as soon as he returned. He was stunned. "I am weakened in every way by his loss," he remarked to Richard Pim.

Mrs Churchill was travelling that day from Leningrad to Moscow. She had flown to Russia at the invitation of the Soviet Government to inspect Russian hopitals and see how the equipment supplied by her Aid to Russia Fund was being used. Her train, bound for Stalingrad, was not scheduled to stop for more than a minute or two in the capital, but as it drew in a great crowd was waiting silently, and she saw Molotov and his wife at the front of the platform. "We come with bad news . . ." Molotov said when he boarded the train; "President Roosevelt is dead." At Mrs Churchill's suggestion they sat silent for two minutes in the carriage, and then she resumed her long journey south.

In England Parliament adjourned. When it met on April 17 the Prime Minister paid a moving tribute to Roosevelt's leadership. He ranged back over his long and momentous association with the President, mentioning that their exchange of correspondence since the start of the war had comprised over 1700 messages; they had had nine meetings, which had brought one hundred and twenty days of close personal contact. He ended—"For us it remains only to say that in Franklin Roosevelt there died the greatest American friend we have ever known, and the greatest champion of freedom who has ever brought help and comfort from the New World to the Old."

The Prime Minister's first instinct was to fly to America to attend the funeral, and he told Tommy to alert the crew of the Skymaster. But in Europe events were moving with headlong speed, and although the new President added his own pressing invitation, suggesting that Mr Churchill should stay on in Washington for talks after the funeral, the Prime Minister was forced to abandon the idea. The war was reaching its grand climacteric. More than ever now the Western world looked for guidance to Downing Street.

[8] C. R. Thompson, Notes.

39

Victory—and the End of the Coalition

IN THE first three weeks of April over a million Germans were taken prisoner and Berlin was surrounded by the Russians. In Italy a general offensive carried Alexander's armies across the Po and the Italian Partisans rose against the German forces as they withdrew northward. Panic-stricken, the bedraggled remnants of Mussolini's Fascist Government fled from Lake Garda, and the Duce himself was captured by the Partisans as he tried to escape into Switzerland in a German convoy.

He and his mistress, Clara Petacci, were driven to Mezzegra, on the shore of Lake Como, and there, on the roadside, they were shot by a Communist 'Colonel' of the Partisans named Audisio. Their bodies were then taken to a garage in Milan—where less than a year before a number of Partisans had been executed—and strung up, head downward, together with the corpses of several other prominent Fascists, including Starace and Farinacci. Mussolini's own countrymen had exacted a terrible and degrading retribution. On the same day an armistice was signed at Caserta, and the Italian campaign came to an end.

In Whitehall rejoicing was tempered by grave anxiety. All through April the unrelenting struggle over Poland had continued, with the Russians thwarting every attempt to gain a fair hearing for the Polish case. As if to underline their repudiation of Yalta they had now set up a provisional Government of their own in Vienna—and once again they had refused to admit Allied observers. Deciding on a personal appeal to Stalin, Churchill sounded a note of warning:

> There is not much comfort in looking into a future where you and the countries you dominate, plus the Communist parties in many other

States, are all drawn up on one side and those who rally to the English-speaking nations and their associates or Dominions are on the other. It is quite obvious that their quarrel would tear the world to pieces. . . . Do not, I beg of you, my friend Stalin, underrate the divergences which are opening about matters which you may think are small to us, but which are symbolic of the way the English-speaking democracies look at life.[1]

On the day that all German forces in Holland and North-west Germany surrendered the Prime Minister received a very disheartening and uncompromising reply. To the Foreign Secretary, in San Francisco, he suggested that only another Three-Power Conference could avert disaster. They had to face the ugly fact that Poland was about to be buried in Russian territory, and that Russia was about to take over permanently the Baltic provinces, a huge slice of Germany, all Czechoslovakia, much of Austria, and all Yugoslavia, Hungary, Roumania, and Bulgaria. "This constitutes an event in the history of Europe to which there has been no parallel . . . ," wrote Churchill to Eden; "nothing can save us from the great catastrophe but a meeting and a show-down as early as possible at some point in Germany which is under American and British control."[2]

* * * * *

Throughout this eventful month of April Churchill had few hours of leisure. He spent the week-ends at Chequers, but a stream of official visitors were invited down for discussions—Baruch and Rosenman; Forde, Evatt, and Fraser; Mikolajczyk and Dr Gerbrandy, the Netherlands Premier. He saw much, too, of Smuts, his most valued counsellor of all in times of crisis. Tommy recalls only one brief escape from Whitehall —a return to Bristol, where as Chancellor of the University the Prime Minister conferred honorary degrees on Ernest Bevin and A. V. Alexander in a setting very different from the scene on his previous visit almost exactly four years earlier, when the city was still in flames after an all-night raid.

After inspecting the gigantic new Brabazon aircraft at Filton Churchill rejoined the train, and a special stop was made at Badminton. Queen Mary, who had been living there for most of the war, had sent a message inviting him and Sarah to dinner.

On their arrival they were shown into a lofty and very cold room where Queen Mary awaited them. She was in full evening dress. Sarah, who was in R.A.F. uniform, was much embarrassed and apologized for having no other clothes with her. "The only reason you see me in this dress is because I have so many of them," said Queen Mary "—and I have no coupons to buy anything else."

* * * * *

[1] Churchill, Vol. VI, pp. 433–434.
[2] *Ibid.*, pp. 438–439.

Although the first German surrender move on the Western Front was made by Himmler through Count Bernadotte of Sweden on April 26, and Hitler died by his own hand in the gloomy concrete air-raid shelter in the Chancellery garden in Berlin four days later it was not until May 8 that Mr Churchill was able to tell the nation that hostilities would cease at midnight.

He spoke from the Cabinet Room at Number Ten. Whitehall was besieged by crowds so dense that when he left Downing Street to go to the House of Commons after his broadcast it took him half an hour to cover the few hundred yards to Parliament Square. The delay brought a touch of comedy to an emotional occasion, for as the House waited impatiently A. P. Herbert, Sir Jocelyn Lucas, and Sir Herbert Williams valiantly strove to fill in the time by cross-examining Sir John Anderson on such richly irrelevant matters as the third reading of the Water Bill, the fate of a Bill dealing with Select Vestries, and the Outlawries Bill. When the Prime Minister finally entered the Chamber he was given a tremendous ovation from every part of the House, Members standing and cheering him to the echo.

Mr Churchill moved that the House should adjourn "to give humble and reverent thanks to Almighty God for our deliverance from the threat of German domination." And, with the bells pealing out overhead, they walked through the cheering crowds to Westminster Abbey. From the Abbey the Prime Minister drove to Buckingham Palace for lunch. Afterwards he went in a small open car to the Ministry of Health building in Whitehall, where he spoke from the balcony.

It was a lovely sunny afternoon, and London looked at its gayest, with flags and paper streamers everywhere. "This is *your* victory!" he said, smiling happily at the sea of faces below him. "It is the victory of the cause of freedom in every land. In all our long history we have never seen a greater day than this."

With Ernest Bevin conducting them the crowd sang "For He's a Jolly Good Fellow." That night Mr Churchill made a further appearance on the balcony, now floodlit, with members of the War Cabinet, and led the singing of "Land of Hope and Glory."

* * * * *

Mrs Churchill was in Moscow on this great day. For weeks she had been touring hospitals and rest-centres from Leningrad in the north to the Crimea and the Caucasus. From the moment she launched her Aid to Russia Fund in the winter of 1941 it had met with an overwhelming response, quickly overshadowing all the Left Wing funds competing for public support. The sponsors of these could barely conceal their resentment, for at a stroke Mrs Churchill's fund had deprived them of a valuable propaganda weapon, and Dr Hewlett Johnson, the "Red Dean" of Canterbury, asserted that it was little short of "poaching." By now the charitable poachers had raised the colossal sum of nearly eight million pounds to buy medical supplies and equipment.

When the Soviet Government first suggested that Mrs Churchill should visit Russia relations with Britain were so tense as a result of the Polish dispute that the Prime Minister hesitated about allowing her to go, but at the beginning of April she flew to Moscow via Cairo in the Skymaster. With her went her personal secretary, Miss Grace Hamblen, and Miss Mabel Johnson, secretary of the Aid to Russia Fund. As interpreter and adviser the Russians provided M. Zinchenko, who had been Maisky's First Secretary in London and was now a senior member of the Soviet Foreign Office staff in Moscow.

They had a rough passage in the final stage of the flight out, bad weather forcing the aircraft down to two hundred feet over the last hundred miles. At the airfield to meet them was Maisky himself, who asked Mrs Churchill if she would like to carry out her tour by air or use a special train which had been placed at her disposal. She chose the train, and a long and exhausting programme began with visits to hospitals in the Moscow area. At the outset she met Stalin, on whom she made a great impression; later she learnt that the Russian Government had conferred on her the Order of the Red Banner for her services to the Russian armies.

After three days in Leningrad Mrs Churchill went south to Stalingrad and Rostov-on-Don, where two hospitals had been entirely equipped by the Fund. She visited the spas in the Caucasus, had a three-day break at Yalta, and then went on to Sevastopol and Odessa. Just before VE Day she returned to Moscow for a final week.

She found there was to be a lunch-party at the British Embassy to listen to the broadcasts by the King and the Prime Minister, and a Service in the Embassy chapel to give thanks for victory. Mr Frank Roberts, the senior British diplomat in Moscow at the time—Sir Archibald Clark Kerr, the British Ambassador, was in San Francisco—had great difficulty in finding anyone to take the Service, for the Embassy had no Chaplain, but eventually a Baptist minister was discovered, serving in the R.A.F. there. So he was persuaded to officiate, but they still had no one to preach the sermon.

Mrs Churchill then had a brainwave. It was rumoured that the "Red Dean"—popularly believed by most Russians to be the Archbishop of Canterbury—was due to arrive in Moscow at midnight on the eve of VE Day. "Let's ask *him* to preach," she suggested. So delighted was Dr Hewlett Johnson that he sat up for the rest of the night and composed a very moving address, taking as his theme the recent death of President Roosevelt.

An unexpected and welcome guest at the official lunch-party was

M. Édouard Herriot, the former Premier of France, who was staying with the French Ambassador, General Catroux. In the afternoon Bill Fraser, who had arrived back in Moscow to fly Mrs Churchill home, rashly ventured out into Red Square with his navigator to see what celebrations were afoot. The two R.A.F. officers were immediately pounced upon by a horde of jubilant Russians and before they realized what was happening they were being hurled into the air, time and again, like small boys being tossed in a blanket in the school dormitory. But each landing was far more hazardous.

Considerably shaken, they retreated as soon as possible to a near-by club frequented by the international Press. Over a drink they were describing their experience when a British journalist who was about to record a broadcast for the B.B.C. asked if, as a special favour, they would return to the Square and run the gauntlet again; it would give him a chance to do a graphic running commentary on Russia's welcome to the Royal Air Force.

Bruised and aching in every limb they reluctantly agreed. At first they thought they might evade attention this time, for when they cautiously emerged the crowd were busy chairing the Red Dean round the far side of the square. But soon some one noticed them and in a moment they were grabbed and tossed violently from one group of cheering spectators to another. "Say something!" shouted the British journalist hovering on the edge of the crowd. Fraser's Russian, limited to one stirring sentence—"Long live the Red Army!"—was greeted with wild applause. And to his great surprise he managed to escape soon afterwards with no bones broken.

* * * * *

Victory celebrations had hardly died down before the Prime Minister found fresh problems on his hands. Tito began to adopt an aggressive attitude towards British troops in Trieste and Venezia Giulia; in the Levant the French, determined to reassert their authority in a country which had been promised its independence, attacked Syrian Army units.

Churchill was much relieved to get a forthright message from President Truman, who advocated immediate steps to restrain Tito before Yugoslavia, following the Russian lead, laid claim to Balkan territory left and right. This was encouraging, but the tone of subsequent messages from Washington was noticeably more cautious. This change of attitude was understandable. With public attention in the United States now focused more and more on the Pacific theatre the President's advisers were anxious to steer clear of incidents which might involve additional military commitments in Europe.

They were anxious, too, to avoid any risk of giving offence to the Soviet Government. When Churchill suggested that President Truman should visit London for preliminary talks on his way to the proposed Three-Power Conference the invitation was hastily declined on the grounds that it would look better if Prime Minister and President arrived separately; a prior meeting between them might suggest to Stalin that they had been concerting some plan against him.

A few days later Mr Truman cabled that he was sending a special envoy to London—Joseph Davies, a former American Ambassador to Moscow, who, to Churchill's astonishment, told him that President Truman was now proposing to meet Stalin on his own, before seeing the Prime Minister. In a long and very frank note which Davies carried back to Washington Mr Churchill reminded the President that Britain and the United States shared the same ideologies; that Russia, with her different philosophy of Communism, had already offended against the spirit of international agreements by enslaving the countries she had occupied; and it would create an unfortunate impression throughout the world if, after all Great Britain and America had gone through together, Britain was to be treated as a junior partner and only summoned to the Three-Power meeting at the conclusion of American talks with Russia. The President sent a friendly reply, and nothing more was heard of the proposal.

In his memorandum Churchill indicated that the most suitable time for the Conference from his point of view would be after the first week of July, "when the British pollings will be over." The Coalition had already been dissolved, and a Caretaker Government had been formed. Although Polling Day had been fixed for July 5 the result of the Election would not be declared for a further three weeks, to enable the votes of Servicemen abroad to be gathered in.

The timing of the first General Election in Britain for nearly ten years roused bitter controversy. For obvious tactical reasons most Conservatives favoured the month of June. Admittedly the Tory machine was in no state of readiness for an early campaign; hundreds of Party agents were serving in the Forces and the constituency organizations throughout the country had virtually ceased operation since 1939, while the Labour Party, on the other hand—with a far higher proportion of its local officials tied to the home front by war production tasks—had remained politically active. But the personal factor of Churchill's leadership in a campaign launched in the very wake of Victory celebrations seemed likely to counterbalance any defects of organization.

Churchill himself felt strongly that he should be given a mandate to continue at the head of a National Government until the war with Japan was over. He therefore proposed to the Labour leaders that approval for this should be sought by national referendum. The holding of a General Election at this critical stage, when the war was still raging in the Far East and grave international problems awaited settlement in Europe, would needlessly interfere with the conduct of foreign affairs, he argued, and at first both Attlee and Bevin seemed disposed to support him.

When they went to Blackpool for the Labour Party Conference, which opened on May 18, they found, however, that Herbert Morrison had already swung opinion firmly against the proposal. While anxious above all to avoid a June election, when the prestige and immense personal popularity of Churchill would exert its maximum effect, the Labour Party Executive flatly refused to support an extension of the Coalition beyond October.

To the Prime Minister, preoccupied with greater issues looming in Europe, this was decisive. If Polling Day was deferred until October electioneering considerations would hamper effective government at every turn. And Britain's authority in international negotiation would be correspondingly weakened. Better by far to settle the matter with all dispatch.

The possibility of defeat did not occur to him. Discussing the tasks which lay ahead, and reflecting, possibly, on flaws in Anglo-American strategy at Yalta, he said to a close friend, "I'm going to be Prime Minister again. Then I can put things right."

To him the shaping of the post-war world was a challenge which far transcended in importance any matter of internal politics. The adamant refusal of the Labour Party to accept his request for a referendum, and their insistence on reverting to partisan rivalry at such a time seemed to Mr Churchill to denote a lack of proportion amounting to irresponsibility. He could not understand how men who had been content to serve loyally under his leadership for so long could desert him now, with the war only half won. But in the ranks of Labour passion and prejudice ran deeper than he realized.

On the day before Parliament reassembled the Prime Minister gave a reception at Number Ten for members of the outgoing Government. In a moving little speech he thanked them for their services, and after Attlee and Sinclair had replied Mr Churchill suggested that they should all move into the garden for a group photograph.

Tommy left the room for a few minutes on an errand for the Prime Minister. As he returned he was surprised to see a prominent public figure hastening towards the front door.

"Aren't you staying for the photograph?" Tommy asked in surprise.

"Not likely!" was the reply. ". . . It wouldn't do me any good at this time to be seen in a group with that lot!"

40

"Vote for Churchill"— A Misjudged Campaign

The Conservative campaign was hampered from the outset by inefficient organization. Even more damaging, Tory tactics showed a complete misconception of the mood of the electorate. After six years of war there was a hunger to escape from an atmosphere of militarism and foreign "entanglements"—a desperate urge to plan for a peaceful future. The Conservative appeal to the country was mainly based, however, on a continuance of Churchill's leadership and the party's wider experience of foreign affairs and defence, with particular reference to the Japanese war. Far too little attention was paid to domestic issues.

Admittedly election addresses stressed the resolve to banish war-time controls. They drew attention also to a National Insurance scheme, a forward-looking policy for Education, and a determination to solve the housing problem. But as a counter to Labour's Five Year Plan Tory candidates were unable to offer any coherent domestic programme. The Beveridge Report cut little ice; its recommendations were regarded as pious hopes rather than promises capable of fulfilment.

This was a considerable handicap, for although the party managers seemed blissfully unaware of the fact the Conservatives were still associated in the minds of many with the widespread unemployment of the thirties. Labour speakers resurrected this bogey. They also hinted that relaxation of controls was only a prelude to renewed exploitation of the working classes by private enterprise.

The attitude of the Service voter was an important factor. Here again the Conservatives were at a disadvantage, for a high proportion of the men in charge of education in Army units held Leftish views. In Current

Affairs discussions they preached the gospel that rigid Tory financial beliefs could lead to a recurrence of the slump and consequent unemployment experienced after the First World War. It was widely believed, too, that under a Conservative Government release from the Forces might well be delayed.

Strangely enough, however, it was the emphasis on Churchill's leadership which unwittingly presented the Socialists with their greatest opportunity. Whereas the Labour Party gave the impression of a co-ordinated team, intent on carrying out a constructive and carefully planned policy, no clear image of the Conservative Party emerged. Their appeal to the electorate was almost naïvely over-simplified. VOTE FOR CHURCHILL AND FREEDOM, urged the posters. . . . VOTE FOR CHURCHILL —HELP HIM TO FINISH THE JOB. There was no mention of the party he represented, nothing to suggest that the Tories had, in fact, anyone else of talent and experience to fill the remaining places in the side.

Since the Prime Minister was already criticized in certain quarters for being too Cromwellian, for holding too much power and desiring even more, this played right into the hands of his opponents. Miss Ellen Wilkinson drew an alarming picture of Churchill as the sole candidate in every constituency; "the Tories offer you merely one man, plus a few airy promises," declared A. V. Alexander. Nevertheless the Prime Minister's popularity worried his opponents. "Some people seem to think the General Election is a vote of thanks," protested Sir Stafford Cripps; "the war was not won by any individual." This remark was prompted by Churchill's triumphal progress through the Provinces in the closing stages of the campaign—but, like the Conservative election managers, Cripps misinterpreted the enthusiasm of the crowds. They cheered the Prime Minister to the echo because they were grateful for what he had done. At the same time there was no widespread conviction that the great war leader was necessarily the right man to entrust with the radically different problems of post-war resettlement.

Many were frankly puzzled by his new rôle. They remembered his fiercely critical attitude towards the Tories before the war. Now that he had become the saviour of his country and a world figure the man in the street found it difficult to understand why Churchill should choose to ally himself to a party he had so violently condemned. And when they heard him attacking Labour politicians who had served under him in responsible posts over a long period they began to mistrust his motives.

Ernest Bevin spoke for many when he deplored the Prime Minister's descent into the political arena. "I told Mr Churchill at Bristol that, having had the loyalty of all parties during the war, it was my profound regret that he did not stand aside, let the parties fight the domestic issues out, and be ready to go back and assist in the great resettlement of the world," he said in a speech just before Polling Day.[1]

Since Bevin had been a member of the War Cabinet he was almost certainly aware that he was advocating the very course which Churchill himself had decided upon not long before. Determined to avoid the mistake of Lloyd George in seeking to remain in office at the end of the First World War, he made up his mind to hand over the leadership of the Conservative Party either at the end or just before the end of the war now in progress. When in 1943 strong pressure was brought to bear by Mr Amery and others for the appointment of Anthony Eden as Viceroy of India the Prime Minister was for this reason extremely reluctant to consider the suggestion. He wished Eden to remain at the Foreign Office, where he was closely in touch with every development on which a future Prime Minister would need to be informed. In this he was strongly supported by the King, who considered that if Eden went to India it might not be practicable to recall him at short notice to succeed Mr Churchill. Consequently Wavell, who had been already proposed as Governor-General of Australia, became Viceroy of India instead.

What had made Churchill change his mind? In all probability it was a growing conviction that his great experience of world affairs could still play a vital part in the reshaping of Europe. As a result, however, he now found himself engaged in a bitter political conflict for which he was by temperament and inclination entirely unsuited.

Humdrum questions of internal politics had always irked him, and never more than now, when his thoughts continually dwelt on the threatening advance of the Russian armies towards the West. He was exhausted, mentally and physically, when the election campaign opened, and, overestimating his personal influence, he took too much on his own shoulders; he tried to go everywhere and do everything. No human being could have striven harder to win the day, but the task he set himself was too great for one man and he was worn out long before the end.

With tiredness his judgment faltered. In his efforts to rouse the country to the dangers of Socialism he overplayed his hand, manufacturing and then magnifying Labour shortcomings to such an extent that few took his warnings seriously.

The fatal damage was done in his first broadcast to the nation. Instead of making a statesmanlike appeal for unity to deal with the tasks ahead, he tried to scare his listeners with an overdrawn picture of the Police State which would emerge if the Labour Party came to power. "No Socialist system can be established without a political police," he warned.... "They

[1] *Daily Telegraph*, June 30, 1945.

would have to fall back on some form of Gestapo, no doubt very humanely directed in the first instance."

In all Churchill delivered four of the ten broadcasts allocated to the Conservative Party, and he returned to this grim Socialist spectre again and again, adding fuel to the synthetic fire with charges that Professor Laski, the Chairman of the National Executive, was the real power behind the Labour movement and his influence threatened the traditional working of the British Constitution. Lord Beaverbrook, the most active and the most outspoken of the supporting Conservative speechmakers, even went so far as to suggest that Laski aimed to destroy the Parliamentary system of Great Britain and establish a dictatorship.

Churchill's first "Gestapo" speech did much to discredit the whole Tory campaign. On the day after the broadcast a prominent Englishman was received in private audience at the Vatican and referring to the Prime Minister's speech Pope Pius expressed his surprise that so wise a man as Mr Churchill could have made such charges. "What he said might conceivably have been true of any country *except* England," the Pope remarked.

Press comment was unfavourable. "Faced with a relatively modest programme of public ownership he leaps to extravagances about totalitarianism and the Gestapo," observed the *Manchester Guardian*. Even *The Times*—not unduly critical of Conservative tactics in the early stages—expressed disappointment with the tone of the Prime Minister's speech. His next broadcast was damned with faint praise, *The Times* commending it as "an improvement" mainly because "it had at least some relevance to the issues of the election." In his third radio speech, however, Churchill returned once again to Professor Laski, and declared that the Socialist Executive would inevitably introduce an Emergency Powers Bill, backed by violence, to enforce their decisions. And at the close of his election tour he dwelt on the danger of State secrets being entrusted to a small caucus who would control British policy irrespective of the will of Parliament.

For the first time in a British election campaign broadcasting played a major part in the bidding for votes. It was therefore doubly unfortunate that Churchill, who commanded a radio audience of half the adult population, should have adopted the extravagant line he did. If the Labour Party had had effective speakers the damage would have been even greater. Attlee, with his sober and restrained replies to the Tory charges, made a good impression, and so did Ernest Bevin, but supporting speeches fell notably below this standard, James Griffiths melodramatically painting a picture of the wicked Tories grinding the faces of the poor and George Tomlinson uttering wild predictions about a return to the bad old days in the docks. Herbert Morrison forecast another "shameful period of national decline" if the Conservatives were returned, and A. V. Alexander delivered himself of some rousing, ranting reflections on the menace of private profit and monopolies.

On the Conservative side Eden, whose illness for much of the campaign threw an additional burden on the Prime Minister, was refreshingly realistic and sensible on both foreign affairs and domestic issues, and the constructive, factual approach of Sir John Anderson and Lord Woolton to the problems of resettlement did more for party prestige than any scaremongering. Up to the half-way stage in the campaign there was little indication, however, that this flood of oratory—in all there were twenty-six of these party political broadcasts—had done anything to clarify the issues.

One fact which did emerge was the indifference of the average voter to the main Tory line of attack. In preparing their able survey of the Election R. B. McCallum and Alison Readman found a marked lack of interest in constitutional issues. In the main the electorate wanted to know "not how the country should be governed, but what the government of the country would do, or give."[2] By tilting at windmills the Tory propaganda machine had largely wasted its opportunity.

On the afternoon of Monday, June 25, Churchill set out from Chequers on a tour which was to take him a thousand miles through England and Scotland. Strangely enough none of the other leading members of the party with the exception of Beaverbrook, who had no seat in the Commons to defend, travelled far afield.

Everywhere, in villages, towns, and the great cities of the Midlands and the North, the Prime Minister received a tumultuous welcome—an ovation so overwhelming, in fact, that Labour leaders were soon accusing him once more of exploiting the celebration of Victory for party advantage. The planning of the tour, however, left much to be desired, and it imposed far too great a strain on a tired man.

When Tommy first saw the draft of the arrangements prepared by the Conservative Central Office he protested at the unrealistic timetable. It allowed no margin for delay in getting from one meeting to another and he pointed out that the Central Office had crammed far too many engagements into each day. Accompanying the Prime Minister everywhere, as he had done for the past five years, Tommy could estimate to a minute or two how long any given programme would take to complete, but the Central Office refused to listen. On the first day Churchill was over two hours late at Coventry; it took him three hours to cover the twenty miles between Coventry and Birmingham, for huge crowds slowed the cars to a walking pace.

As a political gathering the meeting at Coventry was not an unqualified

[2] *The British General Election of 1945*, p. 150.

success, for the amplifiers were damaged by people struggling to secure better vantage-places, and hardly anyone could hear what Churchill said. Most of the huge audience, however, seemed quite content to wave flags and handkerchiefs, and shout "Good old Winnie."

It had been agreed that as the war with Japan was still in progress and the Prime Minister had to carry on the everyday business of government he could continue to use his special train, but he abandoned his official car. An open Humber touring-car was lent to him, and this was fitted with Tannoy equipment. Sarah travelled with her father; Tommy, who had to discard his naval uniform for the duration of the campaign, went ahead in a police car with Elizabeth Layton, one of the Prime Minister's secretaries.

In every city Mr Churchill visited he employed a ruse to find out if the microphones were working. "Are we downhearted?" he would shout. And the crowd would roar back "No!" Fifty thousand people were waiting to hear him at Manchester, where he spoke from a bombed site near the centre of the city. "Whatever you decide, put a strong Government in power . . . a Government that can really carry out what it promises to do," he told them.

He was warned that in Manchester and one or two other places he was to visit Communist gangs might attempt to break up his meetings, but apart from a few faint-hearted boos nothing happened. Even in the drabbest industrial centres of the North every one seemed to be cheering and waving their greetings. Sometimes, admittedly, the greetings were unconventional. As he left one Town Hall a craggy veteran stepped in front of the car and, shaking his fist in mock rebuke, shouted out, "You old bugger!"

"What did he say?" asked the Prime Minister.

When he was told he grinned delightedly, and, craning round in his seat, he gave the old man a special salute.

From Manchester on the second day he drove through Oldham and Huddersfield to Leeds, where he had addressed a public meeting as far back as 1900. He should have reached the Town Hall at 6.15 P.M., but it was nearly eight o'clock when he arrived. Although he was exhausted by another long and arduous day, he made a vigorous fighting speech, urging that it was not the time to plunge the nation into a great organic change; the task was to get the country back on its feet again. "What a pity it would be," he continued, "to break across all these really practical measures which are going to tax our strength and organizing powers to the utmost, with a lot of appeals about Utopias and a lot of windy academic discussions about the theories of the individual and the State and so on."

Each night, when he got back to the train, he faced many hours of work entirely unconnected with the election. On top of this he had to revise his speeches for the morrow, and he was still working on the preparation of his final party broadcast.

The third day of the tour began at Bradford and continued with speeches at Halifax and Queensbury. Then, recrossing the Pennines, he spoke at Burnley and Blackburn. His visit to Preston, where Randolph was fighting to retain his seat, was stage-managed by his son much more efficiently than in most other constituencies, but a discordant note was struck by a Communist agitator who harangued the crowd, warning them that Churchill and his "gang of political parasites" were determined to keep the people in poverty.

Overnight the train carried him to Scotland. Again a tumultuous reception in Glasgow, and an open meeting in the gardens below Princes Street in Edinburgh, where the Prime Minister made his last speech of more than thirty in four days. Here he was given the most rapturous welcome of his whole tour. "I shall never see a scene like this again," he told the vast crowd, ". . . the memory of it will last as long as I live."

While he slept that night the train took him back to London. He lunched at Buckingham Palace, and then drove to Chequers, where he made his fourth and final political broadcast. At this stage it was considered by some observers at Conservative headquarters that the party might get a reasonably large majority, but others were puzzled by the strangely subdued mood of the electorate. They sensed an atmosphere of reserve amounting almost to apathy. Although the Prime Minister's tour had been an undoubted personal success, shrewd judges were not entirely convinced that the cheers for the victorious war leader offered any indication of the way the voting would go. This view, said one leader-writer, seemed to derive not so much from pessimism as a feeling that something unusual was in the wind. TORIES CONFIDENT BUT NOT ARROGANT—NO BOASTING BY LABOUR, ran a *Manchester Guardian* headline.

The strain of the campaign was telling on the Prime Minister now. To Brooke he confessed that he had never been so tired since the days of his escape during the Boer War.[3] In his exhaustion he unwisely resorted once again to attacking personalities—in a speech at Lewisham he lashed out at Herbert Morrison with entirely uncharacteristic viciousness—and he was much upset by the reception he received at some of his evening meetings in the London area. He was loudly booed at Battersea, continuously heckled at Wandsworth and at Norwood, where he spoke for his son-in-law, Duncan Sandys. There was another uproar at Greenwich.

[3] Bryant, *op. cit.*, Vol. II, p. 465.

Churchill, who had fought more election campaigns than any politician living or dead, could deal with heckling as effectively as anyone.[4] But he was distressed by the organized preparations to wreck his meetings, and by the ugly readiness of these London crowds to resort to actual physical violence. At one meeting he was struck by a stone; at Tooting Bec Common a student threw a squib at him which exploded almost in his face.[5] The sorriest performance was reserved for the final meeting of the campaign at Walthamstow, where more than twenty years earlier he had had to be rescued by mounted police.[6]

He arrived at the Stadium to find a hostile crowd of 20,000, who booed, heckled, and jeered so continuously that he had great difficulty in making himself heard at all. He stood facing into the glare of the setting sun, and this worried him so much that he borrowed an old felt hat to shield his eyes. Right from the start it was obvious that a large section of the crowd were determined to deny him a hearing. Most of the uproar came from young hooligans under voting age, and at every place he spoke on his way back to Whitehall that night this hostile element pursued him.

It was a shameful and degrading reception to accord to the man who had led the country through its greatest crisis—and a bitter ordeal to face when he was at the limit of his endurance. During the past ten days he had made sixty speeches, ranging from five to forty-five minutes, and he had visited no fewer than 150 constituencies.

As Polling Day dawned it was obvious that political correspondents and others who had closely studied every aspect of the campaign were still as much in the dark as ever about the outcome of the election. A *Daily Express* poll claimed that 54 per cent. of the population expected a Conservative victory. The *News Chronicle*, employing the most scientific system of analysis of any newspaper—a sampling of opinion taken from carefully chosen age and income groups—indicated that Labour would secure 47 per cent. of the votes, while the Tories and their associates would get 41 per cent.

The influence of Churchill's leadership on the voting still defied assessment. Many people found it difficult to believe that he, and therefore his party, could be rejected after all he had done for the nation. At the same time there was widespread criticism of the tactics he had adopted during

[4] In all he had contested fifteen elections—five at Dundee, four at Epping, two at Oldham, two at Manchester, and one at Leicester and the Abbey Division of Westminster.

[5] When the youth appeared in court next day he told the South-west London magistrate that he did not know why he had thrown the firework, but he was, he said, "anti-Churchill."

[6] In an interview given to a London evening paper at that time he had described the hecklers as "the worst I have ever seen in England in twenty-five years of public life; . . . they were more like Russian slaves than British workmen, howling, foaming, and spitting."

the election. Commenting on the shock of the Prime Minister's first broadcast and his "Gestapo" references to men who had so recently been his colleagues *The Times* said—"His services have set him apart in the eyes of the nation, and the stratagems of the electioneer make him fall short of the rôle for which his countrymen have cast him . . . the campaign has suffered sadly from the attempt to furnish it with inflammatory material capable of stirring the passions or rousing the fears of the electorate."

The *Daily Express* and the *Daily Mail* trumpeted their faith in the Tory cause: the *News Chronicle* asserted that VOTE CHURCHILL was a dangerous slogan: "there is a deep-rooted distrust of the British people for personal government." The situation on the morning of Polling Day was, however, best summed up by an earlier comment in one of the great provincial newspapers which had throughout taken a firmly anti-Tory line. "There was never such an electoral leap in the dark," declared the *Manchester Guardian*.

So, indeed, it seemed. Right to the end the electorate, confused by scares and counter-scares, by appeals to their loyalty which bade them "Vote for Churchill" and the tempting promises of social security from the cradle to the grave offered by the Labour Party, gave little sign that they had made up their minds one way or the other.

41

Holiday at Hendaye—and on to Berlin

MR CHURCHILL was not due to arrive at Potsdam, the scene of the forthcoming Three Power Conference, until the evening of July 15. He badly needed a rest and when the Duke of Westminster offered him his Hunting Lodge at Mimizan, near Bordeaux, he readily accepted. The Duke had, however, had no news of the house since the German occupation and Tommy was therefore dispatched on a reconnaissance trip. By a happy chance the new British Consul at Bordeaux was Bryce Nairn, who had recently been transferred from Marrakesh, and they drove out to Mimizan together.

At first sight the house, set in the middle of a pine-forest not far from the sea, seemed an ideal choice for a secluded holiday. An old Irish retainer of the Duke's—an ex-jockey who had lived there throughout the occupation—told them, however, that there was one serious snag. The main pipeline which carried the water-supply from a near-by lake was badly rusted, and blocked altogether in places. One look convinced them that there was no hope of repairing it in time.

Nairn then thought of a house three miles from the Spanish border, between Saint-Jean-de-Luz and Hendaye, which had been offered to him for his own use. This was the Château Bordabery, owned by a retired industrialist, Brigadier-General Raymond Brutinel, but when they called on him the General explained with some embarrassment that he was hardly in a position to offer suitable hospitality to the Prime Minister. For one thing all his best cutlery was still buried in various parts of the Pyrenees; and with the prevailing food shortage in France it was, he pointed out, impossible for him to act as host to an entire house-party. Nairn hastened to assure him that the Consulate could supply anything which was necessary, and when they went to see the local Prefect of Police the latter readily agreed to provide a guard for the estate.

On July 7 the Skymaster left Northolt for Bordeaux. With the Prime Minister travelled Mrs Churchill and Mary. Also in the party were Lord Moran, Jock Colville, and Tommy, three detectives and two typists. It was a lovely summer afternoon with banks of fleecy cloud turning to gold in the bright sunshine. Mr Churchill complained that he felt battered and worn—he was still brooding unhappily on the attacks which had been made upon him—but during the flight he became absorbed in the book he was reading, a life of Frederick the Great, and by the time the Skymaster landed at Bordeaux he was in a much more cheerful frame of mind.

He took an instant liking to his host, and they quickly found common ground. The General had fought with the Canadian Machine Gun Corps in the First World War, and soon he and Mr Churchill were delightedly recalling the colourful language of a certain "Foghorn Macdonald" at Plug Street!

The week which followed was the happiest time Churchill had spent since his days of convalescence at Marrakesh. As usual, he got through a vast amount of work on papers sent down to him from the Paris Embassy, but the peace and comfort of the château in its lovely setting above the Bay of Biscay, the daily painting and bathing expeditions, and evenings spent in lively conversation with the General, who had much of interest to tell about life in France after the arrival of the Germans, soon banished harsh memories. The Prime Minister could not drive thoughts of the Election entirely from his mind; "the mystery of the ballot boxes and their contents had an ugly trick of knocking on the door and peering in at the windows," he wrote later.[1] And at lunch one day he remarked gloomily, "Soon we shall have to go back to London to see if they've thrown me in the gutter." But from the moment he began to paint again he seemed much more relaxed than they had seen him for a long time.

Painting was his one complete and satisfying solace. At the start of his holiday he said he did not feel in the mood for it: he would just sit in the sun and watch the rest bathe from a beach which the Nairns took them to near Saint-Jean-de-Luz. Nevertheless Cyril Davies, one of his detectives, brought along his paints and "the Juice" (Mr Churchill's own mixture of turpentine and linseed oil), his easel, and the 'shooting stick' chair he always liked to use. Before long the bathing party noticed with relief that Mr Churchill was busy supervising the placing of his easel, and in the shade of a huge umbrella he was soon hard at work. From that moment he grudged every hour of daylight when painting was denied to him.

[1] Churchill, Vol. VI, p. 531.

Although every one in the district knew of his arrival there and was anxious to see him the local inhabitants gave a remarkable display of good manners. Wherever he went on his painting expeditions passers-by neither halted nor stared. They would bow respectfully and continue on their way. A horde of journalists soon descended on Saint-Jean-de-Luz, however, and to give them the slip one day Bryce Nairn suggested a trip up the river to visit an old château on the banks of the Nivelle which had once belonged to the Black Prince. One astute French journalist managed to disguise himself as a member of the crew of the launch, but before they had gone far he was recognized and set ashore to walk four miles home. The rest of the day was spent in peace.

Mr Churchill's first bathe was an impressive occasion. A tent was pitched half-way down the beach. From this he emerged wearing his ten-gallon hat and a pair of large and shapeless drawers. He marched to the water's edge followed by Sawyers, who removed his cigar and his cowboy headgear. Then Mr Churchill took to the water, floating happily to and fro like a contented porpoise.

When he returned to lunch he found that a Basque fête was being staged in his honour in the grounds of the château that afternoon. It was a day of blazing heat, and the Prime Minister, who would have much preferred to spend the afternoon painting on the cliffs, discovered to his alarm that he was expected to appear at an official reception attended by all the local Mayors of the district. This was to be followed by an exhibition of pelota on the court adjoining the château.

Immaculate in royal blue uniform and white cotton gloves a large posse of police arrived. Then, in an ancient lorry, came the pelota-players, accompanied by a drum-and-fife band. The Churchill family were presented with gifts of Basque pottery; for the Prime Minister himself there was a beautifully made sword-stick, the top of which bore the legend JE SUIS LE TERREUR DE MES ENNEMIS! An eloquent speech of welcome was delivered by a young man whose face seemed vaguely familiar. He was, in fact, the journalist who only twenty-four hours earlier had been dumped unceremoniously ashore from the Prime Minister's launch and told to walk home to Saint-Jean-de-Luz!

As soon as they could escape from the festivities the house-party all went back to the beach for a final bathe. There was thunder in the air, and as they swam they watched a tremendous electric storm break over the mountains beyond the Spanish border. All night long the thunder rolled round the château and rain fell in torrents. Next day the sky was overcast, but the Churchills were determined to bathe again, for their holiday was almost at an end.

This particular swimming expedition had an element of high comedy, for a French countess notorious throughout the region as an enthusiastic and passionate collaborator with the Germans made determined efforts to strike up an acquaintance with the Churchills. Swimming tirelessly round and round them she endeavoured to get into conversation with Mrs Churchill and Mary. Forewarned, they promptly headed off each time in the opposite direction until she gave up in disgust.

That night the Mayor of Hendaye gave a *vin d'honneur* at the Casino. Afterwards a traditional spectacle, the Toro del Fuego, was staged in the square outside. The highlight of the entertainment was the entry of two men clothed in a bull's hide. A fearsome and impressive monster, the bull had eyes of flame; from a crown between its horns spurted multi-coloured fireworks; and as the beast ran hither and thither in the crowd more bundles of fire-crackers tied to its tail exploded in showers of sparks.

It was the first time for several years that a Toro del Fuego had been presented there, and when in a grand finale a great spray of Roman candles cascaded from the bull's head the crowd went wild with delight, waving, laughing, and cheering. Then they gathered in front of the tribune where the guest of honour was seated. "Discours!" they shouted. ..."Discours!" Much moved, the Prime Minister stepped forward, and, raising his hand for silence, he said just three words—"Vive la France!"

During the night a violent gale raged over the Landes Forest, uprooting hundreds of trees. The road to Bordeaux was blocked, and it was some time before a way could be cleared for the Prime Minister, waiting to set out for the airfield and the onward journey to Berlin.

On the other side of the world a great storm also raged that night over a remote village called Oscuro. Near by, in the New Mexican desert, vivid flashes of lightning ringed a gaunt steel tower which had just been erected.

A few hours later, from the top of this tall scaffolding, there burst a blazing ball of fire which grew and grew until it seemed to the terrified watchers that it would engulf the whole universe. The fears of Niels Bohr for the future of the world had received terrible confirmation.

* * * * *

The villa in Potsdam allocated to the Prime Minister was set in a large lakeside garden. It had once belonged to Herr Funk, the former Nazi Minister of Economics and President of the Reichbank. Attlee and Eden moved into the house next door, and the rest of the Mission were close at hand, the whole British area being wired in and heavily guarded.

Soon after he arrived Churchill sent for Richard Pim and told him he would want the Downing Street Map Room to show the results of the General Election in detail when the votes were counted in ten days' time. As this involved the installation of a tape machine and the designing of an elaborate display board showing every constituency Pim returned to England to put these arrangements in hand.

Thereafter, preoccupied with the work of the conference, the Prime Minister gave no outward sign that the Election was on his mind, but from random remarks he made as the days passed in Berlin some of his personal staff gained an impression that he was not nearly as confident of the outcome as his advisers were. On the visits he paid to British Army units in the Berlin area the welcome he received from the troops seemed as enthusiastic as ever, but when the leaders of the British delegation appeared at a Victory Parade it was noticeable that Attlee, comparatively unknown to the general public, was greeted just as vociferously as the Prime Minister himself.

One of Churchill's first acts was to pay a formal call on President Truman. "It was strange and rather sad for me to be greeted by new faces," Tommy recalls. "None of the old Presidential retinue I knew so well had survived the change. Even the Secret Service agents were newcomers. Next day Mr Truman came to lunch. He mentioned that he had arranged to visit Stalin that afternoon, but he seemed in no particular hurry to leave. Certainly he had no idea what was ahead of him when we saw him off at three o'clock, but before his conference with Stalin began he found he was expected to eat another complete lunch—and a Russian one at that! It was a gruelling introduction to international diplomacy!"

Churchill had journeyed to Potsdam hopeful that the Conference would bring about agreement with the Russians on a wide range of matters on which hitherto they had shown little disposition to co-operate. Chief among these was the Polish frontier question, now sorely complicated by a new factor. Russian troops had swept forward far beyond the line agreed at Yalta, and Poland, now to all intents and purposes a Russian satellite, had been encouraged to occupy an area of Germany vastly greater than had ever been envisaged by Britain and the United States. As a result, not only had Germany lost at least a quarter of her arable land, but it was already evident that between eight and nine million Germans would have to be resettled by the Western Allies, who had no adequate resources to maintain them.

In his private talks with Churchill Stalin still gave an impression of great affability, reiterating his intention of holding free elections in the countries overrun by the Red Army, professing pained surprise that Britain should criticize Russian moves in Bulgaria and Roumania, and claiming with a great show of sincerity that, far from menacing the West, the Russian Army would shortly be withdrawing, and that large-scale demobilization was imminent.

At the plenary sessions, however, he cleverly baulked every Allied move to examine the boundary question in detail, asserting that since British and American criticism was based on a complete misunderstanding of the situation prevailing in that part of Germany alleged to be controlled by Bierut's Government such criticism could have no validity. In the first place, he said, Poland had not occupied anything like the area which Britain claimed she had; and, secondly, the Poles had every right to take over what territory they had done because the German population had fled, leaving the fields untilled and the mines unworked. In these circumstances the Poles were benefactors, he claimed, and if the Germans who had deserted their homes suffered any hardship as a result then no one should grieve for them.

When Stalin realized that Churchill was determined to pursue the matter he suggested—again playing for time—that the Prime Minister should himself take up the whole question with Bierut and members of his Government. They were summoned to Berlin, and Mr Churchill had two long interviews with the puppet Premier. He made no headway. Well-drilled as ever, Bierut advanced the same double-talk as Stalin, claiming—without offering any factual evidence—that the British had been completely misinformed about Poland's annexations of German territory. When Churchill urged him to re-establish his Government on a broader base, and allow those of his fellow-countrymen who had supported Mikolajczyk to have some say in the future of their homeland, Bierut was equally evasive.

Churchill has himself described the frustrations of this final war-time meeting of the Great Powers. He has also explained his ready assent to Stalin's repeated requests that various important matters discussed during the early plenary sessions at Potsdam should be referred back for further consideration by the Foreign Ministers or other bodies. Since he himself was awaiting a fresh mandate from the British people he felt he was not at this particular stage in a position to take a firm stand. Once confirmed in power, however, he could return to Potsdam and force an issue on many points as yet unresolved, among them the precise form of the Italian peace terms, the disposal of the German Navy, and the immediate future of Austria.

Frustration was not the sum total of all which passed at Potsdam in these final ten days. Churchill had pleasant and useful talks with the new President, and was impressed by his "gay, precise, sparkling manner and obvious power of decision."[2] Truman showed an impressive grasp of international finance and defence matters. And he seemed responsive to Churchill's suggestion that for the time being at least the Joint Chiefs of

[2] Churchill, Vol. VI, p. 545.

Staff organization which had served the world so well should be kept in being.

The Prime Minister had agreeable talks, too, with Stalin, who for all his obdurate defiance during the official sessions seemed in private even more friendly than he had been at their meeting in Moscow in the previous autumn.

On the rare occasions when he was free from conferences and meetings the Prime Minister made several excursions to places of interest in the Berlin area, inspecting Hitler's bunker and closely questioning all who had any knowledge of the Führer's end. In Army uniform he walked freely about the streets of the shattered capital. Around him pressed a motley crowd of Russian soldiers and German civilians, who regarded him with awed fascination.

The news of the successful *Tube Alloy* test had been brought to him almost as soon as he arrived. During the ensuing days he received much fuller details of the experiment. No decision was required from him about the employment of the bomb—approval for its use had already been agreed in principle by the British Government—but Churchill was consulted about the drafting of an ultimatum to Japan, and this was published on the day following his return to England.[3]

"Although in some respects the P.M.'s programme at Potsdam was not as arduous as at some of the earlier conferences, he had very few moments when he could rest, and I was anxious to see that additional engagements were kept to a minimum. Soon after our arrival Admiral Mountbatten rang up and asked for an appointment, mentioning at the same time that he wished to arrange a call on Stalin. Mr Churchill was out at the time. As I was not sure whether he would approve of this visit to Stalin in view of the fact that none of the Chiefs of Staff had as yet called on the Generalissimo I said I would put the Admiral's name on the list, and let him know the answer when the P.M. returned.

"Admiral Mountbatten is, however, a very determined character. Shortly afterwards he presented himself at the villa and announced that he would wait until the Prime Minister appeared. I told him that Mr Churchill had arranged to have a quiet lunch alone and a rest before the afternoon meeting, but Mountbatten insisted that he would only keep him for a few moments. Mr Churchill arrived. Before I could ask him if he would see Mountbatten the latter emerged, and the P.M., always a courteous and considerate host, felt there was nothing for it but to ask him to lunch. So he never got his rest that day.

"This was a problem which was always cropping up on Mr Churchill's

[3] The ultimatum was rejected. Ten days later the first atomic bomb was dropped on Hiroshima.

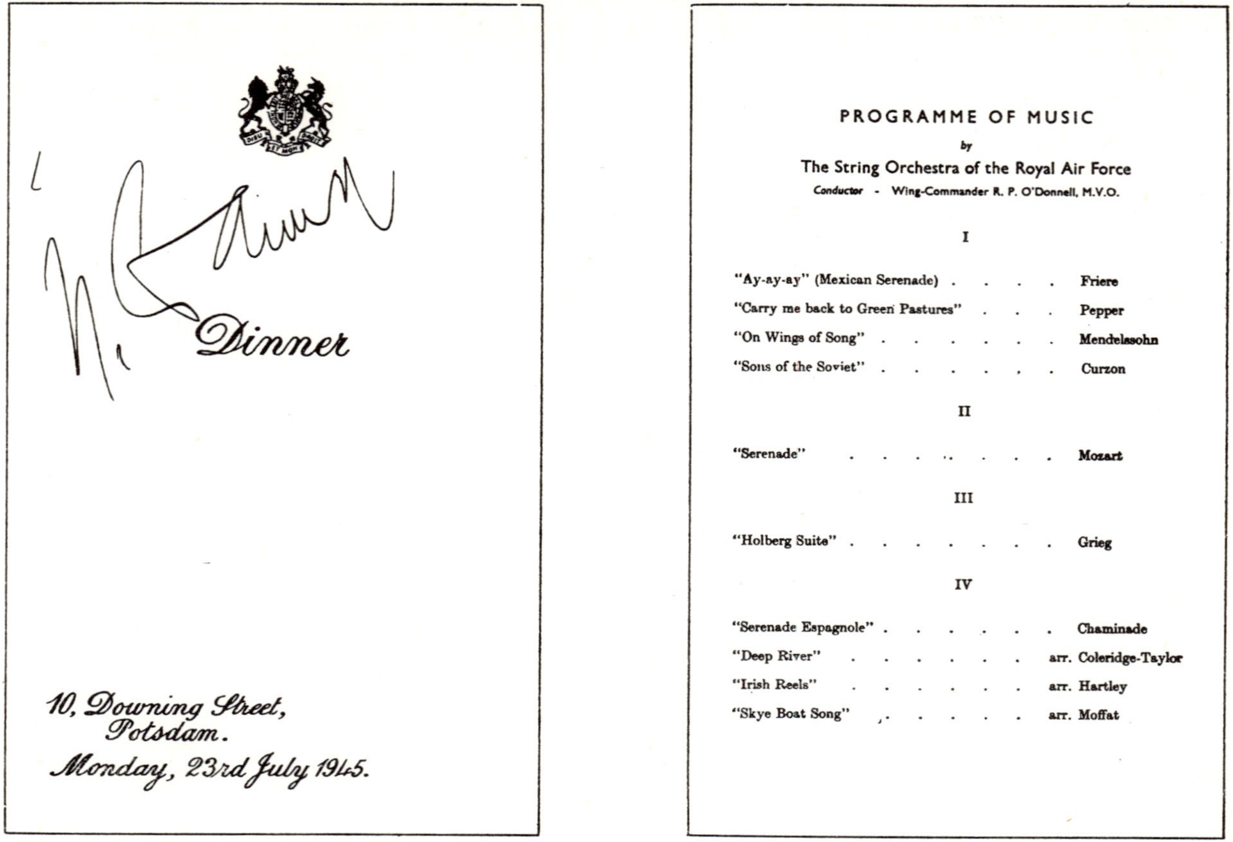

Dinner

10, Downing Street,
Potsdam.

Monday, 23rd July 1945.

PROGRAMME OF MUSIC

by

The String Orchestra of the Royal Air Force

Conductor - Wing-Commander R. P. O'Donnell, M.V.O.

I

"Ay-ay-ay" (Mexican Serenade)	Friere
"Carry me back to Green Pastures" . . .	Pepper
"On Wings of Song"	Mendelssohn
"Sons of the Soviet"	Curzon

II

"Serenade"	Mozart

III

"Holberg Suite"	Grieg

IV

"Serenade Espagnole"	Chaminade
"Deep River"	arr. Coleridge-Taylor
"Irish Reels"	arr. Hartley
"Skye Boat Song"	arr. Moffat

Tommy's Menu Card for the Dinner at Potsdam, which Stalin has inscribed

General of the Army H. H. Arnold	Sir Edward Bridges
Army General A. I. Antonov	Marshal of Aviation F. Ya. Falalev
Field-Marshal the Honble. Sir Harold Alexander	Field-Marshal Sir Bernard Montgomery
Marshal of the Soviet Union G. K. Zhukov	General of the Army G. C. Marshall
Admiral of the Fleet Sir Andrew Cunningham	Marshal of the Royal Air Force Sir Charles Portal
Major A. Birse	Mr. V. N. Pavlov
His Excellency Generalissimo J. V. Stalin	His Excellency Mr. V. M. Molotov
Prime Minister	The Rt. Honble. Anthony Eden
The President of the United States of America	The Honble. James F. Byrnes
Mr Charles E. Bohlen	Field-Marshal Sir Alan Brooke
The Rt. Honble C. R. Attlee	Admiral of the Fleet N. G. Kousnetsov
Fleet Admiral W. D. Leahy	Lord Moran
Field-Marshal Sir Henry Maitland Wilson	Fleet Admiral E. J. King
Commander C. R. Thompson	General Sir Hastings Ismay

Entrance

Table Plan for the Dinner given by the Prime Minister to Stalin and President Truman and the Joint Chiefs of Staff at Potsdam journeys abroad, where there was no Private Office to intercept the continual stream of callers. At Downing Street the Private Secretaries, who dealt with all requests to see him, did their best to ensure that he was never disturbed at this time. They knew that after lunch he liked to retire to his bedroom, where he would fling all his clothes in a heap on the floor, put on a long vest, and get into bed, where he would sleep soundly until Sawyers called him. If I went in with a query just as he was about to take this afternoon nap he would often be fast asleep before I left the room. This short spell in bed deeply refreshed him, but when he was away from England it was far more difficult for him to snatch any rest at all during the day."[4]

Although the entertaining at Potsdam was on a much more restricted scale than at previous conferences the Prime Minister was anxious that the best possible arrangements should be made for the dinner-party he was to give to Stalin, Truman, and the Combined Chiefs of Staff shortly before his departure. Chief Petty Officer Pinfield had again been roped in to take charge of the catering at the villa, but even his versatility was taxed by the food shortage, and at Mr Churchill's suggestion a supply of cold ham was flown out from England to add variety to an unexciting menu. The ham was served, somewhat incongruously, as a special attraction on its own, after the main course.

The preliminaries to the evening were disconcerting, for ignoring the fact that it lay with the Prime Minister to ensure Stalin's safety the Russians poured men into the grounds of the villa, posting them along the lakeside and all round the perimeter of the garden. They were heavily armed, and to avoid any unfortunate incidents Tommy eventually withdrew the British sentries on to the terrace. As this area was brightly lit he felt they were less likely to be shot if they remained there instead of doing their usual patrol.

The dinner proved a gay and surprisingly enjoyable affair. There were twenty guests in addition to the interpreters and the immediate members of the Prime Minister's entourage. Churchill had Truman on his right and Stalin on his left. Facing them across the long table were Eden, Molotov, and Byrnes, the American Secretary of State.

Stalin was in his most genial mood. He was loud in his praise of the music of the R.A.F. String Orchestra, and as the evening wore on he left his seat several times to drink a toast to Wing Commander R. P. O'Donnell, the conductor, and ask for favourite tunes to be played. The only time he seemed at all put out was when, during the speeches, there cropped up a colloquial phrase—recalled by some present as "second to none"—which Stalin promptly queried, reading into Major Birse's inter-

[4] C. R. Thompson, Notes.

pretation a slighting reference to himself. This led to a sharp exchange between the two interpreters, Birse and Pavlov, both of whom were undecided how best to translate the phrase into Russian and still convey the original meaning.

Stalin's irritation was only momentary. By the end of the evening he was walking round among the guests, thrusting a pen at them and asking them to sign his menu card.[5]

On July 24, Churchill's last day in Berlin he invited the British Chiefs of Staff to lunch with him. The subject of the General Election cropped up, and they told him they had gained the impression that the Conservative Party was in real danger of defeat, but the Prime Minister scouted the idea. As they drove out to the airfield to fly to England on the following afternoon the party travelling with Mr Churchill in the Skymaster still felt confident that they would all be returning to Berlin before the week-end.

In this they were encouraged not only by the consistently optimistic forecasts of Lord Beaverbrook; estimates from both Conservative and Labour camps suggested that the Tories held a definite advantage. True, the *News Chronicle*'s Gallup Poll showed a pronounced swing to the Left, but even so this did not seem likely to cut a Conservative majority any lower than fifty seats. In view of all these signs and portents the farewells on the tarmac at Gatow were almost perfunctory. There was no presentiment of what was to come.

Mrs Churchill was waiting at Northolt, and drove back with the Prime Minister to Downing Street. There Randolph joined them for dinner before catching the night train to Preston. He was full of confidence, but Diana, who came in later on with her husband, Duncan Sandys, seemed far from happy.

Duncan Sandys, indeed, was firmly convinced that he would find himself defeated on the morrow, and he sensed that the polling in general had swung against the Tory Party. That night, however, few shared his misgivings.

[5] A reproduction of Stalin's own signature on Tommy's menu card is at p. 394.

42

The End of the Road

WHEN one of his secretaries, Elizabeth Layton, went into the Prime Minister's room at 8.30 next morning he said wearily that although he had taken a sleeping draught he had spent a very restless night. To Mrs Churchill he confessed that for some reason he could not fathom he suddenly felt very despondent about the Conservative chances and feared a stalemate.

While he was dressing there was great activity in the Map Room. The wall facing the Prime Minister's chair now bore an alphabetical list of all the constituencies, with a space beside each for inserting the result and the majority. On the left-hand wall of the room were the names of the Ministers in the late Government, awaiting crosses or ticks to show whether they had been re-elected. To the right was a vast and complicated chart, rather like a tennis tournament score-board, which was to show the gains, losses, and total seats secured by each party at any given moment. In charge of this was Lieutenant-Commander Jack Sayers, one of Pim's assistants. Armed with a piece of chalk and a duster, he had to run up and down a narrow and very insecure plank after the manner of Blondin crossing the Niagara Falls, and as he alone seemed to know how this system of instant reckoning should be operated the rest of the Map Room staff prayed fervently that no harm would befall him during the day.

Richard Pim had set nine o'clock as zero hour. From this moment the Map Room staff prowled anxiously round, arranging and rearranging their pens, pencils, and little piles of chalk. The tape machine whirred and chattered as it relayed test messages, and then, at ten minutes past ten, came the first result—Salford (South), won by Labour.

With the score at twelve Labour wins to four for the Tories Randolph rang up from Preston to find out what was happening.

"Now, now . . . it's not as bad as all that," said Pim as he heard a startled comment. "Everything will be all right; you go back and watch your count." This Randolph did—and saw himself counted out within the hour.

A few minutes later Mr Churchill, clad in his siren suit, entered the Map Room with his brother. He had hardly taken his seat when the news came through of defeat for Harold Macmillan, Walter Womersley, and Brendan Bracken. The Prime Minister received these results without comment, but when the Labour gains had risen to a round dozen he asked to be put through to Sir Robert Topping, the General Director of the Conservative Central Office.

Thereafter the unfortunate Sir Robert had a gruelling time, for he was rung up at intervals of ten minutes for most of the day—so frequently, in fact, that he was eventually asked to station himself nearer the phone to avoid keeping Mr Churchill waiting.

He had told the Prime Minister that he had a list of twenty-five seats he expected to lose to the Socialists.

"How many of these Labour gains have you got on your list?" was Churchill's first demand; ". . . only three, you say?" By this time the board in the Map Room showed thirteen Labour gains and the receiver was abruptly replaced. As the day wore on the preamble to these interrogations grew shorter and shorter until it consisted of one curt monosyllable —a brusque "Well?"

Soon the results were flooding in. The Prime Minister was joined by Lord Beaverbrook, who sat with him for much of the day, leaning back in his chair with his legs comfortably crossed and betraying no visible sign of surprise or emotion, although the voting was running completely counter to all the predictions of his newspapers.

Mrs Churchill and Mary were watching the count at Woodford, where the Prime Minister was opposed by a Northamptonshire farmer named Hancock. Their first inkling of disaster came when this unknown and entirely undistinguished Independent began to amass a surprisingly large number of votes and an anxious call to Storey's Gate brought the startling information that the Socialist gains had mounted to forty-four, against a solitary one for the Conservatives. Mrs Churchill's one thought was to be with her husband, and she dashed back to Whitehall, to find consternation reigning.

"It's a complete debacle," said Jock Colville, who was coming out of the Map Room as she arrived; ". . . it's 1906 all over again." She found Mr Churchill sitting staring blankly at the wall in front of him. Every minute brought news of fresh reverses—Duncan Sandys OUT . . . Leo Amery OUT . . . Ralph Assheton OUT. The first significant pointer to the result came from the Birmingham area, where against all expectations three Tory strongholds fell to the Socialists in quick succession. One member of the Map Room staff who had been an election agent in his time kept repeating hopefully that there was still no need to assume the worst. "You wait till the county constituencies come in . . . they never change," he claimed. But this comforting theory was promptly upset by the returns for Buckinghamshire and Cambridgeshire, both of which showed Labour gains.

Duncan and Diana Sandys arrived looking white and shaken. "I'm so sorry . . . but you're in good company," said the Prime Minister consolingly. By now he had left his seat and was wandering restlessly about the room, but he stopped in his tracks when Diana Lyttelton, the W.A.A.F. officer on Pim's staff, entered with the Woodford result. Pointing a finger dramatically at his chest, he asked, "Am I in?" She read out the figures:

W. S. Churchill (Con)	27,688
A. Hancock (Ind)	10,488

When the Prime Minister heard that his opponent—a man whose manifesto had included the eccentric demand that the working week should be reduced to one day—had polled over ten thousand votes he stared incredulously.

Lunch-time gave the Map Room staff a brief breathing-space. For the Churchill family it was an agonizing interlude. Lord Beaverbrook had made his apologies and departed to lunch with his son who had just scraped home for the Tories at Holborn. The only outside guests were David Margesson and Brendan Bracken. Mrs Churchill did her best to cheer every one up and the Prime Minister fought bravely to hide his feelings but as Sarah and Mary choked their way through the meal they realized how desperately distressed he was.

Mr Churchill himself had confidently expected to be returned to power with a majority of between 80 and 120. Now, bewildered by the extent of the disaster which had overtaken his party he could only say, over and over again, "It is the will of the people."[1]

The long day dragged on. An early visitor to the Map Room after lunch was Oliver Lyttelton, who had gained one of the few respectable Tory majorities. Pim's staff continued to tear paper from the tape

[1] The Duke of Devonshire had warned him that the Labour Party would be returned with a large majority—his actual forecast to friends in Pratt's Club one night before the count was, astonishingly, correct to within a single seat—but Mr Churchill had dismissed this estimate as a complete flight of fancy.

machines, answer the telephone, pass information hourly to Potsdam, and drag back the unhappy Sir Robert Topping for further interrogation by the Prime Minister. One of the detectives looked in to announce gloomily that he was off "across the road"—to Scotland Yard—to put his name down for another job. And Mary Churchill wandered unhappily in and out, trying to devise a plan for retrieving most of her clothes which she had optimistically left in Berlin. The news of a Conservative gain at Berwick-on-Tweed, where Sir William Beveridge lost his seat, produced the only cheerful moment of the afternoon.

By six o'clock all was over. Mr Churchill ordered drinks and cigars to be brought in for the exhausted Map Room staff. Then he set off for Buckingham Palace to tender his resignation. Prime Minister for 1,902 days, he had been turned out of office by one of the greatest political landslides of modern Parliamentary history. Labour had won 393 seats, which gave them a majority of 146 over all other parties and groups. The Conservatives and their allies had lost 193 seats.

On his return from the Palace Mr Churchill reappeared in the Map Room. By now the total votes had been added up and checked, and these were read out to him.

"Five million against us," he said thoughtfully. Then, turning to Richard Pim, he remarked, "We've had good times together. We've seen great days and travelled in many countries. God bless you always!"

Dinner in the Churchill household that night was as melancholy an affair as lunch had been. Mrs Churchill had retired to bed, and although Sarah and Mary, determined to "cheer up Papa," had changed into their smartest evening dresses, they, like every one else, felt too stunned to talk when the time came.

For Mr Churchill the shock of the result had been all the greater because of his intense preoccupation with other matters right up to the moment when the count took place. There was, too, a psychological factor which had accentuated for him the effect of this unforeseen reverse. Throughout his life he had rarely been conscious of opposition as a force to be seriously considered. Living for the most part with his own thoughts, and moving as he did largely within his own intimate circle, he was slow to gauge the strength of adverse opinion.

For that matter he paid little heed to favourable opinion either, and he was completely unaware of the devotion he inspired among those who served him. When Leslie Rowan, normally a reserved and unemotional man, brought him some papers to sign before dinner that evening he was in tears as he stood by the desk. Mr Churchill was astonished, and greatly touched. It had never occurred to him until that moment that members of his staff would be upset by his defeat.

When most of his guests had left after dinner he walked through into the drawing-room, and, finding his youngest daughter with two friends, Robin Maugham and Michael Parish, he sat down and talked to them for some time about the Election and the tasks facing the new Government.[2]

"We must give them a chance," he said. "Let's see what they can do. But let them bear one thing in mind. If they try to tamper with the Constitution we will be at their throats."

Looking intently at his visitors, he went on—"You young people are the hope of the country now. Keep in touch with events. Keep alert. It's *your* turn now. I've thrown the reins on the horse's neck. . . ."

"But you won the race, sir," Michael Parish broke in.

"Yes . . ." said Mr Churchill grimly, ". . . and in consequence I've been warned off the Turf!"

* * * * *

The final days at Downing Street were an ordeal both for the Churchill family and the few members of the staff who stayed on helping to clear up the mass of papers which had accumulated. For Mr Churchill the sudden complete inactivity after months and years when every hour was filled made the shock of defeat doubly hard to bear. The Cabinet War Room was now dark and deserted, the Private Office untenanted. There were no longer any telegrams to deal with, any meetings to attend, any major decisions to be made.

One by one familiar faces disappeared. First the Chiefs of Staff, returning to Potsdam, came to say good-bye. Then Leslie Rowan departed for Germany, and two of the personal detectives, Inspector Hughes and Sergeant Green, left to take up other duties. Few of those who bade him farewell realized what an effort it was for Mr Churchill to maintain his air of calm resignation. Outwardly he seemed almost his old self, and Field-Marshal Brooke, who had never felt temperamentally close to him, was greatly moved by his courage.

By now messages were pouring in, telling how much the change of Government had affected people who had worked with him over the years. One of those who had remained at Potsdam wrote:

> I don't mind the change of Government politically—in fact, I welcome it—but something has gone out of our lives and no birds sing.

[2] He was always interested in young people. Many years earlier he had written, "Twenty to twenty-five, those are the years. Do not be content with things as they are. The earth is yours and the fullness thereof. Enter upon your inheritance, accept your responsibilities . . . do not take 'no' for an answer, never submit to failure. . . . You will make all kinds of mistakes but as long as you are generous and true and also fierce you cannot hurt the world. . . . She was made to be wooed and won by youth." (*My Early Life*, p. 74.)

We chameleons of the Civil Service have to carry on, but we aren't as heartless or as unaffected as we may seem. Babelsburg is suddenly rather colourless. Please understand that we care.

On the Saturday afternoon Tommy drove down to Buckinghamshire with Mr Churchill for the last time. He had arranged for the news reels of the early stages of the Potsdam Conference to be shown at Chequers that evening, followed by an American documentary film, *The True Glory*. The programme ended all too soon, however, and as Mr Churchill made his way back from the Long Gallery he said sadly, "This is where I miss the news . . . no work . . . nothing to do." Invariably he had spent some time in the Private Secretary's room, off the Great Hall, reading the latest telegrams brought by the courier from Whitehall. Now he strode restlessly up and down, paying no attention to the Gilbert and Sullivan records he normally enjoyed so much. When Tommy switched to American and French military marches there was an immediate response, however, and soon Mr Churchill was asking for his special favourites "Run, Rabbit, Run," and the songs from *The Wizard of Oz*. By two o'clock, when he announced that he was ready for bed, he was in a much more cheerful frame of mind.

Several welcome visitors, among them "The Prof," Brendan Bracken, and Gil Winant, arrived at Chequers next morning. It was a lovely summer's day, and after lunch Mr Churchill sat contentedly on the lawn watching his house party playing croquet. With his family and his close friends around him it seemed hard to believe that anything had changed, but in a few hours his guests were signing the Visitors' Book before they retired. Mr Churchill was the last to add his name, and below, at the foot of the page, he wrote the one word—FINIS.

Chequers held too many memories for him now and he seemed almost relieved to be returning to London next morning. But in Downing Street it was even harder to escape from the interminable inquests on the Tory defeat and the chatter of well-meaning sympathizers. One of his lunch guests at Number Ten that day spoke long and angrily of the ingratitude of the electorate. "I wooed them and they spurned me," said Mr Churchill dejectedly; ". . . I ought to have seen it in their eyes."

For a while after lunch he sat alone in the Cabinet Room, reading the early editions of the evening papers. Then he called for his car and drove down to Chartwell with Mary.

The lovely garden where he had sought solace years before, when the desert fighting was at its height, was now tangled and overgrown, but soon it cast its peaceful spell upon him. "It is just like the Sleeping Beauty," he said as they walked slowly round the grounds in the afternoon sunshine. He decided to spend the night in the house. Next morning he was up and about early, directing vigorous nettle-clearing operations which kept him happily occupied till the time came to return to Whitehall.

On the following day he left Downing Street. When Tommy walked across from the Annexe with some final papers for him to sign Number Ten was forlorn and deserted. He found Mr Churchill alone in the Cabinet Room, sitting in his usual chair in the centre of the long table beneath Walpole's picture.

"Well, Tommy," he said, ". . . we've gone a long way since our visit to Scapa Flow."

He had remembered their first journey together, within a fortnight of the outbreak of war . . . a journey prompted by the Prime Minister's anxiety for the safety of the Fleet in its ill-guarded anchorage . . . a journey Mr Churchill had undertaken, too, a quarter of a century earlier to cross-examine Admiral Jellicoe about this selfsame problem.

They talked of other journeys, in other countries, Mr Churchill reliving his visits to America and memorable days they had spent with the President.

"We've had some stirring times together, and I'm very grateful for what you have done," he said. "I want to put your name in my List, and I have recommended you for the C.M.G. If I can help you in any way over a job, now that you're leaving the Navy, you've only got to let me know."

They shook hands. "Keep in touch! This is not the end of the road," were Mr Churchill's final words.

* * * * *

After he left Downing Street Mr Churchill stayed for a while at Claridge's. Still pondering on his dismissal, he was genuinely puzzled by the warmth of the welcome accorded to him when he appeared in public. It was, indeed, an astonishing phenomenon, for wherever he went he was acclaimed with hysterical fervour. He attended a performance of Noel Coward's comedy, *Private Lives*, and the entire audience rose and applauded him for several minutes as soon as he entered the theatre. At the end of the play John Clements made a moving speech about him from the stage, and once again the audience rose and cheered as though they would never stop. When he moved into the flat of his son-in-law, Duncan Sandys, crowds gathered night after night in the hope of seeing him, and searchlights played on the building. At the Savoy, where he dined one evening with James Stuart, every one in the restaurant stood up and clapped and cheered as he passed through the room.

The deliberations at Potsdam came to an end, and on August 16 the new Prime Minister, Clement Attlee, paid a moving tribute to him in the House of Commons:

"However we may be divided politically, . . . I believe I shall be expressing the views of the whole House in making acknowledgment here of the transcendent services rendered by the Right Honourable gentleman to this country, to the Commonwealth and Empire, and to the world. . . . There is a true leadership which means the expression by one man of the soul of a nation and its translation of the common will into action. In the darkest and most dangerous hours of our history this nation found in my Right Honourable friend the man who expressed supremely the courage and determination never to yield which animated all the men and women of this country. In undying phrases he crystallized the unspoken feeling of all. . . . He radiated a stream of energy throughout the machinery of government—indeed, throughout the life of the nation. . . . His place in history is secure."

* * * * *

Winston Churchill was then in his seventy-first year. Six years later he returned to Downing Street as Prime Minister. His service to the nation was not destined to end until he had passed his eightieth birthday.

On an April day in 1955, nearly ten years after the war was over, Tommy was summoned to Number Ten for the last time. He had not served Mr Churchill during the second term of office, for on leaving the Navy he had been appointed a Secretary to the Stewards of the Jockey Club. He had, however, been frequently bidden to family parties which the Churchills gave from time to time, but this particular gathering had a special significance. Every one knew that the Prime Minister's resignation was imminent. It was "the end of the road" at last.

When Mr Churchill bade his former Flag Commander good-bye once again came the familiar injunction "Keep in touch!" As Tommy walked home, past Storey's Gate and on through the Park, memories of the war years came flooding back. . . .

"It suddenly struck me as extraordinary that never, even in the darkest days, had the possibility of defeat occurred to me, simply because the P.M. himself had never considered it. And I recalled a remark of Lord Moran's: "In my heart I think of him as invincible." It seemed then, as it still does, a stroke of unbelievable fortune that the chance came to me to spend the war years at his side."

List of Operational and other Code Names

Admiral Q: President Roosevelt.
Anakim: conquest of Burma.
Anvil: original code-name for South of France landings (subsequently changed to *Dragoon*).
Arcadia: First Washington Conference (Dec. 1941–Jan. 1942).
Argonaut: Yalta Conference (Jan. 1945).
Avalanche: Salerno landings.

Battleaxe: major Allied offensive operations in Western Desert (June 1941).
Bolero: administrative preparations for invasion of France.
Brevity: Allied operations in Western Desert preceding *Battleaxe* and aimed at driving enemy from Sollum and Capuzzo areas.
Buccaneer: projected assault on Andaman Islands.

Cairo Three: Teheran Conference (Nov. 1943).
Caliph: projected Allied landings in Southern and Western France to draw enemy forces away from Normandy beach-head.
Catherine: projected penetration of the Baltic by a special naval squadron.
Colonel Warden: the Prime Minister.
Crusader: operations in Western Desert in Nov. 1941 aimed at recapture of Cyrenaica.
Cultivator: mechanical trench cutter (see *White Rabbit No. 6*).
Culverin: operations against Northern Sumatra.

Dracula: capture of Rangoon.
Dragoon: Allied invasion of South of France (Aug. 1944).
Dynamo: the Royal Navy's plan for the Dunkirk evacuation.

Gymnast: original code-name for *Torch* (North African landings).

Habbakuk: floating ice airfield.
Hercules: plan for capture of Rhodes.
Husky: Allied assault on Sicily.

Jupiter: projected Allied operations in Norway.

Octagon: Second Quebec Conference (Sept. 1944).
Overlord: invasion of Normandy.

Pluto: *P*ipe *L*ine *U*nder *T*he *O*cean (submarine pipeline supplying fuel to Allied invasion forces in N.W. Europe).

Quadrant: First Quebec Conference (Aug. 1943).

Rapid Falls 8833: Top Priority telephone number of No. 10 Downing Street.
Round Up: plan for the liberation of France in 1943.
Royal Marine: mining of the Rhine in 1940.

Sea Lion: German plan for invasion of Britain.
Sextant: Cairo Conference (Nov. 1943).
Shingle: Anzio landings.
Sledgehammer: attack on Brest or Cherbourg planned for 1942.
Supercharge: final stage of the Alamein offensive, designed to force the decisive break through.
Symbol: Casablanca Conference (Jan. 1943).

Terminal: Potsdam Conference (July 1945).
Tiger: passage of a convoy from Gibraltar to Alexandria in 1941 carrying tanks for the Desert Army.
Torch: Allied invasion of French North Africa.
Trident: Third Washington Conference (May 1943).
Tube Alloys: Atomic research project.

Whipcord: plan for an earlier invasion of Sicily, abandoned in Nov. 1941.
White Rabbit No. 6: initial cover title of *Cultivator.*
Workshop: projected attack on Pantelleria in Jan. 1941.

Bibliography

ASPINALL-OGLANDER, CECIL: *Roger Keyes* (Hogarth Press).
BOIS, ELIE J.: *Truth on the Tragedy of France* (Hodder and Stoughton).
BRADLEY, GENERAL OMAR N.: *A Soldier's Story* (Eyre and Spottiswoode).
BROAD, LEWIS: *Winston Churchill* (Hutchinson).
BRYANT, ARTHUR: *The Turn of the Tide* (Collins).
Triumph in the West (Collins).
BUTCHER, HARRY C.: *Three Years with Eisenhower* (Heinemann).
CHURCHILL, WINSTON S.: *The Second World War: Vols. I–VI* (Cassell).
My Early Life (Thornton Butterworth).
The World Crisis (Odhams).
CHURCHILL, RANDOLPH, and GERNSHEIM, HELMUT: *Churchill: His Life in Photographs* (Weidenfeld and Nicolson).
CLARK, GENERAL MARK: *Calculated Risk* (Harrap).
COLVIN, IAN: *Flight 777* (Evans).
CONNELL, JOHN: *Auchinleck* (Cassell).
COOPER, A. DUFF: *Old Men Forget* (Hart-Davis).
COOPER, LADY DIANA: *The Light of Common Day* (Hart-Davis).
COOTE, COLIN, R. (compiled by): *Sir Winston Churchill: a Self Portrait* (Eyre and Spottiswoode).
COWLES, VIRGINIA: *Winston Churchill: the Era and the Man* (Hamish Hamilton).
CUNNINGHAM OF HYNDHOPE, ADMIRAL OF THE FLEET VISCOUNT: *A Sailor's Odyssey* (Hutchinson).
CZARNOMSKI, F. B. (edited by): *The Wisdom of Winston Churchill* (Allen and Unwin).
DE GAULLE, GENERAL CHARLES: *The Call to Honour* (Collins).
Unity (Weidenfeld and Nicolson).

EADE, CHARLES (compiled by): *Secret Session Speeches* (Cassell).
EISENHOWER, GENERAL DWIGHT D.: *Crusade in Europe* (Heinemann).
FISHER OF KILVERSTONE, ADMIRAL OF THE FLEET LORD: *Memories.*
FLEMING, PETER: *Invasion 1940* (Hart-Davis).
FRANK, WOLFGANG: *The Sea Wolves* (Weidenfeld and Nicolson).
FULLER, MAJOR-GENERAL J. F. C.: *Tanks in the Great War* (Murray).
GOEBBELS, JOSEF (edited by Louis P. Lochner): *Diaries* (Hamish Hamilton).
GRENFELL, CAPTAIN RUSSELL: *Main Fleet to Singapore* (Faber and Faber).
GUEDALLA, PHILIP: *Mr Churchill* (Hodder and Stoughton).
HARROD, SIR ROY: *The Prof* (Macmillan).
HART, LIDDELL: *The Rommel Papers* (Collins).
HEDIN, SVEN: *German Diary* (Euphorian Books, Dublin).
HERBERT, SIR ALAN: *Independent Member* (Methuen).
HIGGINS, PROFESSOR TRUMBULL: *Winston Churchill and the Second Front* (Oxford University Press).
HOLLIS, GENERAL SIR LESLIE (with JAMES LEASOR): *One Marine's Tale* (Andre Deutsche). *War at the Top* (Joseph).
JOHNSON, GROUP CAPTAIN J. E.: *Wing Leader* (Chatto and Windus).
JUNGK, DR ROBERT: *Brighter than a Thousand Suns: the Moral and Political History of the Atomic Scientists* (Gollancz and Hart-Davis).
KENNEDY, MAJOR-GENERAL SIR JOHN: *The Business of War* (Hutchinson).
LOW, PROFESSOR A. M.: *Tanks* (Hutchinson).
LOWIS, COMMANDER GEOFFREY: *Fabulous Admirals* (Putnam).
MCCALLUM, R. B., and READMAN, ALISON: *The British General Election of 1945* (Oxford University Press).
MARCHANT, SIR JAMES (edited by): *Winston Spencer Churchill: a Tribute* (Cassell).
MARTIN, HUGH: *Battle* (Gollancz).
MONTGOMERY OF ALAMEIN, FIELD-MARSHAL VISCOUNT: *Memoirs* (Collins).
MORTON, H. V.: *Atlantic Meeting* (Methuen).
NEL, ELIZABETH: *Mr Churchill's Secretary* (Hodder and Stoughton).
PAWLE, GERALD: *The Secret War: 1939–45* (Harrap).
PLAYFAIR, MAJOR-GENERAL I. S. O. (and others): *The Mediterranean and the Middle East*, Vols. I–III (H.M.S.O.).
POSTAN, M.: *British War Production* (H.M.S.O.).
REILLY, MICHAEL, and SLOCUM, WILLIAM J.: *I was Roosevelt's Shadow* (Foulsham).
ROSKILL, CAPTAIN S. W.: *The War at Sea*, Vols. I and II (H.M.S.O.).
ROWSE, A. L.: *The Later Churchills* (Macmillan).
SCHELLENBERG, WALTER (edited by Louis Hagen): *Memoirs* (Andre Deutsch).
SHERWOOD, ROBERT: *The White House Papers of Harry L. Hopkins*, Vols. I and II (Eyre and Spottiswoode).
SLESSOR, MARSHAL OF THE R.A.F. SIR JOHN: *The Central Blue* (Cassell).
SPEARS, MAJOR-GENERAL SIR EDWARD L.: *Prelude to Dunkirk* (Heinemann).
The Fall of France (Heinemann).
SYKES, CHRISTOPHER: *Orde Wingate* (Collins).

TEMPLEWOOD, VISCOUNT: *Nine Troubled Years* (Collins).
THOMPSON, W. H.: *I was Churchill's Shadow* (Johnson).
WESTPHAL, LIEUT-GENERAL SIEGFRIED: *Heer in Fesseln.*
WEYGAND, GENERAL MAXIME: *Memoires: Rappelé au Service* (Flammarion, Paris).
WILMOT, CHESTER: *The Struggle for Europe* (Collins).
WINANT, JOHN GILBERT: *Letter from Grosvenor Square* (Houghton Mifflin).
WRENCH, SIR EVELYN: *Geoffrey Dawson and Our Times* (Hutchinson).

* * * * *

Hansard, Vol. 408 (Feb. 1945) (The Debate on Poland and the Yalta Agreement).
Statements relating to the Atomic Bomb (H.M.S.O.).
Lloyd's Log, Vol. XVII, No. 9.

* * * * *

Where, in footnotes, Sir Winston Churchill is quoted as a source the reference is to his own *Second World War*, Vols. I–VI (published by Cassell), unless otherwise stated.

The lines by A. E. Housman which appear at p. 302 are taken from *A Shropshire Lad*, and are reproduced by permission of Jonathan Cape, the publishers of his *Collected Poems.*

Mrs Christopher Soames and Sir Alan Herbert have kindly allowed me to publish the verses exchanged between H.M.S. *Renown* and H.M.S. *Orwell* on the voyage back from Canada after the first Quebec Conference.

S.G.S.P.

Index

[Titles and Service ranks quoted in this index are in the main those held at the end of the period covered by this book. Operational Code Names are shown in italics.]